The European Atomic Energy Community in the European Union Context

Nijhoff Studies in EU Law

Series Editors

VOLUME 10

Nijhoff Studies in European Union Law is a refereed scholarly monographs series dedicated to the critical analysis of the current state and development of European Union law in a broad sense. Apart from constitutional, institutional and substantive issues of EU law, the series also embraces state-of-the-art interdisciplinary, comparative law and EU policies research with a clear link to European integration. Titles in the *Nijhoff Studies in European Union Law* series will be of particular interest to academics, policy makers and practitioners dealing with eu law and policies, as well as national and international (non-) governmental institutions and bodies.

The titles published in this series are listed at *brill.com/seul*

The European Atomic Energy Community in the European Union Context

The 'Outsider' Within

By

Ilina Cenevska

BRILL
NIJHOFF

LEIDEN | BOSTON

Library of Congress Cataloging-in-Publication Data

Names: Cenevska, Ilina, author.
Title: The European Atomic Energy Community in the European Union context : the 'outsider' within / By Ilina Cenevska.
Description: Leiden : Brill Nijhoff, 2016. | Series: Nijhoff studies in EU law ; 10 | Includes bibliographical references and index. | Description based on print version record and CIP data provided by publisher; resource not viewed.
Identifiers: LCCN 2016000345 (print) | LCCN 2016000255 (ebook) | ISBN 9789004310414 (E-book) | ISBN 9789004310407 (hardback : alk. paper)
Subjects: LCSH: Nuclear energy--Law and legislation--European Union countries. | Euratom. | European Union.
Classification: LCC KJE6858 (print) | LCC KJE6858 .C46 2016 (ebook) | DDC 343.2409/25--dc23
LC record available at http://lccn.loc.gov/2016000345

Typeface for the Latin, Greek, and Cyrillic scripts: 'Brill'. See and download: brill.com/brill-typeface.

ISSN 2210-9765
ISBN 978-90-04-31040-7 (hardback)
ISBN 978-90-04-31041-4 (e-book)

This book is printed on acid-free paper and produced in a sustainable manner.

Contents

Abbreviations IX

Introduction 1

1 **The Nature and the Specificity of the Euratom Community: The Claim for Supranationality** 17

I Three Treaties, One Common Concept 19

II The Nature and Specificity of the Euratom Treaty in the Context of the Founding Treaties 22

III The Institutional Dynamic within the Euratom Compact 29

III.1 *The European Commission and the Council of the EU – The Regulatory Power* 31

III.2 *The Parliament under Euratom: The Quest for Leverage* 38

III.2.1 The Parliament's Legal and Political Struggle 40

III.2.2 The Lisbon Treaty Amendments: (in)Significant? 45

III.3 *The Court of Justice of the EU – The 'Enabler' of Euratom's Competence* 50

III.3.1 Ruling 1/78 52

III.3.2 Commission v Council (Nuclear Safety Convention) 54

III.3.3 Land de Sarre and others v Ministre de l'Industrie (Cattenom) 56

III.3.4 Chernobyl II 57

III.3.5 Commission v Ireland (*MOX Plant*) 59

III.3.6 The Temelín Case 62

IV The Dynamics of Treaty Modification: To Assimilate or Not? 66

IV.1 *The Flexibility Clause of the Euratom Treaty (Article 203) As a Feasible Procedural Option* 69

IV.2 *The Last Word on the Matter: The Convention on the Future of Europe* 71

IV.3 *Calls for Complete Abolishment of the Euratom Treaty* 74

2 **The Interaction between the Euratom Health and Safety Policy and the Union Environmental Policy** 77

I The Possibility for Extending the Application of EU Rules to the Euratom Field 78

I.1 *Lack of Corresponding Provisions in the Euratom Treaty* 80
I.2 *Concurring Competence between Euratom and the EU* 83
I.3 *Transposing General Principles of Union Law to the Euratom Framework* 85
II The Interplay between Environmental and Nuclear Law and Policy 87
II.1.1 The Interface between International Nuclear Law and International Environmental Law Instruments 88
II.1.2 The Interface between Nuclear and Environmental Law before International and Regional Judicial Fora 94
II.2 *Euratom and the EU Environmental Policy* 111
II.2.1 The Health and Safety Policy of Euratom in the Wider Context of Environmental Protection 111
II.2.2 The 'Environmental Approach' to Radiation Protection and Nuclear Safety Endorsed at the International and the EU Level 115
II.2.3 The Overlap between the Euratom-Devised Policies and the Union Environmental Policy through the Use of Secondary Law Instruments 125
II.2.4 Transposing the Principles of Union Environmental Law to the Euratom Field 128

3 Euratom and 'Environmental Democracy': EU Citizens' Access to Information and Participation in Decision-making in the Nuclear Arena 142
I The EU, Euratom and the Concept of 'Environmental Democracy' 143
II The Aarhus Convention Pillars – Key Aspects 155
III The 'Access to Information' Pillar of the Aarhus Convention 160
III.1 *The Access-to-information Pillar Transposed in Union/Euratom Law* 167
IV The Participation-in-decision-making Pillar of the Aarhus Convention 180
IV.1 *Public Participation in Decisions on Specific Activities (Article 6)* 181
IV.2 *Public Participation Concerning Plans, Programmes and Policies Relating to the Environment (Article 7)* 185
IV.3 *Public Participation in the Preparation of Executive Regulations and/or Generally Applicable Legally Binding Normative Instruments (Article 8)* 187

IV.4 *The Participation-in-decision-making Pillar Transposed in Union/Euratom Law* 189
V The Implementation of the Aarhus Convention Obligations 200
VI The Access-to-information and Participation-in-decision-making Requirements in Environmental and Nuclear Matters before International and Regional Judicial Fora 204
VII The Aarhus Convention Access-to-justice Regime in EU Law – An 'Accomplished' Failure 221

4 Euratom and Non-Proliferation of Nuclear Weapons 233
I Non-proliferation and Disarmament – Two Concomitant Objectives of the Treaty on the Non-Proliferation of Nuclear Weapons (The NPT) 236
II The Architecture of the NPT Regime and the IAEA Safeguards Arrangements 241
II.1 *The IAEA Safeguards Agreements* 247
II.2 *The Safeguards Agreement between the IAEA, Euratom and the Member States* 249
II.3 *The Voluntary Offer Agreements with France and the United Kingdom* 251
III The Euratom Safeguards Framework 254
III.1 *The Euratom Treaty Safeguards Provisions* 254
III.2 *Commission Regulation (Euratom) No 302/2005* 257
IV Euratom and EU's Policy on the Non-proliferation of Nuclear Weapons 260
IV.1 *The Raison d'être of EU's Non-proliferation Policy* 260
IV. 2 *EU's Policy on the Non-proliferation of Nuclear Weapons and the Treaty on the Non-Proliferation of Nuclear Weapons (NPT)* 265
IV.3 *The 'Weapons of Mass Destruction (WMD)' Clause in Agreements with Third Countries* 271
IV.4 *The Nuclear Sharing Arrangements under NATO* 276
Legality and Legitimacy Issues Linked to the Practice of Nuclear Weapons Sharing 278
IV.5 *Concluding Observations* 282
V Euratom and Military Uses of Nuclear Energy – A Thundering Silence? 283
V.1 *Concepts and Strategies on Nuclear Energy in Europe Predating the Adoption of the Euratom Treaty* 284
V.1.1 The European Defence Community (EDC) 284

V.1.2 The Western European Union (WEU) 286
V.1.3 The Spaak Report 289
V.1.4 The Draft Minutes of the Venice Conference 291
V.2 *The Euratom Treaty Provisions* 293
V.3 *Clearing the Waters – The CJEU on the Application of the Euratom Treaty to Military Uses of Nuclear Energy* 296
V.3.1 Ruling 1/78 297
V.3.2 T- 219/95 R Danielsson v Commission 298
V.3.3 Case C-61/03 Commission v. UK 299
V.3.4 Joined Cases C-205/10 P, C-217/10 P and C-222/10 P, *Eriksen, Hansen and Lind* 303

5 **Euratom and the European Union: Taking Stock of the Present and Mapping Out the Road Ahead** 309
I The (Dis)Balance of Institutional Power and the Democratic Deficit under the Euratom System 310
II The Relationship between the Euratom Health and Safety Regime and the Union's Environmental Policy 313
III Euratom's Stake in the Field of Environmental Democracy 316
IV Euratom and the Union's Role in the Field of Non-proliferation of Nuclear Weapons and Euratom's Stake in the Field of Military Applications of Nuclear Energy 320
V What Lies Ahead for Euratom 324

Bibliography 329
Index 353

Abbreviations

CD	Conference on Disarmament
CFSP	Common Foreign and Security Policy
CJEU	Court of Justice of the European Union
CTBT Treaty	Complete Nuclear-Test-Ban Treaty
E(E)C	European (Economic) Community
ECHR	European Convention on Human Rights
ECSC	European Coal and Steel Community
ECtHR	European Court of Human Rights
EDC	European Defense Community
EIA	Environmental Impact Assessment
EU	European Union
EURATOM/EAEC	European Atomic Energy Community
IAEA	International Atomic Energy Agency
ICJ	International Court of Justice
ICRP	International Commission on Radiological Protection
NATO	North Atlantic Treaty Organisation
NNWS	Non-Nuclear-Weapon States
NPT	Treaty on the Non-Proliferation of Nuclear Weapons
NWS	Nuclear Weapon States
OSPAR Convention	Convention for the Protection of the Marine Environment of the North-East Atlantic
SEA	Strategic Environmental Assessment
TEC	Treaty establishing the European Community
TEU	Treaty on European Union
TFEU	Treaty on the Functioning of the European Union
UN	United Nations
UNCLOS	United Nations Convention on the Law of the Sea
VOA	Voluntary Offer Agreements
WEU	Western European Union
WHO	World Health Organisation
WMD	Weapons of Mass Destruction

Introduction

Ever since its creation in 1957, the European Atomic Energy Community (EAEC, commonly referred to as Euratom) has been considered as a bold political and legal enterprise of the six founding Member States of the European Community which, alongside to being a futuristic and forward-looking construct, represented a 'threat' to the ever-frowned-upon loss of sovereignty of Member States – possibly greater than the one attributed to the creation of the European Economic Community and the establishment of the comprehensive European Common Market project. In fact, what originally began as a futuristic enterprise promoting the development of the civil nuclear industry grew to become a strange animal of sorts – at least in conceptual and organizational terms. The legal and political system for the civil nuclear industry created under the Euratom Treaty is largely a self-sufficient (almost autarchic) system, something that has been further confirmed by the Euratom Treaty's notorious resistance to change. Namely, the Euratom Treaty has not undergone any substantial modification ever since its adoption, having even managed to evade the most recent vigorous reformatory sweep of the Lisbon Treaty (2007)[1] aimed at rationalizing and consolidating the institutional and structural make-up of the European Union *stricto sensu* (as an entity created under the purview of the Treaty on the functioning of the EU (TFEU) and the Treaty on European Union (TEU), different and differentiable from the Euratom Community as a separate entity).

Nuclear energy is a highly topical subject in Europe, the production of nuclear energy having gone through a true nuclear renaissance in the first decade of the 2000s marked by a surge of new nuclear power plants being built throughout the Union spurred by the conviction that nuclear energy is one of the most effective ways to cope with EU's growing energy demands. However, the nuclear disaster at the Fukushima plant in Japan in 2011 put a halt to

1 Save for several non-substantial changes, the text of the Euratom Treaty has essentially remained the same since 1957. The Euratom Treaty has been amended by the Maastricht Treaty (1992) (Title IV: Provisions amending the Treaty establishing the European Atomic Energy Community and Title VII: Final Provisions which extended the institutional changes introduced to the EC Treaty and the ECSC Treaty to the EAEC Treaty); the Treaty of Amsterdam (1997) (Arts. 1,4,7,8,9,10,11 and relevant protocols applicable to the EAEC); the Treaty of Nice (2001) (Arts. 1,3,7 and 9 and relevant protocols applicable to the EAEC); and lastly, the Treaty of Lisbon (2007)(see, Protocol No. 2 *Amending the Treaty establishing the EAEC* and other protocols applicable to the EAEC).

 | DOI 10.1163/9789004310414_002

the former nuclear upheaval, leading to a reversal in certain national nuclear policies and raising the level of apprehension with regard to the use of nuclear energy which has traditionally been seen as a 'controversial' energy source not solely in terms of the underlying dismay regarding the possible lack of satisfactory health, safety and security standards surrounding the operation of nuclear power plants, but also in terms of the possibility of failure to ensure adequate management, handling and storage of the end-products of the nuclear fuel cycle (notably, nuclear waste).

Presently there are 132 nuclear reactors in operation in 14 Member States of the Union: Belgium, Bulgaria, the Czech Republic, Finland, France, Germany, Hungary, the Netherlands, Romania, Slovakia, Slovenia, Spain, Sweden and the United Kingdom (other states include Lithuania which has 2 reactors that are undergoing decommissioning and four reactors which are under construction).[2] The fact that nuclear power plants cater to around 30% of EU's electricity demand[3] puts nuclear energy high up on EU's energy agenda, bringing to the fore the relevance of the Euratom Treaty as the primary legal source regulating the civil nuclear industry at Union level. Currently, attitudes toward the use of nuclear energy vary significantly from one Member State to another: for instance, Germany, one of the EU 'heavy-weights', introduced a phase-out plan on nuclear energy production in May 2011 under which all nuclear reactors in the country are expected to close by 2022;[4] while France and the United Kingdom, which are at the same time the EU's only nuclear weapon states,[5] are to be found at the very opposite end of the spectrum with national nuclear policies favorable to an additional increase in the countries' dependence on nuclear energy.

2 Nuclear power plants in the EU (updated on 13 June 2013): Belgium: 7 reactors (2 nuclear power plants (NPP)); Bulgaria: 2 reactors (1 NPP); Czech Republic: 6 reactors (2 NPPs); Finland: 4 reactors (2 NPPs); France: 58 reactors (19 NPPs); Germany: 9 reactors (12 NPPs, 17 reactors, 8 were shut down after Fukushima); Hungary: 4 reactors (1 NPP); The Netherlands: 1 reactor (1 NPP); Romania: 2 reactors (1 NPP); Slovakia: 4 reactors (2 NPPs); Slovenia: 1 reactor (1 NPP); Spain: 8 reactors (6 NPPs); Sweden: 10 reactors (3 NPPs); United Kingdom: 16 reactors (10 NPPs); Lithuania: 2 reactors under decommissioning (1 NPP); Four reactors are under construction: Finland: 1 France: 1 Slovakia: 2; Planned reactors: Bulgaria: 1 Czech Republic: 2 Finland: 2 France: 1 Lithuania: 1 The Netherlands: 1 Poland: 2–3 Romania: 2 United Kingdom: 4; (source: http://ec.europa.eu/energy/nuclear/doc/nuclear_power_plants.pdf).

3 http://ec.europa.eu/energy/nuclear/index_en.htm.

4 www.world-nuclear.org/info/Country-Profiles/Countries-G-N/Germany.

5 France and the United Kingdom figure among the five nuclear-weapon-states covered under the terms of the Treaty on the Non-proliferation of Nuclear Weapons (NPT), together with China, the Russian Federation and the United States (http://www.un.org/disarmament/WMD/Nuclear/Repository/submissions_2014.shtml).

Since the very beginning, the Euratom Treaty has acted as the 'outsider within' in the context of the overall European Union framework, having been kept 'at bay' from the mainstream developments in the Union. The former has been confirmed by the Euratom Community having preserved its status as a separate legal entity whereas its contemporary, the European (Economic) Community has been assimilated into the newly created legal personality of the 'Union'. Moreover, pursuant to the language of the Lisbon Treaty amendments, among the current three EU founding treaties in force, the Euratom Treaty acts as a separate treaty from the other two, the TFEU and the TEU which are referred to as the 'Union Treaties'. As a result, the legal personality of the Union exists alongside the singular legal personality of the Euratom Community with the Euratom Treaty having withstood the test of time without any substantial amendments to its text for which reason it has acquired the label of a 'dinosaur' treaty.[6] Hence, while we have witnessed the Common Market Treaty's reason of being evolve and expand with time, that of the Euratom Community seems to have been left untouched or, rather, 'conserved'. Irrespective of whether such a state of affairs is laudable or not – seen from a strictly constitutional perspective, the endurance of the Euratom project is indeed something remarkable.

The status of the Euratom Community is singular not only on account of the nature of its subject matter, but also in terms of the original kind of community of states in the field of nuclear energy it represents – one that has not been matched by any other similar kind of regional or international organization. Euratom is the only organization in the nuclear field that establishes a supranational regulation in an important number of segments of the civil nuclear industry, which, from today's perspective, started out rather humbly – with only six member states – and grew to comprise almost five times the number of its original members. Furthermore, the Euratom Community signifies an original concept not merely from an external viewpoint i.e. in comparison to other international or regional organizations in the nuclear field, but also internally, at the level of the EU. Thus, as much as the European Union itself has been perceived as a *sui generis* creation, Euratom's status can *a fortiori* be regarded as unique where its relationship to the wider Union construct represents a *specificity which exists within the specificity*.

The book focuses on the nuclear safety and radiation protection (health and safety) and nuclear safeguards regimes devised under the scope of the Euratom

6 C. True, Legislative Competences of Euratom and the European Community in the Energy Sector: The Nuclear Package of the Commission, *European Law Review*, 2003, Vol. 28 Issue 5, p. 15.

Treaty which are areas where the Euratom Community lays an undisputed competence that, although short of exclusive, is preponderant to that enjoyed by the Member States and only extends to the civil uses of nuclear energy. The fields of nuclear safeguards, on the one hand, and radiation protection and nuclear safety, on the other, are arguably the two most prominent fields covered by the Euratom Treaty and – according to some – the most viable fields worth preserving should the scenario of the Treaty's abolishment and subsequent assimilation into the Union Treaties materialize.[7] Moreover, it can arguably be held that the fields of nuclear safety, radiation protection and nuclear safeguards as covered under the scope of the Euratom Treaty are ultimately what justifies the existence of the Treaty in the present day[8] and where the specificity and originality thereof predominantly lie.

In this sense, the book explores the following research questions: *How do the Euratom safeguards and health and safety regimes interact with the Union's environmental policy and the Union's non-proliferation policy as their respective proxies developed under the Union framework stricto sensu?*[9] *What are the inconsistencies or lacunae underlying this interaction? Do the two Euratom-devised regimes and the corresponding Union policies they most commonly interact with and are most closely linked to in terms of their respective subject matter fully complement each other or are there any problematic issues or issues of conflict that characterise their relationship? Are such differences reconcilable and surmountable and in what way?* The foregoing research questions serve to test the coherence and the fail-proof character of the Euratom health and safety and safeguards regimes not solely within the boundaries of the Euratom Community, but within the wider context of the European Union in that discerning the 'problem areas' or the 'weak spots' inherent in these two regimes

7 See, similarly, where this has been suggested with regard to the Treaty establishing a Constitution for Europe of 2004 – Contribution by Ms Marie Nagy, Ms Renée Wagner and Mr Neil MacCormick, alternate members of the Convention: 'The Future of the Euratom Treaty in the Framework of the European Constitution' Brussels, 18 February 2003, CONV 563/03, p. 4.

8 J.M. Ayllon Diaz-Gonzalez, *Derecho Nuclear*, Granada, Comares, 1999, p. 302 (as reported in, N. Prieto Serrano, Wakening the Serpent: Reflections on the Possible Modification of the Euratom Treaty, International Journal of Nuclear Law, 2006, Vol. 1, No. 1, 2006, p. 17, ft. 7). The author argues that gradually, the concern [in the Euratom Treaty] for radiological protection, environmental protection and nuclear safety has become accentuated to such an extent that today these functions are, along with control of the non-proliferation of materials, those justifying its existence.

9 Hereinafter in the text the reference 'Union framework' will be used to denote the 'Union framework *stricto sensu*'.

can effectively prepare the ground for the contemplation of feasible solutions aimed at amending or making up for the detected *lacunae*.

In order to adequately respond to the above outlined research questions the analysis employed in order to arrive at the desired answers follows two tenets. The *first tenet* of the analysis explores the correlation between the *Euratom health and safety regime*, on the one hand, and the *Union's environmental protection* regime, on the other, in the context of the interrelationship of the notions of radiation protection, human health protection and environmental protection. Namely, employing an 'environmental' approach towards radiation protection within the framework of Euratom's health and safety policy allows for the notion of radiation protection to be expanded further from the scope of the Euratom Treaty and thus put in the wider context of the notions of 'protection of human health' and 'environmental protection' thereby implicating the corresponding regimes established within the Union legal framework.

The *second tenet* of the analysis concerns the *Euratom nuclear safeguards regime* and scrutinizes the former regime both from an intra-Community and an international perspective, centering on the operation of the safeguards regime at the level of the Euratom Community and inquiring into its relationship with the international safeguards regime created under the auspices of the International Atomic Energy Agency (IAEA). In this context, the non-proliferation role assumed by the European Union carries both an internal and an external component – the *internal* being concerned with the functioning of the Euratom safeguards system (established pursuant to the Euratom Treaty) and the *external* being articulated through the Union's non-proliferation policy (developed within the scope of the Union's Common Foreign and Security Policy and thus belonging to the Union framework *stricto sensu*).

Apart from the Union's environmental policy and non-proliferation policy, Euratom does interact with other Union policies – especially pronounced is the link with the Union's newly introduced energy policy.[10] Being that nuclear

10 For a more basic understanding of the groundlines of EU's energy policy and the stake of the nuclear therein, see, M. Kanellakis, G. Martinopoulos T. Zachariadis, European Energy Policy – A Review, *Energy Policy*, 2013, Issue 62, pp. 1020–1030; T. Maltby, European Union Energy Policy Integration: A Case of European Commission Policy Entrepreneurship and Increasing Supranationalism, *Energy Policy*, 2013, Issue 55, pp. 435–444; A. Pointvogl, Perceptions, Realities, Concession – What is Driving the Integration of European Energy Policies?, *Energy Policy*, 2009, Issue 37, pp. 5704–5716; D. Helm, The European Framework for Energy and Climate Policies, *Energy Policy*, 2014, Issue 64, pp. 29–35; For a general outlook on EU's energy policy, see, J.S. Duffield and V.L. Birchfield (eds.),Toward a Common European Union Energy Policy: Problems, Progress, and Prospects, Palgrave Macmillan, 2011.

energy is a constitutive part of EU's energy mix and the Union's nuclear energy policy is part and parcel of the Union's energy policy in its general sense,[11] it is required that the nuclear policy forged by Euratom adheres to the goals and aligns with the rules relevant to the energy sector set out under the Union framework.[12] Although the link with the Union's energy policy is immanent and *a priori* presumed, the character of the former is nevertheless straightforward and fairly uncontroversial. Furthermore, in comparison to the long track record of EU's nuclear energy policy pursued under Euratom's purview, the Union's energy policy has existed as a separate policy only since after the Lisbon Treaty amendments took effect whereas before that it had merely been considered as a 'presumed', *de facto* policy forged by the EU institutions.[13] For

11 R. Ptasekaite, *The Euratom Treaty v. Treaties of the European Union: Limits of Competence and Interaction*, Swedish Radiation Safety Authority, July 2011, Report number: 2011:32 ISSN: 2000–0456 (available at www.stralsakerhetsmyndigheten.se), p. 98.

The European Commission has pronounced the nuclear energy as forming part of the integral common energy policy (see, e.g., Report from the Commission to the Council on Civil Protection, Tourism and Energy, SEC 1996 496 final (available at: http://aei.pitt.edu/archive/00003938/01/000135 _1.pdf); European Commission White Paper: 'An Energy Policy for the European Union', COM (1995) 682 final).

12 The Euratom regulatory framework does not cover all matters pertaining to the broad scope of nuclear energy to the effect that certain nuclear matters have been left unregulated under the Euratom framework, having been complemented by instruments in the field of energy policy – the example given is the internal electricity market which nuclear energy is part of and which is, however, designated Union competence (see, True, *supra* n. 6, p. 671).

13 Before the chapter on energy was introduced via the Lisbon Treaty amendments, the single reference to energy as a general term was found in the former Art. 3(1)(u) of the EC Treaty (amendment introduced through the Maastricht Treaty), providing for the adoption of '*measures in the spheres of energy, civil protection and tourism*' in the realization of the Community's specific tasks outlined in Art. 2 EC. In the absence of a specific legal basis, Member States had made use of various mechanisms available under different related titles of the EC Treaty as proxy, most notably: Taxation, the Internal Market and the Environment (see, K. Inglis, Anticipating New Union Competences in Energy, *Maastricht Journal of European and Comparative Law*, 2008, Vol. 15 Issue 1, p. 125, 126).

The new Energy chapter of the TFEU reads:

'Energy

Article 194

1. In the context of the establishment and functioning of the internal market and with regard for the need to preserve and improve the environment, Union policy on energy shall aim, in a spirit of solidarity between Member States, to:

(a) ensure the functioning of the energy market;

(b) ensure security of energy supply in the Union;

the reasons given *supra*, the present research is only confined to two aspects of the Euratom domain – health and safety in the nuclear field and nuclear safeguards. In this sense, the Euratom's health and safety field is most immediately and most strongly linked to the field of environmental protection which makes the correlation between Euratom's health and safety policy and the Union's environmental policy the most suitable one for analysis. The same applies *viz.* the field of Euratom safeguards where the exploration of the link between the Euratom nuclear safeguards system and the Union's non-proliferation policy is considered as the most pertinent for the present discussion. Therefore, the choice of the Union's environmental policy and non-proliferation policy as points of reference proves to be most relevant to the nature and scope of outlined research questions. Venturing on an analysis of the interaction between Euratom and the Union's energy policy would effectively exceed the scope of the research questions that the book pursues and thus provides the basis for a different and separate discussion.[14]

The book has been divided into four chapters. *Chapter 1* (*The nature and the specificity of the Euratom Community: the claim for supranationality*) provides an insight into the idiosyncrasies of the Euratom institutional system through an elaboration of the governing balance of institutional powers embedded therein in light of the unique character of the Euratom Treaty as the only founding treaty of the Union which has survived nearly six decades of European

---

(c) promote energy efficiency and energy saving and the development of new and renewable forms of energy; and

(d) promote the interconnection of energy networks.

2. Without prejudice to the application of other provisions of the Treaties, the European Parliament and the Council, acting in accordance with the ordinary legislative procedure, shall establish the measures necessary to achieve the objectives in paragraph 1. Such measures shall be adopted after consultation of the Economic and Social Committee and the Committee of the Regions.

Such measures shall not affect a Member State's right to determine the conditions for exploiting its energy resources, its choice between different energy sources and the general structure of its energy supply, without prejudice to Article 192(2)(c).

3. By way of derogation from paragraph 2, the Council, acting in accordance with a special legislative procedure, shall unanimously and after consulting the European Parliament, establish the measures referred to therein when they are primarily of a fiscal nature.'

14 Exploration of the relationship between the Euratom and the Union's energy policy provides the basis for a separate discussion, different from the present one, necessitating a different methodology employed in the appraisal of the relationship. For a discussion on nuclear energy as part of the common energy policy of the Union and the consequences thereof (see, Ptasekaite, *supra* n. 11, pp. 96–99).

integration almost intact.[15] The analysis pursues the following questions: *Where does the specificity of the Euratom Treaty lie in comparison to the other Community/Union founding treaties? What are the peculiar features of the institutional system and the institutional dynamic established under the Euratom Treaty? Does the governing (dis)balance of institutional powers under the Euratom system correspond to that under the Union framework stricto sensu?*

The chapter begins by exploring the nature and specificity of the Euratom Treaty as a founding treaty in the context of and in comparison to the other two original founding treaties of the Union (the 1951 Treaty establishing the European Coal and Steel Community and the 1957 Treaty establishing the European Economic Community), testing the level of supranationality embedded in each of them and underscoring the essentially promotional and *dirigiste* character of the Euratom Treaty as a distinguishing characteristic thereof. The discussion proceeds with an insight into the governing institutional dynamic within the Euratom construct reflected in the division of competences among the Commission, the Council, the European Parliament and the Court of Justice of the EU as the key institutional actors. All the foregoing institutions are examined separately in terms of the nature and scope of their prerogatives under the Euratom Treaty: the nature and scope of the prerogatives of the Council as the main decision-making organ juxtaposed to the broad scope of prerogatives attributed to the Commission as the main executive organ, on to the prerogatives of the Parliament which has not been endowed with the identical scope of extensive prerogatives as under the Union framework. In this context, the democratic propensity of the Euratom Community is appraised based on the availability of democratic mechanisms under the Euratom Treaty, primarily, judging by the breadth of the prerogatives accorded to the European Parliament as the most democratic of the Union institutions which is directly elected by the Union citizens. The elaboration of the institutional dynamic concludes with the EU Court of Justice as the judicial organ which has had a central role in the consolidation of the singularity and specificity of the legal order created under the Euratom Community and has thus earned the status as the 'enabler' of Euratom's competence, its activist case law enabling for the remit of the Euratom Treaty to be gradually expanded (*Ruling*

15 To the difference of the Euratom Treaty, the other two founding treaties presently in force (the Treaty on the Functioning of the EU (TFEU) and the Treaty on the EU (TEU)) have periodically been subject to important and extensive changes to their structure and content: the TFEU (formerly TEC, dating from 1957) has undergone a substantial transformation over the years having culminated with the Lisbon Treaty amendments while the TEU (dating from 1992) has also been significantly amended by the Lisbon Treaty.

1/78;[16] *Commission v Council (Nuclear Safety Convention);*[17] *Land de Sarre and others v Ministre de l'Industrie (Cattenom);*[18] *Chernobyl II;*[19] *Commission v Ireland (MOX Plant);*[20] *Temelín*[21]). Ultimately, the analysis of the institutional dynamic and institutional power ratio created under the Euratom system aims to establish whether the division of powers that has been established under the Union framework *stricto sensu*, especially in light of the Lisbon Treaty amendments, has been fully translated to the Euratom domain and, in this sense discern the existence of a possible disbalance of prerogatives between the legislative and the executive branch as measured against the model of balance of institutional powers applicable under the Union framework.

The fact that the Euratom Treaty has been often labeled as an 'undemocratic' and 'legitimacy-deficient' treaty, combined with the critique of its vastly technocratic character and notorious resistance to amendment, has lead to the resurgence of a myriad of different case scenarios regarding the future modification of the Treaty. The last section of the chapter contemplates several potential alternatives for the future of the Euratom Treaty (and consequently, the Euratom Community) which range from pleas for treaty revision and/or its assimilation into the Union framework *stricto sensu* to calls for its complete abolishment.

Chapter 2 (*The interaction between the Euratom health and safety policy and the Union environmental policy*) covers the interplay between the health and safety legal framework established under the Euratom Treaty, on the one hand, and the legal framework for environmental protection created under the Treaty on the Functioning of the EU i.e. the Union's environmental policy, on the other. *What are the modalities in which these two regimes interact and what are the areas of concurring or conflicting competence involved therein? Is the practice of extrapolation (spill-over) of legal norms of one framework to the scope of application of the other sufficient for the said competition of competences to be resolved? What are the practical effects entailed by the former practice of extrapolation both for the Union framework and Euratom?*

The chapter commences by expanding on the instances of both concurring and conflicting competences between the Union *stricto sensu* and the Euratom Community in the fields of environmental and human health protection

16 ECR 1978 p. 02151.

17 C-29/99 *Commission v Council* ECR 2002 p. I-1122.

18 C-187/87 *Land de Sarre and others v Ministre de l'Industrie* ECR *1988 p. I-05013.*

19 C-70/88 *European Parliament v Council* ECR *1991 p. I-04529.*

20 C-459/03 *Commission v Ireland* ECR 2006 p. I-4635.

21 C-115/08 *Land Oberösterreich v ČEZ* ECR 2009 p. I-10265.

turning the attention to the nature of these competences and the interplay occurring among the tasks and objectives devised under each of these headings, accordingly. With regard to the notion of concurring/conflicting competences between the Euratom health and safety policy and the Union environmental policy, the discussion elucidates the concept of 'borrowing' or extrapolating legal bases which denotes the practice of extending the scope of Union rules to the Euratom domain, and, conversely, the practice of applying Euratom rules to areas covered by the Union Treaties (the TFEU and the TEU). The practice of extrapolating legal bases mainly occurs in instances of absence of corresponding provisions in the Euratom Treaty or secondary Euratom legislation, instances of concurring competence arising between Euratom and the Union with respect to a particular issue, and instances requiring for a general principle of Union law to be extended to the purview of Euratom.

Further on, for the purpose of pertinently examining the modalities of the interaction between Euratom's health and safety policy and the Union's environmental policy, the discussion builds up from the modalities of interaction occurring between the nuclear and environmental legal orders on the international arena equally reflected in the jurisprudence of the international and regional judicial fora of which the representative cases are looked at (*Nuclear Tests I* (*New Zealand v. France*,[22] *Australia v. France*[23]), *Nuclear Tests II* (*Request for Examination by New Zealand*[24]) and *Opinion on the Legality of the Threat or Use of Nuclear Weapons*[25] (before the International Court of Justice); *the MOX Plant* (before an UNCLOS Arbitral Tribunal);[26] *Balmer-Schafroth,*[27] *Athanassoglou*[28] and *L.C.B. v United Kingdom*[29] (before the European Court of Human Rights)).

Proceeding to the level of the EU, the discussion examines the relationship between Euratom's health and safety policy and the Union's environmental policy through the prism of the extent to which Euratom's health and safety

22 *Nuclear Tests (New Zealand v. France), Judgment, I.C.J. Reports 1974, p. 457.*

23 *Nuclear Tests (Australia v. France), Judgment, I.C.J. Reports 1974, p. 253.*

24 *Request for an Examination of the Situation in Accordance with Paragraph 63 of the Court's Judgment of 20 December 1974 in the Nuclear Tests (New Zealand v. France) Case, I.C.J. Reports 1995, p. 288.*

25 *Legality of the Threat or Use of Nuclear Weapons, Advisory Opinion, I.C.J. Reports 1996, p. 226.*

26 http://pca-cpa.org/upload/files/MOX%20Plant%20Press%20Release%20Order%20No.%206.pdf.

27 *Balmer-Schafroth v Switzerland* (1998) 25 EHRR 598.

28 *Athanassoglou* v Switzerland (2001) 31 EHRR 13.

29 *L.C.B. v United Kingdom* (1998) 27 EHRR 212.

regime is compatible and corresponds with the concept of 'environmental protection' as developed under the Union framework. In this context, the discussion discerns the presence/absence of an 'environmental protection' approach employed in the elaboration of the concepts of radiation protection and nuclear safety under the Euratom framework, looking to see whether the Euratom Treaty and the Euratom secondary legislation have been underpinned by an 'environmental protection' ratio, or, conversely, strictly adhere to the notion of 'protection of human health' thus fully ascribing to the concept of anthropocentricism. In this context, the spill-over effect of the Union's environmental policy rules and mechanisms to Euratom's purview is further appraised with regard to the principles of preventive action and the precautionary principles as principles of the Union's environmental policy and the possibility for their extension to Euratom's purview.

Upon exploring the interface between the Euratom health and safety regime and the Union environmental policy and elaborating the 'environmental protection' aspect of the Euratom health and safety regime, *Chapter 3* (*Euratom and environmental democracy: EU citizens' access to information and participation in decision-making in the nuclear arena*) looks at the 'grass-roots level' and the options available to the EU citizens regarding access to information and involvement in decision-making in the nuclear field in matters which actually or potentially concern the environment. *How reachable is Euratom for the ordinary citizen to the extent that concerns the human health protection and environmental protection aspects of the Euratom regime? What are the available procedural mechanisms for the public to scrutinize and influence the work of the Euratom institutions and be part of the Euratom decision-making process? Has the concept of 'environmental democracy' been adequately translated to the Euratom purview?*

The discussion aims to appraise the level of environmental transparency within the context of the Euratom Community based on the applicability of the procedural standards for 'environmental democracy' fostered under the 1998 *Convention on Access to Information, Public Participation in Decision-making and Access to Justice in Environmental Matters* (the Aarhus Convention) – as the key global charter for environmental democracy – to the remit of Euratom. In this respect, although important segments of Euratom domain are indeed covered by its provisions and come within the scope of the Aarhus Convention,[30] nevertheless it is only the Union and the Member States (not Euratom) that appear as contracting parties to the Aarhus Convention as a mixed agreement which entered into effect for the EU in 2005.

30 Arts. 4,5,6(1)(a) and Annex I of the Aarhus Convention.

Applying the standards of 'environmental democracy' to the Euratom domain is in itself a challenging task in view of the notorious element of secrecy associated with the nuclear field which stems from the inherently dual nature of nuclear energy as an energy source that, from a purely technical perspective, can easily be diverted from civil to military aims and *vice versa*. Therefore, the lack of transparency has traditionally been seen as idiosyncratic to the nuclear field. By contrast, the general tendency, especially pronounced in the past decade, has been to bring the EU closer to the citizens by reinforcing the transparency and accountability mechanisms available under the Union framework. The analysis aims to verify whether the Euratom Community has aligned with the former tendency of increasing the Union's openness and transparency towards its citizens and whether the environmental democracy standards applicable to the Union framework have found an adequate expression within the scope of the Euratom Community.

The chapter starts out by elaborating the procedural requirements set out under the Aarhus Convention (categorized in three different pillars: access to information, participation in decision-making and access to justice) which the EU and the Member States are bound by and thus responsible to ensure the full and correct implementation of. Successively, it looks at the transposing instruments adopted by the Union for the purpose of arriving at an uniform application of the Aarhus Convention requirements both at the EU and the national level adopted – part of which are specific to the nuclear domain (*Directive 2003/4/EC on public access to environmental information,*[31] *Directive 2003/35/EC providing for public participation in respect of the drawing up of certain plans and programmes relating to the environment,*[32] *Regulation No 1367/2006 on the application of the provisions of the Aarhus Convention on Access to Information, Public Participation in Decision-making and Access to Justice in Environmental Matters to Community institutions and bodies* (*the Aarhus Regulation*),[33] etc.). The former instruments are looked at in function to the extent to which the relevant Aarhus Convention obligations have been transposed to the scope of Euratom thus ascertaining the extent to which Euratom is to be considered bound by those obligations. Further on, the discussion inquires into the justiciability of the Aarhus Convention requirements regarding the access to information and participation in decision-making by offering a comparative analysis of the relevant case law of the international and the Union courts and other dispute resolution bodies which is indicative of the general judicial

31 *OJ L 41, 14.2.2003, pp. 26–32.*

32 *OJ L 156, 25/06/2003 pp. 0017–0025.*

33 OJ L 264, 25.9.2006 p. 13.

tendencies in the interpretation and application of the Convention requirements – with a particular focus on the case law pertaining to the nuclear field (*McGinley and Eagan v. United Kingdom*,[34] *L.C.B. v. United Kingdom case*,[35] *Sellafield MOX plant under the OSPAR arbitral tribunal*,[36] etc.).

Lastly, the discussion addresses one of the key shortcomings of the Union regime for procedural protection in environmental matters which is the absence of a specific directive transposing the access-to-justice pillar of the Aarhus Convention. The analysis assesses the void created by the lack of a Union access-to-justice regime in environmental matters to the effect that the former deficiency can be claimed to arguably undermine the overall Union regime for the citizens' procedural protection in environmental matters as prescribed under the Aarhus Convention. Admittedly, the adoption of an access-to-justice directive would not only consolidate the former Union regime, but it would also help gradually eliminate the existent discrepancies in the national legal systems regarding the application of the Aarhus Convention with respect to matters pertaining to the scope of the Union Treaties and the Euratom Treaty.

While Chapters 2 and 3 are concerned with the 'environmental protection' component of the research, *Chapter 4* (*Euratom and Non-Proliferation of Nuclear Weapons*) assesses the correlation between the Euratom safeguards system as representative of Euratom's competence in the area of securing the non-proliferation of nuclear weapons (i.e. the non-diversion of nuclear material intended for civil applications to further military aims), on the one hand, and the Union's non-proliferation policy as a policy belonging to the wider scope of the Union's Common Foreign and Security Policy (CFSP). Namely, as concerns the European Union's non-proliferation role, the *internal* dimension of the objective of non-proliferation of nuclear weapons devolves on the Euratom Community and is represented by the Euratom safeguards system whereas the *external* dimension of non-proliferation[37] is assumed by the Union's non-proliferation policy and is devised via the instruments and

---

34 *McGinley and Egan v. UK* (1998) 27 EHRR 1.

35 *L.C.B. v United Kingdom* (1998) 27 EHRR 212.

36 Final Award 2 July 2003, Ireland v UK, Dispute concerning access to information under Article 9 of the Ospar Convention (http://pca-cpa.org/upload/files/OSPAR%20Award.pdf).

37 For practical reasons, throughout the text the term 'non-proliferation' will sometimes be used interchangeably with the term 'non-proliferation of nuclear weapons', certainly, bearing in mind that the scope of the latter term belongs to the much larger scope of the former.

mechanisms of the Common Foreign and Security Policy as an over-arching Union policy. *What is the extent of the Euratom Community's role in the field of non-proliferation of nuclear weapons? How do the internal and external dimension of the Union's objective of non-proliferation of nuclear weapons interact and which are the issues involved? Has the EU's non-proliferation role been pursued in an adequate and satisfactory manner considering the achievements resulting from the operation of the Euratom safeguards system and the Union's non-proliferation policy, taken cumulatively*?

The chapter commences by examining the non-proliferation regime created under the 1970 *Treaty on the Non-proliferation of nuclear weapon* (the NPT) as the alpha and omega of the global legal regime on non-proliferation of nuclear weapons, looking more closely at the nature and scope of the requirements prescribed for the nuclear-weapon and non-nuclear-weapons states (NWS and NNWS) in the light of the objectives of non-proliferation and disarmament as two concurring objectives pursued by the Non-Proliferation Treaty. The discussion then moves to the nuclear safeguards component of the NPT regime which represents an essential element to the realization of the non-proliferation objective of the NPT regime further instrumentalised through the conclusion of nuclear safeguards agreements between the NPT contracting parties and the International Atomic Energy Agency (IAEA); More particularly, with respect to Euratom, the Member States which are non-nuclear-weapon states are covered under the Safeguards Agreement with the IAEA and the Euratom while the nuclear-weapon states of the EU (France and the United Kingdom) have concluded Voluntary Offer Agreements with the IAEA and the Euratom.

Having established the coordinates of the international safeguards regime, the ensuing discussion turns to the Euratom system of nuclear safeguards as a regional safeguards system devised pursuant to the Euratom Treaty and the related Euratom secondary legislation, primarily, the Commission Regulation (Euratom) No. 302/2005 on the application of Euratom safeguards,[38] where the modalities of the co-existence between the NPT/IAEA and the Euratom safeguards regimes and the level of complementarity between these regimes is assessed with the intention of establishing whether the Euratom safeguards regime as a regional regime fully and adequately follows the international one and whether – in certain respects – it may be considered as introducing an added value thereto.

Further on, the discussion shifts from the internal dimension of EU's non-proliferation role to its external dimension articulated by the Union's

38 OJ 2005 L 54/1.

non-proliferation policy. In this sense, the former policy's relationship with the NPT regime is examined with the aim of establishing its alignment with the objectives and mechanisms of the NPT regime. For this purpose, two segments that belong to the scope of the Union's non-proliferation policy are specifically brought into focus: the practice of inserting clauses relative to non-proliferation of weapons of mass destruction (WMD clauses) in agreements concluded by the Union with third countries (more particularly, the status of the clause and the effects produced by its insertion); and the issue of the NATO nuclear sharing arrangements established between NATO and certain Member States (in their individual capacity, not in the capacity of EU Member States) whereby the latter are required to host NATO nuclear weapons on their territory in peaceful times. The issue of NATO nuclear weapons sharing on European territory does not come under the scope of the Union's non-proliferation policy *per se* but nevertheless has the potential to compromise the Union's adherence to the NPT objectives and thus raises important legality and legitimacy-related issues.

The delineation of Euratom's share of competence in the area of non-proliferation of nuclear weapons would be incomplete should it omit to address the issue of Euratom's ambiguous relationship with the domain of military applications of nuclear energy and the discernment of the boundaries of the Euratom Treaty's scope of application in this regard. The analysis inquires as to whether the scope of the Euratom Treaty can be presumed to cover the domain of military applications of nuclear energy given that, legally speaking, this issue is to be considered a grey area on account of the absence of an express or categorical exclusion of the domain of military (defense) uses of nuclear energy foreseen under the Euratom Treaty or the Euratom secondary legislation. In order to adequately address the issue, the discussion begins by offering insight into the original intentions of the Union's founding fathers with respect to the issue by employing a teleological approach and looking at relevant historical projects and strategies for nuclear energy that have pre-dated the creation of the Euratom Community (the *European Defense Community Treaty*, the *Western European Union Treaty* (the *Modified Brussels Treaty*), the *Spaak Report*, the *Draft minutes of the Venice Conference*). Furthermore, the analysis looks at the provisions of the Euratom Treaty that (directly or indirectly) concern the military (defense) uses of nuclear energy (the chapters on Nuclear Supplies, Nuclear Safeguards and Property Ownership).

Finally, the discussion regarding Euratom's stake in the field of military uses of nuclear energy and thus, the possibility to apply the Euratom Treaty thereto, concludes by elucidating the EU Court of Justice's standpoint in the matter and offering an insight into the relevant case law (C-61/03 *Commission v. UK*;[39] C-65/04 *Commission v. UK*;[40] Joined Cases C-205/10 P, C-217/10 P and C-222/10 P, *Eriksen, Hansen and Lind*[41]). The fact that the former issue is not in the least a clear-cut one has been further confirmed by the differing views expressed by other EU institutions, most notably the Commission and the Parliament, which have clashed with that of the Court of Justice.

Finally, the *Conclusions* part addresses the *lacunae* detected with regard to the Euratom health and safety and safeguards regimes throughout the elaboration of the issues covered in the four chapters of the book, attempting to account for or justify their presence, or, alternatively, suggest possible changes in these regimes. Therefore, certain suggestions are made regarding the discharge of the tasks and activities of Euratom's key institutional actors, and, where applicable, pertinent and feasible modifications of the existent Euratom rules are indicated.

In view of the foregoing, it is important to note that the present text assumes a Euratom-neutral tone by observing the Euratom Community objectively as a unique creation in both legal and conceptual terms all the while avoiding to take a stance pro- or contra- the justifiability of the existence of Euratom, or the justifiability of the use of nuclear energy in general, for that matter. Irrespective of whether the reader declares him or herself a friend or a foe of nuclear energy – or of Euratom as a nuclear energy community – the fact remains that "*(i)t is possible to be against the nuclear and still love the existence of Euratom*".[42]

39 ECR 2005 p. I-2477.

40 ECR 2006 p. I-2239.

41 ECR 2011 p. I-1.

42 Paraphrasing Nina Commeau-Yannoussis, former Head of Unit of Energy Policy and Security of Supply, DG Energy and Transport, in Conference Report: The Euratom Treaty and Future Energy Options: Conditions for a Level Playing Field in the Energy Sector, September 23, 2005, at the Danish Parliament Building Christiansborg, Conference by NOAH – Friends of the Earth Denmark, The Danish Ecological Council and The Danish Organisation for Sustainable Energy (http://www.energyintelligenceforeurope.dk/conf_p6.html), p. 34.

CHAPTER 1

The Nature and the Specificity of the Euratom Community: The Claim for Supranationality

The creation of the European Atomic Energy Community (Euratom) in 1957 meant, in the words of French Prime Minister Guy Mollet, the joining of the atomic destinies of the original six Member States of the then European Coal and Steel Community[1] in a venture which can most succinctly be described as the expression of a subjective ideal (that was integrated Europe) and an objective reality (that was atomic power).[2] Euratom is essentially a *supranational* venture involving concomitant national sovereignty stakes which at its inception was conceived to be the more supranational of the two 1957 Communities (the other being the European Economic Community (EEC)) given that it covered a very specific subject matter which was relatively less controversial and potentially less far-reaching than that of the EEC Treaty. Paradoxically, in spite of the nature of the subject matter the Euratom Treaty being more amenable to supranational regulation,[3] the provisions in the Euratom Treaty owning such a potential are fewer than those of the European Economic Community (EEC) Treaty.[4]

The Euratom Treaty belongs to the 'first' phase in the development of national and international nuclear law, beginning in the late 1940s and early 1950s marked by the adoption of instruments targeting the promotion of the peaceful use of nuclear power.[5] Although it cannot be qualified as an atomic bill of rights because of its prevalent technical character it certainly represents

1 G. Mollet, *Vital Speeches of the Day* (*15 March 1957*), Vol. 23 Issue 11, p. 350.

2 L. Scheinmann, Euratom: Nuclear Integration in Europe, *International Conciliation*, May 1967, No. 563, Carnegie Endowment for International Peace, p. 5.

3 Efron and Nanes considered that by the nature of its subject matter the Euratom Treaty 'bite(s) deeper into the crust of national sovereignty than the Common Market Treaty' (R. Efron and A.S. Nanes, The Common Market and Euratom Treaties: Supranationality and the Integration of Europe, *International and Comparative Law Quarterly*, 1957, Vol. 6, p. 688).

4 Efron and Nanes, *supra*, p. 680.

5 P.D. Cameron, The Revival of Nuclear Power: An Analysis of the Legal Implications, *Journal of Environmental Law*, 2007, Vol. 19 No. 1, p. 72; The author further distinguishes a second phase which heralded by the outbreak of the Chernobyl accident where the use of nuclear law serves as a constraint related to the nuclear safety concerns, as well as a third phase currently taking place, marked by a balancing between the elements of promotion and constraint.

 | DOI 10.1163/9789004310414_003

an 'epoch-making' treaty[6] for European integration. The dynamics in the life of the Euratom Treaty has been characterized by a striving for a perennial balance between two opposite tendencies – one of 'federalizing' (unifying) the nuclear market between Member States and the other of preserving their nuclear 'free will' through the independent development of national nuclear programs and technologies (especially prominent with regard to the delimitation between the civil and the military uses of the atom). The Treaty does not curtail independent military activities of Member States, but nonetheless, the very fact of integrating nuclear human, technical and material potentials under one single treaty invariably impacts national nuclear decisions in the military sphere as well.[7] Thus, apart from the prevalent economic objective, the treaty concomitantly furthers the objective of preserving the peace on the European continent[8] as one of the long-term goals stipulated in the Treaty's preamble. At the time of its adoption, Euratom was seen as a forward-looking and *futuristic* achievement centered on promoting the development of the (then) nascent civil nuclear energy production, the world having already been familiarized with the military nuclear industry and its devastating consequences in the developments throughout the Second World War.

The present chapter explores the unique nature of the Euratom Community as an independent legal entity, different and differentiable from that of the European Union *strict sensu*, positing the former within the overall European Union structure. The chapter inquires into the nature and specificity of the Euratom Treaty as a founding treaty in the context of the *Union* founding treaties (the TFEU and the TEU), proceeding with an insight into the institutional dynamic governing the Euratom construct which has been mirrored in the division of competences among the Commission, the Council, the European Parliament and the Court of Justice of the EU as key institutional actors. The analysis of the institutional dynamic and the institutional power ratio of the Euratom system aims to establish the extent to which the principle of division of powers applicable to the Union framework *stricto sensu* has been translated to the Euratom domain, more particularly, by measuring the breadth of the prerogatives held by the legislative branch against those of the executive branch of institutional power. Further on, the chapter discusses the Euratom Community's predilection for democracy (or, democratic disposition) based on the availability of democratic mechanisms prescribed under the Euratom

6 Efron and Nanes, *supra* n. 3, p. 684.

7 J.G. Polach, *Euratom: Its Background, Issues and Economic Implications*, Oceana Publications, 1964, p. 190.

8 Polach, *supra*, p. 190.

Treaty (or, the Union Treaties and thereby extended to the Euratom domain), using the extent of the prerogatives accorded to the European Parliament as the most democratic of the Union institutions as the main parameter. Lastly, with the intention of painting a clear picture on the viability of the Euratom project for the future and having in mind certain past and ongoing plans for revision of the Euratom Treaty, several case scenarios regarding the future of the Treaty will be elaborated, ranging from pleas for treaty revision or assimilation into the framework of the *Union* Treaties to calls for the Treaty's complete abolishment.

1 Three Treaties, One Common Concept

After the establishment of the European Coal and Steel Community in 1952, the main intention behind the ensuing adoption of the EEC and the Euratom Treaties and creation of two new Communities on the international scene was enable the restart of the engines of European economic integration and exit the stalemate caused by the failure of the European Defense Community in 1954. In this sense, the *relance européenne* was focused on achieving immediate economic goals mainly by employing vertical integration of particular sectors complemented by a horizontal integration of national markets.[9] The initial impetus was provided by the Memorandum prepared by the Benelux governments (the *Benelux Memorandum*) in May 1955 which had outlined transport, conventional energy and atomic energy as economic sectors for vertical integration alongside the envisaged creation of a general common market resulting from the horizontal integration approach.[10] The *Benelux Memorandum* lead to the adoption of the 1955 *Messina Resolution* which entrusted the Intergovernmental Committee (composed of government delegates) under the chairmanship of Belgian Foreign Minister Paul-Henri Spaak with the mandate to reinvigorate the engines of European integration providing a report which would thoroughly explore the possibilities for the future creation of the common market and atomic energy Communities. The Spaak Committee established four commissions consisting of national experts in the fields of the general common market, conventional energy, atomic energy and transport.[11] The work of the Committee was concluded in April 1956 and its achievements were presented in the Spaak Report and adopted at the Venice conference in

9 Polach, *supra*, p. 19.

10 Polach, *supra*, p. 20.

11 Polach, *supra*, p. 21.

June 1956 in order to serve as the groundwork for the preparation of the final treaty proposals.[12] Additional input to the drafting process was provided by the study entitled '*A Target for Euratom*' which reviewed the factors justifying the establishment of Euratom as an economic venture independent from the ECSC and the EEC Communities.[13]

The prevalent conviction among the decision-makers at the time was that the pressing economic needs of Little Europe ('the Six') could be sustained primarily through integration in the nuclear field.[14] Such integration would not entail an assimilation of national nuclear industries into a supranational one: national nuclear industries were to remain independent while being governed by a common supranational authority in the respective fields covered by the Treaty.[15] Nuclear energy was, in a way, believed to be the panacea for the pressing economic problems of 'the Six', having the potential to spur economic growth for the still young and fragile European Community in the short-term.

Effectively, the process that led to the final adoption of both Treaties was certainly not a peaceful sailing. The Euratom Treaty was considered to be Jean Monnet's favorite favorite of the two as it dealt with a brand new economic field, free of any pre-existing Member State claims and thus, standing a better chance of acceptance by the European public than the Common Market Treaty.[16] It was considered that the Euratom Treaty would win over the confidence of European parliamentary bodies more easily, primarily because nuclear energy was still 'virgin territory' where it was believed there were no vested national interests which itself was sufficient guarantee for a smooth acceptance.[17]

The negotiations for the Common Market Treaty that run in parallel did not enjoy the same enthusiastic reception by European audiences, the planned

---

12 Polach, *supra*, p. 23.

13 Polach, *supra*, p. 26; The text of the report 'A Target for Euratom', submitted by Louis Armand, Franz Etzel and Francesco Giordani at the request of the governments of Belgium, France, German Federal Republic, Italy, Luxembourg and the Netherlands in May 1957, can be consulted at http://www.cvce.eu/obj/report_by_the_three_wise_men_on_euratom_4_may_1957-en-e72917a4-3c9d-48b1-b8cb-41307736731e.html (the website of the Centre Virtuel de la Connaissance sur l'Europe).

14 Polach, *supra*, p. 28.

15 Polach, *supra*, p. 28.

16 M. Camps, *Britain and the European Community 1955–1963*, Princeton University Press, 1964, p. 55.

17 European Parliament – Directorate-General for Research, *Working Paper: The European Parliament and the Euratom Treaty: Past, Present and future*, Energy and Research series, ENER 114-EN 2-2002.

establishment of a Common Market having sparked certain animosities between individual Member States.[18] Conceptually from different the Euratom Treaty as a sectoral treaty specifically targeting the nuclear industry, the Common Market Treaty was a much more complex and far-reaching project in terms of its scope and subject matter than. The latter was aimed at coordinating and unifying a multitude of economic policies which provided for the progressive establishment of an area of free movement of goods, workers, services and capital within the territory of the European Community. In a manner of speaking, the fairly uncontroversial response to the Euratom project seems to have served as a means to push the Common Market treaty through the back door since the plan was for the two Treaties to be adopted as a one-package deal, thereby linking together the destinies of the two Treaties.[19] In spite of the fervent instigation of the French side to treat the two projects separately, the predominant view shared by the rest of 'the Six' was for the negotiations on both treaties to run concomitantly and for the two treaties to share a mutual destiny.[20]

In the immediate period prior to the approval of both treaties by the parliamentary bodies of the Member States the future of these two treaties was still hanging in the balance. On this point, the role of the Action Committee proved crucial. The Action Committee, founded in October 1955, was a political elite group consisting of the leaders of all key political parties and trade unions in the Member States and headed by Jean Monnet. It came into existence for the purpose of providing reinforcement to Spaak Committee's *relance* efforts in generating support for the negotiation of the two new treaties, often through informal channels.[21] It is believed that this Committee played a vital role in securing the French Assembly's support for the adoption of the Euratom Treaty in July 1956. In this period France was going through a political turmoil which resulted in change of government, with the Prime Minister Mollet stepping down and Prime Minister Bourges-Maunoury assuming office.[22] However, these events did not substantially affect the ongoing treaty negotiations in any substantial manner thanks to the active lobbying by the French members to the Action Committee.[23]

18 Camps, *supra*, p. 54 et seq.

19 Camps, *supra*, p. 54.

20 Camps, *supra*, p. 54.

21 W. Yondrof, Monnet and the Action Committee: The Formative Period of the European Communties, *International Organization*, 1965, p. 896.

22 Yondrof, *supra*, p. 901.

23 Yondrof, *supra*, p. 901.

While negotiations for the Euratom Treaty did not run as smoothly all the time, the Treaty was eventually fitted to accommodate the positions of all the six Member States, especially France who insisted that military uses of nuclear energy be left outside of the scope of the Treaty. Some argue that the rather benevolent acceptance of the Euratom project had prevented the potential failure of the Common Market project and assured a contemporaneous adoption of the two treaties.[24] The former should nevertheless be taken *cum grano salis* since the general objectives of the two treaties were mutually dependent carrying the danger that the goals of the Euratom Community would have become self-defeating and obsolete should the creation of the Common Market not have been accomplished. In fact, one could plausibly go as far as conceive the existence of an independent, self-standing Common Market Treaty whereas the reverse – an isolated atomic energy Treaty only partially covering the broad-set common market goals of European integration – would seem as a much less viable concept. Another factor which hinders the independent existence of an atomic energy charter as the Euratom Treaty is the delicate dual nature of atomic energy as an energy source that potentially caters to both civil and military needs[25] which draws on the theoretical debate on the suitability of the nuclear field for any functional integration.[26]

II The Nature and Specificity of the Euratom Treaty in the Context of the Founding Treaties

Ever since the adoption of the Paris Treaty and the two Rome Treaties the legal doctrine has inquired into the *sui generis* character of the Treaties and the overarching idea of *supranationality* that characterize the former.[27] The

24 C. Deubner, The expansion of West German Capital and the Founding of Euratom, *International Organization*, 1979, p. 206.

25 See for this also, Scheinmann, *supra* n. 2, p. 61.

26 Scheinmann, *supra*, p. 12.

27 On the supranational character of the treaties, see, R. Efron and A.S. Nanes, The Emerging Concept of Supranationality in Recent International Agreements, *Kentucky Law Journal*, 1955, Issue 44; R. Efron and A.S. Nanes, The Common Market and Euratom Treaties: Supranationality and the Integration of Europe, *International and Comparative Law Quarterly*, 1957, Vol. 6; D.D. Smith, The European Atomic Energy Community (Euratom): The Limits of Supranationalism, *California Western International Law Journal*, 1970 Vol. 1 Issue 33; and, P.M. Houben, The Merger of the Executives of the European Communities, *Common Market Law Review*, 1965–1966, Vol. 3 Issue 37.

following analysis will refer to the three treaties in their original form and content for the purpose of establishing the specific, and therefore different and differentiable character, of the Euratom Treaty with respect to the other two treaties. It will be remembered that of the three founding treaties, the ECSC Treaty has expired with part of its provisions being assimilated to the TFEU, the EC Treaty has been modified and renamed as the TFEU whereas the Euratom Treaty, as the most fortunate of the siblings, has foregone any substantial amendments to its text ever since the original adoption.

The three treaties are international legal acts idiosyncratic in nature both in terms of their legal status and the effect upon the domestic legal orders of Member States. The former have, each in their own domain, established a supranational organization in particular economic and political sectors that had previously not been considered amenable to supranational regulation. The concept of supranational regulation has remained as intrinsic to the institutional and legal order of the Union, accruing from its legal status of an entity that has exceeded the bounds of regional intergovernmental organization, but one which is nonetheless short of a federal state.

An important manifestation of the interdependence between the Euratom, the ECSC and the EEC Treaties are the instances of overlap of their long-term objectives. A textual reading of the original preambles of these three founding treaties reveals that the remits of the treaties' general objectives coincide in two respects: the member states subscribe to the furtherance of *the cause of peace*[28] and to contributing to the *economic growth and the prosperity and well being of the European citizens.*[29] Preserving peace and stability alongside a continuous economic progress benefitting the wellbeing of European citizens have to this day invariably remained to be the bottom-line of the Community/ Union Treaties.

---

28 The preambles of the Euratom Treaty and the TFEU read:

'RECOGNISING that nuclear energy represents an essential resource for the development and invigoration of industry and will permit *the advancement of the cause of peace* (...)' (Euratom Treaty).

'RESOLVED by thus pooling their resources *to preserve and strengthen peace and liberty*, and calling upon the other peoples of Europe who share their ideal to join in their efforts (...)' (TFEU)) [Emphasis added].

29 'RESOLVED to create the conditions necessary for the development of a powerful nuclear industry which will provide extensive energy resources, lead to the modernisation of technical processes and contribute, through its many other applications, *to the prosperity of their peoples* (...)' (Euratom Treaty); 'AFFIRMING as the essential objective of their efforts *the constant improvements of the living and working conditions of their peoples* (...)' (TFEU) [Emphasis added].

Having in mind the undisputed *supranational* character of the Treaties, authors have pointed to the existence of a hierarchy between the Treaties that has been functioned upon the extent of the supranational outreach of their provisions.[30] Even though today belonging to the historical archives, the former ECSC Treaty is a legal document which is emblematic of the supranational effort of the six founding member states and serves as the gold standard against which the potential for supremacy of the other treaties can be measured. In spite of being confined to the domain of the coal and steel industry, the ECSC Treaty was underscored by a powerful integration ratio the intensity of which has not been replicated in the other treaties.[31] Furthermore, while the supranational provisions of the EC Treaty were considered to outnumber those of the Euratom Treaty[32] the latter, by the nature of its field of application, was endowed with a greater potential to affect national sovereignty.[33] Some authors have considered the breadth of the prerogatives belonging to the Commission as a typically supranational organ as the litmus test for judging the supranationality input of the treaties,[34] while others have referred to the autonomous conduct of international relations and progressive assumption of an international personality, which under the Euratom compact has been perceived as comprehensive and fail-proof.[35] However, principally speaking, as will be demonstrated in the subsequent sections, while the *potentiality* for supranationality may be greater for the Euratom Treaty, the *actuality* of supranationality has been predominantly accomplished under the purview of the EC Treaty (today, the TFEU).

In function to the nature of their respective subject matter, the Euratom Treaty and the ECSC Treaty are *sectoral* treaties while the EC Treaty is to be

---

30 Efron and Nanes, *supra* n. 3, p. 680.

31 The text of the Treaty establishing the European Coal and Steel Community expressly refers to the supranational character thereof. Art. 9 of the ECSC Treaty read as follows:

> The members of the High Authority shall exercise their functions in complete independence, in the general interest of the Community. In the fulfillment of their duties, they shall neither solicit nor accept instructions from any government or from any organization. They will abstain from all conduct incompatible with the *supranational character* of their functions. Each Member State agrees to respect this *supranational character* and to make no effort to influence the members of the High Authority in the execution of their duties. [Emphasis added].

32 Efron and Nanes, *supra* n. 3, p. 680.

33 Efron and Nanes, *supra*, p. 683.

34 Efron and Nanes, *supra*, p. 681, 682.

35 H.J. Hahn, Euratom: The Conception of an International Personality, *Harvard Law Review*, April 1958, Vol. 71 Number 6, pp. 1053–1056.

qualified as a *cross-sectoral* treaty.[36] As a sectoral treaty, the Euratom Treaty does not cover the totality of the nuclear energy sector; its scope is confined to the peaceful applications of nuclear energy[37] and extends to the following fields: Promotion of nuclear research (Chapter 1), Dissemination of Information (Chapter 2), Health and Safety (Chapter 3), Investment in nuclear projects (Chapter 4), Joint Undertakings (Chapter 5), Nuclear Supplies (Chapter 6), Nuclear Safeguards (Chapter 7), Property Ownership (Chapter 8), Nuclear Common Market (Chapter 9) and External Relations of Euratom (Chapter 10). In fact, the ambit of application of the Treaty has not been modified by any of the amending treaties and has remained identical ever since its original adoption.

Based on the extent of treaty provisions which are regulatory in nature contained therein, academic literature has categorized the ECSC and EEC Treaties as *regulatory* texts distinguishable from the Euratom Treaty as an essentially *promotional* enterprise[38] by reason of the fact that nuclear industry as a field could not conceivably be created or developed merely through regulations, but rather through concrete actions.[39] Thus, while the main objective of the EC was *to control and regulate* the activities implementing the Common Market policies, the purpose of Euratom was to *promote* the use and development of civil nuclear energy.[40] The task of promoting a new industry is much different than the task of regulating an already established industry. It is imminent that in the exercise of 'promoting' the competent institutions have to encourage, help and provide impetus for the development of a particular nuclear industry and in so doing are driven to promote or favour the operation of certain undertakings (enterprises) which essentially conflicts with the free market logic underpinning the EC Treaty.[41] By being given regulatory powers with relation

---

36 S. Wolf, Euratom before the Court: A Political Theory of Legal Non-Integration, *European Integration Online Papers*, 2011 Vol. 15 – Article 10, http://eiop.or.at/eiop/texte/2011-010a.htm (last accessed in July 2013), p. 8.

37 Nonetheless, the Treaty does not contain an explicit pronouncement in favour of the non-application of its provisions to Member States' military nuclear programmes. For a discussion on whether the Treaty can in certain respects be presumed to apply to the military applications of nuclear energy, see Chapter 3.

38 Scheinmann, *supra* n. 2, p. 56.

39 P. Mathijsen, Some Legal Aspects of Euratom, *Common Market Law Review*, 1965–1966 Issue 3, p. 330.

40 D.D. Smith, The European Atomic Energy Community (Euratom): The Limits of Supranationalism, *California Western International Law Journal*, 1970, Vol. 1, p. 53.

41 T. Cusack, A Tale of Two Treaties, *Common Market Law Review*, 2003, Vol. 40 Issue 117, p. 126. Furthermore, Mathijsen has claimed that the existence of such a close relationship

to existing economic activities, the ECSC and the EC Treaties were comparatively 'better off' than the Euratom Treaty which, in turn, targeted activities that had not yet been introduced or had only existed in a pre-industrial stage.[42] Hence, it was necessary that within the context of an atomic energy treaty the emphasis be put on assistance, *promotion* and cooperation between the Community, the Member States and the enterprises (undertakings) concerned.[43] However, it is important to note that Euratom does possess certain regulatory powers pronounced in the domain of health and safety from radiation protection.[44]

As a typically regulatory legal text, the ECSC Treaty had established a comprehensive institutional and normative framework, leaving little room for legislative action on the part of the institutions.[45] Therefore, instead of providing the basis for law-making, the treaty itself was the law to be applied. Although a sectoral treaty as well, the subject matter of the Euratom Treaty is however not fully comparable to that of the ECSC given that the nuclear industry, unlike the coal and steel industries, was still an experimental field undergoing development in the late 1950s and early 1960s and had not yet progressed to the point where its impact on the economies of Member States could have been accurately assessed.[46]

The former functional distinction between the treaties further leads to distinction between the *market-oriented* characted of the EEC treaty and the Euratom Treaty which was labeled as a *dirigiste* treaty.[47] Namely, the EEC Treaty was modeled to be the typical 'framework' treaty which did not create substantive norms but left it to the institutions to discharge of the legislative functions, thus having an 'almost exclusively constitutional character'.[48] Provided that the nuclear field was a fairly new and experimental field undergoing development, it was considered more suitable that the emphasis be put on assistance, promotion, aid and cooperation between the Euratom Community, the enterprises and the member States, as well as coordination of the activities within the

---

between the Euratom Community and the nuclear industry has given the Community an industrial mindset rather than an administrative one (Mathijsen, *supra*, p. 337).

42 Mathijsen, *supra* n. 39, p. 329.

43 Mathijsen, *supra*, p. 329.

44 Mathijsen, *supra*, p. 334.

45 H. Steiger, An Evaluation of Legal Development on a Regional Basis: The Search for European Unity, *Ohio State Law Journal*, 1961, Vol. 22, p. 505.

46 A. Nanes, The Evolution of Euratom, *International Journal*, 1957–1958, Vol. 16, p. 16.

47 Cusack, *supra* n. 41, p. 125.

48 Steiger, *supra* n. 45, p. 505.

remit of the Community.[49] In this way, the Euratom Community was driven to promote the development of nuclear industries by way of its direct engagement and active involvement in the nuclear field.[50] Such conceptual difference in approaches between Euratom and the other two communities had translated into differences in the prerogatives accorded to the institutions and the decision-making procedures prescribed under each of the treaties.[51]

The Euratom Treaty establishes an institutional framework alongside laying down certain substantive norms (concrete regulations) which is however not to be identified with the purely legislative character of the ECSC Treaty.[52] The former relates to the distinction between the *legislative* and the *quasi-legislative* character of the Treaties. The quasi-legislative character is fully displayed in the EEC Treaty which did not contain any substantive norms, reverting to regulatory action of institutions in creating the norms themselves under the institutional frame provided by the treaty.[53] In this regard, the Euratom Treaty aligns to the EEC Treaty and prevalently performs a quasi-legislative in lieu of a fully-fledged legislative function, laying down a limited number of regulations alongside conferring broader legislative and executive authority on the competent institutions.[54]

In terms of the *nature of the competence* exercised, the Euratom Community, unlike the EEC and the ECSC, has very little to no exclusive competence, except with respect to health protection,[55] a field where it has substantially greater competence than the Member States. The Euratom Community has not followed the trend of increase in the areas of exclusive competence culminating with the Lisbon Treaty amendments.[56] Thus, in the majority of the fields

49 Mathijsen, *supra* n. 39, p. 329.

50 Mathijsen, *supra*, p. 343.

51 Mathijsen, *supra*, p. 343.

52 Steiger, *supra* n. 45, p. 504.

53 Steiger, *supra*, p. 504.

54 Steiger, *supra*, p. 513.

55 Mathijsen, *supra* n. 39, p. 328.

56 The scope of the Union's exclusive competence has been extended via the Lisbon Treaty and covers the following areas (Art. 3(1) TFEU): the customs union, the establishing of the competition rules necessary for the functioning of the internal market, the monetary policy for the Member States whose currency is the euro, the conservation of marine biological resources under the common fisheries policy and the common commercial policy. The Union holds exclusive competence for the conclusion of international agreements when its conclusion is provided for in a legislative act of the Union or is necessary to enable the Union to exercise its internal competence, or in so far as its conclusion may affect common rules or alter their scope (Art. 3(2) TFEU).

covered, the Euratom Community shares the competence with the Member States whereby the functions prescribed for Euratom regarding nuclear integration are less imposing and are complementary in character rather than exclusive.[57]

Another peculiar aspect of the relationship between the Treaties is the *lex general* versus *lex specialis* differentiation. The EC (now, TFEU) Treaty has a broader field of application and is thus considered as *lex generalis* whereas Euratom covers a very narrowly circumscribed field and is therefore qualified as *lex specials*. Also, even if the two treaties had not been contemporaneously adopted, the international law principle *lex posterior derogate legi priori* would prove inapplicable to the relationship between the two particular Treaties. This is because each Treaty is an independent and autonomous entity, equal in statute, precluding the existence of any sort of hierarchical relationship between the two.[58] The Commission has confirmed the *lex specialis* character of the Euratom Treaty considering that in case of conflict or overlap between the Treaties' respective fields of application, it is the special rules of the Euratom Treaty as a sectoral treaty that would apply,[59] perceiving the two Communties as mutually independent frameworks where the legal acts of one Community are not subject to the acts of the other.[60] The former is reflected in the wording of Art. 106a(3) Euratom (the bridging provision between the Euratom Treaty and the TEU and the TFEU) – more particularly, in the guarantee that the provisions of the Treaty on European Union and of the Treaty on the Functioning of the European Union will not derogate from the provisions of the Euratom Treaty.[61] The foregoing division will be further dealt with in Chapter 2 as one determining the direction and the quality of the 'spill-over'

57 Scheinmann, *supra* n. 2, p. 11.

58 Cusack, *supra* n. 41, p. 127.

59 Commission Decision of 21 February 1994, 94/285/Euratom, OJ 1994 L 122/30, para. 21.

60 Commission Decision 94/285/Euratom, para. 22.

61 TITLE III

INSTITUTIONAL AND FINANCIAL PROVISIONS

Application of certain provisions of the Treaty on European Union and of the Treaty on the Functioning of the European Union

Article 106a

1. Article 7, Articles 13 to 19, Article 48(2) to (5), and Articles 49 and 50 of the Treaty on European Union, and Article 15, Articles 223 to 236, Articles 237 to 244, Article 245, Articles 246 to 270, Article 272, 273 and 274, Articles 277 to 281, Articles 285 to 304, Articles 310 to 320, Articles 322 to 325 and Articles 336, 342 and 344 of the Treaty on the Functioning of the European Union, and the Protocol on Transitional Provisions, shall apply to this Treaty.

process occurring between the legal rules adopted under the Euratom framework and those adopted further to the TFEU and the TEU treaties.

Certain of the categories of distinction between the three treaties outlined *supra*, although historical and teleological in nature, should nevertheless not be seen as anachronistic as they can serve to elucidate the current relationship between the Union Treaties (the TFEU and the TEU) and the Euratom Treaty. Conversely, there are also those types of distinction that have been invalidated in view of present day developments, especially those which center on the 'new and experimental character of nuclear industry' accounting for the fundamental conceptual differences between the treaties. What seems striking in this respect is that even though the nuclear industry and nuclear technology are today optimally developed and are thus no more considered as *terra incognita*, the former conceptual difference has been maintained in the present relationship between the Euratom construct and the legal order of the Union *stricto sensu* (established under the TFEU and the TEU treaties). These considerations will be further developed in the sections that follow.

III The Institutional Dynamic within the Euratom Compact

Due to its dominant supranational tendency, the institutional dynamic (the interaction among the institutions and the decision-making procedures) of the European Union *lato sensu* differs in important respects from that of the domestic legal systems of the Member States. It is for this reason that the principle of division of powers is not always consistently applied and strictly followed as in the national systems – namely, the former is most clearly reflected in the prerogatives accorded to the Union's legislative branch (the Council and the Parliament) which, in certain points, find themselves intertwined with those of the Union's executive branch (the Commission). It is quite difficult to categorically differentiate among EU instiutions that can be considered to singularly and exclusively hold the legislative as opposed to the executive power

2. Within the framework of this Treaty, the references to the Union, to the "Treaty on European Union", to the "Treaty on the Functioning of the European Union" or to the "Treaties" in the provisions referred to in paragraph 1 and those in the protocols annexed both to those Treaties and to this Treaty shall be taken, respectively, as references to the European Atomic Energy Community and to this Treaty.

3. The provisions of the Treaty on European Union and of the Treaty on the Functioning of the European Union shall not derogate from the provisions of this Treaty.

and the former, as will be evidenced *infra*, holds true *a fortiori* with respect to the Euratom Community.

What may be described as a certain discrepancy between the decision-making competences under the Union and the Euratom frameworks could be explained with the existent conceptual difference between the Euratom Treaty as a sectoral and the TFEU and the TEU as cross-sectoral treaties with a different propensity for supranationality. Admittedly, the signatories of the Euratom Treaty have transferred significant competences regarding the conduct of the nuclear energy policy to the supranational level (in the fields of nuclear safeguards[62] and nuclear health and safety[63]) while simultaneously forseeing 'deliberative' provisions which revert to the adoption of soft measures (promotion of nuclear research[64]).[65]

The interaction among the EU institutions within the scope of the TFEU and the Euratom Treaty is best conveyed by the concepts of *hierarchical supranationalism* and *deliberative supranationalism* as competing modes of governance.[66] The exercise of weighing out the supranational against the national interests in the context of these two modes of governance is performed at EU level.[67] *Hierarchical supranationalism* signifies the promotion of supranational interests in a particular field with Member States being barred from intervening via unilateral regulation.[68] The *deliberative supranationalism* approach employs a balancing act between supranational and national interests whereby the solution is reached at supranational level through a deliberative process that favors a compromise to be achieved among the institutions and the Member States instead of the use of majority voting.[69]

The following sections will consecutively look at the most relevant prerogatives of the key institutional players in the Euratom system – the Commission, the Council, the Parliament and the Court of Justice of the EU – in function to the respective fields covered by each of the Treaty chapters. As the goal is to

62 Arts. 77–85 Euratom.

63 Arts. 30–39 Euratom.

64 Arts. 4–11 Euratom.

65 See, Wolf, *supra* n. 36, p. 5.

66 For this see, S. Wolf, Euratom, the European Court of Justice, and the Limits of Nuclear Integration in Europe, *German Law Journal*, 2011, Vol. 12 No. 8, pp. 1650–1653. The concept of deliberative supranationalism was largely elaborated in, C. Joerges, 'Deliberative Supranationalism' – Two Defences, *European Law Journal* 2002 Issue 8; and, C. Joerges and J. Neyer, 'Deliberative Supranationalism' Revisited, EUI Working Paper LAW No. 2006/20.

67 Wolf, *supra*, p. 1650.

68 Wolf, *supra*, p. 1650.

69 Wolf, *supra*, p. 1652.

adopt an analytical rather than a descriptive approach, only those prerogatives which are representative of the instiutions' involvement in the field will be referred to.

III.1 *The European Commission and the Council of the EU – The Regulatory Power*

The regulatory power under the Euratom system is vested with the European Commission and the Council of the EU, with the extent of prerogatives belonging to the Commission as a central decision-making organ being preponderant to those of the Council. As the institution where the dominant part of the regulatory, supervisory and executive power under the Euratom Treaty is concentrated, the Commission exercises a functional control over national and sub-national actors as well as actors at the EU level (such as the Euratom Supply Agency created under the *Supplies* chapter of the Treaty). These prerogatives of control are administrative in nature and (and in most cases) are exercised on the Commission's own motion.[70]

In its capacity of an executive organ, the Commission dispenses of important administrative tasks which reverts to the pervasive technocratic character of the Treaty, which proved indispensable at the 'promotional stage' in the first decades of Euratom's existence when nuclear energy production was still considered an obscure area. Since nuclear energy in Europe has now grown well past the promotional era, the impending question is whether such a technocratic approach is still justified and should be reconsidered.

The Commission also carries the legislative initiative under the Euratom Treaty while the legislative power *per se* is held by the Council – although, in principle, the 'real' power and authority within the Euratom Community rests with the Commission given its extensive decision-making powers.

Throughout the 'formative' years of Euratom especially, the Commission was known to act as an *enabling agent* in the broad construction of the Euratom Treaty provisions leading to a gradual explicit and implicit enlargement of the former's scope of application. It has played an invaluable role in actualizing the specificity and uniformity of the Euratom legal order by advocating the *effet utile* – type of interpretation of the Treaty provisions assuring that the Euratom competences are adequately delineated, or in certain cases, indeed broadened.[71] In addition, the Commission assumes a quasi-judicial role in the

70 H.J. Hahn, Control under the Euratom Compact, *The American Journal of Comparative Law*, 1958, Vol. 7, p. 28.

71 Such are the Ruling 1/78, the *Nuclear Safety Convention* case, the *Mox* case, which will be considered in detail *infra*.

domain of *Nuclear Safeguards*, where it is entitled to impose sanctions on persons and undertakings that are in breach of the safeguards provisions of the Euratom Treaty and related secondary legislation thus performing a quasi-judicial function.

In the area of *Promotion of nuclear research* (Chapter 1) the role of the Commission is central as the forum responsible to promote and facilitate nuclear research in the Member States which is to be complemented by conducting the Community research and training programme and all the operational tasks linked thereto – the former role is more supervisory than regulatory being that the main goal of these provisions is promotional.[72]

The *Dissemination of Information* chapter (Chapter 2) establishes the regime for information over which the Community has the power of disposal where the Commission is empowered to grant licenses and sublicenses and has full authority over the dissemination of that information[73] and other type of information the dissemination of which is performed by amicable agreement and information which is subject to compulsory communication to the Commission.[74] The Council also has an active role which is to adopt security regulations that lay down various security gradings, modify a particular security grading or declassify certain information via unanimous decision.[75]

The basic standards for the protection of the health of workers and the general public against the dangers of ionizing radiations (*Health and Safety* (Chapter 3)) are drafted by the Commission, having beforehand obtained the opinion of a group of persons appointed by the Scientific and Technical Committee (among which scientific experts, in particular public health experts, from the Member States), as well as the opinion of the Economic and Social Committee. The Council further adopts the basic standards acting by a qualified majority, after consulting the European Parliament and taking account of the opinions expressed by the two relevant Committees.[76]

72 Arts. 4–11.

73 Arts. 12, 13.

74 Arts. 14–23; For a more elaborate overview of the role of the two institutions in the field, see Council Directive 96/29/Euratom of 13 May 1996 laying down basic safety standards for the protection of the health of workers and the general public against the dangers arising from ionizing radiation (*OJ L 159, 29.6.1996, p. 1–114*) and the proposal for a new Directive laying down basic safety standards for protection against the dangers arising from exposure to ionising radiation, Brussels, 30.5.2012 COM (2012) 242 final.

75 Art. 24.

76 Art. 31.

Under the *Investment* chapter (Chapter 4), the Commission is under the duty to stimulate action by persons and undertakings and to facilitate coordinated development of their investment in the nuclear field, *inter alia*, by periodically publishing illustrative programmes revealing particular nuclear energy production targets and scoping the types of investment required for their attainment.[77] The investment projects thus established are to be communicated to the Commission.[78]

The provisions on *Joint Undertakings* (Chapter 5) point to a collaborative effort between the Commission and the Council – namely, those undertakings which are of essential importance to the development of the nuclear industry in the Community can qualify to be established as Joint Undertakings[79] while projects aimed at establishing such a Joint Undertaking previously undergo an inquiry conducted by the Commission.[80] The Commission subsequently forwards the project for establishing a Joint Undertaking to the Council together with a reasoned opinion; provided the opinion is favorable, it further submits to the Council relevant proposals along with a detailed report on the project as a whole.[81] The Council reaches the final decision approving the establishment of the joint undertaking by a qualified majority, taking all of the former factors into consideration.[82]

In the field of *Nuclear Supplies* title (Chapter 6) a common supply policy is established based on the principle of equal access to sources of supply, whereby the supply of ores, source materials and special fissile materials is guaranteed.[83] The Euratom Supply Agency has been established to pursue these tasks

77 Art. 40.

78 Art. 42.

79 Art. 45.

80 Art. 46(1).

81 Art. 46(2).

82 Art. 47(3).

83 Art. 52(1); For the purposes of the Euratom Treaty, pursuant to Art. 197 thereof:
1. "Special fissile materials" means plutonium 239; uranium 233; uranium enriched in uranium 235 or uranium 233; and any substance containing one or more of the foregoing isotopes and such other fissile materials as may be specified by the Council, acting by a qualified majority on a proposal from the Commission; the expression "special fissile materials" does not, however, include source materials.
[...] 3. "Source materials" means uranium containing the mixture of isotopes occurring in nature; uranium whose content in uranium 235 is less than the normal; thorium; any of the foregoing in the form of metal, alloy, chemical compound or concentrate; any other substance containing one or more of the foregoing in such a concentration as shall be specified by the Council, acting by a qualified majority on a proposal from the Commission.

under direct supervision of the Commission, which in turn can issue directives to the Agency and disposes of a right of veto over the Agency's decisions.[84]

Under the *Safeguards* title (Chapter 7), the Commission ensures that in the territories of Member States ores, source materials and special fissile materials are not diverted from their intended uses as declared by the users.[85] The Commission can issue directives urging Member States concerned to take all measures necessary to rectify infringements of their safeguards obligations and informs the Council thereof.[86] It can also impose sanctions on persons and undertakings that have breached the safeguards provisions.[87] The Commission requires the relevant authorities in Member States to keep and produce operating records in order to allow accounting for ores, source materials and special fissile materials used or produced.[88] The nature and the extent of these requirements are defined by the Commission in Regulation (Euratom) No 302/2005 the application of Euratom safeguards, approved by the Council.[89]

For the establishment of the *Nuclear Common Market* (Chapter 9) Member States have been required to prohibit all customs duties on imports and exports or charges having equivalent effect, as well as all quantitative restrictions on imports and exports of the nuclear goods and products specified in Annex IV to the Euratom Treaty.[90] Thus, all restrictions based on nationality potentially affecting the right of nationals of any Member State to take skilled employment in the field of nuclear energy have been abolished.[91] The Council may issue directives to implement the former requirement, acting by a qualified

4. "Ores" means any ore containing, in such average concentration as shall be specified by the Council acting by a qualified majority on a proposal from the Commission, substances from which the source materials defined above may be obtained by the appropriate chemical and physical processing (...).

84 Art. 53(1).

85 Art. 81.

86 Art. 82(3). The safeguards procedures and the role of the Commission therein are further discussed in Chapter 4, Section II.

87 Art. 83.

88 Art. 83.

89 Commission Regulation (Euratom) No 302/2005 of 8 February 2005 on the application of Euratom safeguards (*OJ L 54, 28.2.2005, p. 1–71*). Also, for the modalities of application of the former regulation, see Commission Recommendation of 15 December 2005 on guidelines for the application of Regulation (Euratom) No 302/2005 on the application of Euratom safeguards (notified under document number C (2005) 5127), *OJ L 028, 01/02/2006 P. 0001–0085*.

90 Art. 93.

91 Art. 96(1).

majority on a proposal from the Commission (the latter having previously obtained the opinion of the Economic and Social Committee).[92]

When it comes to the preponderance of institutional decision-making powers under the Euratom system, the 'rule of thumb' would be that for decisions of a financial nature or with financial repercussions the Council as the intergovernmental body has the ultimate power of approval – acting pursuant to a proposal from the Commission (e.g., in taking measures necessary to facilitate the conclusion of insurance contracts covering nuclear risks (Art. 98); under the supply policy, the Council is competent to fix prices, acting unanimously on a proposal from the Commission (Art. 69); the Commission can decide to build up emergency stocks – the method of financing those stocks being approved by the Council by a qualified majority on a proposal from the former (Art. 72(2)); The Council may, acting unanimously on a proposal from the Commission make applicable to each Joint Undertaking any or all of the advantages listed in Annex III to the Euratom Treaty (Art. 48(1)); etc.);

In the realm of the *External relations* of Euratom (Chapter 10) the role of the Commission is fairly extensive, almost short from exclusive. From the very beginning, Euratom was endowed with a comprehensive set of external prerogatives, at a time when the EEC's respective external competences were still rudimentary. From the very beginning, the Euratom Community owned the capacity to enter into obligations by concluding agreements or contracts with a third State, an international organisation or a national of a third State, those agreements or contracts being negotiated by the Commission in accordance with directives from the Council and finally concluded by the Commission with the approval of the Council acting by a qualified majority.[93] Furthermore, agreements or contracts whose implementation does not require action by the Council are to be negotiated and concluded solely by the Commission – to the extent that the Commission keeps the Council informed on the developments.

In conducting their nuclear foreign policy, Member States have the duty to communicate to the Commission draft agreements or contracts with a third State, an international organisation or a national of a third State where such agreements or contracts concern matters falling within the purview of the Euratom Treaty.[94] Member States are not allowed to conclude the proposed agreement or contract until the observations of the Commission have been met, and, furthermore, they have the option to proceed an application to the

92 Art. 96(2).

93 Art. 101(2).

94 Art. 103 (1).

CJEU after having received the comments of the Commission concerning the compatibility of the envisaged agreement with the provisions of the Euratom Treaty.[95] In comparison to the procedure for the conclusion of international agreements foreseen in Arts. 216–219 TFEU pursuant to which the Parliament is either consulted or its consent is required for the conclusion of international agreements envisaged under the Union framework, the corresponding procedure under the Euratom Treaty is legitimacy-deficient as it completely excludes the involvement of the Parliament.[96] The regime is different only with respect to agreements that Euratom concludes with States or international organizations, establishing an association involving reciprocal rights and obligations and common action which are concluded by the Council acting unanimously after consulting the European Parliament.[97]

What is additionally to be perceived as a deficiency inherent in the Euratom external relations regime is the inability for the Commission or any other institution to request an opinion from the CJEU on the compatibility of an envisaged international agreement with the Euratom Treaty as this possibility is only reserved for Member States. In contrast, Art. 218(11) TFEU enables the Member States, the Parliament, the Council and the Commission to obtain the opinion of the CJEU regarding the compliance of the envisaged agreement with the rules of the TFEU and the TEU. The CJEU has remarked on this shortcoming both in *Ruling 1/78* and in the *Nuclear Safety Convention*[98] case (the two judgments being almost 25 years apart from each other) whereas the said inconsistency has failed to be corrected by any subsequent treaty modification. Thus, in *Ruling 1/78* it was the Belgian Government that appeared before the CJEU although it was clearly effectively voicing the Commission's stance in the matter (which itself was unable to refer to the Court under the Euratom Treaty). The Court resolved the problem by stating that the former procedural deficiency can be overcome by reverting to the annulment procedure, namely, by requesting the review of the legality of an act approving a decision to conclude an international agreement since bringing an action for annulment is an undisputed prerogative of the institutions under the Euratom system.[99]

95 Art. 103(3).

96 This is to be contrasted to the view expressed by certain authors in the 1950s who have commended the external relations regime established under the Euratom Treaty to be forward-looking and revolutionary (see, Hahn, *supra* n. 35).

97 Art. 206.

98 C-29/99 Commission v Council (Nuclear Safety Convention), ECR 2002 p. I–11221, paras. 52, 54.

99 Para. 54.

The overall impression when examining the decision-making procedures applicable within the Euratom framework is that the administrative powers are predominantly dispensed by Commission while in the legislative arena it is the Council that appears as the main legislator. The latter departs from the legislative procedure applicable under the Union framework where both the Council and the Parliament appear as co-legislators for a great majority of the legislative acts i.e. acts adopted through the ordinary legislative procedure (Art. 294 TFEU et seq.) as the pervasive legislative procedure under the Union framework. Namely, Art. 289 TFEU institutes two types of procedures for the adoption of legal acts, applicable both to the Union and the Euratom regimes: the ordinary and the special legislative procedure. Under the ordinary legislative procedure the European Parliament and the Council jointly adopt the legislative acts on a proposal from the Commission whereas in the special legislative procedure the Parliament adopts an act with the participation of the Council, or the latter with the participation of the Parliament.[100] The failure to incorporate the former changes into the consolidated version of the Euratom Treaty published subsequently to the coming into force of the Lisbon Treaty[101] indicates that a significant procedural inconsistency is to be observed in the fact that while the TFEU provisions relating to the ordinary legislative procedure have been formally extended to apply to the remit of the Euratom Treaty via Art. 106a Euratom, the applicable Euratom decision-making procedures outlined *supra* have not been impacted. The former is, deplorably, an indication of the purely perfunctory character of the extension.

The problematic aspect of the decision-making procedures within Euratom is that along with a manifest lack of actual legislative power for the Parliament there is a prevalence of a Euratom-specific type of a legislative procedure which only involves the Council and the Commission. Consequently, the dominant legislative procedure under Euratom's auspices is the special

100 Article 289 TFEU

1. The *ordinary legislative procedure* shall consist in the joint adoption by the European Parliament and the Council of a regulation, directive or decision on a proposal from the Commission. This procedure is defined in Article 294.

2. In the specific cases provided for by the Treaties, the adoption of a regulation, directive or decision by the European Parliament with the participation of the Council, or by the latter with the participation of the European Parliament, shall constitute a *special legislative procedure*. (...) [Emphasis added].

101 *Consolidated version of the Treaty establishing the European Atomic Energy Community*, OJ 2012/C 327/01.

legislative procedure where the negligible legislative role of the Parliament involves consultation with the Council (Arts. 31, 76, 85, 90, 96, 98, 203, 206 of the Euratom Treaty).

Irrespective of the arguments purporting the delicate nature and distinct character of the Euratom Community, it seems difficult to reconcile the foregoing divergent tendencies: one of enlarging the field of application of the ordinary legislative procedure (pioneered under the Union framework) and the contrasting tendency to discredit any attempts to expand the Parliamentary legislative powers under the Euratom remit. It is a worrying *status quo* being that both of these tendencies exist under the same roof, that of the European Union which is striving to keep up an exemplary image as a fully democratic political system both in the eyes of the international community and its own Member States.

III.2 *The Parliament under Euratom: The Quest for Leverage*

Ever since Euratom came into existence, the European Parliament and the Euratom Community have been experiencing their share of what can be described as a standing strenuous relationship due both to the elevated degree of democratic deficit inherent to the Euratom Treaty and its rigidity as a legal document that has 'survived' any substantial amendments. Even though democratic deficit is seen as a feature intrinsic to the nature of the overall European Union construct,[102] its presence seems more pronounced with regard to Euratom.

Euratom has been commonly regarded as a democracy deficient community chiefly on account of the Parliament's insufficient involvement in the Euratom decision-making.[103] The concept of EU's democratic deficit presupposes the existence of legitimacy deficit – in fact, the main reason that is usually invoked for the existence of EU's democratic deficit is the lack of transparency and accountability in the work of certain of its institutions

102 See T.D. Zweifel, *Democratic Deficit? The European Union, Switzerland, and the United States in Comparative Perspective*, 2002, Lixington Books, pp. 11–44. For further reading on the democratic deficit in the EU see also, A. Von Bogdandy, A Disputed Idea Becomes Law: Remarks on European Democracy as a Legal Principle in, B. Kohler-Koch and B. Bittberger (eds.), *Debating the Democratic Legitimacy of the European Union*, Rowman & Littlefield, 2007, p. 36, 37; and, R. Balme and D. Chabanet, *European Governance and Democracy: Power and Protest in the EU*, Rowman & Littlefield, 2008, p. 202 et seq.

103 Comments in this direction have been voiced by the European Parliament, the Member States and NGO sector, covered in the last section of this chapter.

and bodies with respect to the citizens[104] (i.e. legitimacy deficit). In addition, the European Parliament has been usually regarded as a legitimacy-deficient institution in view of the decreasing trend in the European Parliament elections turnout.[105] The tremendous input of the Treaty of Lisbon in this respect consists of both substantiating and expanding the prerogatives of the Parliament under the Union framework and thus making up, to the extent possible, for the impending legitimacy deficit in the Union. Unfortunately, the enlargement of the Parliament's powers under the Union framework has not been paralleled by a corresponding enlargement within the Euratom remit.

As was observed in the preceding section, the only involvement in the legislative process foreseen for the Parliament under the Euratom Treaty was through the special legislative procedure where the Council adopts the act after the Parliament has been consulted. This procedure has been provided under the *Health and Safety* chapter for the adoption of basic standards for radiation protection.[106] Further on, regarding the possibility to modify the provisions belonging to the chapters on *Supply*,[107] *Safeguards*[108] and *Property Ownership*,[109] the Treaty prescribes that in case of a change in circumstances or a compelling need, the provisions under each of these chapters may be subject to change requiring a unanimous decision of the Council acting from a proposal from the Commission and after consulting the Parliament.

In the context of the *Nuclear common market*, for the purpose of abolishment of nationality-based restrictions so that nationals of any Member State are able to acquire the right to take skilled employment in the field of nuclear energy – subject to the limitations resulting from the basic requirements of public policy, public security or public health – the Council can issue directives acting by a qualified majority upon consultation with the Parliament.[110] Furthermore, in the effort for Member States to facilitate the conclusion of

---

104 J. Crowley and L. Giorgi, The Political Sociology of the European Public Sphere in, Giorgi, Von Homeyer and Parsons (eds.), *Democracy in The European Union: Towards the Emergence of a Public Sphere*, Routledge, 2006, p. 1.

105 The 1999 European Parliament elections turn-out was estimated to be 49.51%, decreasing in 2004 to 45.47% and to 43% in 2009 (source: http://www.europarl.europa.eu/parliament/archive/elections2009/en/turnout_en.html.

106 Art. 31.

107 Art. 76.

108 Art. 85.

109 Art. 90.

110 Art. 96.

insurance contracts covering nuclear risks, the Council can issue directives acting by a qualified majority after consulting the Parliament.[111]

In addition to the foregoing, the Parliament is consulted also regarding the activation of the 'flexibility' clause of Art. 203 Euratom ('extension clause'[112]) which acts as supplementary legal basis for Euratom action where the Treaty itself has not provided for the necessary powers. Should such action prove necessary for the attainment of the objectives of Euratom, the Council can take the appropriate measures by acting unanimously on a proposal from the Commission and after consulting the European Parliament. The mirroring procedure established in Art. 352(1) TFEU is to be distinguished from the former in that it raises the threshold for Parliamentary involvement requiring that in addition to a unanimous vote in the Council and a proposal coming from the Commission, the consent of the Parliament is to be obtained. In this way, the Parliament's consent is decisive to the final outcome of the procedure. This enhancement to the 'open-ended' competence procedure under the TFEU has been introduced by the Lisbon Treaty – the former Art. 308 TEC only requiring consultation with the Parliament.

Lastly, with relation to the budgetary procedure, the TFEU provisions applicable thereto (Arts. 314 et seq. TFEU) have been extended to the Euratom Treaty via Art. 106a enabling for the European Parliament to be given equal weight with the Council in deciding on the final adoption of the budget.

III.2.1 The Parliament's Legal and Political Struggle

The story of the Parliament struggling to find its place in European nuclear territory has been an enduring one. The only legal challenge that the Parliament has initiated so far in favour of expanding its competences under Euratom is the *Parliament v Council (Chernobyl II)*[113] case, where it succeeded to assure its prerogative as an institution to bring actions for annulment of Community measures before the CJEU. The Parliament further demanded the annulment of *Regulation 3954/87 (Euratom) laying down maximum permitted levels of radioactive contamination of foodstuffs and of feeding-stuffs following a nuclear accident or any other case of radiological emergency*[114] claiming that Art. 31 Euratom (the health and safety provisions) which foresees a

111 Art. 98.

112 A reference coined by H.J. Hahn (Hahn, *supra* n. 35, p. 1040).

113 *Parliament v Council* (C-70/88) [1991] ECR I-04529.

114 Regulation 3954/87 (Euratom) laying down maximum permitted levels of radioactive contamination of foodstuffs and of feeding-stuffs following a nuclear accident or any other case of radiological emergency [1987] OJ L371/11.

consultation procedure, was not the correct legal basis and that the act should have been adopted under Art. 100a EC (now Art. 114 TFEU; provision on harmonisation of laws) – if necessary in conjunction with Art. 31. The latter provision provided for a co-operation procedure which would have ensured the Parliament a more decisive role in the legislative procedure. However, the Court held that the purpose of the Regulation was to protect the population against the dangers arising from foodstuffs and feeding-stuffs which have undergone radioactive contamination[115] and the fact that the Regulation contains a provision on the prohibition on the placing on the markets of certain products with level of contamination that exceeds the maximum permitted levels only served to enable the application of the maximum permitted levels.[116] The Regulation therefore simply had an incidental harmonising effect on the free movement of goods[117] leading the Court to uphold Art. 31 Euratom as the correct legal basis.[118]

---

115 *Parliament v Council* (C-70/88) [1991] E.C.R. I-04529, para. 12.

116 Para. 16.

117 Para. 17.

118 The *Chernobyl II* case will be further examined *infra* in Section III.3; Another very recent example of a turf war between the Parliament and the Council regarding the choice of a legal basis for an act falling under the Euratom domain is case C-48/14 *Parliament v Council* (ECLI:EU:C:2015:91) in which the Parliament had seeked annulment of *Directive 2013/51/Euratom of 22 October 2013 laying down requirements for the protection of the health of the general public with regard to radioactive substances in water intended for human consumption* (OJ 2013 L 296/12) claiming that Art. 31 Euratom concerning the adoption of the basic standards relating to the protection of the health of workers and the general public against the dangers arising from ionising radiations under which the Directive had been adopted was the incorrect legal basis and that the former should have instead been adopted under the Union's environmental protection provisions of Art. 192(1) TFEU – more particularly 'the objectives of the protection of human health and the prudent and rational use of natural resource as listed in Art. 191(1) TFEU'. Under Art. 31 Euratom, the Council adopts the act after consulting the Parliament whereas under Art. 192(1) Parliament would have benefitted from the ordinary legislative procedure. By relying on the *lex specialis/lex generalis* rule, the Court of Justice asserted that the purpose and content of the contested Directive corresponded to the purpose and content of a basic standard within the meaning of Art. 30 Euratom (Paras. 32, 33) in that Art. 31 Euratom constituted a *more specific legal basis* for protecting the health of populations against radioactive substances in water intended for human consumption than the general legal basis resulting from Art. 192(1) TFEU (Paras. 37, 38). Moreover, the Parliament even went as far as claiming that by having chosen this particular legal basis for the act the Council had breached the principle of sincere cooperation among the institutions laid down in Art. 13(2) TEU, which the Court readily dismissed.

Apart from legal challenges, the Parliament has also attempted to 'politically' challenge the imbalance of institutional competences under the Euratom Treaty and be more closely associated with the developments under Euratom auspices, mainly by issuing reports or adopting various legislative and non-legislative resolutions. In following, reference will be made to several recent European Parliament reports and resolutions where the Parliament has given its own assessment of the overall Euratom structure and its *modus operandi*.

The *Maldeikis Report*[119] which was drafted on the occasion of the 50th anniversary of the Euratom Community, offers an insight into the Parliament's view on the issue of Euratom's democratic deficit and possible modalities for correcting this lacuna. The report notes that (by the time of adopting the report, 2007) the Euratom Treaty had been amended only once in 50 years, its core provisions having remained unchanged.[120] Regret is expressed about the fact that the growth in Parliamentary powers and the operation of the co-decision procedure (now, ordinary legislative procedure) with regard to most of EU legislation has not been extended to Euratom. It sees the current situation, where the Parliament is almost completely excluded from the Euratom legislative process, as evidence of an 'unacceptable democratic deficit', the practice of involving the Parliament in the preparatory phase and final drafting, as well as taking its opinions into consideration, being regarded as insufficient.[121]

The *Hökmark Report*[122] offers a discussion on the choice of the legal basis for the (then, proposed) Directive setting up a Community framework for nuclear safety of nuclear installations[123] where the Parliament, although ending up by giving an affirmative appraisal of the proposed legal basis, examines several other possibly relevant legal bases which foresee a greater stake for it in the

---

Clearly, C-48/14 *Parliament v Council* represents yet another of the Parliament's failed attempts to influence the Euratom decision-making process 'through the back-door', however, by exhibiting a blatant (possibly, intentional) disregard of the *lex specialis/lex generalis* rule governing the interaction between the Union and the Euratom legal frameworks and the principle according to which the provisions of the TFEU are not to derogate from the provisions of the EAEC Treaty.

119 European Parliament, Committee on Industry, Research and Energy, Rapporteur : E. Maldeikis, Report on Assessing Euratom: 50 years of European nuclear energy policy (*Maldeikis Report*) A6-0129/2007.

120 European Parliament, *Maldeikis Report*, p. 5.

121 European Parliament, *Maldeikis Report*, p. 5.

122 European Parliament, *Report on the proposal for a Council Directive (Euratom) setting up a Community framework for nuclear safety of nuclear installations* A6-0236/2009.

123 Directive 2009/71/Euratom establishing a Community framework for the nuclear safety of nuclear installations [2009] OJ L172/18.

procedure for the adoption of the directive. The Directive lays down uniform standards for the safety of nuclear installations and is based on Arts. 31 and 32 Euratom, provisions on the protection of the health and safety of workers and the general public against dangers arising from ionising radiations. Concerning the appropriate legal basis, the European Parliament Committee on Legal Affairs examined the question whether Art. 175 EC (now 192 TFEU) on protection of the environment should be added as a supplementary legal basis, giving the Parliament the benefit of the co-decision procedure.[124] As an alternative, the possible use of Art. 203 Euratom in conjunction with or instead of Arts. 31 and 32 was argued for, with the intention of covering both the technological aspects of nuclear safety and the environmental effects from the functioning of nuclear installations.[125] Finally, the Parliament concluded that none of the provisions of the proposed measure deal specifically with protection against threats to the environment, finding that Arts. 31 and 32 Euratom were the correct legal bases.[126] Therefore, it was suggested that the reference to 'protection of the air, water and soil' be scrapped off which is something the Commission and the Council had conceded to in the final version of the Directive where in the definition for nuclear safety contained in Art. 3(2) reference is made solely to 'protection of workers and the general public from radiation arising from ionising radiations from nuclear installations'.

An important amendment to the text proposed by the Parliament was included in Art. 9 on the reporting procedure for the implementation of the Directive. Namely, the rapporteur stressed the need for the European Parliament to be kept well informed on activities in the field of nuclear safety, proposing that the Commission should be obliged to submit reports on the progress made in the implementation of the Directive not solely to the Council, but also to the Parliament.[127] The wording of the present Art. 9(2) reflects this demand.

The Parliament has developed a keen interest in matters of nuclear safety and often feels called upon to state its opinions in this area which is of most immediate concern to the EU citizens. Thus, in a recent *Resolution on risk and safety assessments ('stress tests') of nuclear power plants in the European Union and related activities*,[128] the Parliament stressed the need for EU citizens to be

124 European Parliament, *Report on the proposal for a Council Directive (Euratom)* A6-0236/2009, p. 40.

125 *Idem*, p. 41.

126 *Idem*, p. 47.

127 *Idem*, p. 39.

128 European Parliament *Resolution of 14 March 2013 on risk and safety assessments ('stress tests') of nuclear power plants in the European Union and related activities*, 2012/2830(RSP).

fully informed and consulted on nuclear safety in the Union.[129] It welcomed the proposed revision of the Nuclear Safety Directive as an ambitious project aiming to introduce major improvements in safety procedures through the definition and implementation of binding nuclear safety standards which reflect modern technical, regulatory and operational practices in the EU,[130] and called on the EU and the Member States to treat nuclear power equally to the other energy sources under the Treaty on the Functioning of the European Union, in accordance with the notions of democracy, involvement of the European Parliament, transparency and full public access to information.[131]

The Parliament passed *Resolution of 10 May 2007 on the public health consequences of the 1968 Thule crash* (*Petition 720/2002*) (*2006/2012(INI)*) in response to a citizens' petition, urging Member States to implement and apply without delay the Basic Safety Standards Directive 96/29/Euratom[132] and expressing great concern about the existence of a gap in the protection of the health of the general public regarding the use of nuclear energy for military purposes.[133] In order for the former lacuna to be made up, it has suggested the Commission to draft a proposal addressing the public health and environmental effects of the use of nuclear energy.[134]

In a report prepared regarding the (then) proposal for a *Council Directive laying down basic safety standards for protection against the dangers arising from exposure to ionising radiation,*[135] the Parliament cemented its eco-centric approach to nuclear safety and radiation protection which encompasses the protection of both the human and the non-human environment, suggesting a

---

The resolution was issued pursuant to the Commission communication of 4 October 2012 on the comprehensive risk and safety assessments ('stress tests') of nuclear power plants in the European Union and related activities (COM(2012)0571). See also, the European Parliament *Resolution on the problem of nuclear safety fifteen years after the Chernobyl accident*, B5-0321/2001; and, European Parliament *Legislative Resolution on the draft Council regulation establishing an Instrument for Nuclear Safety and Security Assistance* (9037/2006 – C6-0153/2006 – 2006/0802(CNS)A6-0397/2006).

129 Point 15.

130 Point 26.

131 Point 31.

132 Point 9.

133 Point 11.

134 Point 12.

135 European Parliament Committee on the Environment, Public Health and Food Safety (Draft Report) on the proposal for a Council directive laying down basic safety standards for protection against the dangers arising from exposure to ionising radiation (COM(2012)0242 – C7-0151/2012 – 2011/0254(NLE)) (Rapporteur: Thomas Ulmer).

bold stand on environmental protection in matters pertaining to the protection against the dangers arising from exposure to ionising radiation. The inclusion of a chapter on environmental protection in the proposed directive was welcomed, the former introducing environmental criteria that guarantee the protection of humans and laying down rules on the protection of non-human species.[136] Nevertheless, the Parliamentary Committee that authored the report considered that at this point there was not any sufficient scientific basis to determine the impact of radiation on non-human species.[137] Thus, it was proposed that the chapter on environmental protection be deleted from the directive and a separate legal act specifically dealing with the protection of the environment against ionising radiation be drawn up once sufficient scientific data becomes available.[138] Interestingly, the Committee takes the view that such an act ought to be adopted under the TFEU environmental protection provisions (in the ordinary legislative procedure) since Arts. 30 and 31 Euratom cannot be taken as adequate legal basis due to their relevance specifically to the protection of the health of workers and the general public.[139] Effectively, a view is taken that Euratom lacks competence to espouse an environmental approach to radiation protection.[140] Therefore, If the Commission decides to concede with the former suggestion and drafts such an act, the Parliament will be given the benefit to co-legislate with the Council instead of only be consulted were the act to be based on the Euratom Treaty provisions.

III.2.2 The Lisbon Treaty Amendments: (in)Significant?

Prior to the Lisbon Treaty, the only envisaged legislative procedure involving the Parliament under the Euratom Treaty was the consultation procedure. The only change that has been achieved with the Lisbon Treaty amendments in this respect is purely nominal in that the consultation procedure has been assimilated into the new, broader notion of 'special legislative procedure'.

The modifications to the Euratom Treaty have been produced in the *Protocol Amending the Treaty Establishing the European Atomic Energy Community*[141] attached to the Lisbon Treaty. The Protocol, apart from making

136 p. 15.

137 p. 15.

138 p. 16.

139 p. 16.

140 For a different approach, see Chapter 2, Section II.2.

141 Art. 3 of the Protocol Amending the Treaty Establishing the European Atomic Energy Community, inserting the new Art. 106a to the Euratom Treaty.

certain institutional adjustments and repealing a number of Treaty articles, does not insert any new substantial provisions into the Treaty. Among the repealed provisions are those concerning the legislative procedures on account of extending the legislative procedures provided under the Arts 288 et seq. TFEU (i.e. legislative procedures for *Union* acts) to the Euratom remit, which, as was argued in the sections above, is a change of a merely perfunctory nature.

The fact that the Parliament's role in the legislative process under Euratom has not matured past *consultation* actualizes the significance of those *Union* acts (adopted under the TFEU) which regulate particular aspects of the nuclear sector and their potential to partially make up for the democratic deficit in the nuclear field.[142] In this way, the increase in the Parliament's legislative powers under the Union framework offsets Euratom's democratic deficit through the use of *Union* acts in the adoption of which the European Parliament co-legislates with the Council. The Union acts that pertain to the nuclear domain are chiefly acts based on the environmental protection provisions of Art. 192 TFEU (former Art. 175 TEC); Such acts pertaining to the nuclear field are: the *Criminal Penalties Directive,*[143] *Directive 2003/4/EC on public access to environmental information,*[144] *Directive 2003/35 providing public participation in respect of the drawing up of certain plans and programmes relating to the environment,*[145] etc.

---

142 The European Parliament has fostered the possibility of such a cross-over of legal bases. In the *Maldeikis Report* (A6-0129/2007) it notes that ordinary law laid down by the EC Treaty applies to nuclear activities (p. 8), whereas in the *Hökmark Report* (A6-0236/2009) it asserts the possibility of directives based on the EC Treaty to (also) regulate nuclear installations (p. 48 of the report).

143 Directive 2008/99 on the protection of the environment through criminal law [2008] OJ L328/28 (Criminal Penalties Directive); The Criminal Penalties Directive applies *inter alia* to activities covered by the Euratom Treaty and the legislation adopted pursuant thereto (Art. 2) where the offences to which it applies include 'the operation of a plant in which a dangerous activity is carried out or in which dangerous substances or preparations are stored or used and which, outside the plant, causes or is likely to cause death or serious injury to any person or substantial damage to the quality of air, the quality of soil or the quality of water, or to animals or plants' (Art. 3).

144 *OJ L 41, 14.2.2003, p. 26–32;* The 2003 Access-to-information Directive guarantees the right of access to environmental information held by or for public authorities, while the definition of environmental information contained in Art. 2(b) refers also to 'factors, such as substances, energy, noise, radiation or waste, including radioactive waste, emissions, discharges and other releases into the environment, affecting or likely to affect the elements of the environment'.

145 Directive 2003/35 providing for public participation in respect of the drawing up of certain plans and programmes relating to the environment [2003] OJ L156/17; In addition, the

In addition, the Union commercial policy provisions can also potentially affect the nuclear field. The applicable legislative procedure for the title on the Union commercial policy has been amended after Lisbon, namely, the present Art. 207 TFEU (ex Art. 133 TEC) forsees the ordinary legislative procedure. An example of a Union commercial policy act relating to the nuclear field is *Regulation 428/2009 setting up a Community regime for the control of exports, transfer, brokering and transit of dual-use items*[146] which was adopted on the basis of ex-Art. 133 TEC which then required a qualified majority in the Council, excepting any involvement of the Parliament.

Regrettably, it would be unrealistic to consider that reliance on the former and similar TFEU provisions as legal bases providing for the ordinary legislative procedure can mitigate the Euratom democratic deficit in any significant manner, especially since the number of such Union acts is highly limited.

There exists nevertheless another possibility for reduction in the democratic deficit to be accomplished through the involvement of national parliaments which according to the Lisbon amendments have been enabled to participate in the democratic review of legislative proposals. The involement of the national parliaments as democratic actors has been forseen in the *Protocol on the role of national parliaments in the European Union*[147] (annexed to the TEU, the TFEU and the Euratom Treaty) complemented by the *Protocol on the application of the principles of subsidiarity and proportionality*[148] (only annexed to the TEU and the TFEU). The former protocols have enabled Member States' parliaments to become more closely involved in the EU decision-making process as *de facto*

Directive 85/337/EEC of 27 June 1985 on the assessment of the effects of certain public and private projects on the environment (the *Environmental Impact Assessment Directive*) *OJ L 175, 5.7.1985, p. 40–48* (as amended by the 2003/35/EC Directive) applies to nuclear power stations (Art. 4(1)) and, in specific cases, environmental impact assessment can be conducted with respect to installations for the production or enrichment of nuclear fuels as well as installations for the reprocessing of irradiated nuclear fuels (Art. 4(2)). The former two directives transpose the majority of the Aarhus Convention provisions to which the EU has been a party since May 2005 (http://ec.europa.eu/environment/aarhus/). It is believed there might be some degree of legal uncertainty in this regard given that the Aarhus Convention was signed under the auspices of the EC Treaty rather than the Euratom Treaty (http://ec.europa.eu/energy/nuclear/governance_en.htm). A discussion on this point will be further developed in Chapter 3, Section 1.

146 Regulation 428/2009 setting up a Community regime for the control of exports, transfer, brokering and transit of dual-use items [2009] OJ L134/1.

147 *Protocol on the role of national parliaments in the European Union* [2007] OJ C306/148.

148 *Protocol on the application of the principles of subsidiarity and proportionality* [2007] OJ C306/150; The Protocol is annexed only to the TEU and the TFEU.

co-legislators. According to the protocols, draft legislative acts are forwarded to national parliaments which, should they consider it pertinent, can send a reasoned opinion to the Presidents of the European Parliament, the Council and the Commission on whether a draft legislative act complies with the principle of subsidiarity.[149] Each national parliament is assigned two votes so that where the reasoned opinions on a draft legislative act's non-compliance with the principle of subsidiarity represent at least one third of all the votes allocated to national parliaments, the draft concerned must be reviewed.[150] Concerning the acts adopted in the ordinary legislative procedure, the threshold for mandatory review is even lower and represents a simple majority of the votes allocated to the national parliaments.[151]

An important debilitating factor regarding the application of the former Protocol to the Euratom field is that neither the *Protocol on the application of the principles of subsidiarity and proportionality* nor Art. 5 TEU which codifies the former two principles have not been foreseen to apply to Euratom. Conversely, it is manifest that the assessment performed in light of the principle of subsidiarity is instrumental to the discharge of the newly accorded role of national parliaments in the legislative process under the *Protocol on the role of national parliaments in the European Union* which has been extended to Euratom's purview.[152] Such a loophole in the parliamentary participatory regime leaves it unclear as to how the national parliaments are expected to fully discharge of their roles concerning their involvement in the Euratom legislative process in a situation where the principle of subsidiarity is *de jure* inapplicable to the scope of the Euratom Treaty. In spite of that, should one take an *effet utile* approach, the fact that the *Protocol on the application of the principles of subsidiarity and proportionality* was not foreseen to apply to Euratom does not hinder a *per extensiam* application of certain of its provisions since Art. 3(1) of the Protocol on the role of the national parliaments makes direct reference to the provisions of the former Protocol which lay down the procedure involving the national parliaments.

149 *Protocol on the application of the principles of subsidiarity and proportionality*, Arts. 4, 5.

150 *Idem*, Art. 7(1) and (2).

151 *Idem*, Art. 7(3).

152 Art. 3 of the *Protocol on the role of national parliaments in the EU*:

> National Parliaments may send to the Presidents of the European Parliament, the Council and the Commission a reasoned opinion on whether a draft legislative act complies with the *principle of subsidiarity*, in accordance with the procedure laid down in the Protocol on the application of the principles of subsidiarity and proportionality.(…) [Emphasis added.].

In addition to the foregoing, the Lisbon Treaty attempts to empower the EU citizens as active participants in the Union legislative process by laying down the principle of representative democracy in Art. 10(1) TEU and establishing direct democracy mechanisms for the EU citizens such as consultations with interested parties and citizens' initiatives, envisaged in Art. 11 TEU. Most importantly, Art. 11(4) TEU offers the possibility for at least one million citizens of a significant number of Member States to take the initiative of inviting the European Commission to submit a proposal on matters where citizens consider that a legal act of the Union is required for the purpose of implementing the Treaties. These enabling democracy mechanisms for European citizens, unfortunately, have no impact on the Euratom regime since Art. 11 TEU has not been extended to the field of application of the Euratom Treaty. In legitimacy terms, this is a serious shortcoming which cannot be compensated by simply employing an extensive interpretation of the relevant TFEU provisions. That being said, notwithstanding the great potential of these democratic mechanisms, it ultimately devolves on the authority of the Commission as the initiator of Union legislation to give full effect to Art. 11(4) TEU by deciding, on its own discretion, whether a citizens' initiative will eventually be materialized in a legislative proposal or not.[153]

Having escaped the Lisbon democratic reform, the Euratom Community remains sheltered from any satisfactory level of scrutiny and supervision from the European Parliament, the national parliaments and the EU citizens with the Euratom Treaty preserving its reputation of an 'undemocratic treaty'. Even if one uses European Parliament's lack of legitimacy to downplay the striking democratic deficit within the Euratom system (especially in view of the argument as to whether the European Parliament indeed effectively voices the needs of European citizens), the fact remains that the Parliament is still the most democratic of all the Union institutions.[154] Moreover, it is plausibly the nature and composition of the Parliament that hinder it from having any greater bite on the decision-making in the nuclear realm. Being composed

153 See, B. Kohler-Koch and B. Rittberger, Charting Crowded Territory: Debating the Democratic Legitimacy of The European Union, in, Giorgi, Von Homeyer and Parsons (eds.), *Democracy in The European Union: Towards the Emergence of a Public Sphere*, Routledge, 2006, p. 11.

154 This argument actually goes both ways since, according to some authors, there is the option that the overcoming of the democratic deficit should presumably be followed by a reduction of the legitimacy deficit (J. Crowley and L. Giorgi, The Political Sociology of the European Public Sphere in, Giorgi, Von Homeyer and Parsons (eds.), *Democracy in The European Union: Towards the Emergence of a Public Sphere*, Routledge, 2006, p. 1.).

of directly elected and independent representatives of the peoples of the Member States, the Parliament truly represents an 'invention' from the perspective of nuclear decision-making since it does not have a counterpart in any other international and regional nuclear energy organization such as the IAEA, the OECD NEA, etc. as the former organizations do not possess deliberative bodies formed by directly elected independent representatives.[155] Furthermore, it seems to be a common feature inherited from the national systems that the nuclear domain is typically less stringently supervised by national parliaments on account of different national security considerations.[156]

Effectively, there exists a persistent discrepancy between the decision-making patterns set out under the *Union* framework and the Euratom framework which has become increasingly pronounced in recent years with the adoption of the Lisbon Treaty which democratized the decision-making procedures within the *Union* framework, leaving the Euratom decision-making almost untouched. In this sense, as was shown *supra*, the expansion of the legislative powers of the European Parliament under the Union structure has failed to be been matched by a corresponding reform within the Euratom compact. Therefore, in the presence of limited institutional reforms extended to the Euratom Community via the Lisbon Treaty, it is difficult to speak of an accomplished balance of institutional powers under the Euratom Treaty. The Parliament has maintained its fairly marginal role in Euratom's decision-making procedures and disposes of *mutatis mutandis* the same 'embryonic' prerogatives[157] ever since the Euratom Treaty was adopted whereas the Council, as an equally important legislative organ, does not dispose of the full legislative powers it has been endowed with under the Union framework. The former is a startling indication of a fractured institutional balance within the Euratom system where the main institutional weight is carried by one single institution (the Commission) which possesses an extensive array of executive, quasi-legislative and quasi-judicial prerogatives, leaving much to be desired in both democracy and legitimacy terms.

III.3 *The Court of Justice of the EU – The 'Enabler' of Euratom's Competence*

The judicial control over the Euratom compact is exercized by the Court of Justice of the EU, which from the very creation of the three Communties has

155 Hahn, *supra* n. 70, in ft. 33 on p. 30.

156 *Idem.*

157 *Idem*, p. 31. Although this observation dates as far back as 1958, it still stands valid today.

been perceived as the strongest integrating factor of these Communities[158] on account of its undisputed prerogative to review the work of the institutions and ensure a correct and effective interpretation and application of Euratom and European Union law both by the institutions and the Member States. In terms of the nature and scope of its powers, within the Euratom Community the CJEU can be seen as the most non-controversial institution in comparison to the often frowned upon 'technocratic' Commission and meagerly potent Parliament. The Court's tendency to frequently apply a broad interpretation of the Euratom Treaty provisions has even gone as far as being described as an exercise of 'breathing (...) new life into the moribund Euratom Treaty'.[159]

The judgments of the Court have served to reinforce Euratom's legal and political regime mainly in two ways: (1) by confirming or clarifying an already existent Euratom competence or, (2) by employing an extensive interpretation of the Euratom Treaty which practically leads to enlargement of the Euratom Treaty's scope of application. The latter is what authors call a 'spill-over' of Euratom provisions to fields which are not covered by the Euratom Treaty which corresponds to the neo-functionalist approach employed with regard to the legal and institutional dynamic of the Euratom Community.[160] In fact, the two key assumptions of a law-based neo-functionalism that are presumed to trigger a spill-over effect of Euratom regulation to other (Union) fields/policies are the (i) sub-national actors trying to overcome national law in order to pursue their interests by means of the preliminary reference proceedings before the CJEU, and the (ii) political dynamics which is the consequence to a general strategy of the Commission to widen the scope of Euratom which has been manifested, for the most part, in the infringement actions against Member States initiated by the former.[161] The spill-over of Euratom measures to neighboring policies is justified by functional reasons[162] so that by allowing for such a spill over to occur the CJEU is effectively extending the competences of Euratom, irrespective of whether such an extension has previously been occurring *via facti* and is subsequently merely acknowledged by the Court or, alternatively, is an extension that stems directly from the Court's reasoning (i.e. an exercise of 'deliberative supranationalism').

158 *Idem*, p. 31.

159 J. Woodliffe, Making Sense of Article 37 of the Euratom Treaty, *European Law Review*, 1989, Vol. 14 Issue 2, p. 101.

160 For an elaborate account of how the neo-functionalist approach can be applied to the Euratom scope, see, Wolf, *supra* n. 36.

161 *Idem*, p. 3.

162 *Idem*, p. 8.

Following is an analysis of several CJEU judgments which have produced a powerful spill-over effect of the kind referred to *supra*, having both served to enable and reinforce Euratom's competences. These 'Euratom-empowering' judgments majorly concern Euratom's policy on the health and safety of workers and the general public as a competence exercised internally and safeguarded externally i.e. through the Community's involvement in the international sphere.

III.3.1 Ruling 1/78

In Ruling 1/78[163] the CJEU was requested to examine the necessity for the Euratom Community to participate in the *Convention on the Physical protection of Nuclear Material* alongside its Member States in the light of Art. 103 Euratom.[164] Having noted that the draft Convention concerns in various ways matters which fell within the purview of the Euratom Treaty,[165] the Court considered that the field of application of the Convention and that of the Treaty overlap, both covering the same type of materials and nuclear facilities.[166] In order to examine whether the absence of the Community as a party to the Convention would potentially hinder the application of the Euratom Treaty, it examined the relevant chapters of the Treaty (the Supply arrangements, the Nuclear common market, the Safeguards and the Property Ownership of the Community) concluding that the Euratom Community had exclusive jurisdiction over the domain of nuclear supplies along with a general responsibility for the proper functioning of the nuclear common market.[167] Hence, it was held that those Convention obligations corresponding to the former field were to be applied by the Member States in conjunction with the participation of the Community.[168] With respect to Euratom's competence in the area of safeguards which was not as clear-cut, an exercise of 'extension' was performed by the

163 Ruling 1/78, ECR 1978 p. 02151.

164 Council Decision of 9 June 1980 approving the conclusion by the Commission of the *International Convention on the physical protection of nuclear material* (80/565/Euratom, OJ L149 1980 p. 41). The adoption of the new *Convention on the Physical Protection of Nuclear Material and Nuclear Facilities* was followed by the adoption of Council Decision 2007/513/Euratom of 10 July 2007 approving the accession of the European Atomic Energy Community to the amended Convention on the Physical Protection of Nuclear Material and Nuclear Facilities (OJ L 190, 21.7.2007, p. 12–14).

165 Para. 12.

166 Para. 12.

167 Para. 12.

168 Para. 18.

Court which inferred that the actual and potential dangers the draft Convention aimed to counter were not as pressing for the negotiators and to the general public at the time when the Euratom Treaty was drawn up and implemented[169] so that the exclusion of the Euratom Community from the draft Convention in this respect would have an impeding effect and would compromise the subsequent development of the Euratom safeguards system to its full scope.[170] Moreover, it was considered that the exclusion of the Community from participation in the Convention would detrimentally affect the powers conferred on it by the Treaty regarding supply and the nuclear common market, its right of ownership and the safeguards responsibilities.[171]

In addition, the Court called on the duty of Member States to take all appropriate measures to ensure fulfilment of the obligations that arise from the Euratom Treaty or resulting from action taken by the institutions of the Euratom Community, prescribed in Art. 192 Euratom.[172] The former corresponds to the duty of cooperation between the institutions and the Member States in the field covered by the Treaty implying that individual or collective action by Member States excluding the Community would undermine some of the essential functions of the Community and detrimentally affect the latter's independent action in external relations.[173] Therefore, the draft Convention could only be adequately implemented through a close association between the institutions and the Member States in the process of negotiation, conclusion and implementation of the Convention[174] given that the subject matter of the agreement fell partly within the power and jurisdiction and partly within that of the Member States.[175] Furthermore, the Court sided with Commission's claim that it was not necessary to determine in advance, regarding other parties to the Convention, the division of powers between the Community and the Member States being that the former may change in the course of time.[176]

Apart from clarifying the external competence of Euratom in terms of the subject matter of the Convention, from a purely technical standpoint the CJEU ruling elucidates the deficiencies of the Art. 103 Euratom procedure for obtaining the CJEU's opinion from the CJEU on the compatibility of an envisaged

169 Para. 20.
170 Para. 23.
171 Para. 33.
172 Para. 33.
173 Para. 33.
174 Para. 34.
175 Para. 34.
176 Para. 35.

agreement with the Euratom Treaty which, especially in comparison to the corresponding Art. 218 TFEU (then, Art. 228 TEC) does not seem tenable. The judgment leaves the option open for the Euratom's Community competence in the matter covered by the Convention to grow as a result of the former's participation thereto and the fact that the Convention was to be regarded as an integral part of the Euratom Community legal order.[177] Undisputedly, the judgment can be considered as an example of extending the 'field for mainoeuvre' for Euratom's external relations achieved through judicial means, revealing an evolutive approach exhibited on the part of the CJEU.

III.3.2 Commission v Council (Nuclear Safety Convention)

The *Nuclear Safety Convention* case[178] is another case arising in the context of Euratom's external competence in the field of nuclear safety where the Commission had requested the partial annulment of the Council Decision of 7 December 1998 approving the accession of the European Atomic Energy Community to the Nuclear Safety Convention, claiming that the 'Declaration of competence' which was part of the contested decision was incomplete in that it failed to enlist all the existent Euratom competences in the fields covered by the Convention.[179] The judgment displays CJEU's deferential attitude towards a broad interpretation of Euratom's competences and evidences a spill-over to fields that the Euratom Treaty does not (at least, nominally) cover but which are functionally and imminently linked to its scope of application.

The safety of nuclear installations (nuclear safety) was formerly considered as inherent Member State competence as opposed to the safety of nuclear materials (radiation protection) which falls under the objectives set out in Art. 2 of the Euratom Treaty and thus comes within the purview of Euratom's competence. The Court was asked to determine the scope of Euratom's competence as a signatory party to the Nuclear Safety Convention in the areas covered by the Convention, where in the absence of a specific title in the Euratom Treaty particular to the safety of nuclear installations the Court embarked on an interpretation of the health and safety provisions of Chapter 3 of the Treaty.[180] It pointed out that the protection of the health of workers and of the general public could not be achieved without controlling the

177 J.A. Usher, International Competence of Euratom (Comment on Ruling 1/78 of November 14, 1978), *European Law Review*, 1979, Vol. 4, p. 306.

178 C-29/99 *Commission v Council* [2002] ECR I-1122.

179 Para. 57.

180 Para. 74.

sources of harmful radiation[181] to the effect that the interpretation of the former provisions required that the Euratom Treaty's preambular objective to 'create the conditions of safety necessary to eliminate hazards to the life and health of the public' is duly taken into account.[182] Concurring with Advocate General Jacobs' Opinion, the Court observed that there existed a significant overlap between the fields of radiation protection as a health protection objective of the Treaty, on the one hand, and the safety of nuclear installations, on the other, which warranted an extensive approach towards establishing Euratom's competence in the latter field which would supersede the artificial distinction between protection of the health of the general public and the safety of the sources of ionizing radiation.[183] The Court went further than what was suggested by AG Jacobs and decided that the 'Declaration of competence' should have included not only Art. 17 of the Convention that concerns the siting of nuclear installations, but additionally, Arts. 18 and 19 concerning the design, construction and operation of nuclear installations. Thus, manifestly, the Court broadened Euratom's regulatory competence to the field of technological aspects of nuclear safety, supported by the argument that there was no clear dividing line between nuclear safety in purely technological terms and general nuclear safety.[184]

It is important to note that the Court reached the former conclusion without previously relying on any contemporary scientific developments in order to corroborate its broad and dynamic construction of the Treaty provisions which, according to commentators, in view of the technical nature of the subject matter would have been a more adequate route to take in order for the 'effet utile' approach to be better substantiated.[185]

The Opinion of AG Jacobs in the case is further instructive in that it offers important directions as to the methodology to be applied in interpreting those provisions of the Euratom Treaty that have not been updated. Namely, with respect to the health and safety provisions of the Treaty it was suggested that the former are interpreted in the light of subsequent practice and, particularly, Euratom's Basic Safety Standards Directive of 1996.[186] Such 'interpretation in the light subsequent practice' is to be employed regarding provisions drafted

181 Para. 76.

182 Para. 75.

183 Para. 82.

184 P. Koutrakos, Case note on Case C-29/99 Commission v Council (re: Nuclear Safety Convention), *Common Market Law Review*, 2004, Vol. 41, p. 205.

185 *Idem*, p. 201.

186 Para. 147.

long ago, which have not been amended since and where there 'is a common and consistent practice of all actors entitled to interpret, apply or modify the rules in question'.[187] AG Jacobs considers the Health and safety, Supplies and Safeguards chapters of the Treaty as most appropriate to be subjected to the former method of interpretation since, on their own these provisions could not be pertinently interpreted and understood without relying on the practice in their application.[188]

By producing a clear spill-over effect, the *Nuclear Safety Convention* judgment unequivocally confirms that Euratom's external competence can arise in the presence of an internal Euratom rule which prescribes minimum or less detailed/ less concrete Euratom Community prerogatives in a particular field.[189] This goes beyond the famous *ERTA* doctrine where the Court derived the European Community's external competence in the field of road transport from the existence of already clearly prescribed Community internal rules.[190]

III.3.3 Land de Sarre and others v Ministre de l'Industrie (Cattenom)

The two cases that follow have had a more modest impact in comparison to the former two. Namely in the *Cattenom*[191] and *Chernobyl II*[192] cases the CJEU, by way of a functional i.e. *effet utile* interpretation has helped circumscribe an already foreseen competence for Euratom which however neither resulted

187 Para. 148.

188 Para. 149.

189 Koutrakos, *supra* n. 184, p. 203.

190 C-22/70 Commission v Council (*ERTA* (*European Agreement on Road Transport*) *case*) ECR 1971 p. 0263; For more regarding this doctrine and how it evolved in the subsequent case law of the CJEU, see , the *ILO* (International Labour Organization) Opinion (Opinion 2/91 ECR 1993 p. I-01061) and the *Lugano II* Opinion (Opinion 1/03 ECR 2006 p. I-1145).

The EU legislators felt compelled to align with the *Nuclear Safety Convention* judgment – following the delivery of the judgment in December 2002, the Council drew up a proposal in 2004 for a Directive laying down basic obligations and general principles on the safety of nuclear installations (Proposal for a Council Directive (Euratom) laying down basic obligations and general principles on the safety of nuclear installations, COM(2004) 526 final), which was eventually adopted as *Directive 2009/71/Euratom establishing a Community framework for the nuclear safety of nuclear installations* in June 2009 (OJ L 172/18). The preamble of the Directive makes an express reference to the case law of the CJEU, among which the *Nuclear Safety Convention* judgment (Para. 4 of the preamble).

191 C-187/87 Land de Sarre and others v Ministre de l'Industrie, des P et T et du Tourisme, ECR 1988 p. I-05013.

192 C-70/88 European Parliament v Council of the European Communities ECR 1991 p. I-04529.

nor was intended to result in further expansion of the scope of Euratom's competence.

The Cattenom case concerned the validity of French inter-ministerial orders authorizing the disposal of liquid and gaseous radioactive waste from the Cattenom nuclear power-station in France, the Court being seized with interpreting the scope of Art. 37 Euratom requirement for Member States to provide the Commission with general data relating to plans for the disposal of radioactive waste allowing the latter to determine whether the implementation of such plans would be liable to result in the radioactive contamination of the water, soil or airspace of another Member State. The issue was to ascertain the exact point in time when the data is to be supplied to the Commission: whether it should be done before any disposal of waste is actually effected (regardless of whether such disposal may have been authorized by national authorities before the Commission had been notified),[193] or, whether the data is to be provided prior to the authorization of such disposal by the competent national authorities. The Court noted that the Commission possesses powers of considerable scope under the *Health and Safety* Chapter of the Euratom Treaty[194] so that its contribution in the application of Art. 37 Euratom was of great importance to the Member State concerned on account of 'the Commission's unique overview of developments in the nuclear power industry throughout the territory of the Community'.[195] It was indispensable that for Art. 37 Euratom to attain its full effectiveness, the former was to be interpreted to the effect that Member States carried the obligation to provide the Commission with general data relating to a plan for the disposal of radioactive waste *before*[196] definitive authorization for such disposal was granted by the competent national authorities of the Member State.[197]

III.3.4 Chernobyl II

While the previous judgment aimed to delineate the Commission's prerogatives in a particular area, the *Chernobyl II*[198] case examines the choice of the correct legal basis for an act adopted under the Euratom Treaty and the

193 Para. 5.

194 Para. 11.

195 Para. 13.

196 Emphasis added.

197 Para. 19.

198 C-70/88 European Parliament v Council of the European Communities ECR 1991 p. I-04529.

scope of the Parliament's prerogatives pertinent to the adoption thereof. Namely, the Parliament had requested the annulment of *Regulation (Euratom) No. 3954/87 laying down maximum permitted levels of radioactive contamination of foodstuffs and of feedingstuffs following a nuclear accident or any other case of radiological emergency* which was adopted on the basis of Art. 31 Euratom which lays down the procedure for the adoption by the Council of basic standards for the protection of the health of workers and the general public against the dangers caused by ionizing radiation, under which the Parliament is merely consulted. The regulation prohibits the placing on the market of foodstuffs and feedingstuffs which own a level of contamination exceeding the maximum permitted levels that have been set out in a measure adopted in accordance with the provisions of the Regulation.[199] Since the Parliament claimed that Art. 31 was the wrong legal basis the Court examined the purpose of the Regulation in the light of its aim and content which was to protect the population against the dangers arising from foodstuffs and feedingstuffs that have been subjected to radioactive contamination.[200] In this sense, the Regulation clearly did not represent a harmonization measure as the Parliament had indicated since the effect of the Regulation on the harmonization of the conditions for free movement of goods within the Community was only incidental and merely served to ensure the effectiveness of the maximum permitted levels.[201]

The Court refused to take a restrictive stance in its response to the Parliament's contention that Art. 30 et seq. of the Euratom Treaty failed to apply to 'secondary' radiation (radiation emanating from contaminated products) and thus only concerned the protection of persons directly involved in the nuclear industry.[202] *A fortiori*, it held that the purpose of the former articles was to ensure a consistent and effective protection of the health of the general public against the dangers of ionizing radiations, regardless of their source and regardless of the categories of persons exposed to those radiations.[203]

---

199 Para. 2.

200 Para. 12.

201 Para. 17.

202 Para. 13.

203 Para. 14; Such broad approach has equally been observed in the subsequent case-law of the Court, namely, in the *Nuclear Safety Convention* judgment (Para. 80) as well as in AG Jacobs's Opinion in the same case (Para. 150).

III.3.5 Commission v Ireland (*MOX Plant*)

The last two cases to be covered in this section are the *MOX Plant*[204] and the *Temelin*[205] cases as representative of a type of CJEU cases where what was accomplished was an affirmation of a *de facto* extension of Euratom's competences accompanied by a strong empowerment of both Euratom's/Union's internal legal order by way of establishing a particular external competence for the Community/Union. Both of these cases related to disputes that had (intentionally or not) 'strayed' from the Union legal order *sensu lato* risking for the application of pertinent Euratom/Union rules to be circumvented. More specifically, in the *Temelin* case, the national court referring the case considered the dispute to fall under the scope of the TFEU (then, TEC) and, consequently, the questions it had put out to the CJEU solely concerned the application of the former Treaty. In the *MOX* case, on the other hand, Ireland had initially brought before a foreign (non-EU) judicial forum a dispute which essentially fell within the Union's jurisdiction.

The Commission in the *MOX* case alleged that by having instituted dispute-settlement proceedings against the United Kingdom under the auspices of the United Nations Convention on the Law of the Sea (UNCLOS) concerning the operation of the MOX nuclear power plant located at Sellafield, Ireland had breached its obligations under Arts. 10 TEC (now Art. 4(3) TEU; the duty of cooperation of Member States) and Art. 292 EC (now Art. 344 TFEU).[206] Pursuant to the former provisions, Member States undertake not to submit a dispute concerning the interpretation or application of the TFEU to any method of settlement other than those provided for therein. The former two articles have been mirrored in Arts. 192 and 193 Euratom.[207]

---

204 C-459/03 *Commission v Ireland* ECR 2006 p. I-4635.

205 C-115/08 *Land Oberösterreich v ČEZ* ECR 2009 p. I-10265.

206 The legal saga surrounding the operation of the Sellafield MOX plant will also be examined from the perspective of the other international jurisdictions involved (other than that of the EU) in Chapter 2, Section II.

207 Article 193 Euratom:

> 'Member States undertake not to submit a dispute concerning the interpretation or application of this Treaty to any method of settlement other than those provided for therein'.
>
> Article 192 Euratom:
>
> 'Member States shall take all appropriate measures, whether general or particular, to ensure fulfilment of the obligations arising out of this Treaty or resulting from action taken by the institutions of the Community. They shall facilitate the achievement of the Community's tasks.
>
> They shall abstain from any measure which could jeopardize the attainment of the objectives of this Treaty'.

The disputed claim Ireland had lodged before the UNCLOS Arbitral Tribunal was not confined to the immediate consequences arising from the operation MOX plant and covered the totality of the effects arising from the establishment and operation of the MOX plant.[208] Ireland held that the UNCLOS imposed on the United Kingdom obligations concerning the protection of the marine environment, the prevention and control of pollution and co-operation between the two States, and demanded that the Tribunal decide on appropriate remedies against the United Kingdom.[209] The Commission insisted that the fact that Ireland had submitted the matter to a jurisdiction other than that of the Union constituted a failure to respect the exclusive jurisdiction the CJEU enjoyed under to Art. 292 EC (now, 344 TFEU) which was to rule on any dispute concerning the interpretation and application of Union law.[210] It was alleged that Ireland had breached Arts. 292 EC and 193 EA by referring to an arbitral tribunal a dispute which necessitates interpretation and application of measures of Community law for its resolution.[211] Furthermore, Ireland was considered to have allegedly breached the duty of cooperation devolving on Member States (under ex-Art. 10 EC (now Art. 4(3) TEU) and Art. 192 Euratom) by exercising a competence that originally belongs to the Community and by omitting to inform or consult with the competent Union institutions prior to taking such a step.[212]

The CJEU brought the dispute between Ireland and the UK fully within the scope of the EU legal order by stating *inter alia* that the (former) *Directive 80/836/Euratom laying down the basic safety standards for the health protection of the general public and workers against the dangers of ionizing radiation*[213]

208 Para. 11.

209 Para. 12.

210 Para. 59.

211 Para. 59.

212 Para. 59; The Commission had been closely associated with the issues linked to the Selafield site. In fact, on 11 February 1997 the Commission, based on information supplied by the United Kingdom Government, delivered an opinion pursuant to Art. 37 Euratom on the plan for the disposal of radioactive waste arising from the operation of the MOX facility (OJ 1997 C 68, p. 4) in which it had concluded that the radioactive waste arising from the operation of the BNFL Sellafield mixed oxide fuel plant was not liable to result in radioactive contamination regarding the water, soil or airspace of another Member State. Furthermore, an assessment of the economic justification for the MOX plant was carried out by a private consulting firm ('the PA report') pursuant to the requirements set out in Directive 80/836/Euratom of 15 July 1980 amending the Directives laying down the basic safety standards for the health protection of the general public and workers against the dangers of ionizing radiation (OJ 1980 L 246, p. 1).

213 OJ 1980 L 246, p. 1.

was applicable to the issue of the radioactive discharge from the Mox plant into the marine environment of the Irish Sea[214] whereas UK's refusal to provide Ireland with certain types of information was to be considered as coming within the scope of (former) *Directive 90/313/EEC of 7 June 1990 on the freedom of access to information on the environment.*[215]

Regarding the choice of the appropriate dispute settlement mechanism, the Court unequivocally held that in spite of the available procedures for the resolution of disputes pursuant to Art. 282 of the UNCLOS, it was nevertheless the system for the resolution of disputes established under the EC (TFEU) Treaty that must take precedence.[216] The Court considered the relevant provisions of the UNCLOS (a mixed international agreement) as belonging to the scope of Community competence as competence that the Community has exercised by acceding to the UNCLOS, thus making the former provisions an integral part of the Community legal order.[217] Therefore, the dispute in the Mox case was considered as pertaining to the interpretation or application of the EC (TFEU) Treaty according to the terms of Art. 292 EC[218] whereby the institution of proceedings before the Arbitral Tribunal carried a manifest risk for EU's established jurisdictional order and the autonomy of the Union's legal system to be potentially adversely affected.[219]

As regards Ireland's failure to respect the duty of cooperation by bringing proceedings unilaterally, without having informed and consulted the Community institutions beforehand, the Court reiterated the Member States' obligation of close cooperation with the Union institutions primarily since the subject matter of the UNCLOS as a mixed agreement related to a field (protection and preservation of the marine environment) where the respective areas of competence of the Community and the Member States could potentially overlap[220] so that submission of the dispute to an external judicial forum entailed the risk that the

214 Para. 111.

215 OJ 1990 L 158, p. 56; Para. 117.

216 Para. 125.

217 Para. 126; For an elaborate treatise of the concept of mixed international agreements, see, Hillion, C. and Koutrakos, P. (eds.), Mixed agreements revisited: The EU and its Member States in the World, Hart Publishing, 2010; More particularly, on the typology of mixed bilateral agreements – the concept of bilateral mixity and the different categories of mixed bilateral agreements – see, M. Maresceau, A Typology of Mixed Bilateral Agreements, in, Hillion, C. and Koutrakos, P. (eds.), Mixed agreements revisited: The EU and its Member States in the World, Hart Publishing, 2010, pp. 11–29.

218 Para. 127.

219 Para. 154.

220 Para. 176.

former forum could become competent to rule or at least attempt to rule on the scope of the obligations carried by Member States under Community law.[221]

The practical implications of the judgment go beyond strictly the Euratom scope, confirming the exclusive character of the CJEU's jurisdiction regarding mixed international agreements that have become part of Union law and reinforcing the autonomy and coherence of the Union legal order.[222] The former completely removes any possibility for an external, non-EU jurisdiction to offer a more specialized grasp on a particular issue and thus be better suited to apply the relevant international legal rules.[223] With this judgment, the CJEU has permanently curtailed the possibility for international judicial fora to settle disputes which concern the Union Treaties' scope of application thus preventing the Member States from instituting proceedings outside of the Union jurisdiction in this way, or, otherwise, be brought before the CJEU for incompliance.[224] Hereinafter, a Member State which brings a case against another Member State under an international public law dispute settlement system relating to the provisions of an international agreement within EU competence would be considered as acting in direct breach of its Union law obligations.[225]

III.3.6 The Temelín Case

Another remarkable case is *Temelín* which is to be regarded as a typical 'spill-over' case on many fronts. It concerned the official authorisations for the construction and operation of the Czech nuclear power plant *Temelín* located near the Austrian border[226] where the Land Oberösterreich and other private owners had brought actions under the Austrian Civil Code requesting that an order is adopted to terminate the actual and potential nuisance relating to the

221 Para. 177.

222 S. Marsden, MOX Plant and the Espoo Convention: Can Member State Disputes Concerning Mixed Environmental Agreements be Resolved Outside EC Law?, *Review of European Community and International Environmental Law,* 2009, Vol. 18 Issue 3, p. 315.

223 *Idem*, p. 316.

224 *Idem*, p. 316.

225 I. Govaere, Beware of the Trojan Horse: Dispute Settlement in (Mixed) Agreements and the Autonomy of the EU Legal Order, in, C. Hillion and P. Koutrakos (eds.), Mixed agreements revisited: The EU and its Member States in the World, Hart Publishing, 2010, p. 202; Govaere further raises another important point which may prove to be a complicating factor in adhereing to the CJEU's categorical stance which is the possibility for the action undertaken by one Member State against another to be perfectly valid from the perspective of public international law all the while potentially leading to a different outcome from that under EU law (See, *idem*, p. 203).

226 Para. 38.

ionizing radiation emanating from the Czech nuclear power plant.[227] More particularly, according to the Austrian Civil Code an undertaking in possession of the necessary official authorisations for operating a nuclear power plant situated in the territory of another Member State (in the case in point, the Czech Republic) is liable to be the subject of an action for an injunction to prevent an actual or potential nuisance to neighbouring property emanating from that installation.[228] Conversely, undertakings that have their industrial installation situated in the Member State where the action for injunction is brought and are in possession of an official authorisation may not be the subject of such an action and are only liable to be the subject of a claim for damages for harm caused to a neighbouring property.[229] Thus, the Austrian rules in question effectively established a *prima faciae* difference in treatment based on the national territory where the power generating installations have been set up.

Although the questions referred from the national court related to issues arising under the EC Treaty and requested the interpretation of EC Treaty provisions which the national court presumed to be applicable to the case, the CJEU nevertheless decided to put the matter completely within the purview of the Euratom Treaty. It was insisted by the Commission that the case concerned the application of the principle of non-discrimination espoused in Art. 18 TFEU (ex-Art. 12 EC)[230] which was equally considered applicable to the Euratom Treaty and thus making the difference in treatment arising under the application of the Austrian legislation impossible to justify.[231] Given that the Euratom Treaty does not contain a general non-discrimination clause corresponding to that of the TFEU, the CJEU decided to extend the scope of application of the principle of prohibition of discrimination as a general principle of Union law to the purview of the Euratom Treaty,[232] considering it to be unsuitable both to the purpose and the consistency of the treaties to allow discrimination on grounds of nationality which is prohibited under the TFEU to be tolerated within the purview of the Euratom Treaty.[233]

227 Para. 41.

228 Para. 139.

229 Para. 139.

230 Art. 18 TFEU reads: 'Within the scope of application of the Treaties, and without prejudice to any special provisions contained therein, any discrimination on grounds of nationality shall be prohibited (…)'.

231 Paras. 72, 73.

232 Para. 91.

233 Para. 90.

Acknowledging that the Euratom Treaty does not contain a title on the safety of nuclear installations, the Court drew on its crucial pronouncement in the *Nuclear Safety Convention* case indicating that in defining Euratom's competences it would be inappropriate to uphold an artificial distinction between the protection of the health of the general public and the safety of sources of ionising radiation.[234] The Court opined that the granting of official authorisations for the construction and operation of nuclear installations, to the extent that it relates to health protection against the dangers of ionising radiations for the general public, is to be considered as coming within the scope of application of the Euratom Treaty.[235] After establishing the existence of a difference in treatment, the Court sought to find a legitimate justification for such a difference in the form of objective consideration irrespective of nationality which is proportionate to the legitimately pursued objective.[236] In order to examine the justifications relating to health protection that lie behind the difference in treatment between the official authorisations granted to industrial installations situated in Austria and those granted regarding nuclear power plants situated in another Member State, the Court looked at the basic safety standards laid out in Chapter 3 of the Euratom Treaty and the related secondary legislation which has been amended in line with scientific developments in the field of radiation protection.[237] It was noted that the applicable health and safety protection regime under Euratom was not restricted to establishing basic standards, but additionally included important compliance and monitoring mechanisms supplementing the basic standards.[238] Furthermore, the Commission and the Council were, in line with their respective tasks, closely involved in the nuclear safety evaluation of the *Temelín* plant, having issued safety reports and opinions which concluded in the affirmative i.e. that the checks carried out under the health and safety requirements of the Euratom Treaty indicated a satisfactory level of nuclear safety, compliant with the relevant Euratom legislation.[239]

The judgment confirmed that the Member States have a comprehensive system of legal remedies at their disposal to curb any arising deficiency in the Euratom health and safety protection system,[240] indicating that the level of protection provided under the former system was satisfactory and discounting

234 Para. 102.

235 Para. 105.

236 Para. 108.

237 Paras. 110–116.

238 Para. 117 et seq.

239 Paras. 45–49.

240 Para. 131 et seq.

any possibility for a difference in treatment such as that foreseen by the Austrian legislation that could be regarded as necessary for the purposes of health protection and that could be considered as fulfilling the proportionality requirement.[241]

Temelín is a spill-over case which contributes to the strengthening of Euratom's nuclear safety regime by prioritizing Euratom Community's authority in the field of nuclear safety over particular Member States' nuclear safety policies, even in cases occurring in Member States such as Austria[242] which is a country with a strong national anti-nuclear sentiment where nuclear energy policy is a highly sensitive and delicate political issue.[243] The judgment conveys the message that Member States' unilateral measures that undermine the established Euratom nuclear safety regime (especially those of a discriminatory nature) should be outright dismissed. Consequently, nuclear activities carried out in the territory of a Member State that meet the requirements of Euratom legislation and satisfy the Commission's scrutiny cannot be subject to national discriminatory measures of other Member States.[244] Aside from reinforcing Euratom's position in the field of nuclear safety,[245] the judgment will presumably also have an impact on the relationship between the Euratom Community and the Member States, highlighting the extensive prerogatives of the Commission and making it more difficult for Member States to question its authority.[246]

The cases in the present section have evidenced the spill-over effect produced by CJEU's case law mainly concerning the scope of Euratom's competence in the fields of radiation protection and nuclear safety. The foregoing analysis has shown that such spill-over fostered by the CJEU is largely initiated by the Commission (via the infringement procedure) or the subnational actors appearing before the Court (via the preliminary reference procedure). Nevertheless, the Commission's stake in the spill-over process is much more substantial than that of subnational actors mostly due to the rather modest number of influential actors at the national level involved in the nuclear field (nuclear operators, concerned individuals) and, generally speaking, the limited knowledge on Euratom law and the workings of Euratom as a

241 Para. 136.

242 Austria has been an anti-nuclear country since 1978.

243 W. Schärf, 'The Temelín-Judgement of the European Court of Justice', *Nuclear Law Bulletin*, Vol. 2010/1, p. 79.

244 *Idem*, p. 85.

245 *Idem*, p. 79.

246 *Idem*, p. 91.

community.[247] On its own part, the CJEU appears to be selective of the potential spill-over possibilities it creates and is generally more inclined towards allowing a spill-over in cases that involve the basic principles of the Union legal order, the Union's scope of competence in a particular policy field, or, cases that implicate its own prerogatives as a judicial organ.[248] Notwithstanding the CJEU's decisive role in the spill-over process, there will equally be instances where an activist CJEU judgment will not materialize in an actual spill-over due to lack of agreement among Member States on the particular Euratom measures to be taken to achieve the spill-over effect.[249]

IV The Dynamics of Treaty Modification: To Assimilate or Not?

The objective of the foregoing discussion was to offer a more general and basic insight into the nature and the workings of the Euratom Community as a separate entity existing under the hat of the Union. Such a discussion would prove incompete should it omit to cover the issue of the future of Euratom and the planned alternatives elaborated with relation thereto. In the past decade, commentary on the future of the European Atomic Energy Community has ranged from calls urging its revision to pleas for its abolition, making the *ratio essendi* of the Euratom Treaty somewhat questionable, with as many foes as friends on its side. Many of the foes tend to point to the highly technocratic character of its provisions as one of the reasons why the Euratom Community has traditionally been kept at the outskirts of the EU's legal and political framework, however questionable this argument might be in terms of justifying the 'renegade' status that the Euratom Treaty enjoys in relation to the other founding treaties of the Union. One of the peculiar features of this Treaty is that it has withheld the test of time, since its present text (save for several non-substantial changes)[250] has essentially remained the same since its adoption in 1957 which is a far cry from the destiny that lay in wait for the EAEC's sibling, the European (Economic) Community.

247 Wolf, *supra* n. 36, p. 15, 16.

248 *Idem*, p. 18.

249 *Idem*, p. 16.

250 Amended by the TEU (Title IV: Provisions amending the Treaty establishing the European Atomic Energy Community and Title VII: Final Provisions which extended the institutional changes introduced to the EC Treaty and the ECSC treaty to the EAEC Treaty); the Treaty of Amsterdam (Arts. 1, 4, 7, 8, 9, 10, 11 and relevant protocols applicable to the EAEC); Treaty of Nice (Arts. 1, 3, 7 and 9 and relevant protocols applicable to the EAEC); and lastly, the Treaty of Lisbon – Protocol No. 2 *Amending the Treaty establishing the EAEC* and other protocols applicable to the EAEC.

The calls for a reform of the Euratom Treaty coming from the EU institutions,[251] the Member States[252] and the non-governmental sector[253] as well as the academic community,[254] became increasingly loud throughout the Union 'reform period' from 2001–2007 which had been marked by the drafting of the *Treaty establishing a Constitution for Europe* (the Constitutional Treaty) in 2004 which subsequently failed to be ratified by all the Member States thereupon followed by the signature of the reformatory Lisbon Treaty in 2007. With regard to the possibility for a Treaty reform, all of the former commonly consider the urgent need to add more democratic flesh to the Euratom construct in the direction of increasing the European Parliament's involvement in the decision-making process.[255] Although the Lisbon treaty's reformatory sweep

---

251 European Parliament, *Report on Assessing Euratom – 50 Years of European Nuclear Energy Policy* (*Maldeikis Report*) A6-0129/2007 final, p. 9, 11; European Parliament Resolution of 10 May 2007 on the public health consequences of the 1968 Thule crash (Petition 720/2002) (2006/2012(INI)), point 13.

252 Final Act of the Intergovernmental Conference on the Lisbon Treaty, *Declaration made by Germany, Ireland, Hungary, Austria and Sweden* [2007] OJ C306/268:
54. Declaration by the Federal Republic of Germany, Ireland, the Republic of Hungary, the Republic of Austria, the Kingdom of Sweden – *Germany, Ireland, Hungary, Austria and Sweden note that the core provisions of the Treaty establishing the European Atomic Energy Community have not been substantially amended since its entry into force and need to be brought up to date. They therefore support the idea of a Conference of the Representatives of the Governments of the Member States, which should be convened as soon as possible.*

253 Friends of the Earth Europe, 'Will the New EU Constitution Promote Nuclear Energy? – Paper Analyzing the Role of the EURATOM Treaty in the New EU Constitution' available at http://www.foeeurope.org/publications/2005/euratom_and_constitution_may2005.pdf, p. 8; Ahead of the 50th anniversary of the EU and its pro-nuclear Euratom Treaty, 780 organisations and 630,000 individuals have demanded abolition of the Euratom and a phase-out of nuclear power across Europe (from the website of the European initiative against nuclear power: http://million-against-nuclear.net/).

254 See P.M. Barnes, The nuclear industry: A particular challenge to democracy in Europe, *Managerial Law*, 2006, Issue 48, p. 425; J. Grunwald, Euratom Treaty History and The Way Forward in, *Nuclear Inter Jura 2007 Proceedings*, Bruylant, 2008, p. 1079; P.D. Cameron, Energy: Efficiency, Security and the Environment, in M. Dougan and S. Currie (eds.), *50 Years of The European Treaties: Looking Back and Thinking Forward*, Hart Publishing, 2009, p. 263.

255 For example, the *Maldeikis Report* demanded an upgrade of the decision-making procedures under the Euratom Treaty, enabling the Parliament to be more closely involved thus allowing for greater transparency and involvement of the Union citizens. The Council and the Commission were called upon to address the 'democratic deficit inherent in the Euratom Treaty' (point 43) whereby Art. 203 Euratom was suggested as the legal basis for treaty reform (point 44). On the strengthening of the democratic legitimacy of the Euratom, see also, Contribution by Mr. Hannes Farnleitner, Mr. Caspar Einem and

did not significantly affect the Euratom Treaty and preserved the singular legal status of the Euratom Community, it would be appropriate to look at the possible ways in which the destiny of the Euratom Treaty will develop in the future in view of the still very topical character of the issue.

The reasons indicated in the pleas for imminent Treaty reform have been mostly centered on the out-datedness of certain Treaty provisions, the potentially distortive and unbalancing effect of the Treaty provisions both upon the Union's common market and the Union's competition rules coupled with the perennial lack of consensus among Member States regarding nuclear energy use especially in light of certain Member States governments' decisions to completely de-nuclearise (Austria) or phase-out nuclear energy in the foreseeable future (Germany).

The proposals for a future Euratom Treaty reform have mainly revolved around three avenues. The first avenue concerns a revision intended to update the Treaty whereby its integrity and singular legal status would be maintained (to be accomplished by relying on the flexibility clause of Art. 203 Euratom, the Art. 48 TEU treaty revision procedure , or, by utilizing the relevant rules of the Vienna Convention on the Law of Treaties[256]). The second avenue is represented by the option to repeal the Treaty, deleting the outdated provisions or those which duplicate the corresponding TFEU provisions, and incorporate the remainder of the Euratom Treaty provisions into the TFEU either in a separate chapter or into the existent 'Energy' chapter. Consequently to the former, the Euratom Community will be extinguished and its legal personality relinquished. The third option is the most radical of the three and suggests the abolishment of the Treaty and all of its provisions in their entirety – a scenario most fervently advocated by the European anti-nuclear lobby represented by the 'green' political parties and the anti-nuclear NGOs who believe the Euratom Treaty to be an obsolete treaty that does not reflect the nuclear reality in the EU and propose that the current EU nuclear policy should be brought back to the national field and thus become re-nationalized.

Mr.Reinhard E. Bösch, members of the Convention for the future of Europe: 'A single legal personality – On the future of Euratom', CONV 358/02, p. 4, 5.

256 See the transcript from the presentation 'The Legal Perspective: The Euratom treaty and the new Constitution' by Dörte Fouquet, attorney from the European Renewable Energies Association, prepared for the conference titled 'The Euratom Treaty and Future Energy Options: Conditions for a Level Playing Field in the Energy Sector', organized by Friends of the Earth-Denmark, The Danish Ecological Council and The Danish Organisation for Sustainable Energy (http://www.energyintelligenceforeurope.dk/conf_p6.html).

IV.1 *The Flexibility Clause of the Euratom Treaty (Article 203) As a Feasible Procedural Option*

The use of the flexibility clause of Art. 203 Euratom was suggested by the Parliament Committee on Industry, Research and Energy in the Maldeikis Report as the means pertinent to make any necessary adjustments to the text of the Euratom Treaty.[257] Pursuant to Art. 203 Euratom (analogous to Art. 352 TFEU), if action by the Community proves necessary for the attainment of the objectives of the Community while in the absence of necessary powers provided by the Treaty, the Council is entitled to take the appropriate measures.[258] The former Committee considered that the option of deleting certain Treaty chapters or that of merging certain treaty provisions into the TFEU would 'unbalance the Euratom Treaty as a whole by weakening supervision of nuclear energy use in Europe'.[259] It held that in the decades of its existence the Treaty has demonstrated the usefulness of its provisions and merging certain of its provisions into an 'Energy' chapter in the TFEU Treaty would undermine the legal supervision over nuclear energy in Europe and obliterate the existent specific nuclear control procedures established under the Treaty.[260] However, the Committee did require a comprehensive revision of the Treaty as one that would amend the democratic deficit and reinforce the safety and security framework of nuclear activities of the EU and the Member States.[261] In the Opinion of the Parliament Committee on Constitutional Affairs addressed to the Committee on Industry, Research and Energy which has been attached to the Maldeikis Report[262] the former Committee expressed the need for the convening of an intergovernmental conference in order for a comprehensive revision to be accomplished by repealing of the outdated Treaty provisions and revision of the remaining provisions in the light of a sustainable energy policy which would subsequently be incorporated into the Constitutional Treaty, in a

257 Point 30.

258 Art. 203 Euratom: 'If action by the Community should prove necessary to attain one of the objectives of the Community and this Treaty has not provided the necessary powers, the Council shall, acting unanimously on a proposal from the Commission and after consulting the European Parliament, take the appropriate measures'.

259 Point 39.

260 Point 40.

261 Point 43.

262 Opinion of the Committee on Constitutional Affairs of the European Parliament (included in the *Report on Assessing Euratom – 50 Years of European Nuclear Energy Policy* (*Maldeikis Report*) A6-0129/2007 final) (2006/2230(INI)), Draftsman: Johannes Voggenhuber.

separate energy chapter.[263] There is a noticeable inconsistency in approach between the two Committees as to the destiny of the Euratom Treaty – the Industry, Research and Energy Committee being inclined towards safeguarding the integrity of the Euratom Treaty and the Euratom Community and the Constitutional Affairs Committee being in favor for the nuclear policy established under the Euratom Treaty to be assimilated into the wider scope of the Union's energy policy. Manifestly, there is a clear division in perceptions within the European Parliament concerning the future of the Euratom Treaty. Nevertheless, what is certain is that there does not exist any important political majority within the European Parliament that is against nuclear power and requires a complete abolishment of the Euratom Treaty, provided that the 'Greens' are the only political group in the Parliament that opposes nuclear energy use in a consistent manner in parliamentary votes.[264] In turn, the former corroborates the European Parliament's support for the longevity of the European nuclear energy policy and the coherence of the nuclear legal framework established at the EU level.

One important advantage of the Euratom Treaty which makes it impervious to radical change is the nature of its text which for the most part is perfectly flexible[265] (especially the Chapter 6 on supply, Chapter 7 on safeguards and Chapter 8 on the system of ownership which have been drafted in such a way that makes them adaptable to newly arising circumstances (labeled as the Treaty's 'ability to learn'[266]). In this sense, utilizing the flexibility clause of Art. 203 would prove as a more suitable way in order to effectuate Treaty adjustments while not affecting the overall Treaty structure and circumventing the application of the Art. 48 TEU treaty modification procedure which requires that an inter-governmental conference is convened for the purpose.

While Art. 203 Euratom can be relied on for enforcing simple adjustments to the Treaty, should a more substantial revision of the Treaty be required, the use of the ordinary treaty revision procedure of Art. 48 EU would be the more pertinent solution (by virtue of Art. 106a Euratom, the former article is equally applicable to the ambit of the Euratom Treaty). Art. 48 TEU introduces the 'small' option for minor treaty adjustments (without Convention) and the 'big'

263 Point 6.

264 http://archive.greens-efa.eu/cms/topics/dok/172/172579.euratom_50_years_too_much@en.htm.

265 N.P. Serrano, Wakening the serpent: reflections on the possible modification of the Euratom Treaty, *International Journal of Nuclear Law*, 2006, Vol. 1 No. 1, p. 13.

266 *Idem*, p. 14.

option which necessitates that a Convention is assembled.[267] The latter allows the Member States' governments, the European Parliament or the Commission to introduce proposals for the amendment of the Treaties directed at increasing or reducing the competences conferred on the Union under the Treaties.[268] Thereby, the European Council consults the European Parliament and the Commission and adopts a decision granting an examination of the proposed amendments, entrusting the President of the European Council with the task of convening a *convention* composed of representatives of the national Parliaments, of the Heads of State or Government of the Member States, of the European Parliament and of the Commission.[269] Should the European Council decide, after obtaining the consent of the European Parliament, not to convene a Convention justified by the extent of the proposed amendments, the European Council sets out the terms of reference for a *conference* of representatives of the governments of the Member States to be held.[270] Regardless of whether the option to hold a Convention is triggered or not, the amendments which are to be introduced to the Treaties are determined by common accord through a conference of representatives of the governments of the Member States that is to be convened by the President of the Council.[271]

The option concerning the employment of the ordinary revision procedure in this respect had been formally raised in Declaration No. 54 of the Final Act of the Intergovernmental Conference on the Lisbon Treaty, where the governments of five Member States (*Germany, Ireland, Hungary, Austria and Sweden*) expressed their support for the convening of a conference of the representatives of the governments as soon as possible for the purpose of bringing the Euratom Treaty provisions up to date.

iv.2 *The Last Word on the Matter: The Convention on the Future of Europe*

In the course of the preparation of the text of the (now defunct) Treaty establishing a Constitution for Europe (the Constitutional Treaty) within the framework of the *Convention on the future of Europe*, a number of proposals of a

267 For a discussion on this point, see, W. Kilb, The Europan Atomic Energy Community and Its Primary and Secondary Law, in, *International Nuclear Law: History, Evolution and Outlook*, 2010, OECD NEA publication (downloadable at http://www.oecd-nea.org/law/isnl/10th/isnl-10th-anniversary.pdf), pp. 83–86.

268 Art. 48(2).

269 Art. 48(3).

270 Art. 48(3).

271 Art. 48(4).

more radical nature had surfaced which related to the dissolution of the Euratom Community and the merging of the 'viable' provisions of the Euratom Treaty into the TFEU. The Declaration adopted at the 2001 European Council Summit in Laeken heralded the start of a reform process for the Union that was to be crowned with the drafting of a new constitutional treaty which was to rationalize the Union's institutional set-up and streamline Union's policies. The former mandate was entrusted to the European Convention (the Convention on the Future of Europe) whose members were representatives of the national parliaments of the Member States, the European Parliament, the European Commission as well as representatives of heads of state and government of the Member States. The mandate of the Convention ran from December 2001 through July 2003 when it was finalized with the Convention producing the final draft of the Treaty establishing a Constitution for Europe.[272]

The Praesidium of the European Convention did not address the issue of reform of the Euratom Treaty considering that the former exceeded both its mandate and the timetable of the Convention so that it failed to find any basis for the Convention as a body to venture on substantially amending the provisions of the Euratom Treaty, regarding it as inappropriate for it to perform a task of that nature.[273] The actual changes to the Euratom Treaty were instead included in a protocol to the Constitutional Treaty[274] and were merely formal and unsubstantial in nature (concerning certain institutional and financial adjustments), leaving the substantive rules of the Treaty untouched. The Protocol intended to *amend* the Euratom Treaty in order to bring it in line with the newly-introduced institutional, financial and procedural arrangements. The amendments set out in the Lisbon Treaty follow the same pattern of *amending* the Euratom Treaty rather than engaging in a substantial revision thereof.

Even though the Convention's deliberations resulted in a decision to amend the Treaty to a limited extent (which was obviously performed via the Art. 48 TEU 'Convention' mechanism for treaty revision), it would nonetheless be instructive to also look at certain formal and less formal proposals that had arisen in the course of the work of the Convention.

272 The official documents of the European Convention as well as the contributions from the members of the Convention can be found at the Convention's official website (http://european-convention.eu.int/EN/bienvenue/bienvenue2352.html?lang=EN).

273 Note of the Presidium of the European Convention dated from 14 March 2003, CONV. 621/03.

274 Protocol no. 36 amending the Treaty Establishing the European Atomic Energy Community, OJ 310/391.

The *Feasibility study on the Constitution of the European Union*, issued in December 2002, was a working document (also known as the 'Penelope document') commissioned by then President of the Commission Mr. Romano Prodi the drafters of which were required to provide viable solutions for the rationalization of the Treaties and the simplification of the Union's policies.[275] Apart from the draft constitutional text, the Penelope document contained five additional acts, Additional Act No. 2 of which was entitled 'Peaceful uses of nuclear energy' which incorporated all the existing provisions of the Euratom Treaty save for those deemed to have become obsolete with time or those that duplicate the general provisions of the constitutional text.[276] The provisions retained were those of Chapter III (Health and Safety), Chapter IV (Investments), Chapter V (Joint Undertakings), Chapter VI (Supplies) and Chapter VII (Safeguards), amounting to a total of forty-five articles and two short annexes. Thus, the constitutional text proposed by the Penelope document was to abolish the legal personality of the Euratom Community, assimilating it into the singular and indivisible personality of the *Union*. Nevertheless, the Commission never submitted the Penelope document before the Convention so that it never became part of the official deliberations held within the framework of the Convention.[277]

In addition, several contributions issued by members of the Convention were brought to the attention of the Convention body dealing specifically with the future status of the Euratom Treaty, their authors having expressed the necessity for the reform of the Euratom Treaty to be placed at the Convention's agenda (which the Presidium however subsequently did not concede to).[278] The proposals ranged from requests for revision and modification of the Treaty to requests urging that the Treaty is abolished and its still 'current' provisions incorporated into one general and comprehensive treaty (be it a Constitution or another document of a constitutional nature). In fact, a possible route examined in one of the proposals was to repeal the

---

275 p. III of the Penelope document.

276 p. III of the Penelope document.

277 Serrano, *supra* n. 265, p. 15.

278 Contribution from Mr. Hannes Farnleitner, Mr. Caspar Einem and Mr. Reinhard E. Bösch, members of the Convention: 'A single legal personality – On the future of EURATOM' Brussels, 22 October 2002, CONV 358/02; Contribution by Ms Marie Nagy, Ms Renée Wagner and Mr Neil MacCormick, alternate members of the Convention: 'The Future of the Euratom Treaty in the Framework of the European Constitution' Brussels, 18 February 2003, CONV 563/03; Contribution from Mr Klaus Hänsch, member of the Convention: 'Future of the Euratom Treaty' Brussels, 14 October 2002 CONV 344/02.

obsolete Treaty provisions and transfer the provisions relating to health and safety, safeguards and non-proliferation (as the only 'viable' provisions of the Euratom Treaty) to the text of the new Constitution.[279] The former comes with an important *caveat* reflected in the legal and practical ramifications of assimilating the Euratom Treaty provisions to the existent Union framework for the purpose of of rationalizing the bulky and technical treaty, which have not been sufficiently examined and are not easily predictable.[280]

IV.3 *Calls for Complete Abolishment of the Euratom Treaty*

The third case scenario for the future of the Euratom Treaty is the option for a complete abolishment of the Treaty which would entail the extinguishment of Euratom's legal personality and the conduct of Member States' nuclear policies being brought back to the hands of national governments. It is a possibility which the EU institutions are for the time being not inclined to accept as they are decidedly the ones that are competent to initiate any Treaty change in such direction. Within the European Parliament, the political group of the European Greens has been adamant in promoting a nuclear-free agenda for the European Union according to which the use of nuclear power could not be regarded as a solution for Europe's energy needs. The former claims have won the support of a certain portion of the EU citizens, which was observed in the recent pan-European initiative launched on the occasion of the 50th anniversary of the Euratom Treaty.[281] On the same occasion, (then) EU Energy Commissioner Piebalgs received 630 000 signatures against nuclear energy

279 Contribution by Ms Marie Nagy, Ms Renée Wagner and Mr Neil MacCormick, alternate members of the Convention: 'The Future of the Euratom Treaty in the Framework of the European Constitution' Brussels, 18 February 2003, CONV 563/03, p. 4. The former proposal is in line with the view that it is indeed the radiological protection, environmental protection, nuclear safety and non-proliferation which are the components that justify the existence of the Treaty in the present day (as reported in N. Prieto Serrano, Wakening the Serpent: Reflections on the Possible Modification of the Euratom Treaty, International Journal of Nuclear Law, Vol. 1, No. 1, 2006, at p. 17, ft. 7).

280 This was confirmed in the Final report of the Convention's Working Group on Legal Personality, 1st October 2002, CONV 305/02, at point 15.

281 The Greens/European Free Alliance group in the European Parliament hosted a conference titled 'Euratom – 50 years too much: Nuclear error since 1957' where the issues of nuclear safety, nuclear proliferation and the future of the Euratom were discussed. For the Report from the Conference, see: http://archive.greens-efa.eu/cms/topics/dok/172/172579.euratom_50_years_too_much@en.htm.

from individuals and over 750 from organisations from all over the EU.[282] The signatories of the petition called for a complete phase-out of nuclear energy production across the EU and the abolishment of the Euratom Treaty.[283]

The underlying reasons for the present *status quo* attitude towards the Euratom Treaty may well be political and socio-economic in nature and mutually intertwined (the EU institutions being wary of openly discussing them). At the time of the ratification of the Constitutional Treaty, certain observers argued that the reason why the Euratom Community had been intentionally kept outside of the framework of the Constitutional Treaty *stricto sensu* was to avoid that the text of the future Constitution becomes 'contaminated' by the outdated nuclear text.[284] Another argument that has been put forward centers on the rationalization of any future attempts to revise the Euratom Treaty making it possible for the Treaty to be amended or even completely repealed without having to revise the Constitutional Treaty *per se*.[285] Furthermore, it is also important to acknowledge that none of the contributions submitted to the *Convention on the future of Europe* supported the prospect of a complete extinguishment of the Euratom Treaty, considering the former as an untenable solution especially in view of the pressing nature of the issues of nuclear waste disposal and nuclear safety that would be difficult to coordinate and tackle among the Member States in the absence of a nuclear treaty.[286]

The ultimate word on the future of the Euratom Treaty coming from an official intergovernmental forum of the Union has been the ambiguous pronouncement of the Convention's Praesidium that a discussion on the future of the Euratom Community surpasses the mandate of the Convention – pointing to a lack of consensus among and within the Member States on the justifiability of the use of nuclear technology in the future.[287] Given that only five Member States have signed the fore-mentioned Declaration urging the updating of the

282 http://archive.greens-efa.eu/cms/default/dok/173/173688.nuclear_error_since_1957@en.htm.

283 *Idem.*

284 Friends of the Earth Europe, 'Will the New EU Constitution Promote Nuclear Energy?' available at http://www.foeeurope.org/publications/2005/euratom_and_constitution_may2005.pdf, p. 3.

285 P. Norman, The Accidental Constitution: The Story of The European Convention, *Euro-Comment* (2003), p. 267.

286 Contribution from Mr Klaus Hänsch, member of the Convention: 'Future of the Euratom Treaty', Brussels, 14 October 2002, CONV 344/02, p. 5.

287 C. True, Legislative Competences of Euratom and the European Community in the energy sector: The Nuclear Package of the Commission, *European Law Review*, 2003, Vol. 28 Issue 5, p. 15.

Euratom Treaty, it is safe to conclude that for the time being the majority of Member States still consider the issue of the future of the Euratom project to be too politically sensitive to be addressed among the pro- and anti-nuclear energy states of the Union.[288]

However, the matter of deciding on the definitive future of the Euratom Community will become more pressing in the future, on account of the increasingly divergent national attitudes towards the use of nuclear power: on the one end of the spectrum there are Member States with active phase-out policies in place (Austria, Germany), while on the other end there are those Member States which consider the nuclear as essential to their nation state identity (France, the UK). Such a diverse nuclear landscape in the Union of today significantly overshadows the initial nuclear consensus among the founding Member States out of which the Euratom Community was born.[289]

288 Kilb, *supra* n. 267, p. 85.

289 On a similar note, see Contribution from Nagy, Wagner and MacCormick, *supra* n. 279, p. 3.

CHAPTER 2

The Interaction between the Euratom Health and Safety Policy and the Union Environmental Policy

The present chapter draws on the interaction between the Euratom health and safety policy as a policy developed under the Euratom Treaty, on the one side, and the Union envirironmental policy as a policy pursued within the scope of the Treaty on the functioning of the European Union (formerly, the European Community Treaty). It examines the concurring as well as the conflicting areas of competence between the Euratom Community and the Union with respect to the two above designated areas of focus, the nature of the competences thereby exercised and the interplay occurring among the respective tasks and objectives employed in the elaboration of the two policies. The transformation undergone by the European Community Treaty (TEC) into a Treaty on the functioning of the European Union (TFEU), pursuant to the Lisbon Treaty amendments, has nevertheless left the core objectives and respective policies developed under each of the three founding treaties (TFEU, TEU, Euratom Treaty) virtually unaltered. Therefore, the analysis of the pre-Lisbon relationship between the Euratom Community and the European Community/Union stands valid post-Lisbon as well, with the important difference that European Community's legal personality has now been assumed by that of the 'European Union'.

By observing the modalities of interaction between the environmental and the nuclear health and safety legal frameworks created under the purview of Euratom and the Union, accordingly, the discussion inquires into the instances of both concurring and conflicting competences between Euratom and the Union exercised in this respect. Drawing on the aspect of concurring competences between the Euratom health and safety policy and the Union environmental policy, the discussion elaborates the concept of 'borrowing' of legal bases signifying the practice of extending the scope of Union rules to the Euratom domain, and, conversely, the practice of applying Euratom rules to areas covered by the Union Treaties (the TFEU and the TEU). The practice of 'borrowing' legal bases from the Union Treaties mainly occurs in instances of absence of corresponding provisions in the Euratom Treaty or secondary Euratom legislation, instances of concurring competence arising between Euratom and the Union regarding a particular issue, as well as instances requiring for a general principle of Union law to be extended to the purview of Euratom.

 | DOI 10.1163/9789004310414_004

For the purpose of adequately positing the link between Euratom's health and safety policy and the Union's environmental policy, the analysis starts out by observing the interaction between the nuclear and environmental legal orders on the international arena, proceeding with the EU level and the issue of the role accorded to the the concept of 'environmental protection' within the scope of the Euratom health and safety regime. Relying on the concept of environmental protection to create the bridge between the Euratom health and safety policy and the Union environmental policy, the text examines the extent to which the former concept has been factored into Euratom's policy on nuclear health and safety as well as the extent to which it corresponds with and is compatible with the concept of environmental protection as elaborated under the Union environmental protection policy. In this context, the analysis discerns the presence/absence of an 'environmental protection' approach employed in the elaboration of the concepts of radiation protection and nuclear safety under the Euratom framework, looking to see whether the former have been underpinned by an 'environmental protection' ratio, or, are rather strictly confined to the notion of 'protection of human health' thus fully ascribing to the concept of anthropocentricism.

I The Possibility for Extending the Application of EU Rules to the Euratom Field

Following the diverse nature of the subject matter covered accordingly by the Union (formerly, Community; the common market and the policies linked to the creation and development thereof) and the Euratom Community (confined to the development of the civil nuclear industry), it is imminent that competition among the different Euratom and Union policies in particular fields frequently occurs, resulting in the practice of 'extrapolation' or 'borrowing' of legal bases. The 'borrowing' of legal bases covers the practice of extending the scope of EU rules to the Euratom domain (which is more frequent), or, conversely, applying Euratom rules to areas covered by the Union Treaties (the TFEU and the TEU). The 'extrapolation' of Union measures to the nuclear domain, even though common in practice, has not sufficiently been dealt with in academic literature. Examining the links between these two closely knit legal frameworks contributes to a better understanding of the delicate relationship between their respective legal orders and is instrumental in adequately positioning the Euratom Community's singular legal personality within the complex legal and political make-up of the European Union.

With regard to the intersection among the competences belonging to the Union and Euratom, a pattern is to be discerned regarding the modalities in which Union legal rules can be presumed to apply to Euratom's field of application, and vice versa. The reliance on the principle *lex specialis/lex generalis* seems pertinent to this end. The correct application of this principle to the relationship between the Union and the Euratom legal frameworks is contingent on the correct interpretation of the Treaties' 'bridging provisions'. The 'bridging provisions' articulate the lex specialis/lex generalis formula and represent the basic link between the two separate legal orders which sets the foundations from which their interaction builds up. Prior to the Lisbon Treaty, the bridging provision for the EC/Euratom/ECSC Treaties was found in ex-Art.305 EC which stipulated that:

1. The provisions of this Treaty [EC Treaty] *shall not affect*[1] the provisions of the Treaty establishing the European Coal and Steel Community, in particular as regards the rights and obligations of Member States, the powers of the institutions of that Community and the rules laid down by that Treaty for the functioning of the common market in coal and steel.
2. The provisions of this Treaty *shall not derogate*[2] from those of the Treaty establishing the European Atomic Energy Community.

The cited article performs the task of linking together the legal frameworks of the (then) three Communities (EC, Euratom and ECSC). Certain authors have argued that the term '*affect*' used to describe the correlation between the ECSC and the EC and the term '*derogate*' used with regard to Euratom are not to be construed as synonyms.[3] The key argument here is that the difference in wording exemplifies the essentially different character of the Treaties: the ECSC Treaty had established an almost autarchic legal system which could effectively function without any sort of European Community involvement much unlike the Euratom compact which does not benefit from such an elevated degree of autonomy.

After the termination of the ECSC and the adoption of the Lisbon amendments, the provision which governs the relationship between the Euratom Treaty, the Treaty on the Functioning of the European Union (successor of the EC Treaty) and the Treaty on the European Union is found in the Chapter

1 Emphasis added.

2 Emphasis added.

3 A. Nikpay and J. Faull, *The EC Law of competition*, Oxford University Press, 1999, p. 733.

entitled '*Application of certain provisions of the Treaty on European Union and of the Treaty on the Functioning of the European Union*', Art.106(a)(3) Euratom:

(…) 3. The provisions of the Treaty on European Union and of the Treaty on the Functioning of the European Union *shall not derogate* from the provisions of this Treaty.[4]

Ever since the creation of the European Community and Euratom, both the Union's law-makers and the Union's highest judicial body have been faced with the task to adequately and correctly interpret and apply the requirement that the provisions of the EC Treaty as *lex generalis* not derogate from those of the Euratom Treaty as *lex specialis*. Provided that the respective subject matter of the two legal regimes are in constant and intensive interaction, the need to utilise EU rules in order to regulate issues primarily falling under Euratom purview, in the absence of corresponding Euratom rules or Euratom legal bases, inevitably arises. Thus, the absence of relevant provisions both in the Euratom Treaty and secondary implementing legislation underscores the importance of the exercise of determining the exact scope and content of the duty '*not to derogate*'. Namely, such a duty arises either in instances where for an issue in the nuclear domain the Euratom legal framework has not provided an applicable legal rule thus resulting in a legal void to be filled through applying corresponding EU rules, or, alternatively, instances where the competence for regulating a particular issue falls equally under the general scope of the TFEU/TEU and the more subject-specific scope of the Euratom Treaty so that both of the legal framework potentially provide for an applicable legal rule (concurring competence).

1.1 *Lack of Corresponding Provisions in the Euratom Treaty*

The practice of extrapolating EC (EU) norms to the Euratom field was endorsed by the Court of Justice of the EU (CJEU) in a number of cases where the CJEU has allowed for such an extrapolation to occur solely with respect to Euratom-related issues that are *at want of regulation* (i.e. where the Euratom Treaty and/or the secondary implementing legislation have failed to provide a pertinent legal rule to be applied). In this sense, the CJEU does not confine the possibility for extension to only certain types of nuclear issues, but rather endorses the 'spill-over' option as a general possibility. Thus far, the Court has dealt with cases involving extension of rules relating to the following *Union* policies: the

4 Emphasis added.

common commercial policy, the competition policy (in the field of state aids and anti-dumping), health policy and environment policy. However the absence of *caveats* in the Court's dicta should not be taken for granted as, presumably, there could be issues potentially arising in the nuclear field which would prove unsuitable for regulation by strictly *Union* instruments.

An important analogy regarding the Union-Euratom regulatory interaction can be drawn from the Advocate General Slynn's Opinion in the *Deutsche Babcock*[5] case where the AG summarizes the co-existence of the EEC (European Ecnomic Community) and the ECSC (European Coal and Steel Community) legal frameworks through the spectrum of the requirement that the EC Treaty provisions *are not to affect* those of ECSC Treaty which does not imply "(...) that the EEC Treaty is not concerned with coal and steel and that legislation made under it may not make rules in respect of coal and steel (...) It would have been perfectly simple to provide that nothing in the EEC Treaty related to coal and steel products or to the coal and steel industry if that had been intended. That was not done. Instead the limitation imposed is that the provision of the EEC Treaty shall not "affect the provision" of the earlier Treaty, in particular as regards the matters specified (...)". *In nuce*, AG Slynn suggested that the EC Treaty may apply to the coal and steel industry to the extent that the particular matter at hand has not been covered by the ECSC Treaty rules or implementing secondary legislation under this Treaty. *Per analogiam*, the former reasoning could be extended to the EU-Euratom relationship in that it would be highly impractical and inopportune to deny or completely exclude the EU regulatory framework from matters falling within the remit of the Euratom Treaty.

In following reference will be made to several cases which showcase the CJEU and the General Court's approach to the matter of extrapolation of Union (then, EC) rules to the purview of Euratom.

In the joined cases C-188-190/80 *France v Commission, Italy v Commission, UK v Commission*,[6] the Court dealt with the possibility of applying the EC rules on state aids to undertakings in the nuclear sector. The Commission contended that the absence of provisions on state aids in the Euratom Treaty allowed for Arts.92 and 93 EC (now, Arts.86 and 87 TFEU) to be applied to the nuclear sector, subject to the exceptions provided in the Directive 80/723/EEC of 25 June 1980 on the transparency of financial relations between Member States and public undertakings.[7] In keeping with the '*not to derogate*' obligation, the Court accepted the former argument and concluded that the provisions of the

5 C-328/85, ECR 1987 Page 05119.

6 ECR 1982 p. 2545.

7 OJ 1980L 195/35; Para. 29 of judgment.

Directive did not depart from or compromise the effect of the Euratom Treaty provisions.[8]

Similarly, in *Opinion 1/94*[9] the Court remarked on the common concession made on the part of the Council and the Member States to the Commission's claim that the (then) European Community had exclusive competence to conclude the Multilateral Agreements on Trade in Goods in so far as the former apply to Euratom products.[10] Reiterating the *'not to derogate'* principle, it accepted that the lack of Euratom provisions on external trade warranted that agreements dealing with international trade in Euratom products to be concluded on the basis of the common commercial policy provisions of Art.113 EC (now, Art.207 TFEU).

In the *ENU v Commission* case,[11] the EU General Court examined the Euratom Supply Agency's right of option and exclusive right to conclude contracts for the supply of nuclear ores, while not neglecting to indicate that, in principle, there was nothing hindering the application of the EC Treaty antidumping provisions to the nuclear sector, in the absence of corresponding antidumping rules in the Euratom Treaty itself.

Another instance in which the CJEU sanctioned the possibility to extend the outreach of EU (EC) legal rules to the Euratom scope concerned the delicate issue of radioactive waste stemming from military nuclear installations. Namely, in *Commission v UK*,[12] the Court ruled out the possibility to apply the Euratom health and safety provisions (more precisely, the Art.37 Euratom provisions on disposal of radioactive waste) to military applications of nuclear energy and instead, suggested the use of appropriate EU (EC) measures that carry the same objective of protecting the health of the public and the environment against the dangers related to the use of nuclear energy.[13] The reason why

8 Para. 32.

9 Opinion 1/94 of 15 November 1994, ECR 1994 p. I-5267.

10 Para. 23 of Opinion.

11 T-458/93 and T-523/93, ECR 1995 p. II-2459.

12 C-61/03 ECR 2005 p. I-2477.

13 Para. 44 of judgment; To corroborate its claim, the Court offered the example of Case C-62/88 *Greece* v *Council*. The pertinence of such analogy seems questionable as the former case concerned the choice between two legal bases i.e. two different sets of provisions (the Euratom health and safety provisions and the EC commercial policy provisions). The particular case, however, did not involve any *lacunae* in the Euratom Treaty warranting an extension of EU (EC) rules to the Euratom matter in question.

Furthermore, Advocates General Geelhoed and Van Gerven have also offered their views on the interaction between the Euratom and the EU(EC)-devised policies. AG Geelhoed in C-61/03 *Commission v UK* considered it possible to utilize the Art.346 TFEU

the Euratom provisions were considered inapplicable to the case was the fact that the Euratom Treaty in its entirety did not cover the realm of military use of nuclear energy.[14]

1.2 *Concurring Competence between Euratom and the EU*

Apart from instances of lack of applicable provisions in the Euratom Treaty and/or implementing legislation, there have also been instances of 'competition' between existent Euratom Treaty and/or secondary Euratom legislation on the one hand, and *Union* legal rules, on the other which is ordinarily resolved by applying the *lex specialis/lex generalis* principle by virtue of which the Euratom rules take priority. Given that the former is a well-established principle, a competition of norms of this type is mostly resolved in a straightforward and non-controversial manner.

The competition between the Euratom and Union legal rules can best be observed with regard to the balancing exercise performed when chosing the correct legal basis for the adoption of a particular act and in instances where regulatory action can only be performed *either* through the use of a Euratom *or* a EU measure. In this sense, it is to be reminded that it is settled case law that where a measure pursues a twofold purpose, one of which can be identified as the main or predominant purpose, that measure must be founded on the legal basis required by the predominant purpose.[15] Alternatively and by way of exception from the former, a measure can simultaneously pursue several inextricably linked objectives, none of which is predominant and both of which are equally important to attaining the purpose of the measure – such a measure must be founded on multiple legal bases.[16] However, thus far, such measures which fully or partly regulate nuclear issues while at the same time being founded on a double legal basis (of both the TFEU/TEU and the Euratom Treaty) have not been adopted.

(ex-Art.296 EC) conditions for Member States to derogate from their Treaty obligations in order to safeguard national defense interests (see, para. 107 of Opinion). With regard to the possible ways to interpret the scope of the Euratom-devised policies, AG Van Gerven, in case C-70/88 Parliament v Council (para. 23) opined that he: "(…) *see*[*s*] *no valid reason for interpreting the scope of a policy laid down by the EAEC Treaty according to rules different from those relating to the scope of a policy laid down by the EEC Treaty* (…)".

14 For more on the military applications of nuclear energy and the Euratom and a more elaborate discussion on the *Commission v. UK* case, see Chapter 4, Section V.3.

15 See, *Energy Star Agreement* (C-281/01 Commission v Council, ECR 2002 p. I-12049, para. 34). Also, see C-36/98 Spain v Council [2001] ECR I-779, para. 59.

16 See, *inter alia* para. 35 of *Energy Star Agreement* case.

Following the catastrophic Chernobyl nuclear accident, the CJEU was asked to review the legal bases of two EC measures that concerned the nuclear field, namely, *Regulation (EEC) No 3955/87 on the conditions governing imports of agricultural products originating in third countries following the accident at the Chernobyl nuclear power-station*[17] and *Regulation (Euratom) No 3954/87 laying down maximum permitted levels of radioactive contamination of foodstuffs and of feedingstuffs following a nuclear accident or any other case of radiological emergency*.[18] The validity of the former regulation was contested in the *Chernobyl I* case[19] whereas the validity of the latter was at issue in *Chernobyl II*.

In *Chernobyl I* the applicant (Greece) claimed that the Council could not adopt the Regulation on the basis of the EU (EC) commercial policy provisions since it considered the predominant objective of the measure to be the protection of the environment and the health of the public thus viewing the Art.31 Euratom provisions on protection of the health of workers and the general public against the dangers of ionizing radiations *or* Art.192 TFEU (formerly, Art.130(r)(s) EEC) environment protection provisions as the appropriate legal basis for the measure. The Court found that the preponderant objective of the Regulation was to regulate trade between the Community and non-member countries[20] and concluded that the fact that the concerned measure additionally pursues an ancillary health protection objective was not sufficient to support the contention that the Euratom health and safety provisions (Art.31 Euratom et seq.) or the EU (EC) environmental protection provisions should have been chosen as the adequate legal basis. The former line of reasoning was further substantiated by the observance of the principle of integration of environmental policy into other Union (Community) policies pursuant to which the concept of environmental protection is to be made an additional component of the other Union (Community) policies.[21]

Later on, the *Chernobyl II* case[22] concerned the legal basis of Regulation (Euratom) No 3954/87 laying down maximum permitted levels of radioactive contamination of foodstuffs and of feeding stuffs following a nuclear accident or any other case of radiological emergency, was at issue where the Parliament insisted that Art.31 Euratom was the wrong legal basis for the Regulation which

17 Regulation (EEC) No 3955/87 of 22 December 1987, OJ 1987, L 371, p. 14.

18 No 3954/87 of 22 December 1987, OJ 1987L 371, p. 11.

19 C-62/88 *Greece v Council* ECR 1990 p. I-1527.

20 Para. 17.

21 Para. 20.

22 Case C-70/88 *Parliament v Council* ECR 1991 p. I-4529.

ought to have been adopted under the harmonization provisions of Art.100a EC (presently, Art.114 TFEU). The Court found that the aim of the Regulation was to establish uniform safety standards for the protection of the health of workers and the general public[23] and that the former only had an incidental effect on harmonizing the conditions for the free movement of goods within the Community by preventing the interference of unilateral national measures in the area of trade in foodstuffs and feedingstuffs that have undergone radioactive contamination.[24] According to the Court, this was not sufficient to qualify the regulation as a harmonization measure within the meaning of Art.114 TFEU (then, Art.100a EC) and therefore upheld the Euratom legal basis.

In addition, there have been instances where the application of a Euratom rule has actually or potentially hindered the application of a Union rule which, however, very rarely occur. The problematic was addressed within the scope of the Euratom supply policy, namely, in Commission Decision 94/285/Euratom[25] where the German company Kernkraftwerke Lippe-Ems (KLE) in its reference letters to the Commission[26] alleged that the Euratom Supply Agency, in applying the Euratom supply policy provisions, interfered with the Community commercial policy provisions.[27] In response to these claims, the Commission relied on the *lex specialis* status of the Euratom Treaty as a treaty containing special rules pertaining to the nuclear supply policy which "(…) *takes precedence over the general provisions of the EC Treaty*".[28] Moreover, the Commission pointed out that the precedence in question does not flow solely from the *lex specialis* status of the Euratom Treaty, but is also derived from the (then) Art 232 EC '*shall not derogate*' requirement which determines the relationship between the two respective legal frameworks.[29]

1.3 *Transposing General Principles of Union Law to the Euratom Framework*

There is a *caveat* attached to the duty '*not to derogate*' that is to be observed regarding the issue of binding the Euratom Community to the general principles of EU law as primary source of EU law and espoused as such (strictly formally speaking) under the *Union* Treaties. These general legal principles are

23 Para. 10 of judgment.

24 Para. 17.

25 Commission Decision 94/285/Euratom OJ 1994L 122/30.

26 Point 7 et seq. of Decision.

27 Point 22 of Decision.

28 Point 22 of Decision.

29 Point 22 of Decision.

nevertheless presumed equally to apply to the Euratom domain given that the Euratom Community is not merely attached to, but is one of the constitutive components of the legal and institutional system of the European Union.

In this sense, the EU Court of Justice in the *Temelin* case[30] recently departed from its settled practice of 'extrapolating' EC/EU rules to the Euratom domain. Namely, one of the issues raised was the application of the principle of non-discrimination enshrined in Art.18 TFEU (ex-Art.12 EC) to the Euratom remit and it was the first time that the Court was confronted with the issue of transposing a general principle of Union law to the Euratom legal framework. The case concerned Austrian national rules introducing different set of criteria for bringing actions for injunction to prevent actual or potential nuisance for nuclear installations on Austrian territory from those situated in the territory of another Member State. The Court noted that the Euratom Treaty does not contain any express provisions on the prohibition of discrimination, analogous to that of Art.12 EC (now, Art.18 TFEU) which precludes all discrimination on grounds of nationality within the scope of application of the EC Treaty.[31] The former prohibition was considered by the Court as "(...) *a specific expression of the general principle of equality, which itself is one of the fundamental principles of Community law*".[32] Deciding to circumvent the application of the EC provision, it directly applied the principle of non-discrimination as a general principle of Union law and one that equally covers the scope of the Euratom Treaty. By refraining from an automatic, *by-default* extension of the EC (EU) provisions, the Court deferred to the integrity and autonomy of the Euratom legal order as one that is both different and differentiable from the legal order established under the the TFEU (EC) Treaty, but one that nevertheless abides by the general principles of the Union legal system.[33] Conversely, it could be argued that the Court essentially sanctioned an existent state of affairs – the requirement of non-discrimination is not foreign to the Euratom system, especially in view of, *inter alia*, the provisions of the Euratom Treaty relevant to the nuclear common market (Arts.92-100

30 Case C-115/08, ECR 2009 p. I-10265; For a consideration of a different aspect of the *Temelin* case, see Chapter 1, III.3.6.

31 Para. 88 of judgment.

32 Para. 89.

33 See, also, W. Schärf, The Temelín-Judgement of the European Court of Justice", *Nuclear Law Bulletin*, Vol. 2010/1, p. 85; The author sees the judgment as one that reinforces the autonomy and integrity of the Euratom Treaty in many ways. For more on the integrative role played by the Court in rendering the ČEZ judgment, see, S. Wolf, *supra* S. Wolf, Euratom Before the Court: A Political Theory of Legal Non-Integration, *European Integration Online Papers*, 2011 Vol.15, p. 13 et seq.

Euratom) which preclude the existence of any nationality-based restrictions and indicate that a compelling non-discrimination ratio has been embedded in the Euratom Treaty's provisions.

The foregoing case has been the only time that the CJEU has had the opportunity to pronounce itself on the issue of applying the general principle of Union law to matters falling within the Euratom domain. Nonetheless, by analogy to the reasoning employed by the Court in *Temelin*, it could be inferred that the other general principles of Union law can be equally presumed applicable to Euratom's purview (e.g., the principle of protection of fundamental rights, the principle of legal certainty, the principle of proportionality, etc.).[34]

II The Interplay between Environmental and Nuclear Law and Policy

II.1 *The Interface between 'Environmental' and 'Nuclear'*

The link between nuclear and environmental law and policy, given the nature of their respective subject matter, is intrinsic and immanent, regardless of whether the former are devised on a global, regional or national level. The primary objective of nuclear law is the regulation of nuclear energy production whereas the undisputed ancillary objective which enables the effectiveness of the primary objective is the protection of the environment and the health of the population (directly or indirectly) exposed to radiation. Effectively, one cannot adequately safeguard and legitimize the use of nuclear power without offering accompanying guarantees relative to environmental and human health protection. The global nuclear and environmental legal systems have their unique characteristics which are underpinned by different rationales and ideologies, but, undoubtedly, the ultimate goal shared by both is safeguarding the health of the population and the environment.[35]

From the perspective of environmental law, a distinction is to be made with respect to the manner in which environmental law relates to the nuclear field – *direct* or *indirect*.[36] The relation is direct when particular nuclear aspects

34 The issue of the applicability of horizontal Union principles (such as the principles of subsidiarity and proportionality) to the Euratom domain has been addressed in Chapter 1, Section III.2.

35 See, S. Emmerechts, Environmental Law and Nuclear Law: A Growing Symbiosis, *Nuclear Law Bulletin*, 2008-I, p. 92; P. Reyners, Le droit nucléaire confronté au droit de l'environnement: autonomie ou complementarité?, *Revue québécoise de droit international*, 2007, Hors-série ed., p. 184.

36 Emmerechts, *supra*, p. 92 et seq.

are made subject to international environmental regulation; and indirect in instances where different international nuclear law instruments touch upon aspects of environmental protection.[37] Effectively, environmental considerations are essential to the existence of the law and policy on nuclear energy which is reflected in the fact that for a long time practitioners of nuclear law have also inadvertently been creators of environmental law.[38] The former has even lead certain authors to go to the extent of denying the autonomous character of nuclear law as a legal framework which covers activities that predominantly belong to the scope of other, already existent legal frameworks (energy law, health law, etc.).[39]

When dealing with the law on environmental protection as an autonomous legal system it is important to note there are views that ascribe to a 'narrow' definition of 'environmental law' as the law that protects the ecosystem i.e. soil, water, air and biodiversity (flora and fauna)[40] versus a 'broad' definition thereof. The difference is that the narrow definition fails to include the concept of human health protection within its scope.[41] The choice between a broad as opposed to a narrow circumscription of the scope of environmental law influences the modalities of interplay between the environmental and the nuclear legal frameworks and thus determines the direction of the inquiry into the complex nature of the correlation between the nuclear and the environmental legal orders. Namely, once a restrictive view on the notion of *environment protection* is taken, the link between nuclear energy and the environment becomes more remote, given that the 'environmental' aspect of nuclear law is chiefly concerned with the *protection of human health* while the environmental protection component *stricto sensu* appears as somewhat secondary.[42]

II.1.1 The Interface between International Nuclear Law and International Environmental Law Instruments

The practice of back and forth 'borrowing' of legal instrumentaria occurring between the nuclear and the environmental policy as two mutually intertwined policies is both natural and intuitive, mostly prominent in cases where a measure originally adopted within the framework of one policy touches upon or, indeed, regulates an issue belonging to the scope of the other policy (understandably, in the *absence* of an applicable rule adopted under the

37 *Idem*, p. 92.

38 Reyners, *supra*, p. 184.

39 *Idem*, p. 163.

40 Emmerechts, *supra*, p. 92.

41 *Idem*.

42 For further reading, see, Emmerechts, *supra*, p. 91.

framework of the latter). The list of international environmental law instruments whose provisions directly or indirectly concern the activities in the nuclear field is a non-exhaustive one, for which reason a reference shall be made to the more prominent of them. The same approach will be followed in relation to international nuclear law instruments applicable to the field of environmental protection. Pursuant to the devastating effects of the 1986 Chernobyl accident, there has been a noticeable increase in the body of international nuclear law documents dealing with environment and health protection since this nuclear predicament served as the turning point for raising the global awareness of the potentially catastrophic and far-reaching effects of nuclear radiation on the environment and the people.[43] More recently, the 2011 Fukushima nuclear disaster in Japan which, after Chernobyl, is the world's worst nuclear distaster in recent years, further spurred the awareness of the international community with regard to the issue of nuclear safety and lead to certain policy improvements both at the level of the International Atomic Energy Agency (IAEA) and the EU.[44]

For this reason, it is to be noted that a number of treaties adopted in the nuclear field endorse a kind of a health protection/environmental protection dichotomy.[45] Among the nuclear law instruments there are those that merely make a passing, declarative reference to environmental protection and those that lay down concrete substantive rules and/or obligations thereto. An example of the former are the texts of the *Partial Nuclear-Test-Ban Treaty* (Treaty Banning Nuclear Weapons Tests in the Atmosphere, in Outer Space and Underwater signed on 5 August 1963), the signatories of which unequivocally declared their desire to put an end to "*the contamination of man's environment by radioactive substances*" (Preamble); and the *Complete Nuclear-Test-Ban Treaty* (CTBT),[46] signed in September 1996, banning all nuclear explosions on

43 V.P. Nanda, International Environmental Norms Applicable to Nuclear Activities, with Particular Focus on Decisions of International Tribunals and International Settlements, Denver Journal of International Law, 2006, Vol. 35 Issue 1, p. 49.

44 The *IAEA Action Plan on Nuclear Safety* was adopted in September 2011, the ultimate aim of which is to strengthen nuclear safety worldwide (see, www.iaea.org/newscenter/focus/actionplan/); On the part of the EU, in order to enhance the safety of nuclear installations in the Union, the 2009 *Nuclear Safety Directive* was amended in July 2014 (see, *Council Directive 2014/87/Euratom amending Directive 2009/71/Euratom establishing a Community framework for nuclear safety of nuclear installations*, OJ L 219, pp. 42–52).

45 This will be further discussed in Section II.2 of the present chapter.

46 http://www.ctbto.org/fileadmin/content/treaty/treaty_text.pdf.

Earth, both for military and peaceful purposes and acknowledging the hope that the CTBT Treaty could contribute to the protection of the environment.[47]

One of the oldest conventions in the field of nuclear law that deals more substantially with environment protection is the *Convention on Physical Protection of Nuclear Material* (1979), which, apart from a brief reference to the "*protection of public health, safety, the environment and national and international security*",[48] criminalizes the intentional commission of certain types of acts that cause or are likely to cause "*death or serious injury to any person or substantial damage to property or to the environment*".[49] Another international nuclear law instrument that fosters the protection of life, property and the environment from the effects of radioactive releases as one of its objectives is the *Convention on Assistance in Nuclear Accident and Radiological Emergency* (1986).[50] The *Convention on Nuclear Safety* (1994) and the *Convention on Spent Fuel and Radioactive Waste Management* (1997) have both identified among their objectives the protection of "*individuals, society and the environment from harmful effects of ionizing radiation*" (see the first article in both conventions).[51] Further on, the 'Liability Conventions' (The *Protocol to Amend the 1963 Vienna*

47 See, Preamble to the Treaty; The *Complete Nuclear-Test-Ban Treaty* is not yet in force.

48 From the Preamble to the Convention.

49 Art.7 of the Convention on Physical Protection of Nuclear Material criminalizes the intentional commission of:

> (…) (a) an act without lawful authority which constitutes the receipt, possession, use, transfer, alteration, disposal or dispersal of nuclear material and which causes or is likely to cause death or serious injury to any person or substantial damage to property or to the environment; (…)
>
> (e) an act directed against a nuclear facility, or an act interfering with the operation of a nuclear facility, where the offender intentionally causes, or where he knows that the act is likely to cause, death or serious injury to any person or substantial damage to property or to the environment by exposure to radiation or release of radioactive substances, unless the act is undertaken in conformity with the national law of the State Party in the territory of which he nuclear facility is situated; (…)
>
> (g) a threat:
>
> (i) to use nuclear material to cause death or serious injury to any person or substantial damage to property or to the environment or to commit the offence described in sub-paragraph (e)… (…)

50 Art.1.

51 The reference to 'individuals, society and the environment' is also present in Arts.4,6,11,13 of the Convention on Spent Fuel and Radioactive Waste Management used regarding the scope of the safety measures for the operation of nuclear facilities.

Furthermore, concerning the siting of nuclear installations, Art.17(d) of the Nuclear Safety Convention reads as follows:

Convention on Civil Liability for Nuclear Damage (1997), the *Convention on Supplementary Compensation for Nuclear Damage* (1997) and the *Protocol to Amend the Paris Convention on Nuclear Third Party Liability* (2004)) have been additionally modified to accommodate certain upgraded liability requirements related to the environment. Under the former regime nuclear operators can be held liable for nuclear damage by incurring the cost of measures for reinstating a significantly impaired environment or for economic loss deriving from an economic interest in the use or enjoyment of the environment that has been significantly impaired due to a nuclear incident.[52]

Conversely, as was indicated *supra*, there equally exist a number of international environmental law instruments that pertain to the nuclear domain. These are the *London Convention on the Prevention of Marine Pollution by Dumping of Waste and Other Matter* (1972) and its Protocol of 1996 covering the prevention of pollution to the marine environment caused by the introduction of, inter alia, radioactive wastes in the sea; followed by the *Convention on Environmental Impact Assessment in a Trans-boundary Context* (1991) ("Espoo Convention") which requires states to conduct environmental impact assessment for nuclear energy activities liable to cause a significantly adverse trans-boundary impact.[53]

The *Convention for the Protection of the Marine Environment of the North-East Atlantic* (OSPAR Convention, 1992) and the *Aarhus Convention on Access to*

Each Contracting Party shall take the appropriate steps to ensure that appropriate procedures are established and implemented: (i) for evaluating all relevant site-related factors likely to affect the safety of a nuclear installation for its projected life-time; (ii) for evaluating the likely safety impact of a proposed nuclear installation on *individuals, society and the environment* (...) [Emphasis added].

52 See also on this, Emmerechts, *supra* n. 35, p. 93. For more on the concept of environmental damage caused by nuclear incidents see, Emmerechts, *supra*, p. 99 et seq.

53 Appendix I of the OSPAR Convention:

List of activities

1. Crude oil refineries (excluding undertakings manufacturing only lubricants from crude oil) and installations for the gasification and liquefaction of 500 tonnes or more of coal or bituminous shale per day.

2. Thermal power stations and other combustion installations with a heat output of 300 megawatts or more and nuclear power stations and other nuclear reactors (except research installations for the production and conversion of fissionable and fertile materials, whose maximum power does not exceed 1 kilowatt continuous thermal load).

3. Installations solely designed for the production or enrichment of nuclear fuels, for the reprocessing of irradiated nuclear fuels or for the storage, disposal and processing of radioactive waste (...).

Information, Public Participation in Decision-Making and Access to Justice in Environmental Matters (1998) are two highly comprehensive environmental legal instruments that just as importantly influence the nuclear field. The OSPAR Convention targets the prevention and elimination of pollution to the marine environment from land-based sources, offshore sources as well as pollution from dumping or incineration of wastes and other matter as well as pollution from radioactive substances (including waste) (Arts.3, 4 and 5).[54] The Aarhus Convention,[55] in turn, deals with the procedural aspects of environment protection by introducing a sort of an *ex ante* control over measures liable to have a damaging effect on the environment and establishing an extensive array of procedural requirements for the public authorities to provide access for the public to environmental information related to the nuclear field as well as enabling the public to participate in the decision-making regarding specific nuclear projects and activities.[56]

---

54 For the types of radioactive substances covered by the OSPAR Convention see Annexes I, II and III of the Convention.

55 The three pillars of the Aarhus Convention (access to information, participation in decision-making and access to justice) will be dealt with in greater detail *infra* in Chapter 3.

56 See, for that matter, Art.6 and related Annex I of the Aarhus Convention:

> Article 6
> Public Participation in Decisions on Specific Activities
> 1. Each Party:
> (a) Shall apply the provisions of this article with respect to decisions on whether to permit proposed activities listed in annex I; (...)
> (contd.) (...)
> Annex I
> List of Activities Referred to in Article 6, Paragraph 1 (a)
> 1. Energy sector:
> – Mineral oil and gas refineries;
> – Installations for gasification and liquefaction;
> – Thermal power stations and other combustion installations with a heat input of 50 megawatts (MW) or more;
> – Coke ovens;
> – Nuclear power stations and other nuclear reactors including the dismantling or decommissioning of such power stations or reactors 1/ (except research installations for the production and conversion of fissionable and fertile materials whose maximum power does not exceed 1kW continuous thermal load);
> – Installations for the reprocessing of irradiated nuclear fuel;
> – Installations designed:
> – For the production or enrichment of nuclear fuel;
> – For the processing of irradiated nuclear fuel or high-level radioactive waste;
> – For the final disposal of irradiated nuclear fuel;

Another instrument that merits attention in this respect is the draft international framework document that codifies the existing legal principles related to environment and development, the *Draft International Covenant on Environment and Development*, originally launched at the UN Congress on Public International Law in March 1995. Although a document lacking binding force, the Covenant serves as an authoritative reference for all stakeholders worldwide in their efforts to ensure that principles and rules of international environmental law are satisfactorily incorporated into regional and national legislation and policies.[57] The 2010 updated edition of the Draft Covenant makes no express mention of nuclear activities and is altogether more general in wording compared to its previous versions, most probably due to the intention of its drafters to give an all-encompassing character to the Draft Covenant as a reference document. Although from the commentary to the text of the Draft Covenant it is to be deduced that nuclear activities are indeed covered by its provisions, a retreat is nevertheless to be observed in the language used regarding protection from radioactive substances. For example, Art.28 dealing with 'Pollution' provides that "(t)he Parties shall take, individually or jointly, all appropriate measures to prevent, reduce, control and eliminate, to the fullest extent possible, detrimental changes in the environment from all forms of pollution (....)", to the difference of the 1995 edition of the Draft Covenant which provided a direct reference to radioactive substances as potential source of pollution ("Parties shall take individually or jointly, as appropriate, all measures that are necessary to prevent, reduce and control pollution of any part of the environment, *in particular* from radioactive, toxic and other hazardous substances (...)").[58]

As an exception to the above outlined spill-over of legal rules between the environmental and the nuclear legal frameworks, there also exist international environmental law instruments that *explicitly exclude* nuclear activities from their scope mainly due to the fact that the particular nuclear domain has already been specifically and comprehensively regulated under a different international legal instrument.[59] An example for such 'exclusionary clauses'

– Solely for the final disposal of radioactive waste;
– Solely for the storage (planned for more than 10years) of irradiated nuclear fuels or radioactive waste (...).

57 The text of the most recently updated 2010 edition of the Covenant can be found at http://www.portals.iucn.org/library/efiles/documents/EPLP-031-rev3.pdf.

58 Emphasis added; The original version of the Covenant has been reproduced in, E. Molodtsova, Nuclear Enrgy Law and International Environmental Law: an Integrated Approach, *Journal of Energy and Natural Resources Law*, 1995, p. 277.

59 Emmerechts, *supra* n. 35, p. 93.

are provided in the *Basel Convention on the control of transboundary movements of hazardous wastes and their disposal* (1989), the *Convention on the Transboundary Effects of Industrial Accidents* (1992), etc.[60]

II.1.2 The Interface between Nuclear and Environmental Law before International and Regional Judicial Fora

The role of international and regional judicial fora has markedly contributed to acquiring a correct understanding of the active interplay occurring between the nuclear and environmental global and regional normative frameworks. Regarding the interpretation and application of international environmental law, generally speaking, the case law of international judicial bodies exhibits a certain degree of judicial self-restraint and caution[61] which possibly accounts for the wariness on the part of international judges in extending the scope of application of international environmental norms to the nuclear field. Nevertheless, in practice, the transposition of nuclear legal rules to the scope of environmental law is much less frequent than the opposite occurrence.

While not always expressly endowed with the competence to adjudicate cases involving environmental protection, international judicial bodies have nonetheless accomplished this result either through *extensive interpretation of the legal texts* before them (which, as will be shown *infra* in the present section, is usually performed by the European Court of Human Rights (ECtHR)), or through a marginal reference to environmental protection in the judgment which, given the undisputed authority of the judicial organ making the reference, serves as the basis for the creation of *opinio juris* encouraging future application of environmental legal norms (as is most commonly done by the International Court of Justice (ICJ)).

The former observations on the role of international judicial forums are predicated on guaranteeing the right to a clean environment as the bedrock of environmental human rights, which is a relatively recent concept in legal history. Unlike the ICJ or the ECtHR, the Court of Justice of EU did not, prior to the entry into force of the EU Charter of fundamental rights, enjoy the status of a forum for human rights adjudication – in spite of the Court of Justice's irrefutable competence to apply the general principles of Union law, one of which is the principle on protection of fundamental rights. The CJEU's take on the interface between the Union nuclear and environmental legal orders will be

60 For more on this see, Emmerechts, *supra* n. 35, p. 94.

61 See for this, N. Klein, Settlement of International Environmental Law Disputes, in, D.M. Ong, P. Merkouris and M. Fitzmaurice (eds.), *Handbook on International Environmental Law*, Edward Edgar Publishing, 2010, p. 391.

examined *infra* in the section dealing with the health and safety provisions of the Euratom Treaty and the modalities of their application devised by the Court.[62] With regard to environment protection in the context of fundamental rights, Art.37 of the Charter of Fundamental Rights of the EU speaks of securing a high level of environmental protection and improving the quality of the environment which is to be integrated into the policies of the Union (an expression of the integration principle of Union environmental law), but nonetheless fails to introduce a specific right to a clean environment as a fundamental right of Union citizens. Due to its general nature and lack of prescriptive force, it is doubtful whether the requirement to integrate a high level of environmental protection awareness into the Union policies is justiciable on its own and can effectively act as legal grounds for claims made before both the CJEU and the national courts.

a *The International Court of Justice (ICJ)*

The International Court of Justice's role as a forum for environmental dispute settlement was only relatively recently instituted (since the early 1990s)[63] and frequently involves cases that are not strictly confined to environmental legal issues and simultaneously raise a conundrum of legal issues from other fields of international law.[64] While the ICJ cannot be qualified as an international environmental court *per se*, the Court has, on a number of occasions, made important pronouncements on the pre-eminence attached to the observance of international environmental protection requirements. *Exempli gratia*, in its judgments in the *Nuclear Tests* cases as well as the Advisory Opinions on the *Legality of the Threat or Use of Nuclear Weapons* and the *Legality of the Use by a State of Nuclear Weapons in Armed Conflict*, the ICJ has offered its insights on the delicate correlation between the use of nuclear weapons and environment protection. These cases did not directly concern the application of international environmental rules to the domain of the use of nuclear energy as the ICJ was requested to rule on the *legality* of the threat or use of nuclear weapons.[65]

---

62 For further elaboration, consult Section II.2 of the present chapter.

63 For more on the history of the Court's involvement in environmental law disputes, see, M.A. Fitzmaurice, *International Protection of the Environment* (*Collected Courses of the Hague Academy of International Law*), Martinus Nijhoff Publishers, 2001, p. 363 et seq.

64 *Idem*, p. 364.

65 The first case heard by the ICJ where the subject of the dispute *primarily* concerned environmental issues was the 1997 Gabcikovo-Nagymaros case relating to the Gabcikovo-Nagymaros project concluded between Hungary and Slovakia (see on this, Nanda, *supra* n. 43, pp. 58–60).

The *Nuclear Tests I* (*New Zealand v. France*,[66] *Australia v. France*[67]) and *Nuclear Tests II* (*Request for Examination by New Zealand*[68]) saga before the ICJ concerned French nuclear testing in the South Pacific region with the radioactive fallout, byproduct of the nuclear testing carried out in this area, being considered a great source of concern for people in the Pacific region. The main difference between the contentions made by both Australia and New Zealand before the Court was that Australia relied on the dispersion of radioactive fallout as a violation of Australian sovereignty while New Zealand based its request for interim measures on the potentially harmful contamination borne by French nuclear tests on the environment.[69] The Court did not rule on the matter, considering New Zealand's claim to be immaterial because at the time France, through a series of statements to that effect, had undertaken to refrain from further *atmospheric* nuclear testing in the South Pacific region.[70]

Subsequently, in *Nuclear Tests II*, New Zealand requested that the Court examines whether its previous judgment in *Nuclear Tests I* had been affected by France's actions, demanding of the Court to order France to stop the ongoing underground nuclear tests in the South Pacific in line with its previously undertaken obligation of discontinuation of nuclear testing. New Zealand considered that the former obligation, in addition to atmospheric testing, comprised all other types of nuclear testing. France held the opposite view: it held that the case was solely concerned with *atmospheric* tests, so that underground tests fell outside the scope of New Zealand's application given that France's commitment not to undertake further atmospheric tests had not been "*indissociably linked to its announcement of its intention to carry out underground tests*".[71] New Zealand argued that the only reason to confine the issue to atmospheric tests was because at the material time of depositing the original application before the ICJ in 1973 there existed no indication that underground nuclear testing might lead to environmental consequences similar to those from atmospheric testing.[72] In support to this, New Zealand referred to recent scientific evidence indicating the potentially detrimental effects of underground testing

66 *Nuclear Tests (New Zealand v. France), Judgment, I. C. J. Reports 1974, p. 457.*

67 *Nuclear Tests (Australia v. France), Judgment, I. C. J. Reports 1974, p. 253.*

68 *Request for an Examination of the Situation in Accordance with Paragraph 63 of the Court's Judgment of 20 December 1974 in the Nuclear Tests (New Zealand v. France) Case, I. C. J. Reports 1995, p. 288.*

69 See, *Nuclear Tests I*, para. 37 et seq. Also, see Fitzmaurice, *supra* n. 63, pp. 370,371.

70 Para. 59.

71 *Nuclear Tests II*, para. 22.

72 Para. 32.

in the South Pacific regions of Mururoa and Fangataufa.[73] In addition to this, New Zealand invoked the precautionary principle in environmental law according to which the burden of proof fell on the State wishing to engage in potentially damaging environmental conduct to show in advance that its activities would not cause contamination[74] so that by virtue of this principle, France was required to carry out an environmental impact assessment as a precondition for undertaking the tests, thereby demonstrating there was no risk associated thereto.[75] Stating that its Order in the instant case did not prejudice the obligations of States to respect and protect the natural environment,[76] the Court concluded that the basis of its 1974 judgment had not been affected by France's actions and therefore dismissed New Zealand's request.[77] Failing to pronounce itself on the merits, the Court gave a judgment that imposed strict limits on its jurisdiction and offered complete deference to France's sovereignty concerns.[78] Judge Weeramantry in his Dissenting Opinion appealed to a missed chance to further develop the concepts of precaution, environmental impact assessment and take stock of the environmental consequences for future generations, while in his Opinion judge Palmer deplored the fact that the Court, for purely technical and formalistic reasons, failed to address such an important problem of international environmental law.[79]

Evidenced by the above, it is to be observed that the arguments presented by France were consistent with its overall ambiguous attitude towards participation in international nuclear treaties, especially those treaties dealing with the effects on the environment. France never became signatory to the 1963 *Partial Nuclear-Test-Ban Treaty* (PTBT) which banned nuclear weapon tests in the atmosphere, outer space and under water and recognized the existence of a threat to human health and the environment caused by nuclear testing,[80] nor did it become party to the 1985 *South Pacific Nuclear Free Zone Treaty* (*Rarotonga Treaty*) banning all testing of nuclear explosive devices in the South Pacific[81] – in spite of having

73 Para. 33.

74 Para. 34.

75 Para. 35.

76 Para. 64.

77 Para. 65.

78 Fitzmaurice, *supra* n. 63, p. 376.

79 For further reading on the *Nuclear Tests* cases see, Klein, *supra* n. 61, pp. 391,392.

80 See, P. Birnie, A. Boyle and C. Redgewell (eds.), *International Law and the Environment*, Oxford University Press, 2009, p. 490.

81 There was also popular resistance to the French nuclear tests in the Pacific headed by Greenpeace as global non-governmental organization, as a response to which the French government reportedly engaged in lethal sabotage against the Greenpeace vessel, *The*

formally declaring its intention to cease all atmospheric testing in the early 1970s and nevertheless having continued with underground nuclear testing. Arguably, the reasons behind France's reticence to adhere to the former treaties are similar, if not identical, to those that lie at the bottom of its refusal to sign the 1968 *Non-Proliferation Treaty*.[82] Eventually, however, France came around in September 1996 and concluded the *Comprehensive Test Ban Treaty* (CTBT) which has not yet entered into force.[83]

Following the *Nuclear Tests* cases, the ICJ was seized by a similarly delicate political issue – the *legality of the threat or use of nuclear weapons*. In 1995 the Court was referred a request for an Opinion by the UN General Assembly regarding whether the threat or use of nuclear weapons was in any circumstance illegal under international law. Although the 1996 *Advisory Opinion on the Legality of the Threat or Use of Nuclear Weapons*[84] did not particularly deal with the environmental 'justifiability' of nuclear weapons, the Court nonetheless felt urged to additionally consider this aspect at the insistence of a number of UN Members States which in their written and oral statements had argued that any sort of use of nuclear weapons should be considered unlawful in view of the existing international norms on safeguarding and protection of the environment.[85] Therein, a specific reference was made, *inter alia*, to the 1977 Additional Protocol I to the 1949 Geneva Conventions which prohibits the employment of "methods or

---

Rainbow Warrior in 1985 while the ship was docked in the harbor at Auckland, New Zealand (for this, see the oral and written arguments by Australia and New Zealand in the Nuclear Tests Cases; also, see, R. Falk, The Second Cycle of Ecological Urgency: An Environmental Justice Perspective, in, J. Ebbesson and P. Okowa (eds.), *Environmental Law and Justice in Context*, Cambridge University Press, 2009, p. 47).

82 For more on Frances's initial reticence towards abiding by its international non-proliferation obligations, see Chapter 4, Section I.I.;

The Partial Test-Ban Treaty and the Non-Proliferation Treaty were not primarily concerned with environment protection considerations. Nonetheless, these treaties followed an important subsidiary objective of protecting the environment against the dangers of nuclear radiation and are therefore often included in the category of international environmental agreements (see, D. Bodansky, *The Art and Craft of International Environmental Law*, Harvard University Press, 2010, p. 27).

83 Although 162 out of a total of 183 signatories have ratified the CTBT, according to Annex 2 of the Treaty it is mandatory for countries such as, inter alia, the United States, Israel, Iran, Republic of North Korea to ratify in order for the Treaty to enter into force (www.ctbto.org/map/#status).

84 *Legality of the Threat or Use of Nuclear Weapons, Advisory Opinion*, I. C. J. Reports 1996, p. 226.

85 Para. 27.

means of warfare which are intended, or may be expected, to cause widespread, long-term and severe damage to the natural environment" (Art.35(3)); and the 1977 *Convention on the Prohibition of Military or Any Other Hostile Use of Environmental Modification Techniques* which prohibits the use of weapons that have *widespread, long-lasting or severe effects* on the environment (Art.1). Also cited were Principle 21 of the 1972 *Stockholm Declaration* and Principle 2 of the 1992 Rio Declaration which articulate the common conviction regarding the existence of a duty among states "to ensure that activities within their jurisdiction or control do not cause damage to the environment of other States or of areas beyond the limits of national jurisdiction".[86]

The Court recognized that nuclear weapons could constitute a catastrophe for the environment,[87] the term environment taken to encompass 'the living space, quality of life and the health of human beings, including the unborn generations'.[88] Thus, it factored in the respect for the environment as one of the parameters to be used in assessing whether an action pursuing a military objective is in conformity with the principles of necessity and proportionality.[89] The Court considered that the existing body of international environmental law did not prohibit the use of nuclear weapons as such, but, however, suggested that environmental factors needed to be taken into account when rules and principles of the law applicable in armed conflict are given effect.[90] It referred to the seriousness of the use of nuclear weapons and the potentially catastrophic effect thereof as well as their immense and indiscriminate destructive power on civilization and the eco-system of the planet[91] all the while confirming the potential damaging effect to future generations attributed to the ionizing radiation's potential to damage the future environment, food and marine ecosystem, and to cause genetic defects and illness in future generations.[92] For these reasons, the Court esteemed it indispensable that in order to correctly apply the UN Charter law on the use of force and the law applicable in armed conflict, account needed to be taken of the unique characteristics of nuclear weapons and their destructive capacity to cause damage to the present and future generations.[93]

86 Para. 29.

87 Para. 29.

88 Para. 29.

89 Para. 30.

90 Para. 33.

91 Para. 35.

92 Para. 35.

93 Para. 36; More on the theory of intergenerational equity as a concept that has largely influenced the development of international environmental law (see Fitzmaurice, *supra*,

Effectively, the Court did not intend to reach a conclusion that would in any way undermine the states' right of self-defence under international law, much less if this would have been done through the application of environmental treaty obligations,[94] esteeming that the use of weapons with potentially destructive effect needs to be restricted, but however, not prohibited.[95] The foregoing is an example of international environmental rights and obligations being in competition with rights and obligations under the international law of armed conflict before the ICJ where the latter superseded.[96]

Two years prior to the reguest for Opinion lodged by the UN General Assembly, in 1993, the World Health Assembly (the parliamentary organ of the World Health Organization (WHO)) called upon the ICJ to render an Opinion on whether, in view of the health and environmental effects related thereto, the use of nuclear weapons by a state in war or other armed conflict would be a breach of its obligations under international law including the WHO Constitution.[97] The reasons that lead the WHO to make a request for an ICJ Opinion was achieving 'primary prevention' as the most appropriate means in tackling the health and environmental effects of the use of nuclear weapons.[98] The WHO was strongly convinced that the primary prevention from the health hazards engendered by nuclear weapons use required a preliminary clarification regarding the latter's status under international law.[99] From an environmental law perspective it is important that the WHO had centered its request on the application of the principle of prevention in international environmental law, inquiring as to whether in the light of this principle the use of nuclear weapons should be presumed to be illegal. Judge Weeramantry in his dissenting opinion offers a similar reasoning, basing his views on the compelling medical facts surrounding the use of nuclear weapons and thus, the necessary attention that is to be given to the notion of prevention.[100]

---

n. 63, p. 186 et seq.); For further commentary on this judgment, see, Nanda, *supra* n. 43, pp. 57,58.

94 Birnie, *supra* n. 80, p. 207.

95 *Idem*, p. 208.

96 J. Ebbesson and P. Okowa, Environmental Justice in Situations of Armed Conflict, in, P. Okowa (ed.), *Environmental Law and Justice in Context*, Cambridge University Press, 2009, p. 238.

97 *Legality of the Use by a State of Nuclear Weapons in Armed Conflict, Advisory Opinion, I. C. J. Reports 1996, p. 66.*

98 Para. 1 of Advisory Opinion.

99 Para. 1.

100 Judge Christopher Gregory Weeramantry at point 5: "The futility of medical treatment after a nuclear catastrophe is a reason that cries out aloud for attention in the fields of

However, from the outset the Court observed that the question put before it related *not to the effects* of the use of nuclear weapons on health, but to the *legality* of the use of such weapons *in view of their health and environmental effects* (*emphasis added in the Advisory Opinion*).[101] In this sense, it was considered that declaring the *character of the use* of nuclear weapons to be legal or illegal did not have any influence on the *effects of their use* or the requisite measures aimed at tackling these effects.[102] On a more substantive note, the Court considered that it could not give the requested opinion since WHO's request did not relate to a question arising within the *scope of the activities* of that Organization, thus failing to satisfy the essential condition for founding the Court's jurisdiction (Art.96(2) of the UN Charter enables specialized agencies to request advisory opinions of the Court on legal questions arising within the scope of their activities).[103]

While the ICJ adopted a fail-safe approach by making a statement on the potentially devastating effects of the use of nuclear weapons, it nevertheless failed to make a direct link between the UN Charter law on armed conflicts and the global environmental law regime. The former validates the academic commentary regarding the ICJ's history of '*tentative endorsement of international environmental law*'[104] and the Court's tendency to interpret international environmental norms restrictively resulting in *jus cogens* rules of international law prevailing over environmental considerations.[105]

b The Tribunals Under the UNCLOS Framework

The focus of the discussion will now turn to the cumbersome *MOX* litigation where the origin of the issue concerned the discharges into the Irish Sea coming from the mixed oxide (MOX) fuel plant at the Sellafield nuclear facility in

planning and prevention, and it would be an irresponsible custodian of global health that stands aloof from that question, waiting for the medical catastrophe to occur in which it is powerless to extend any meaningful medical assistance".

101 Para. 21.

102 Para. 22.

103 Para. 31; For a critique, see point 5 of the Dissenting opinion Judge Christopher Gregory Weeramantry who argues that the it is not a case of lack of jurisdiction, but rather, fault regarding the status of the applicant requesting an opinion from the Court thus overstepping its prerogatives as a specialized agency. He considers that the compelling medical facts surrounding the use of nuclear weapons trump over this procedural 'snag', affording the WHO as a protector of global health the prerogative to seize itself with the issue of the legality of nuclear weapons.

104 Klein, *supra* n. 61, p. 391.

105 *Idem*, p. 393.

the UK. One part of the *MOX* legal saga was dealt with under the Union judicial system while the rest was covered before different international judicial fora. Originally, Ireland instituted proceeding against the UK relying on the *Convention for the Protection of the Marine Environment of the North-East Atlantic* (*OSPAR*) Art.9(2) regarding the Contracting Parties' obligation to provide access to any available information on activities or measures adversely affecting or likely to affect the maritime area. The OSPAR Arbitral Tribunal found that the UK did not breach the former provision (Final Award 2 July 2003, Ireland v UK, Dispute concerning access to information under Art.9 of the Ospar Convention).[106]

Almost coincidentally with instituting the OSPAR proceedings, Ireland commenced arbitral proceedings against the UK before a *UNCLOS* (*United Nations Convention on the Law of the Sea*) Arbitral Tribunal. Pending the constitution of the arbitral tribunal, Ireland requested the International Tribunal for the Law of the Sea (ITLOS) to rule on provisional measures which consisted of ordering the UK to immediately suspend the authorisation of the operating license of the Sellafield MOX plant or alternatively, take appropriate measures to prevent, with immediate effect, the operation of the MOX plant. Additionally, Ireland requested that the UK immediately ensure there were no movements into or out of the waters under Irish jurisdiction of any radioactive substances, materials or wastes associated with the operation or the preparatory activities for the operation of the MOX plant.[107] The ITLOS did not rule on the material aspects of the case, but suggested that the UK and Ireland cooperate and enter into consultations in order to exchange information on the consequences for the Irish Sea arising from the commissioning of the MOX plant, monitor the effects on the Irish Sea of the operation of the MOX plant and introduce appropriate measures to counter the pollution of the marine environment linked thereto. The ITLOS did not grant the provisional measures requested by Ireland, putting the stress on the duty of cooperation as a fundamental principle in the prevention of pollution of the marine environment. The decision not to grant Ireland the requested provisional measures can be seen as evidence of the facilitative role courts and tribunals play in relation to international environmental law disputes as the former frequently tend to reach an outcome that would be satisfactory to both parties i.e. one that emphasizes the importance of reaching a solution through mutual cooperation rather than normative

106 http://pca-cpa.org/upload/files/OSPAR%20Award.pdf.

107 International Tribunal for the Law of the Sea, *MOX Plant Case* (*Ireland v. United Kingdom*), *case no. 10, Order of 3 December 2001*, para. 27.

regulation.[108] Such an approach is to be attributed to the uncertainties and ambiguities related to the extent of the normative character of international environmental law.[109]

Concomitantly, the proceedings instituted before the UNCLOS Arbitral Tribunal were suspended since problems closely related to Community law had arisen implicating crucial procedural issues such as Ireland's and the United Kingdom's standing before the Arbitral Tribunal, the division of competences between the European Union (Community) and its Member States with respect to the scope of the Convention, as well as the scope of the jurisdiction of the Court of Justice of the EU in the matter that initially gave rise to the proceedings.[110] The UNCLOS Arbitral Tribunal took the view that, given the risk of reaching conflicting decisions and for the purpose of maintaining mutual respect and co-existence between the judicial organs, it would not have been appropriate to continue the proceedings without prior resolution of the issues that were related to Community law.[111]

Being that the jurisdiction to review the matter hade been primarily deferred to the EU judicial fora, the issue appeared before the Court of Justice of the EU in *Commission v Ireland* (*MOX*)[112] where the CJEU sanctioned Ireland for bringing proceedings under the dispute-settlement system instituted under the UNCLOS without previously informing and consulting with the competent Union institutions, thus failing to comply with its duty of cooperation under Arts. 10 EC and 192 EA.[113] Essentially, the Court found that Ireland's *locus standi* before the UNCLOS Tribunal had been pre-empted both by its duty of cooperation as a Member State under EU law and by the competence that the Union enjoys with regard to the matter at issue.[114]

The chapter on the MOX saga finally closed in June 2008 when the UNCLOS Arbitral Tribunal issued Order No.6,[115] officialising the withdrawal of Ireland's

108 Klein, *supra* n. 61, p. 394.

109 *Idem*, p. 394.

110 See, C-459/03 Commission v Ireland (MoX), para. 43. Also, see *Order No.3 on Susprension of Proceedings on Jurisdiction and Merits*... (http://www.pca-cpa.org/showpage.asp?pag_id=1148).

111 Para. 46.

112 C-459/03 Commission v Ireland (MoX), *ECR 2006 p. I-4635*.

113 Para. 182 of judgment; On the genesis of the MOX Plant dispute see also, N. Lavranos, The Epilogue in the MOX Plant Dispute: An End Without Findings, *European Energy and Environmental Law Review*, 2009 (June), pp. 180–184.

114 For more on the *Commission v Ireland* (*MoX*) case, see *supra*, Chapter 1, Section III.3.5.

115 http://pca-cpa.org/upload/files/MOX%20Plant%20Press%20Release%20Order%20No.%206.pdf.

claim against the UK and the termination of the proceedings. Unfortunately, due to procedural defects, the substantive aspects of the issue were left untouched and therefore never decided upon. It is therefore still open for speculation what the decision on the merits of the case would have been had the issue of radioactive discharges originating from the MOX plant been dealt with *in meritum* either by the UNCLOS Arbitral Tribunal or the EU Court of Justice.[116]

c *The European Court of Human Rights*

The text of the European Convention of Human Rights (hereinafter, the Convention) does not contain provisions laying down environmental human rights guarantees. The reason for this is that in the early 1950s, when the Convention was originally adopted the universal need for environmental protection had not been as apparent.[117] To counter these shortcomings, the European Court of Human Rights (ECtHR) has developed an activist judicial approach by considering the Convention as a living instrument and thus, occasionally, opening the way for extensive interpretation thereof in the light of the dynamism of changing conditions.[118] In the field of environmental protection, this resulted in the *right to a healthy environment* being fitted into the wider scope of the *right to respect for private and family file.*[119] The right to a healthy environment understood in this sense encompasses the right to protection against various types of pollution and nuisances (such as those caused by harmful chemicals, offensive smells, noise etc.).[120] Moreover, as a direct consequence of this sort of progressive interpretation there has been a rise in the level of protection of rights and freedoms guaranteed under the Convention.[121] In cases involving environmental pollution and nuisances, the ECtHR has taken the position that severe environmental pollution is liable to affect the well-being of individuals in that it is disruptive on the enjoyment of their private and family life, while not necessarily seriously endangering their health (para. 51 of the 1994 *Lopez Ostra*[122] judgment, reiterated in para. 60 of the 1998 *Guerra*[123] judgment).

---

116 For an insight into the MOX litigation from the perspective of the rights of access to information and participation in decision-making, see Chapter 3, Section VI.

117 Point 2 of Joint Dissenting Opinion of Judges Costa, Ress, Turmen, Zupancic and Steiner in *Hatton II* case.

118 Point 2 of the Joint Dissenting Opinion.

119 Point 2 of the Joint Dissenting Opinion.

120 *Idem.*

121 *Idem.*

122 *Lopez Ostra v Spain* (1994) 20 EHRR 277.

123 *Guerra v Italy* (1998) 26 EHRR 357.

Generally, applicants before the ECtHR have traditionally attempted *three* alternative routes in order to be able to fit these types of violations by states within the scope of the Convention, that is by relying on *Art.2* (*right to life*), *Art.6* (*right to a fair trial*) and *Art.8* (*right to respect for a person's private and family life*) of the Convention.

Article 2: Right to Life

1. Everyone's right to life shall be protected by law. No one shall be deprived of his life intentionally save in the execution of a sentence of a court following his conviction of a crime for which this penalty is provided by law.
2. Deprivation of life shall not be regarded as inflicted in contravention of this Article when it results from the use of force which is no more than abso-lutely necessary:
   (a) in defence of any person from unlawful violence;
   (b) in order to effect a lawful arrest or to prevent the escape of a person lawfully detained;
   (c) in action lawfully taken for the purpose of quelling a riot or insurrection.(…)

Article 6: Right to a Fair Trial

1. In the determination of his civil rights and obligations or of any criminal charge against him, everyone is entitled to a fair and public hearing within a reasonable time by an independent and impartial tribunal established by law.

   Judgment shall be pronounced publicly but the press and public may be excluded from all or part of the trial in the interests of morals, public order or national security in a democratic society, where the interests of juveniles or the protection of the private life of the parties so require, or to the extent strictly necessary in the opinion of the court in special circumstances where publicity would prejudice the interests of justice.
2. Everyone charged with a criminal offence shall be presumed innocent until proved guilty according to law.
3. Everyone charged with a criminal offence has the following minimum rights:
   (a) to be informed promptly, in a language which he understands and indetail, of the nature and cause of the accusation against him;
   (b) to have adequate time and facilities for the preparation of his defence;

(c) to defend himself in person or through legal assistance of his own choosing or, if he has not sufficient means to pay for legal assistance, to be given it free when the interests of justice so require;

(d) to examine or have examined witnesses against him and to obtain the attendance and examination of wit-nesses on his behalf under the same conditions as witnesses against him;

(e) to have the free assistance of an interpreter if he cannot understand or speak the language used in court.

(...)

Article 8: Right to Respect for Private and Family Life

1. Everyone has the right to respect for his private and family life, his home and his correspondence.
2. There shall be no interference by a public authority with the exercise of this right except such as is in accordance with the law and is necessary in a democratic society in the interests of national security, public safety or the economic well-being of the country, for the prevention of disorder or crime, for the protection of health or morals, or for the protection of the rights and freedoms of others.;

Article 8 of the ECHR is most commonly invoked as legal grounds for claims concerning human health and environmental protection; it guarantees the individual's right to respect for his private and family life, his home and his correspondence while precluding the interference on the part of public authorities in the exercise of this right.[124] Pursuant to the text of the article, the State bears a positive obligation to ensure the enjoyment of the individual's right and a negative obligation not to interfere in the said enjoyment.[125] Thus, Art.8 is applicable both to environmental cases where pollution is directly caused by the State and cases where the State is responsible for its failure to act.[126] Regardless of whether a case is examined in the light of the positive duty of the State to take reasonable and appropriate measures to secure the applicant's rights or, from the perspective of the duty of non-interference by a public

124 On how the protection of the right to privacy and home life has evolved in ECtHR's case law see, D. Shelton, Human Rights and the Environment: Substantive Rights, in, D.M. Ong, P. Merkouris and M. Fitzmaurice (eds.), *Research Handbook on International Environmental Law*, Edward Elgar Publishing, 2010, pp. 275–279.

125 See, Case of *Hatton and Others v. United Kingdom* (Application no. 36022/97, judgment of 8 July 2003), para. 98.

126 Para. 98 of the Hatton II judgment.

authority, the applicable principles are similar.[127] Taking into account the tests on the proportionate balancing of interests with respect to the first and second paragraph of Art.8, the margin of appreciation is considerably wider in the case of positive obligations[128] and is predicated on the existence of a procedural parameter for assessing the scope of the 'positive obligation' of the State, especially in environmental cases.[129]

Cases of environmental damage directly caused by a State's actions are rare in comparison to those where environmental damage is caused by other persons or entities whereby the authorities have not provided for an adequate redress.[130] The ECtHR has on occasion demonstrated a certain degree of self-restraint in establishing the referential procedural parameter: e.g. in the *Hatton II*[131] case pertaining to the noise nuisance from London's Heathrow Airport, the Court failed to address the existence of a different procedural parameter and confined the examination to whether the state had acted within its margin of appreciation in striking a balance between its own interests and environment protection concerns, stating that "(...)it would not be appropriate for the Court to adopt a special approach in this respect by reference to a special status of environmental human rights".[132]

The ECtHR has dealt with several cases related to nuclear energy projects with potential impact on the environment and the population that involved the application of Arts.2, 6 and 8. In *Balmer-Schafroth*,[133] regarding the extension of the operating license of a Swiss nuclear power plant, the applicants maintained that such an extension would have a nugatory effect on the life and health of the local population.[134] They originally brought the matter before the Swiss Federal Council (as part of the Swiss government executive) relying on the right to have their physical integrity protected from the risks connected to the use of nuclear energy.[135] In spite of the applicant's claim, the Federal Council reached a decision in favor of extending the operating license based

127 Para. 98 of the Hatton II judgment.

128 D.J. Harris, M. O'Boyle, E.P. Bates and C.M. Buckley, *Law of the European Convention on Human Rights*, Oxford University Press, 2009, p. 391.

129 *Idem*, p. 392.

130 J.G. Merrills and A.H. Robertson, *Human Rights in Europe: A study of the European Convention on Human Rights*, Manchester University Press, 2001, p. 156.

131 *Hatton and Others v. United Kingdom* (Application no. 36022/97, judgment of 8 July 2003).

132 Para. 122 of *Hutton II* judgment.

133 *Balmer-Schafroth v Switzerland* (1998) 25 EHRR 598.

134 Para. 33.

135 Para. 33.

on the technical data it was provided with,[136] which the applicants did not consider as a judicial decision and demanded that a Swiss judicial body re-evaluate the issue, invoking Art.6(1) ("In the determination of his civil rights and obligations or of any criminal charge against him, everyone is entitled to a fair and public hearing within a reasonable time by an independent and impartial tribunal established by law(...)"[137]). Regarding the applicability of Art.2 of the Convention, the Court held that the applicants had not established a *direct link* between the operating conditions of the power station they contested and their right to protection of their physical integrity since they failed to show that the power station exposed them personally to a danger "that was not only serious but also specific and above all imminent".[138] Therefore, the connection between the Federal Council's decision and the right invoked by the applicants was regarded as too tenuous and remote.[139]

However, Judge Pettiti in his Dissenting Opinion (joined by judges Gölküklü, Walsh, Russo, Valticos, Lopes Rocha and Jambrek) suggested that in order for Art.6 (1) to apply, the applicant does not need to prove from the outset that a risk exists or what the exact consequences are. *Likelihood* for the occurrence of risk and damage should be sufficient proof of the existence of a link. He does not neglect to mention that the Court had been oblivious to a growing trend in international institutions and public international law as evident in the EU and the Council of Europe instruments on the environment, especially with regard to the application of the precautionary principle and the principle of conservation of the common heritage. The judge was also highly critical of the Court's insistence on the tenuous character of the connection and the absence of an imminent danger to the environment and the population, thus begging the question whether the population first needs to be irradiated in order to be entitled to exercise the right to a remedy.

The case *Athanassoglou*[140] was very similar to *Balmer-Schafroth* in that it involved the granting the extension for the operating license of a Swiss nuclear plant bringing into play the identical applicable domestic rules and the same grounds for raising the complaint (Art.6(1)).[141] Applying the same reasoning as in the previous case, the Court considered the former article to be inapplicable to the facts of the case. In contrast to this, the Joint Dissenting Opinion of

136 Para. 37.

137 Para. 36.

138 Para. 40.

139 Para. 40.

140 *Athanassoglou* v Switzerland (2001) 31 EHRR 13.

141 Para. 42.

judges Costa, Tulkens, Fischbach, Casadevall and Maruste found there had indeed been a violation of Art.6(1) since it was impossible to determine if the applicants had been personally exposed to a danger that was serious, specific and above all, imminent. The judges supported their claim with the argument that nuclear catastrophes that have happened in a number of countries were unforeseeable or in any event, unforeseen. In addition to this, they suggested there was also a violation of Art.13 ECHR according to which everyone whose rights have been violated under the Convention is entitled to an effective remedy before a national authority notwithstanding that the violation has been committed by persons acting in official capacity. They found that the Federal Council's decision on extending the operating license (as a decision of an executive body) should be subject to judicial review under national law. According to the judges, the ECtHR in the instant case had acted as court of first instance, thus allowing for a governmental body to act as both judge and party given that the option to raise a challenge before the Swiss Federal Council against which body there was no appeal under Swiss law, did not in itself constitute an effective legal remedy.

The disclosure of documents on radiation exposure levels of service personnel at the time of the UK Christmas Island nuclear tests used in support to their pension claims made before the UK Pensions Appeal Tribunal was at issue in the case *McGinley and Egan*.[142] The ECtHR found there had been no violation of Art.6(1) as the applicants failed to exhaust all available national procedures for the disclosure of documents. The Court equally considered Art.8 to be inapplicable to the case. Namely, the right of respect for private and family life presupposed an effective and accessible procedure to be established under national law enabling the persons to demand the relevant information.[143] The Court considered the available national procedures to be sufficient since they assured the applicants' access to all the relevant and available information on radiation exposure levels surrounding the conducted nuclear tests as a hazardous activity that might have lead to adverse consequences on the health of those involved.[144] Nonetheless, the Court reminded that "the exposure to high levels of radiation is known to have hidden, but serious and long-lasting effects on health, it is not unnatural that the applicants' uncertainty as to whether or not they had been put at risk in this way caused them substantial anxiety and distress".[145] Judge

142 *McGinley and Egan v UK* (1998) 27 EHRR 1; For further commentary on the case, see Chapter 3, Section VI.

143 Para. 101.

144 Para. 101.

145 Para. 99.

Pekkanen, in his Dissenting Opinion, was not persuaded that it had been satisfactorily demonstrated that the national procedures offered the applicants sufficient means to obtain the disclosure of documents.[146] According to the judge, the national procedure the Court had advised the applicants to avail themselves of did not exhaust the State's positive obligation to provide the necessary means for the applicants to obtain access to information.[147]

Another relevant case in this regard is *L.C.B. v United Kingdom*[148] which, unlike the previous cases, deals with the application of Art.2(1) ECHR (right to life). The material time of the facts of the case was once again the period of UK's Christmas Island nuclear tests. The applicant, diagnosed with leukemia, claimed that the State's failure to warn her parents of the possible risks to her health caused by her father's participation in the nuclear tests and its earlier failure to monitor her father's radiation dose levels gave rise to violations of Art 2(1) of the Convention.[149] However, the Court could not establish a causal link between the radiation exposure of the father and the diagnosed leukemia in a child subsequently conceived.[150] This position stemmed from the Court's consideration that the information available to the State at the relevant time concerning the likelihood of the applicant's father having been exposed to dangerous levels of radiation and of this creating a risk to the health of his unborn child was not conclusive. Therefore, it could not have been expected from the State to act on its own motion to notify the parents on the matter or take any other special action in relation thereto.[151] The judgment offers an important clarification with regard to the degree of scrutiny the ECtHR is prepared to perform in assessing the State's Art.2(1) positive obligation to protect the individual's right to life. The Court reminded that its task in the present case was confined to determining "(...) whether, given the circumstances of the case, the State did all that could have been required of it to prevent the applicant's life from being avoidably put at risk".[152]

In defence of the ECtHR's reticence to apply a more generous standard of appreciation in the nuclear-related cases, what needs to be taken into consideration is both the complex and delicate nature of the nuclear field and the

146 Point 4.

147 Point 5.

148 *L.C.B. v United Kingdom* (1998) 27 EHRR 212. For further commentary on the case, see Chapter 3, Section VI.

149 Para. 24.

150 Para. 39.

151 Para. 41.

152 Para. 36; For an elaborate account, see, Harris, *supra* n. 128, p. 42.

issues arising therefrom as a result of which it is often difficult to successfully establish the existence of the requisite causal link between the State's action/inaction and the harmful effects of radiation on the population and the environment. It could be argued that the foregoing cases demonstrate a 'politically correct' approach on the part of the Court, which, *inter alia*, considered the issue of nuclear testing to be inherent to the national security interests of States. Quite plausibly, one could further suggest that the ECtHR was indeed in a position to make up for the enounced procedural deficiencies by attempting a preventive or, even, a precautionary approach to the matter which, in turn, is not always as straightforward to substantiate. The result is that, at least for the time being, the environmental and human health effects attributed to nuclear activities have evaded any substantive scrutiny before the Strasbourg court. By comparison, the ECtHR's Luxembourg counterpart has had a relatively better track record of being more receptive to arguments relative to health and environmental protection in the nuclear field, however, not always to the fully desirable extent.[153]

II.2 *Euratom and the EU Environmental Policy*

II.2.1 The Health and Safety Policy of Euratom in the Wider Context of Environmental Protection

The intrinsic and indivisible link that exists between the health and safety policy developed under the Euratom Treaty and the Union environmental policy has engendered a significant interface between the two respective legislative frameworks created thereunder. The health and safety provisions of the Euratom Treaty take up a substantial part of the subject matter covered by the Treaty and their prominence, in retrospect, proves all the greater given that these provisions were considered to be the closest reference to 'environmental protection' included in the founding treaties.[154] The provisions relative to environmental protection under the Union construct *stricto sensu* and thus, the Union (Community) environmental policy, were introduced into the Union Treaties as late as in 1987 with the adoption of the Single European Act.[155] For this reason, certain authors consider the most significant environmentally

153 On the case law of the CJEU on nuclear health and safety, consult *infra* Section II.2.

154 D. Edward and W. Robinson, The Court of Justice and Environmental Protection, in, D.S. MacDougall and T.W. Wälde (eds.), *European Community Energy Law: Selected Topics*, Graham&Trotman/Martinus Nijhoff, 1994, p. 152.

155 On the stages of the development of European Community environmental policy, see, J.H. Jans and H.B. Vedder, *European Environmental Law*, Europa Law Publishing, 2008, p. 3 et seq.

relevant legal bases outside of the Union framework to be found in the Euratom Treaty.[156] The nature of the former argument may seem slightly one-sided given that it is questionable whether the Euratom Treaty provisions can be presumed as being specifically directed at *environmental protection* as an integral concept, or, indeed, only partially cover the former concept i.e. to the extent that it concerns the *protection of human health*.[157]

For the purpose of determining the extent and the intensity of the interface between the Euratom health and safety policy and the Union environmental policy, the aim and objective of the Euratom health and safety provisions need to be looked at more closely and placed into the wider context of the concept of environmental protection. To begin with, the core objective enounced under the 'Health and Safety' chapter of the Euratom Treaty (Arts.30 et seq.) is to lay down the basic standards within the Community for the protection of the health of workers and the general public against the dangers arising from ionizing radiations[158] while Art.35 Euratom introduces an obligation for Member States regarding the establishment of the necessary facilities that perform continuous monitoring of the level of radioactivity in the *air, water and soil* (the Commission having the right of access to such facilities in order to verify their operation and efficiency).[159]

Further on, under Art.37 Euratom, dealing with the disposal of radioactive waste, Member States are obligated to communicate to the Commission the general data relating to any plan for the disposal of radioactive waste in whatever form which enables the former to determine whether "the implementation of such plan is liable to result in the radioactive contamination of the *water, soil or airspace* of another Member State". By virtue of Art.38, in the execution of its tasks, the Commission makes recommendations to the Member States regarding

156 *Idem*, p. 81.

157 L. Kramer, EC *Environmental Law*, Sweet&Maxwell, 2000, p. 269; Kramer argues that energy measures based on the Euratom Treaty do not target the impact of nuclear energy on the environment in any significant way since they mainly consider the effects borne on human health by nuclear energy, not on the fauna and flora or any other environmental assets.

158 According to Art.30 Euratom, the term 'basic standards' refers to:
"(a) maximum permissible doses compatible with adequate safety;
(b) maximum permissible levels of exposure and contamination;
(c) the fundamental principles governing the health surveillance of workers."

159 Under Art.36 Euratom, the competent national authorities periodically communicate information on the checks referred to in Art.35 to the Commission, keeping the former informed of the level of radioactivity to which the public is exposed.

the levels of radioactivity in the air, water and soil (the reference to 'fauna and flora' being absent from the treaty text).

As can be inferred from the foregoing language of the Euratom Treaty, while the human health protection objective is clearly predominant and overarching, the aspect that provides the link between the health and safety provisions and the objective of environmental protection lies in the reference to 'air, water and soil' as a reference which, in turn, only partially covers the 'broad' definition of the concept of environmental protection (and the 'narrow' definition, for that matter, being that the difference between the two is that the latter excludes the notion of protection of human health).[160] Hence, the narrowly defined concept of 'environment protection' which comprises the protection of 'water, air, soil, and fauna and flora' as environmental assets, has been incompletely and non-exhaustively covered by the Euratom Treaty. Moreover, to the difference of the provisions of the 'Health and Safety' chapter which specifically target the protection of the health of workers and the general public (Arts.30 et seq.), Arts.37 and 38 Euratom have no real regulatory 'bite' as they do not lend themselves as potential legal bases for the adoption of legislative measures and can only be relied upon as grounds for conducting the data collection and the adoption of recommendations.[161]

It follows that the emphasis in the Euratom Treaty is put primarily on the protection of the health of humans (the workers and the general public), which in itself is not sufficient so as to conclude that the Euratom Treaty *completely* excludes environmental protection from its scope and consequently

160 Literature has not been very prescriptive in defining for the elusive term 'environment'. Authors disagree as to whether the scope of the term should be confined to the notion of natural environment or also include other elements of the environment, such as human health (See, Fitzmaurice, *supra* n. 63, p. 24). An erratic pattern of approaches is discernible with regard to the definition for 'environment', fostered by a number of prominent international environmental law instruments. For a wider discussion on this, see, Fitzmaurice, *supra* n. 63, pp. 22–28.

161 See, Hökmark Report, *supra* n. 183, p. 48; The extent to which the the institutions have made use of their prerogatives flowing from Arts.37 and 38 Euratom is a different matter. For an analysis, consult the following documents: 1999/829/Euratom: Commission Recommendation of 6 December 1999 on the application of Article 37 of the Euratom Treaty OJ *L 324, 16/12/1999 p. 0023–0043*; 2000/473/Euratom Commission Recommendation of 8 June 2000 on the application of Article 36 of the Euratom Treaty concerning the monitoring of the levels of radioactivity in the environment for the purpose of assessing the exposure of the population as a whole (notified under document number C(2000) 1299); 2010/635/Euratom: Commission Recommendation of 11 October 2010 on the application of Article 37 of the Euratom Treaty OJ L 279, 23.10.2010, p. 36–67.

does not endorse an *environmental approach* towards radiation protection. In fact, even if the Treaty fails to ascribe to a broad definition of environmental protection or even comprehensively uphold the narrow definition thereof, the reality is that one could not artificially divorce the 'human health protection' component from the 'protection of air, water, soil' as the former would, effectively, amount to depriving the Euratom Treaty's health and safety provisions from attaining their full effect. Manifestly, the former two concepts are inextricably linked since the quality of the health of humans is directly derived from and dependent on the quality of their living environment i.e. the surrounding 'air, water and soil' space.[162]

162 By comparison, under the head of the Union's environmental policy a clearly broad approach towards the notion of 'environment protection' has been embraced. In fact, the protection of human health figures among the objectives of the Union environmental policy (Art.192(1) TFEU). However, in this respect, a different problem of interpretation has arisen with the introduction of a separate chapter for the Union's public health policy in the TFEU, different from that of the Union's environmental policy. The dividing line between the two policies has proven to be significantly blurred both in the practice of EU institutions and the case law of the EU Court of Justice.

For this reason, the differentiation between the notions of *'human health'* as covered under Art.192 TFEU et seq. (the Union environmental policy), and the notions of *'public health'* and *'human health'* as used in the context of Art.168 TFEU et seq. (the Union public health policy) persists to be unclear (On this, see, Kramer, EC Environmental Law, Sweet and Maxwell, 2003, p. 12 (ft.49)). Kramer gives the example of Case C-293/97 Standley (1999 ECR I-2603) where the Court considered *Directive 91/676 on the protection of water from nitrates pollution* to be aimed at protecting public health in spite of its 'environmental protection' legal basis (then, Art.130 EC on the EC environmental policy).

Furthemore, regarding the use of the concepts of public health and human health interchangeably, the *Chernobyl I* case concerned the choice of a correct legal basis for Regulation No.3955/87 fixing maximum permitted levels of radioactive contamination in response to a concern to protect public health, where the EU Court of Justice stated that, *"the protection of public health is also one of the objectives of Community action in environmental matters* (...)". *Contra* to the Court's reasoning, Advocate General Darmon was reluctant to accept that protection of public health falls entirely within the concept of environment since contributing to the protection of human health as one of the objectives of Union's (Community) action relating to the environment does not entail that all "(...) *preoccupations of that kind are exclusively reserved to the sphere of environmental matter*". The reason for the Court's 'inclusive' approach may have been the fact that the separate treaty chapter on public health did not exist at the material time of the case as it was introduced later on with the Maastricht Treaty (1992). Hence, in the absence of an express treaty basis specific to the protection of human health, the provisions on the Union environmental policy were considered as the most suitable 'proxy' to attaining the

II.2.2 The 'Environmental Approach' to Radiation Protection and Nuclear Safety Endorsed at the International and the EU Level

In the context of examining the breadth of the outreach of the Euratom Treaty's health and safety provisions regarding the concept of environmental protection, another concept that equally deserves attention is '*radiation protection*' which is a concept which fully encapsulates and is inherently linked with the objectives of health protection and nuclear safety enounced under the Euratom Treaty. Similarly to the evasive definition of 'environmental protection', a broad and a narrow approach to radiation protection have been advanced, predicated upon the choice of a broad as opposed to a narrow approach applied in examining the relationship between EU's human health protection and environmental protection frameworks.

From the outset, a preliminary clarification is required regarding the definition of the terms '*radiation protection*' and '*nuclear safety*'. The former implies the setting out of parameters for radiation doses and radioactivity levels originating from various sources of radiation, whereas the latter relates to the safety of the design and operation of nuclear power plants and other nuclear facilities as sources of radiation.[163] The way in which the two concepts complement each other has been reflected in the definition espoused by the

objective of protection of human health. However, in view of the imminent correlation between human health protection and environment protection, these two policies will in the future persist to be subjected to a frequent intertwining between of respective legal bases.

The former approach has been consistently followed by the Union legislators in their choice between the treaty provisions on public health and those on environmental protection as potential legal basis for Union/Euratom acts (See, for example,Directive 2002/98/EC of the European Parliament and of the Council of 27 January 2003 setting standards of quality and safety for the collection, testing, processing, storage and distribution of human blood and blood components and amending Directive 2001/83/EC (based on then, Art.168 TFEU (ex-Art.152 EC) on public health); Directive 2004/23/EC of the European Parliament and of the Council of 31 March 2004 on setting standards of quality and safety for the donation, procurement, testing, processing, preservation, storage and distribution of human tissues and cells (based on Art.168 TFEU (ex-Art.152 EC)) which have a clear public health protection objective.Conversely see, Council Directive 1999/13/EC of 11 March 1999 on the limitation of emissions of volatile organic compounds due to the use of organic solvents in certain activities and installations, which also mentions the protection of human health as one of its objectives and is however based on Art.192 TFEU (ex-Art.130 EC; the Union environmental policy provisions).

163 Molodstova, E. "Nuclear Energy and Environmental Protection: Responses of International Law." *Pace Environmental Law Review*, 1994, p. 190.

IAEA for radiation protection and nuclear safety. According to *IAEA's Safety Glossary – Terminology Used in Nuclear Safety and Radiation Protection*,[164] radiation protection is understood as the protection of people and the environment against radiation risks, while nuclear safety represents the safety of facilities and activities giving rise to radiation risks.[165] The EU Court of Justice embraced the former definitions in the *Nuclear Safety Convention* Case C-29/99, where in order to define the Union (Community) competence in the field of nuclear safety it refused to draw an artificial distinction between the *protection of the health of the general public* and the *safety of sources of ionising radiation*,[166] thus aligning with the appraisal of the evolution of the disciplines of 'nuclear safety' and 'radiation protection' offered in AG Jacobs's Opinion in the same case.[167] According to AG Jacobs, the two concepts had originally been treated as separate and not impinging upon each other with nuclear safety being focused on the technological safety of nuclear installations and radiation protection being concerned with the maximum exposure levels and dose limits for workers and the population.[168] However, the rapidly changing conditions in the global nuclear sector inevitably lead to the two formerly separate and autonomous domains to partially coincide: in addition to its core technological aspect, nuclear safety gradually developed a radiation protection aspect thereto, whereas radiation protection grew increasingly concerned with limiting radiation exposures through strengthening of the control over radiation sources (including nuclear installations).[169]

The dynamic concept of radiation protection and the different approaches adopted with regard thereto will now be elaborated. In this sense, once more, a *broad* and a *narrow* view on radiation protection are to be put forward, where the broad view is one which couples the human health protection requirements together with the requirements specific to the protection of 'air, water, soil, flora and fauna' (i.e. the narrowly construed notion of 'environment'). In practical terms, adopting a broad approach to radiation protection presupposes an 'environmental protection' approach to radiation protection as opposed to the narrow one which implies a restrictive view that only includes 'human health protection'. In order to arrive at the 'correct approach' to be

164 International Atomic Energy Agency (IAEA) Safety Glossary: Terminology used in Nuclear Safety and Radiation Protection, 2007 edition, IAEA, 2007.

165 P. 2 of the Glossary.

166 Para. 82 of judgment.

167 Para. 81 of the judgment; See also, Paras.123–132 of Opinion.

168 Para. 132 of Opinion.

169 Para. 132 of Opinion.

followed, first and foremost, an insight must be provided into the approaches taken in the texts of various international and regional instruments, followed by a comparative view of individual EU institutions' views on the matter (the Parliament, the Council, the Commission and the EU Court of Justice).

The approaches regarding radiation protection devised at both the international and the EU level have varied from inclusive to completely exclusionary in view of the extent of their endorsement of the concept of 'environment protection'. According to the original definition of radiological protection given by the *International Commission on Radiological Protection* (ICRP), the environment is to be considered as sufficiently protected as long as human beings are deemed sufficiently protected being preoccupied with the issue of radiation protection only to the extent that the former coincides with the concept of human environment i.e. to the extent that the radiological protection of man is directly affected.[170] Since the 1990s there has been a departure from this restrictive view spurred by the rise in prominence of environmental protection concerns and the increased proliferation of international and regional legal instruments in the field of environmental protection. Therefore, the ICRP is no longer predicating 'environment protection' on 'human health protection', but rather offers a unique and independent outlook on the former concept by introducing a more extensive approach to the relationship between radiation protection and the environment which aims to prevent/reduce "(...) radiation effects in the environment to a level where they would have a negligible impact on the maintenance of biological diversity, the conservation of species, or the health and status of natural habitats, communities, and ecosystems".[171] The foregoing is evidence to an extension in the scope of the ICRP definition of

---

170 Molodstova, *supra* n. 163, p. 192.

171 Abstract of *Annals of the ICRP*, vol 38 issues 4–6, 2008: ICRP Publication 108 – *Environmental Protection – the Concept and Use of Reference Animals and Plants* (http://www.icrp.org/publication.asp?id=ICRP%20Publication%20108);

In addition, in the Abstract of *Annals of the ICRP*, vol 38 issues 4–6, 2008: ICRP Publication 108 – *Environmental Protection – the Concept and Use of Reference Animals and Plants*, the International Commission on Radiological Protection considered it necessary "(...) to address, directly, the subject of protection of the environment, although it acknowledged that there is no simple or single universal definition of 'environmental protection', and that the concept differs between countries and from one circumstance to another. It is a very large and complicated subject. Nevertheless, the Commission did consider it appropriate to set out some high-level ambitions with regard to environmental protection and the specific issue of potential radiation effects, and thus included within its general aims those of wishing to prevent or reduce the frequency of deleterious radiation effects in the environment to a level where they would have a negligible impact on

radiation protection as one which is not confined to the notion of 'human environment', but equally aims to include the broader eco-system.[172]

The *International Atomic Energy Agency* (IAEA)'s approach to radiation protection has also been one to evolve with time. The IAEA Statute as the Agency's founding act fails to provide a specific and concrete reference to environment protection, the closest reference thereto being found in the provisions on 'Health and Safety' of Article III. It has been speculated that the absence of an express reference is accounted for by the fact that at the time the IAEA Statute was adopted the potential risks inherent to the peaceful uses of nuclear energy had not been as evident as those resulting from military uses.[173] Nevertheless, other IAEA official documents and publications such as the recently reviewed IAEA Safety Standards of 2014 accord equal importance to the protection of humans and the environment from the harmful effects of ionizing radiation.[174] The former exhibits an important shift in approach in comparison to the language used in the 1996 IAEA Basic Safety Standards which predominantly focused on the protection of *people* against exposure to ionizing radiation and the safety of radiation sources.[175]

In addition, a significant change in IAEA's view can equally be observed in the 2007 *IAEA Safety Glossary – Terminology Used in Nuclear Safety and Radiation Protection* where a prevalent use of the phrase 'safety standards for

---

the maintenance of biological diversity, the conservation of species, or the health and status of natural habitats, communities, and ecosystems.

The Commission also stated, however, that it believed that its approach to environmental protection should be commensurate with the overall level of risk (and thus optimised), and that it should be compatible with other approaches being made to protect the environment" (http://www.icrp.org/publication.asp?id=ICRP%20Publication%20108).

172 See, also, ICRP, *Protection of the Environment under Different Exposure Situtation*, ICRP Publication 124, Ann. ICRP 43(1).

173 Molodstova, *supra* n. 163, p. 201.

174 The IAEA Safety Standards set out the basic requirements for protection of people against exposure to ionizing radiation and for the safety of radiation sources. See, *Safety Standards for protecting people and the environment: Radiation Protection and Safety of Radiation Sources: International Basic Safety Standards*, IAEA, 2014 (http://www-pub.iaea.org/MTCD/Publications/PDF/Pub1578_web-57265295.pdf), pp. 17, 18, 21, 22 and 24.

175 Safety Series No. 115, IAEA 1996, International Basic Safety Standards for Protection against Ionizing Radiation and for the Safety of Radiation Sources, http://www-pub.iaea.org/MTCD/publications/PDF/Pub996_EN.pdf;

For a discussion on the legal status of the IAEA Safety Standards, see, Veuchelen, L., The Legal Value of General Principles, Technical Norms and Standards in European Nuclear Safety Law: The Imbalance Between Soft and Hard Law and the Need for Global Regulatory Governance, *European Energy and Environmental Law Review*, 2009, Vol. 18 Issue 4, p. 219 et seq.

protecting people *and the environment* from harmful effects of ionizing radiation' can be observed. In addition, it needs to be reminded that under various other official IAEA documents, the term radiation protection has been construed as 'protection of people and the environment against radiation risks'.[176] Furthermore, an environmental approach to radiation protection has also been fully endorsed in Principle 8 of the IAEA fundamental principles which reads as follows: "Whereas the effects of radiation exposure on human health are relatively well understood, albeit with uncertainties, *the effects of radiation on the environment* have been less thoroughly investigated (...) The general intent of the measures taken for the purposes of environmental protection has been *to protect ecosystems against radiation exposure* that would have adverse consequences for populations of a species (as distinct from individual organisms)".[177]

Coming to the EU level, it follows from the discussion *supra* regarding the areas of intersection between the Euratom health and safety policy and the Union's environmental policy that the Euratom Treaty has only to a limited extent ascribed to an 'environmental protection' approach to radiation protection. The Treaty's reference to 'air, water and soil', which neglects to include 'fauna and flora' as a crucial component of the environment, additionally prevents that the Euratom's approach to radiation protection be qualified as fully 'environmental'. However, the former is not completely indicative of Euratom's overall approach to radiation protection which has further evolved pursuant to the terminology employed in *Directive 96/29/EURATOM of 13 May 1996 laying down basic safety standards for the protection of the health of workers and the general public against the dangers arising from ionizing radiation* and its successor, *Directive 2013/59/EURATOM laying down basic safety standards for protection against the dangers arising from exposure to ionising radiation*.[178] Namely, while both the directives carry a prevalent human health protection objective, the former attempted an 'environmental' definition for the term 'radioactive contamination' defining the term as "*the contamination of any material, surface or environment or of an individual by radioactive substances*".[179] The 2013 Directive, however, clearly

176 IAEA Safety Glossary: Terminology used in Nuclear Safety and Radiation Protection, IAEA, 2007; Also, for a list of recent IAEA publications, see http://www-ns.iaea.org/standards/documents/recent-pubs.asp?s=11&l=84.

177 IAEA Safety Standards Series No. SF-1 (2006); Emphasis added.

178 OJ 2014L 13/1.

179 See, Title I Definitions; See also on this, Molodstova, *supra* n. 163, p. 229 (Molodstova discusses the Basic Safety Standards Directive's pre-cursor – Directive 80/836/Euratom where the identical approach to radiation protection was upheld).

puts the emphasis on the protection of the health of individuals subject to occupational, medical and public exposures against the dangers arising from ionising radiation,[180] stipulating that its provisions apply to risks "from exposure to ionising radiation which cannot be disregarded from a radiation protection point of view or *with regard to the environment in view of long-term human health protection*".[181]

In establishing the existence of an 'environmental' approach to radiation protection, it would also prove useful to gain insight into the stance of the EU institutions in the matter which can be qualified as mostly environmental, but, however, short of consistent. Among the majority of institutions, there is a noticeable tendency not to prioritize or in any way favor the health protection over the environmental protection objective.

The *European Parliament* was involved in a back-and-forth with the Commission regarding the initial proposal for the *Directive establishing a Community framework for the nuclear safety of nuclear installations*[182] where the Parliament's Legal Affairs Committee examined the possibility of basing the Directive on the Treaty's environmental policy provisions thus accommodating both the technological aspects and environmental aspects of nuclear safety.[183] The Legal Affairs Committee remarked the insistence on the part of the Parliament's Industry Committee that environmental protection considerations be incorporated into the scope of the Directive through the insertion of a provision regarding the IAEA fundamental principles reflecting the environmental

180 Art.1 of Directive.

181 Emphasis added; Art.2 of the Directive. In the course of preparation of the final text of the 2013 Directive, there was a version of the draft directive (Proposal for a Council Directive laying down basic safety standards for protection against the dangers arising from exposure to ionising radiation, European Commission, Brussels, 30.5.2012 COM(2012) 242 final 2011/0254 (NLE)) which carried an eco-centric component, consisting of targeting the reinforcement of the Euratom regime for the protection of the non-human environment (and including a separate chapter on 'Protection of the environment' for this purpose). The text of the proposed directive was not solely aimed at reinforcing the overall health and safety protection regime under the Euratom; it went on further in developing a broader notion of environmental protection as encompassing both the human and the non-human environment.

182 Council Directive 2009/71/Euratom of 25 June 2009 establishing a Community framework for the nuclear safety of nuclear installations, OJ *L 172 pp. 0018–0022.*

183 Hökmark Report, European Parliament Report on the proposal for a Council Directive (Euratom) setting up a Community framework for nuclear safety of nuclear installations, A6-0236/2009, p. 40.

protection concerns.[184] The former Committee took special note of Art.2 of the draft Directive which defined "nuclear safety" as "the achievement of proper operating conditions through measures taken with a view to the prevention of accidents or mitigation of accident consequences, resulting in protection of *workers, general public* and *the air, water and soil* from undue radiation hazards arising from nuclear installations".[185]

It appeared that the centre of gravity of the proposed directive was nuclear safety in general, the main objective being to supplement the basic standards previously laid down in the Basic Safety Standards Directive 96/29/Euratom in order to ensure that a high level of safety of nuclear installations is attained and constantly improved.[186] The explicit reference to environment in Art.2 had indicated that, for the purposes of the Directive, nuclear safety needed to include environment protection requirements, in addition to the requirements regarding the protection of the health of workers and the general public.[187] However, being that the main thrust of the instrument was considered to be in the enhancement of the existing system of radiation standards laid down by Directive 96/29/Euratom whereas none of the provisions set out in the proposed directive were specifically aimed at protection against threats to the environment.[188] Eventually, the Committee inferred that in spite of the 'inclusive' definition for nuclear safety in Art.2, the protection of the environment was not covered by Art.31 Euratom (basic health and safety standards provision) whereas it regarded the 'air, water and soil' reference of Arts.37 and 38 Euratom as lacking the potential to provide a legal basis for the adoption of legislative measures and therefore upheld Arts.31 and 32 as the Directive's appropriate 'center of gravity'.[189]

The Commission took an important cue from the Parliamentary Committee's appraisal and the Art.2 reference to 'air, water and soil' was removed from the definition of nuclear safety in the final text of the Directive adopted in June 2009. In the present text "nuclear safety" is defined as the achievement of proper operating conditions, prevention of accidents and mitigation of accident consequences, resulting in protection of workers and the general public from dangers arising from ionizing radiations from nuclear installations.[190]

184 Hökmark Report, p. 46.

185 Emphasis added; Hökmark Report, p. 45.

186 Hökmark Report, p. 46.

187 Hökmark Report, p. 46.

188 Hökmark Report, p. 47.

189 Hökmark Report, p. 48.

190 Art.2 of the Directive; Although the Directive was subsequently amended by Directive 2014/87/EURATOM amending Directive 2009/71/Euratom establishing a Community

Nevertheless, the lawmakers did not go completely oblivious to 'environment protection', the former having found its place in the Directive's preamble: "(...) the provisions of Chapter 3 of the [Euratom] Treaty, related to health and safety, form a coherent whole conferring upon the Commission powers of some considerable scope in order to protect *the population and the environment* against risks of nuclear contamination".[191]

Unlike the European Parliament, the *Commission* has not been as keen on the prospect of widening the scope of the Euratom health and safety provisions which is to be expected bearing in mind the role accorded to the Commission in the legislative process as the institution holding the monopoly over Union legislation proposal. Namely, the Commission could not venture on drafting a legislative act that would depart from the circumscribed scope of application of the Euratom Treaty provisions thereby risking the act to be declared invalid before the Court of Justice. By exception, the former would arguably be possible in the presence of progressive case law of the EU courts paving the way for a broad construction of the Euratom Treaty's provisions concerning radiation protection.[192] Nevertheless, there have been a panoply of Commission policy documents pertaining to radiation protection that have acknowledged the importance of environmental protection, while viewing it as an objective which is distinct and subsidiary to the original health protection objective written into the Euratom Treaty.[193]

---

framework for the nuclear safety of nuclear installations (OJ 2014L 219/42), the definition for 'nuclear safety' provided therein has remained unaffected.

191 Emphasis added; Recital 5 of the Preamble; For this, see also, European Parliament, *Report on Assessing Euratom – 50 Years of European nuclear energy policy*, FINAL A6-0129/2007; The Parliament considered that the provisions of the Euratom Treaty that have helped prevent the proliferation of nuclear materials along with those which address health, safety and the prevention of radiological contamination, should be carefully coordinated with the health and safety provisions of the EC Treaty (point 26 of Report).

192 For example, the Preamble of the Nuclear Safety Directive makes a direct reference to the case law of the EU Court of Justice, at point 4.

193 For an overview of the Commission's stance, see the following documents: Commission Communication to the Council, The Development of Community measures for the application of Chapter 3 of the Euratom Treaty 'Health and Safety' COM/86/434FINAL; 1999/829/Euratom: Commission Recommendation of 6 December 1999 on the application of Article 37 of the Euratom Treaty (notified under document number C (1999) 3932) *Official Journal L 324, 16/12/1999 p. 0023–0043*; 2000/473/Euratom: Commission recommendation of 8 June 2000 on the application of Article 36 of the Euratom Treaty concerning the monitoring of the levels of radioactivity in the environment for the purpose of assessing the exposure of the population as a whole (notified under document number C(2000)

In the context of nuclear safety, the *Council of the EU* has been open to pairing the concept of protection of the health of the population and workers together with the concept of protection of the environment from dangers resulting from ionizing radiation, recognizing the progress the Union has been making in providing a satisfactory threshold of protection thereof in a number of resolutions specifically related to the matter.[194]

The role of the *EU Court of Justice* in this respect is equally not to be neglected as the former has directly contributed to a progressive extension of the scope of application of the Euratom Treaty provisions pertaining to radiation protection. Back in the late 1980s, in its *Cattenom*[195] judgment concerning the disposal of radioactive waste from a French nuclear power plant in Cattenom, the EU Court of Justice noted that the health and safety provisions of the Euratom Treaty conferred upon the Commission powers of considerable scope in the protection of the population *and the environment* against the risks of nuclear contamination.[196] This statement conveys a fully-embraced environmental approach on the part of the Court stemming from its tendency to interpret the Euratom health and safety provisions extensively so as to include environment protection into their scope.[197] In the *Chernobyl I* case, confronted with the

1299); 2010/635/Euratom: Commission Recommendation of 11 October 2010 on the application of Article 37 of the Euratom Treaty OJ L 279, 23.10.2010, p. 36–67;

To the contrary, in the oral proceedings in the C-29/99 *Nuclear Safety Convention* case, where the CJEU examined Euratom's competence in the field of nuclear safety, the Commission expressed the view that Arts.30 et seq. of the Euratom Treaty and the relevant articles of the Nuclear Safety Convention pursued the same core objective, which was that of protection of the people and *the environment* against ionizing radiation (see para. 117 AG Jacobs Opinion in C-29/99).

194 See, Preamble of Council Resolution of 18 June 1992 on the technological problems of nuclear safety (92/C 172/02); and, Council Resolution of 18 June 1992 on the technological problems of nuclear safety OJ C 172, 8.7.1992, pp. 2–3.

> (…) Whereas the issue of nuclear safety is an important one, particularly with regard to the protection of the health of the population and of workers as well as the protection of the environment from the dangers resulting from ionizing radiation, particularly in the view of the developments which have taken place throughout Europe (…)
>
> RECOGNIZES the progress towards an equivalent and satisfactory degree of protection of the population and of the environment in the Community at the highest practical safety levels, as called for in the 1975 resolution, and in contributing to the international acceptance of similar high safety levels (…).

195 C-187/87 *Saarland v. Minister for Industry* ECR 1988 p. 5013. For an appraisal of a different aspect of the *Cattenom* judgment, see *supra*, Chapter 1, Section III.3.3.

196 Para. 11 of judgment.

197 The Opinion of AG Slynn in the *Cattenom* case follows the same approach.

issue of maximum permitted levels of radioactive contamination being fixed in response to a concern to protect public health, the Court viewed the protection of public health as one of the objectives of Community action in environmental matters,[198] quite the opposite from AG Darmon, who was not convinced that the protection of public health fell entirely and exclusively within the concept of environment.[199] According to AG Darmon, the fact that protection of human health falls under one of the objectives of Community environmental action does not presuppose that issues of that kind are exclusively reserved to the sphere of environmental matters.[200] It also needs to be pointed out that at the time of the deliberation of these cases the Union's public health policy had not yet been introduced as such. Nevertheless, the former was not determinative for the Court's willingness to couple the public health and the environmental protection objectives for the purpose of tackling with the dangers arising from the use of nuclear energy. The Court did not subsequently abandon its broad approach, as both in *C-61/03 Commission v UK* and *C-65/04 Commission v UK* it again referred to the "(…) the vital importance of the objective of protecting the health of *the public and the environment* against the dangers related to the use of nuclear energy (…)".[201]

Finally, in the *Temelin*[202] case where the Court discussed the potentially nugatory effects of the operation of a Czech nuclear power plant on part of the Austrian population living at the border with the Czech Republic, it recognized that it was "(…) common ground that [the Euratom] Treaty contains a set of rules relating precisely *to the protection of populations and the environment* against ionising radiations"[203] and reiterated its *Cattenom* judgment *dictum* that the provisions of Chapter 3 of the Euratom Treaty form a coherent whole conferring upon the Commission powers of considerable scope for the

198 Para. 18 of judgment.

199 Para. 33 of Opinion.

200 Para. 33 of Opinion.

201 Emphasis added; Para. 44 of the former and Para. 28 of the latter judgment; See, for a similar favorable extension, AG Geelhoed's Opinion in *C-61/03 Commission v UK*: "(…) the objectives underpinning Chapter 3 of the EAEC Treaty – public health and safety and environmental protection – have, since the entry into force of the Treaty, consistently been viewed as being of the utmost importance". (Para. 77 of Opinion); Both *C-61/03 Commission v UK* and *C-65/04 Commission v UK* will be looked at more closely, however from a different angle, *infra*, in Chapter 4, Section IV.3.

202 For the *Temelin* judgment, see also *supra*, Chapter 1, Section III.3.6 and Chapter 2, Section I.3.

203 Emphasis added; Para. 83 of judgment.

purpose of protecting *the population and the environment* against the risks of nuclear contamination.[204]

Consequently, it can be firmly held that the EU Court of Justice has endorsed an environmental approach to radiation protection, treating the concepts of 'radiation protection' and 'environmental protection' as inextricably linked and giving a green light to the practice of extrapolation of the Euratom health and safety provisions to the field of environmental protection.[205] It would seem that the Court sees the former as 'impliedly' written into the Euratom Treaty to the extent that the linking of the two concepts is most often a natural occurrence in the wider context of the application of the Euratom Treaty, independent of any hidden agendas or deeply rooted political motives.

II.2.3 The Overlap between the Euratom-Devised Policies and the Union Environmental Policy through the Use of Secondary Law Instruments

Coming again to the issue of extrapolation of legal rules between the domains of nuclear energy and the environment (elaborated *supra* for the international level) what follows is an insight into the patterns of extrapolation discerned at the EU level where there are a number of Union acts containing provisions which, comprehensively or marginally, cover a particular nuclear energy aspect (e.g., radioactive waste or other radioactive matter-related nuisances, nuclear power plant construction planning), and vice versa. The former type of extension of legal rules occurs more frequently and concerns issues which have not been regulated under the scope of Euratom, either due to lack of an *express competence* prescribed under the Euratom Treaty for regulation to occur or due to the fact that Euratom has not yet acted in the direction of regulating a particular area, thus making way for the Union to be 'impliedly' allowed to step in and regulate instead of Euratom.

Directive 85/337/EEC on assessment of the effects of certain public and private projects on the environment[206] lays down an obligation for assessment to be conducted regarding the environmental effects of public and private projects likely to have significant effects on the environment, thereby covering nuclear power stations and other nuclear reactors and installations

204 Para. 118.

205 Some authors consider that any confusion regarding application of the environmental policy standards and principles to the Euratom field would be removed when the scenario of assimilating the Euratom Treaty to the TFEU materializes (see, C. True, Legislative Competences of Euratom and the European Community in the energy sector: The Nuclear Package of the Commission, *European Law Review*, 2003, Vol. 28 Issue 5, p. 15).

206 OJ 1985L 175/40.

designed for permanent storage or final disposal of radioactive waste. Although primarily targeting environmental protection, the Directive was adopted under Arts.114 and 352 TFEU (then, Arts.100 and 235 EC; i.e. the open-ended clause for establishing Community competence and the provisions on legal harmonization) since at the time of its adoption a separate Community environmental policy was still not envisaged under the Treaties. The Directive was later on amended by *Directive 2001/42/EC of the European Parliament and of the Council of 27 June 2001 on the assessment of the effects of certain plans and programmes on the environment*[207] which was based on Art.192(1) TFEU (ex-Art.175(1)EC – the Union's environment policy provisions), complementing and reinforcing the Union's existent environmental impact assessment regime.

Directive 2003/4/EC of the European Parliament and of the Council of 28 January 2003 on public access to environmental information[208] (based on Art.192(1) TFEU (ex-Art.175(1)EC)) guarantees the right of access to environmental information held by or for public authorities,whereby the term 'environmental information' covers any information in written, visual, aural, electronic or any other material form on factors, among other, radiation and waste, including radioactive waste, emissions, discharges and other releases into the environment affecting or likely to affect the elements of the environment.[209] These elements of the environment comprise the air and atmosphere, water, soil, land, landscape and natural sites including wetlands, coastal and marine areas, as well as biological diversity and its components, including genetically modified organisms.[210]

The much debated upon *Directive 2008/99/EC on the protection of the environment through criminal law*[211] had a curious life cycle as it was originally adopted under the EU Treaty provisions in the form of *Council Framework Decision 2003/80/JHA of 27 January 2003 on the protection of the environment through criminal law*. Subsequently, the Commission challenged the choice of legal basis for the said Framework Decision in *C-176/03 Commission v Council*[212] where the EU Court of Justice sanctioned the use of a Community measure as a first pillar instrument for harmonizing the national regimes on environmental offences which entailed the imposition of penalties on the part of the

207 OJ 2001L 197/ 30.

208 OJ 2003L 41/ 26.

209 Art.2.

210 See, Art.2 'Definitions'.

211 OJ 2008L 328/28.

212 ECR 2005 p. I-7879.

Member States which are *effective, proportionate and dissuasive* in nature.[213] With respect to the nuclear field, The Directive treats the following type of conduct as criminal offence, when unlawful and committed intentionally or with at least serious negligence: "(...) (a) the discharge, emission or introduction of a quantity of materials or *ionising radiation* into air, soil or water, which causes or is likely to cause death or serious injury to any person or substantial damage to the quality of air, the quality of soil or the quality of water, or to animals or plants; (...) and (...) (e) the production,processing, handling, use, holding, storage, transport, import, export or disposal of *nuclear materials* or other *hazardous radioactive substances* which causes or is likely to cause death or serious injury to any person or substantial damage to the quality of air, the quality of soil or the quality of water, or to animals or plants".[214]

Conversely, there have been a few Euratom legislative acts that have directly or indirectly impacted on the scope of the Union's environmental policy since, generally speaking, Euratom acts regularly refer to the observance of 'environmental considerations' applicable to the nuclear field being that the prevention/protection from risks liable to adversely affect the environment is a vital corollary objective of the Euratom rules. In this vein, the Preamble of the *Directive 2009/71/Euratom establishing a Community framework for nuclear safety*[215] invokes the general aim of the Euratom health and safety rules to protect "the population and the environment against risks of nuclear contamination" (albeit the Euratom Treaty text does not mention the concept of 'environment protection' *per se*).[216] In a similar manner, *Directive 2006/117/Euratom on the supervision and control of shipments of radioactive waste and spent fuel*[217] couples together the notions of human health protection and environment protection,[218] as is the case with *Council Directive 2003/122/Euratom of 22 December 2003 on the control of high-activity sealed radioactive sources and orphan sources*[219] where a reference is made to the potential risks for human health and the environment caused by high-activity sources.[220]

213 Emphasis added; See, paras.46 et seq. of judgment. The Court had considered that this type of measure could only appropriately be based on Art.192 TFEU (ex-Art.175 EC) as its main purpose was undisputedly, the protection of the environment (para. 51 of judgment).

214 Emphasis added; Art.3 of the Directive.

215 OJ 2009L172/18.

216 Recital 5 of Preamble. For further discussion, see Section IV.2 of this chapter.

217 OJ 2006L 337/21.

218 Recital 11 of Preamble.

219 OJ 2003L 346/57.

220 Recital 8 of Preamble.

What the former three directives have in common is that their texts merely make a passing mention of the importance of the objective of environment protection in the nuclear sphere where those provisions seem to be intended more as declaratory statements rather provisions of a regulatory nature. In contrast to this, the former *Directive 96/29/Euratom laying down basic safety standards for the protection of the health of workers and the general public against the dangers arising from ionizing radiation*, as was discussed in the preceding section, was not strictly confined to the objective human health protection and contained operative provisions with a direct, regulatory effect on the environment.[221] Although the new 2013 Basic Safety Standards Directive exhibits a retreat in the 'environmental' language used, it nevertheless contains important operative provisions concerning the protection of the environment as such.[222]

II.2.4 Transposing the Principles of Union Environmental Law to the Euratom Field

Another issue corollary to the issue of extending the scope of Union environmental rules to the Euratom domain is the possibility for applying the principles of the Union environmental policy to the Euratom framework. These principles have a status different from that of the general principles of EU law which rank as primary sources of Union law in that there exists a certain controversy regarding their legally binding effect (some authors consider these principles as merely a policy orienteer lacking any binding force[223] while others claim that the Union environmental policy principles cannot be completely denied of having any legal effect[224]).

Article 191(2) TFEU (ex. Art.174(2)) enumerates the following as principles that the Union policy on the environment is based upon: the *precautionary principle*, the *principle of preventive action*, the principle that *environmental damage should be rectified at the source* and the *polluter-pays principle*. The TFEU is silent as to the precise content and binding nature (if any) of these principles making it difficult to adopt one general position regarding the potential of these principles to produce any legal effects.[225] In view of the

221 See, Arts. 19, 22, 44, 45 and 47 of the Directive.

222 See Arts. 28(4), 67(1), 68, 72, 73 of the 2013 Directive.

223 See, Kramer, *supra*, n. 162, p. 14; Kramer, *supra*, n. 157, p. 10.

224 See, A. Epiney, Environmental Principles, in, R. Macrory (ed.), *Reflections on 30 Years of EU Environmental Law: High Level of Protection?*, Europa Law Publishing, 2006, pp. 22,33.

225 Nevertheless, the EU General Court has boldly stepped out on one occasion by referring to the precautionary principle as a 'general principle of Union law' (See, *Artegodan and*

uncertainty as to their status as legal principles, it is to be gathered that the former principles have greater prominence in international environmental law (as a legal system predominantly based on soft law instruments) while as far as the Union environmental law is concerned, they have, to a large extent, already been translated into binding Union acts.[226]

The principles of the Union's environmental policy have been characterized as *guiding principles* of a *policy nature* which decision-makers use to justify the planned adoption of a measure[227] and which are only enforceable by courts in instances of 'systematic disregard' thereof.[228] Thus, it would be difficult to deny these principles of having (at a minimum) an indirect legal effect given that the former often serve to reinforce the justification for the choice of a particular legal basis of a measure and have, in addition, been instrumental to the process of interpreting secondary Union legislation.[229] It may be somewhat misleading to discuss the legal character of these environmental principles in general terms (by treating all the principles as a whole), making it more appropriate to examine their individual ('legal') effects by considering all the principles separately.[230] From the perspective of EU law, the practical consequence of acknowledging the legally binding nature of the environmental policy principles is to impose an obligation for the Union institutions to act upon them.[231] However, the imposition of an obligation to act would only occur by exception in view of the difficulty to comprehensively determine the scope and content of these principles so as to allow for an obligation to act which is both enforceable and definable to be discerned.[232] In turn, it would be virtually impossible for the EU courts to precisely determine the 'failure to act' at issue, because the type of action required to be taken in application of the principles is not sufficiently clear in the first place.[233]

others v Commission (T-74/00, T-76/00, T-83/00, T-84/00, T-85/00, T-132/00, T-137/00 and T-141/00), ECR 2002 p. II-4945. For more commentary on the case, see, J. Scott, The Precautionary Principle before the European Courts, in, R. Macrory (ed.), *Principles of European Environmental Law (Proceedings of the Avosetta Group of Europan Environmental Lawyers)*, Europea Law Publishing, 2004, pp. 53–56).

226 Kramer, *supra*, n. 157, p. 10.

227 Kramer, *supra*, n. 162, p. 14.

228 Kramer *supra*, n. 157, p. 10.

229 *Idem*, p. 11.

230 See on this, P. Sands, Principles of International Environmental Law (2nd ed.), Cambridge University Press, 2003, pp. 231, 232.

231 Epiney, *supra* n. 224, p. 33.

232 *Idem*, p. 33.

233 *Idem*, p. 34.

The CJEU has pronounced itself on the matter of the legal effect of the principles of Union's environmental policy by considering the former as judicially reviewable only in exceptional cases where there is a *systematic disregard* of their aim and content.[234] In *Safety Hi-Tech*[235] the Court of Justice opined that the Union institutions were bound by the principles enshrined in Art.192 TFEU (ex-Art.130 TEC), deciding to regard this particular Treaty article as one that "(...) sets a series of objectives, principles and criteria which the Community legislature must respect in implementing the environmental policy (...)".[236] The Court held that, in view of the need to strike a balance between certain of the objectives and principles mentioned in Art.130r (present Art.191(2) TFEU) and of the complexity of the implementation of these criteria, the review by the Court must necessarily be limited to the question whether the Council, by adopting the Regulation, committed a manifest error of appraisal regarding the conditions for the application of Art.130r of the Treaty (present Art.191(2)).[237] It follows that once the Union has decided to act, the principles are presumed to have a binding effect for the institutions only where there has been a manifest breach of the obligation to act in which case the EU courts would be competent to rule on a violation of these principles.[238] Again, the notoriously difficult task of establishing what would exactly constitute a 'manifest error of appraisal' committed on the part of the Union institutions comes to the fore in this regard.

a *The Prevention Principle and the Precautionary Principle as Principles of EU Environmental Action*

The two most prominent of the Union environmental policy principles, the principle of prevention (principle of preventive action) and the precautionary principle, are equally the most evasive in terms of defining their exact content.[239] The principle of prevention, which concerns the notion of "(...) preventing the creation of pollution or nuisances at source, rather than

234 See for this, Kramer, *supra* n. 157, p. 10.

235 *C-341/95 European Court Reports 1998 Page I-04355.*

236 Para. 34 of judgment.

237 Para. 35; Emphasis added.

238 Epiney, *supra* n. 224, p. 34.

239 For more on the principle of preventive action and the precautionary principle as principles of international environmental law, see, P. Sands and J. Peel (eds.), Principles of International Environmental Law (3rd edition), Cambridge University Press, 2012, pp. 200–203 and 217–228.

subsequently trying to counteract their effects",[240] was introduced as a principle of the Union's environmental policy through the Single European Act (1987) and was the first environmental principle to be included earlier on in the EC's First Environmental Action Programme in 1973.[241] With the precautionary principle being introduced to the Union framework later on with the Maastricht Treaty (1992), the temporal difference regarding the inauguration of the two principles accounts for the previously established practice of blurring the boundaries between them, which, in turn, resulted in perceiving the two principles as mutually intertwined in terms of their respective aim and content.[242]

The precautionary principle, as it is understood and applied today, is one that is both different and differentiable from the prevention principle. It is a highly controversial principle given that the required degree of certainty for indentifying the extent of environmental danger in the activities covered by its scope of application[243] is still considered as ambiguous and largely dependent on the *context* in which the principle is applied. The most distinct features of the precautionary principle are that it mainly applies to instances of *lack of conclusive scientific evidence*, where the existence of a threat is *not tangible* and there is *no concrete causal link* between the activity and the potentiality of the harm.[244] For these reasons, the principle has also been labeled as a '*in dubio pro natura*' principle.[245]

Principle 15 of the Rio Declaration on Environment and Development defines the precautionary approach in the following terms: "(...) Where there

240 P. 9 of the Action Programme; See on this, L. Kramer, The Genesis of EC Environmental Principles, in, R. Macrory (ed.), *Principles of European Environmental Law* (Proceedings of the Avosetta Group of Europan Environmental Lawyers), Europa Law Publishing, 2004, p. 38.

241 Programme of Action of the EC on the Environment (1973) OJ C 112 p. 1.

242 Hence, prior to the Maastricht Treaty, all cases of scientific uncertainty that would have otherwise triggered the application of the precautionary principle were subsumed under the notion of prevention (Kramer, *supra* n. 240, p. 39).

243 See, Fitzmaurice, *supra* n. 63, pp. 263, 274.

244 N. de Sadeleer, The Principles of Prevention and Precaution: Two Heads of the Same Coin?, in, Ong, Merkouris and Fitzmaurice (eds.), *Research Handbook on International Environmental Law*, Edward Elgar Publishing, 2011, p. 184. Fitzmaurice, on the other hand, distinguishes three common features of the precautionary principle: (1) regulatory inaction threatening non-negligible harm, (2) lack of scientific certainty on the cause and effect relationship and (3) under the circumstances regulatory inaction is unjustified (Fitzmaurice, *supra* n. 63, pp. 263, 264).

245 As reported in, Jans, *supra* n. 155, p. 38.

are threats of serious or irreversible damage, *lack of full scientific certainty* shall not be used as a reason for postponing cost-effective measures to prevent environmental degradation".[246] Alternatively, the OSPAR Convention (Convention for the Protection of the Marine Environment of the North-East Atlantic) considers the precautionary principle as a principle "(…) by virtue of which measures are taken when there are reasonable grounds for concern that substances or energy introduced directly or indirectly into the environment may bring about damage to human health, or harm living resources, even where there is *no conclusive evidence of a causal relationship between the inputs and effects*"[247] to be applied by the State Parties. The definition of the precautionary principle that the Union has endorsed is more in line with the OSPAR definition,[248] as can be observed, *inter alia*, in the Commission's *Communication on the Precautionary principle*.[249] The Communication serves to establish a common understanding of the factors leading to recourse to the precautionary principle and introduce practical guidelines for its application.[250] According to the Communication, the decision to invoke the precautionary principle is exercised where scientific information is insufficient, inconclusive, or uncertain and where there are indications that the effects on the environment or the human, animal or plant health may be potentially dangerous.[251] As for the legal nature of the principle, the Commission considers that it devolves on the decision-makers and (if necessary, the courts) to materialize it,[252] reminding that the former practice is not contingent on the adoption of legally binding instruments which are subject to judicial review.[253]

Regarding the scope of application of the precautionary principles, the Commission distinguishes between the terms 'scientific evaluation' and 'risk assessment', insisting that every decision must be "(…) preceded by an examination of all the *available scientific data* and, if possible, *a risk evaluation* that is as objective and comprehensive as possible".[254] In this sense, the Commission

---

246 Emphasis added; For an overview of the wording of other international law instruments that follow the wording of Principle 15 of the Rio Declaration, see, Annex II of the *Communication from the Commission on the Precautionary principle* COM/2000/0001 final.

247 Emphasis added; p. 3, (1998) OJ L 104.

248 Kramer, *supra* n. 240, p. 40.

249 Communication from the Commission on the Precautionary principle COM/2000/0001 final.

250 P. 8 of Communication.

251 P. 7.

252 P. 9.

253 P. 15.

254 P. 21; Emphasis added.

considers the scientific evaluation as mandatory, while the requirement to perform a risk assessment is seen as complementary and optional thus making the 'risk assessment' requirement one susceptible to manipulation liable to potentially downplay the importance of the application of the principle in a particular case and effectively reduce its field of application.[255]

The application of the precautionary principle under the Union framework is not confined to the field of environmental protection and can be extended to other fields in "(...) *specific circumstances where scientific evidence is insufficient, inconclusive or uncertain and there are indications through preliminary objective scientific evaluation that there are reasonable grounds for concern that the potentially dangerous effects on the environment, human, animal or plant health may be inconsistent with the chosen level of protection*"[256] A similar sort of 'extension' is equally taken to apply with regard to the prevention principle.[257]

The extension of the scope of application of the precautionary principle was equally acknowledged by the EU's General Court in the *Artegodan* case[258] where the Court decided to extend the scope of application of the principle beyond the concept of 'environmental protection' *stricto sensu*. It considered the scope of the principle to additionally cover the "(...) protection of health, consumer safety and the environment in all the Community's spheres of activity (...)", substantiating its approach by referring to "(...) the requirements relating to that high level of protection of the environment and human health [which] are expressly integrated into the definition and implementation of all Community policies and activities under Art.6 EC [11 TFEU] and Art.152(1) EC [168(1) TFEU], respectively".[259] Evidently, the Court attempted to promote an 'environmental' approach to the field of human health protection, performing a 'coupling' of the environment protection and the human health protection

255 Kramer, *supra* n. 157, p. 17.

In the *BSE* case (C-157/96 A998 ECR I-2211 and C-180/96 1998 ECR I-2265) the Court did not consider that it was required of the Commission to have should have made a risk assessment before pronouncing an export ban for British beef. (See, Kramer, *supra* n. 162, p. 22). Contrary to this, Jans considers that protective measures could be adopted on the condition that a risk assessment is conducted that would be as complete as the peculiarities of the case in question allow it to be (Jans, *supra* n. 155, p. 39).

256 Commission Communication, p. 9.

257 The use of the precautionary and the prevention principles has been extended to other fields such as health protection and food safety (De Sadeleer, *supra* n. 244, p. 184).

258 *Artegodan and others v Commission (T-74/00, T-76/00, T-83/00, T-84/00, T-85/00, T-132/00, T-137/00 and T-141/00), ECR 2002 p. II-4945.*

259 Para. 183 of judgment.

objective by relying on the use of the *integration principle*[260] of the Union's environmental policy.[261]

A certain pattern can be discerned in the Union courts' treatment of the application of the precautionary principle depending on whether the case at hand is health/food safety-related or environment protection-related.[262] The former is an area where scientific knowledge is much more advanced than the strictly environmental protection sector where the existence of scientific uncertainty is greater given the growing difficulty in foreseeing the ways in which ecosystems would potentially react to various ecological risks.[263] In consequence, the Union courts have acquired a stricter approach when examining the application of the principle with respect to the health and food safety cases than the environmental protection cases.[264]

As a sublimation of the foregoing, it is clear that the dividing line between precaution and prevention is very thin and often times not as evident,[265] the crucial characteristic differentiating the two principles lying in the (in)existence of a *causal link* i.e. sufficient scientific evidence that links the behavior or the existence of a threat with the subsequent potentially dangerous effect.[266]

---

260 For more on the integration principle and how it can be used to extend the application of the prevention and the precautionary principles to the Euratom framework, see, *infra* in the present chapter.

261 The General Court's activism exhibited in this particular judgment did not stop there as it courageously went on to award the precautionary principle the status of *general principle of Union law*, defining the principle as one requiring the competent authorities to take appropriate measures to prevent potential risks to *public health, safety and the environment* (Para. 184 of judgment). The EU Court of Justice however did not come back to these points when reviewing the case on appeal in *Commission v Artegodan and others* (*C-39/03 P, ECR 2003 p. I-7885*). In the second *Artegodan* judgment (*Artegodan II Judgment of 3 March 2010, Artegodan/Commission* (*T-429/05*), *on appeal C-221/10*), the General Court was noticeably more reserved regarding the legal status of the precautionary principle, considering the former as merely a 'corollary' to the principle of pre-eminence (primacy) of public health protection which itself was qualified as a 'general principle' (Paras. 106 and 125 of judgment).

262 De Sadeleer, *supra* n. 244, p. 194.

263 *Idem.*

264 *Idem.*

265 Similarly, Kramer, *supra* n. 157, p. 17.

266 According to Fitzmaurice, it would seem erroneous to view the two principles as having the same features in the legal and economic content they are applied to (Fitzmaurice, *supra* n. 63, p. 275); The issue of applying the precautionary principle was raised before the ICJ in *Gabickovo-Nagymaros* and *Nuclear Tests II*, where the dissenting opinions expressed by the judges in the latter case have been valuable to the legal discourse on the precautionary principle (see for this, Fitzmaurice, *supra* n. 63, pp. 266,267). Moreover,

The former has been confirmed by the EU Court of Justice in C-180/96 *BSE*[267] where the Court, intentionally or not, practically equated the scope of application of the two principles, by referring to the *uncertainty* of the existence of harmful effects (which would typically lead to the application of the precautionary principle) in the context of the application of the principle of preventive action.[268] According to the Court, the uncertainty as to the existence or extent of risks to human health opens way for the institutions to take protective measures without having to wait until the reality and seriousness of those risks become fully apparent.[269] The Court supported this approach by invoking Art.191(1) TFEU (ex-Art.30r(1) EC), pursuant to which the Union policy on the environment is to follow, *inter alia*, the objective of protecting human health[270] as well as Art.191(1) TFEU which foresees that the environmental policy is to be based, among other, on the principle that *preventive action* should be taken, in addition to the obligation to integrate the environmental protection requirements into the definition and implementation of other Community policies.[271] This is an example of how an environmental policy principle (in this instance, the prevention principle) can be applied with relation to human health protection by way of liaison performed via the *integration principle* (principle which requires that environment protection requirements are integrated into the definition and implementation of the Union's policies). In this way, the integration principle has been commonly used as a tool to justify the 'exportation' of Union environmental principles to fields other than environmental protection, and even (as will be shown *infra*) fields and activities that do not necessarily belong to the Union framework *stricto sensu*.

b *The Precautionary and the Prevention Principles Examined under the Euratom Framework*

The previous sections of the present chapter dealt with the interface between the Union environmental policy and the Euratom health and safety policy and

---

Sand distinguishes among those European states that are 'precaution' countries (such as Germany, the Netherlands, Sweden) and those that are 'protection' countries (France, the UK) (see, P. Sand, The Precautionary Principle: Coping with Risk, *Indian Journal of International Law*, January-March 2000, No. 1, pp. 1–13).

267 OJ 1998 ECR I-2265.

268 See on this, Kramer, *supra* n. 162, p. 22; Kramer observes that the English version of the text of para. 100 of CJEU's *BSE* judgment only mentions *prevention* while the German and other versions mention both *prevention* and *precaution*.

269 Para. 99.

270 Para. 100.

271 Para. 100.

the possibility to apply the Union environmental provisions to the Euratom domain. In this vein, it is pertinent to inquire into the possibility of *integrating* the principles of the Union environmental policy into the Euratom-devised policies, more particularly, Euratom's health and safety policy. The discussion will focus on the principle of prevention and the precautionary principles where, in view of the confirmed possibility for Union environmental provisions to apply to the Euratom domain, by implication, the principles underlying these environmental provisions would equally be presumed to apply.

Curiously enough, at this point there are no international nuclear law instruments in existence which provide a direct reference to the precautionary principle.[272] International courts have thus far equally shied away from taking a view on whether the precautionary principle applies to risks stemming from the use of nuclear energy. The application of the principle was unsuccessfully invoked by states before international and regional judicial bodies on several occasions (e.g., New Zealand relied on the principle in the *Nuclear Tests II* case; Ireland raised the relevance of the principle before the UNCLOS Arbitral Tribunal in the proceedings against the UK concerning the MOX nuclear plant; the ECtHR equally failed to address the issue of 'precaution' in the *McGinley* and *LCB* since as it failed to see a sufficient causal relationship between the action/inaction of the national authorities and the potential/actual damage).[273]

All the while, the 'preventive' character of certain international nuclear law instruments cannot be denied, as the objectives they convey are often underpinned by the notion of prevention of potentially harmful effects. The *Convention on Nuclear Safety*, aims, among other, to *prevent* the occurrence of accidents with radiological consequences and mitigate the effects of such consequences (Art.1(iii)); while the *Convention on Assistance in the case of a Nuclear Accident or Radiological Emergency* refers to *preventing* or minimising injury and/or damage which may result from a nuclear accident or radiological emergency (Art.1). Similarly, the Preamble of the *Convention on Early*

272 De Sadeleer, *supra* n. 244, p. 192.

273 For a more extensive elaboration on the missed opportunities for applying the precautionary principle in the nuclear field, see, De Sadeleer, *supra*, p. 193; Furthermore, the application of the precautionary principle to the nuclear field has been examined in the context of its relationship with the ALARA principle (the principle according to which radiation doses should be kept 'as low as reasonably achievable') where the former has been regarded as a risk assessment tool whereas the latter as a principle of risk management (see, Lierman, S. and Veuchelen, L., The Optimisation Approach of ALARA in Nuclear Practice: An Early Application of the Precautionary Principle? Scientific Uncertainty versus Legal Uncertainty and its Role in Tort Law, *European Environmental Law Review*, 2006, Vol. 15 Issue 4, p. 8 et seq.).

Notification of a Nuclear Accident ascribes to *preventing* nuclear accidents and minimising the consequences of any such accident, should they occur; the *Joint Convention for the management of spent fuel* targets the *prevention* of accidents with radiological consequences and the mitigation of their consequences should they occur during any stage of spent fuel or radioactive waste management (Art.1(iii)); while *the Convention on the Physical Protection of Nuclear Material and Nuclear Facilities* speaks of necessary *precautions* regarding the levels of physical protection for nuclear material during international transport.[274] The latter use of the term 'precaution' is not linked to the precautionary principle as defined *supra*, the aim and content of the text suggest the term 'precaution' used here serves as synonym for 'prevention'.

In spite of the lack of an express reference in the text of the Euratom Treaty endorsing the application of the principle of prevention and/or the precautionary principle,[275] what can be inferred from the character and aim of the health and safety provisions of the Treaty is that the health protection (and to a certain extent, the environmental protection) objective these provisions carry is effectively underpinned by the concept of *prevention*. Thus, the principle of prevention can arguably be presumed to be, at the very least, impliedly written into the Euratom Treaty. It is doubtful, however, whether the same applies to the precautionary principle in view of the relatively recent coinage

274 "Annex I

(...) 2. Levels of physical protection for nuclear material during international transport include:

(a) For Category II and III materials, transportation shall take place under special precautions including prior arrangements among sender, receiver, and carrier, and prior agreement between natural or legal persons subject to the jurisdiction and regulation of exporting and importing States, specifying time, place and procedures for transferring transport responsibility;

(b) For Category I materials, transportation shall take place under special precautions identified above for transportation of Category II and III materials, and in addition, under constant surveillance by escorts and under conditions which assure close communication with appropriate response forces (...)".

275 Alternatively, it may be argued that the precautionary principle fails to apply with regard to the field of the Euratom and thus with regard to nuclear radiation altogether given that the dangers arising from nuclear radiation are *a priori* presumed. However, the former claim would be difficult to substantiate with regard to all applications of nuclear energy, especially, provided the requirements of nuclear health and safety as well as nuclear security (the security of nuclear installations) have been satisfied. In this respect, what would be the most pertinent approach to follow is that a scientific assessment of the entirety of related risks is conducted on a case-by-case basis.

of the principle in international legal instruments and especially since the Euratom Treaty has not undergone, since its adoption, any substantial changes to its text. The former, as is the case with most of the 'old' texts of a constitutional nature, enables that a dynamic interpretation of the Euratom Treaty's provisions is permitted in this respect.

The Euratom secondary legislation has translated the implied 'prevention' requirement in the following way: the 2009 *Directive establishing a Community framework for the nuclear safety of nuclear installations*[276] defines "nuclear safety" as the achievement of proper operating conditions, *prevention* of accidents and mitigation of accident consequences, resulting in protection of workers and the general public from dangers arising from ionizing radiations from nuclear installations;[277] the wording used throughout *Directive 2013/59/Euratom laying down basic safety standards for protection against the dangers arising from exposure to ionizing radiation*[278] indicates that the concept of *prevention* underpins the overall objectives of this Directive; the aim of *prevention* of potential pollution and nuisances also underpins *Directive 2003/4/EC of the European Parliament and of the Council of 28 January 2003 on public access to environmental information* (extended to the Euratom domain). Finally, Directive 2003/122/Euratom *on the control of high-activity sealed radioactive sources and orphan sources* in Art.1(1) identifies the *prevention* from exposure to ionizing radiation of workers and the general public as one of its objectives.

Judging by the way in which the aforementioned Euratom measures have been phrased with regard to the concepts of 'prevention' and 'precaution', it cannot be definitively concluded whether the intention of the Union legislators had been to introduce these principles 'through the back door' to the Euratom domain, in the absence of an express legal basis in the Euratom Treaty or the Union Treaties warranting an extension of the Union environmental

276 *Directive 2009/71/Euratom establishing a Community framework for the nuclear safety of nuclear installations* OJ L 172/18; The former has been amended by *Council Directive 2014/87/Euratom amending Directive 2009/71/Euratom establishing a Community framework for the nuclear safety of nuclear installations*, OJ L 219/42.

277 Art.3.

278 *Directive 2013/59/Euratom of 5 December 2013 laying down basic safety standards for protection against the dangers arising from exposure to ionizing radiation and repealing Directives 89/618/Euratom, 90/641/Euratom, 96/29/Euratom, 97/43/Euratom and 2003/122/Euratom* OJ L 13pp. 1–73; The former directive is largely based on the text of the former 1996 Basic Safety Standards Directive (*Directive 96/29*/Euratom *laying down basic safety standards for the protection of the health of workers and the general public against the dangers arising from ionizing* radiation, OJ L 159, pp. 1–114).

policy principles. The answer possibly lies in examining the boundaries of the scope of application of the integration principle enshrined in Art.11 TFEU, more specifically, by predicating the option for extending the prevention and the precautionary principles to the Euratom framework upon the possibility for extending the scope of the integration principle to the said framework.

The integration principle, enshrined in Art.11 TFEU, is a typically horizontal principle which is primarily directed at the Union institutions, concerning the definition and implementation of the Union's policies and activities. Under the former article, "[e]nvironmental protection requirements *must be integrated into the definition and implementation* of the Union's policies and activities, in particular with a view to promoting sustainable development".[279] Unlike its previous versions,[280] the current Art.11 TFEU avoids a *numeris clausus* approach of enumerating the Union policies and activities that the integration principle is to apply to, and instead, makes a general reference to *all* Union policies.

On the point of what the integration requirement functionally entails, it has been argued that the practical implications of the principle are only visible at the level of elaboration of Union *policies* while with respect to individual measures the approach is not as straightforward being that in the latter instance the Union institutions enjoy a greater discretion in the implementation of the integration requirement.[281] In comparison, the 1987 version of the integration principle introduced via the Single European Act creates a greater 'obligatory'

---

279 Emphasis added.

280 Prior to being officially inaugurated in Art.130-r (2.2) of the Single European Act (1987) (in the following terms: "Environment protection requirements *shall be a component* of the Community's other policies".), the integration principle had already been part of the Union's Environmental Action Programmes (in its rudimentary version,it was initially inserted in the 1973 First Commission Environmental Action Programme (*Programme of action of the EC on the environment* OJ 1973 C 112 p. 1) with a reference to the activities of the Communities that *must take into account* concerns related to the protection and improvement of the environment where those concerns need to be *taken into consideration* in the elaboration and implementation of these policies (Kramer, *supra* n. 240, p. 33)). A similar reference was found in the Second, Third and Fourth Action Programme (Kramer, *idem*, pp. 34, 35);

The Maastricht Treaty version of the integration principle read: "Environment protection requirements *must be integrated* into the definition and implementation of other Community policies" while the Amsterdam Treaty subsequently introduced a new Art.6 TEC according to which: "Environment protection requirements *must be integrated into* the definition and implementation of the Community policies and activities referred to in Art.3 [TEC] (...)".

281 Kramer, *supra* n. 157, pp. 1–26.

effect ("Environment protection requirements *shall be* a component (…)" (Art.130-r)) rather than the principle's present version which centers on the *necessity* to integrate environment protection requirements into the Union's policies and activities. The former casts doubt as to the legal consequences produced by Art.11 TFEU provided that compliance with the integration requirement depends largely on the political will of the institutions making it highly unlikely for the principle to be judicially reviewable on its own before the Union courts.[282] By contrast, there have been views that, regarding the possibility for reviewing the validity of secondary legislation in the light of the integration principle, consider the present version of the integration principle to be formulated 'more forcefully' than that of the Single European Act,[283] thus opening the possibility for judicial review of measures in the light of the environmental principles (including the integration principle).[284] However, irrespective of whether an act can in exceptional cases be open to annulment on grounds of non-compliance with the Union's environmental objectives, the obligation to interpret secondary European legislation in the light of the Union's environmental objectives still remains.[285]

Furthermore, another clarification is to be made with regard to defining the exact content of the integration requirement i.e. *what* effectively needs to be integrated. The conundrum of environmental requirements that need to be integrated include, primarily, the Art.191 TFEU environmental principles[286] which adds credit to the assumption that predicating the application of the Art.191 TFEU principles upon the application of the integration principle would instrumentalize the transposition of the former principles to the Euratom domain. However, the Euratom policies and activities *per se* have not been included under Art.11 TFEU[287] and cannot be fitted within the scope of the term 'Union policies and activities' (the Euratom Community having remained a separate legal personality from that of the Union). *A fortiori*, Art.11 TFEU does not figure among the Euratom Treaty's bridging provisions that

---

282 *Idem.*

283 Jans and Vedder, *supra* n. 155, p. 17.

284 Even though the integration principle figures in treaty article separate from that of the Union environmental principles, it is nonetheless treated as a Union environmental principle (See the tables of contents of both, Jans and Vedder, *supra* and Kramer (2003), *supra*).

285 Jans and Vedder, *supra* n. 155, p. 5.

286 *Idem*, p. 15.

287 See, N. Dhondt, *Integration of Envrionmental Protection into Other EC Policies*, Europa law Publishing, 2003, p. 43.

concern the extension of the application of certain TFEU and TEU provisions to the Euratom domain (Title III, Art.106a of the Euratom Treaty). The former is indicative of a lack of a clear intention on the part of the treaty makers to broaden the purview of the integration principle to policies and activities covered under the Euratom Treaty,[288] while the reasons for such exclusion remain obscure.[289]

The foregoing claims are made with regard to an explicit extension of the integration principle to the Euratom field. In this sense, the shortcoming of adopting a purely legalist and formalistic approach on the matter ostensibly undermines the potential for applying the Art.191 TFEU environmental principles to the Euratom sphere, and more particularly, the prevention and the precautionary principles, being that the concepts of prevention and precaution are concepts which are inherently and indissociably attached to the field of nuclear health and safety.

288 *Idem*, p. 44.

289 *Idem*, p. 47; A comparison with the principles of subsidiarity and proportionality as horizontal principles of Union action seems pertinent in this regard. The two principles have been stipulated in Art.5 TFEU and while they have not been formally extended to the Euratom domain (through Art.106a Euratom), the *Protocol on the role of national parliaments in the European Union* which, annexed to the TEU, TFEU and the Euratom Treaty, establishes the option for national parliaments to appraise legislative acts in the light of the principle of subsidiarity (Art.3). The former protocol is complemented by the *Protocol on the application of the principles of subsidiarity and proportionality* which, in turn, has solely been annexed to the TEU and the TFEU. In spite of the evident mismatch of applicable instruments, the former is evidence of yet another *implied* extension of Union principles to the Euratom domain given that the subsidiarity and proportionality principles are *presumed* to apply thereto.

CHAPTER 3

Euratom and 'Environmental Democracy': EU Citizens' Access to Information and Participation in Decision-making in the Nuclear Arena

Having established the link between the Euratom health and safety regime and the Union environmental policy, and, in this sense, more generally, Euratom's relationship with environmental protection as a concept, the present chapter proceeds with a discussion on the issue of environmental transparency within the Euratom framework, focusing on the options available to EU citizens regarding access to information and involvement in the decision-making in the nuclear field in matters which actually or potentially concern the environment. In this sense, the level of 'environmental democracy' under the Euratom framework will be appraised in light of the procedural standards for 'environmental democracy' fostered under the 1998 Aarhus Convention on Access to Information, Public Participation in Decision-making and Access to Justice in Environmental Matters as the ruling international legal document in the field of environmental democracy. The analysis aims to verify whether the Euratom Community has aligned with the prevalent tendency within the Union of increasing the Union's openness and transparency towards its citizens and, thus, whether the 'environmental democracy' standards applicable to the Union framework have found an adequate expression within the scope of Euratom.

The chapter examines the procedural requirements set out under the Aarhus Convention which the EU and the Member States are bound by and thus responsible to ensure the full and correct implementation of, both at the EU and the national level. For the purpose of arriving at an uniform application of the Aarhus Convention requirements both at the EU and the national level, the EU has adopted a series of transposing instruments in the form of directives and regulations, part of which are specific to the nuclear domain. The former instruments are looked at in function to the extent to which the relevant Aarhus Convention obligations extend to the scope of Euratom thus ascertaining the extent to which Euratom is to be considered bound by these obligations. The discussion proceeds by inquiring into the justiciability of the Aarhus Convention requirements relative to access to information and participation in decision-making both before the international and the Union courts by offering a comparative analysis of the relevant case law which is indicative of the general judicial tendencies in the interpretation and application of the

 | DOI 10.1163/9789004310414_005

former requirements, with a particular focus on the case law pertaining to the nuclear field.

Lastly, the chapter addresses one of the key shortcomings of the Union regime for the procedural protection in environmental matters and that is the absence of a directive transposing the access-to-justice requirements of the Aarhus Convention, namely the justiciability of the Convention obligations pertaining to the access to information and the participation in the decision-making process. The adoption of an access-to-justice directive would not only consolidate and reinforce the Union standards for procedural protection in environmental matters, it would also gradually help eliminate the existent discrepancies in the national legal systems regarding the application of the Aarhus Convention requirements regarding access to justice in the former field.

1 The EU, Euratom and the Concept of 'Environmental Democracy'

The United Nations Economic Commission for Europe (UNECE) *Convention on Access to Information, Public Participation in Decision-making and Access to Justice in Environmental Matters* of 1998 (the Aarhus Convention) is arguably the most prominent international legal instrument of environmental democracy[1] which represents a successful attempt of linking together two different sets of rights: human rights and environmental rights.[2] The adoption of the Convention constitutes a crucial step forward in the nascent field of 'information governance' in environmental matters understood as the kind of governance where information, information technologies and information processes play a central role.[3]

The notion of 'environmental democracy' signifies the balance between representative and participatory decision-making, reflecting the will of those with an essential stake in the outcome and bringing environmental values into the policy-making process.[4] The notion can be further described as the achievement of a satisfactory level of transparent, inclusive and accountable decision-making

1 See, J. Wates, The Aarhus Convention: A Driving Force for Environmental Democracy, *Journal of European Environmental and Planning Law*, 2005, Issue 1, p.2.

2 See, L. Lavrysen, The Aarhus Convention: Between Environmental Protection and Human Rights, in, *Liège, Strasbourg, Bruxelles: parcours des droits de l'homme. Liber amicorium Michel Melchior*, 2010, Anthemis, p. 653. The article provides a general overview of and explanatory commentary on the Aarhus Convention.

3 Mason, M. Mason, Information Disclosure and Environmental Rights: the Aarhus Convention, *Global Environmental Politics* August 2010 Vol. 10 Issue 3, p. 13.

4 J. Foti et al., *Voice and Choice: Opening the Door to Environmental Democracy*, 2008, World Resources Institute (available at http://pdf.wri.org/voice_and_choice.pdf), p. 4.

processes galvanised through the provision of access to information, public participation and access to justice.[5] Furthermore, it would be a grave oversight to omit the notion of environmental justice from the discourse involving environmental democracy. Much like environmental democracy, 'environmental justice' is a term that is both delicate and complex and does not yield to a simplified definition. 'Environmental justice' is frequently referred to as the fair treatment and meaningful involvement of the public in the development, implementation, and enforcement of environmental laws, regulations, and policies whereby everyone is entitled to the same degree of protection from environmental and health hazards and afforded equal access to the decision-making process concerning a healthy environment in which to live, learn, and work.[6] In international environmental law terms, it encompasses the *rational sharing of the burdens and costs of environmental protection, discharged through the procedural and substantive adjustment of rights and duties*.[7] Construed in more basic terms, the environmental justice frame consists of four major components: the right to obtain information about one's situation; the right to a serious hearing when contamination claims are raised; the right to compensation from those who have polluted a certain environment; and the right of democratic participation in deciding the future of the 'contaminated community'.[8]

Prior to discussing the nature and the scope of the rights covered under the Aarhus Convention, it is to be reminded that the legal doctrine is not unanimous as to the issue of whether human rights and environmental rights are different sets of rights which are complementary and thus intrinsically related, or, are, to the contrary, essentially irreconcilable.[9] The former division notwithstanding, the Aarhus Convention establishes a link between procedural

---

5 *Idem*, p. X.

6 This is the way the US Environmental Agency defines environmental democracy http://www.epa.gov/environmentaljustice/; For this and more on the notion of environmental justice in the context of the EU, see, L. Kramer, Environmental Justice in the European Court of Justice, in J. Ebbeson and P. Okowa (eds.), *Environmetal law and justice in context*, 2009, Cambridge University Press, p. 197 et seq.

7 D. Shelton, Describing the Elephant: International Justice and Environmental Law, in J. Ebbeson and P. Okowa (eds.), *Environmetal law and justice in context*, 2009, Cambridge University Press, p. 72.

8 S.M. Capek, The 'Environmental Justice' Frame: a Conceptual Discussion and an Application, *Social Problems*, 1993 Issue 40, pp. 5–24; The former definition only takes into account the contamination occurring *ex post* (rather than *ex ante*) and disregards the equally important 'prevention' aspect of the notion of environmental justice.

9 D. Shelton, Resolving Conflicts between Human Rights and Environmental Protection: Is there a Hierarchy?, in, E. de Wet and J. Vidmar (eds.), *Hierarchy in International law*, 2012,

rights and the right to a healthy environment and attempts to address the most common difficulty associated to the human right to clean environment which is that of lack of effective implementation,[10] without intending to introduce a substantive right to a clean environment and thus being strictly concerned with the procedural aspects of the realization of this right. The procedural aspect to the right to a clean environment, covered by the Aarhus Convention, is considered instrumental to the attainment of the goal of '(...) *protection of the right of every person of present and future generations to live in an environment adequate to his or her health and well-being,* [whereby] each Party shall guarantee the rights of access to information, public participation in decision-making, and access to justice in environmental matters in accordance with the provisions of [the] Convention'.[11] Effectively, the procedural rights established there under carry the objective of maintaining an adequate and decent environment for people and serve to reinforce the substantive aspect of the right to clean and healthy environment.[12] In a certain way, the rights espoused by the Aarhus Convention act as a cross-section between procedural entitlements and substantive environmental quality requirements[13] in which regard the Convention builds up from the foundations previously laid down by the 1972

Oxford University Press, p. 207; The article offers further insight into the conflicts and convergences between human rights and environment rights.

10 United Nations Economic Commission for Europe (UN ECE), *The Aarhus Convention: An Implementation Guide*, ECE/CEP/72 (prepared by S. Stec and S. Casey- Lefkowitz in collaboration with J. Jendroska (Editorial Adviser)), December 2000 (available at http://www.unece.org/fileadmin/DAM/env/pp/acig.pdf), p. 29.

The Guide is not a legally binding document, it is reference document of a great interpretative value intended to assist Signatories and potential Parties to the Aarhus Convention in implementing the Convention, and in understanding its implications in order facilitate its ratification and entry into force (p. ix of the Guide).

11 Art.1 of the Aarhus Convention (Emphasis added). The Convention espouses a clear anthropo-centric approach to the right to clean environment as it deals with the concept of environment only to the extent that the former concerns the human beings.

12 O.W. Pedersen, European Environmental Human Rights and Environmental Rights: A Long Time Coming?, *Georgetown International Environmental Law Review*, 2008, Vol. 21 No. 1, p. 35.

13 Mason, *supra* n. 3, p. 17; Mason holds that the absence of substantive environmental standards in the Convention poses a certain restriction on the enjoyment of human rights since it allows that information disclosure and public participation become more of a means to legitimize rather than scrutinize the national institutions (p. 26).

Stockholm Declaration and the 1992 Rio Declaration[14] as international environmental soft law instruments that have majorly contributed to developing and reinforcing the right of humans to a clean and decent environment adequate to their needs. The Principle 10 of the Rio Declaration[15] represents the milestone for the development of procedural rights in an environmental context, endorsing the three key aspects of environmental democracy which were subsequently elevated to the level of procedural rights under the Aarhus Convention – the access to information, the public participation, and the access to justice.[16]

The Aarhus Convention was adopted at the United Nations Economic Commission for Europe's Fourth Ministerial Conference 'Environment for Europe' in Aarhus, Denmark, on 25 June 1998, presently comprising 46 State Parties, 29 Parties to the Convention *Protocol on Pollutant Release and Transfer Registers* (PRTRS) and 27 Parties to the *Amendment on public participation in decisions on the deliberate release into the environment and placing on the market of genetically modified organisms* (GMOS).[17] Both the EU and all of the Member States[18] have acceded to the Aarhus Convention; the EU ratified the

14 *Principle 1 of the Rio Declaration*: 'Human beings are at the centre of concerns for sustainable development. They are entitled to a healthy and productive life in harmony with nature (…)';

Principle 1 o of the Stockholm Declaration:' Man has the fundamental right to freedom, equality and adequate conditions of life, in an environment of a quality that permits a life of dignity and well-being, and he bears a solemn responsibility to protect and improve the environment for present and future generations. In this respect, policies promoting or perpetuating apartheid, racial segregation, discrimination, colonial and other forms of oppression and foreign domination stand condemned and must be eliminated'.

15 *Principle 1 of the Rio Declaration*: '(…) Environmental issues are best handled with participation of all concerned citizens, at the relevant level. At the national level, each individual shall have appropriate access to information concerning the environment that is held by public authorities, including information on hazardous materials and activities in their communities, and the opportunity to participate in decision-making processes. States shall facilitate and encourage public awareness and participation by making information widely available. Effective access to judicial and administrative proceedings, including redress and remedy, shall be provided'.

16 *The Aarhus Convention: An Implementation Guide*, p. 13.

17 For an overview of the parties to the Convention, consult the following UNECE webpage: http://www.unece.org/env/pp/ratification.html.

18 Ireland was the last one to ratify the Convention as late as in June 2012. (http://treaties.un.org/Pages/ViewDetails.aspx?src=TREATY&mtdsg_no=XXVII-13&chapter=27&lang=en); Ireland officials have been sketchy in revealing the factors that accounted for the late ratification http://www.environ.ie/en/Environment/News/MainBody,30480,en.htm.

Convention in 2005 via the adoption of Council Decision 2005/370/EC[19] and the Convention is applicable in the EU as of 18 May 2005, with a large majority of Member States having already acceded by that time. Given that the material scope of the Aarhus Convention covers important segments of the nuclear field,[20] the Euratom Community, nevertheless, does not appear as contracting party to the Aarhus Convention.

The *Declaration of competence* annexed to the Council Decision 2005/370/EC on EU's conclusion of the Aarhus Convention confirms the external competence of the EU to enter into environmental agreements, indicating the areas in the field of environmental protection with regard to which the Union is competent to enter into international agreements: preserving, protecting and improving the quality of the environment; protecting human health; prudent and rational utilization of natural resources and promoting measures at international level to deal with regional or worldwide environmental problems.[21] The former, thus, coincides with the scope of the objectives of the Union's environmental policy listed in Art.191(1) TFEU. Additionally, the Union remarks that it has already adopted several legal instruments, binding on its Member States, which implement the provisions of the Aarhus Convention. The fairly laconic manner in which the Union's scope of competence in the matter covered by the Aarhus Convention has been delimited fails to offer any real guidance for third parties to be able to comprehend whether a particular provision of the Aarhus Convention is to be implemented by the EU or by the Member States.[22] From merely mentioning the Union's objectives in the environmental field (as is done in the Declaration of competence) it does not follow that the Union would own full competence over the scope of the Aarhus Convention.[23] Namely, environmental protection is a field of shared competence, where, by

---

19 Council Decision 2005/370/EC of 17 February 2005 on the conclusion, on behalf of the European Community, of the Convention on access to information, public participation in decision-making and access to justice in environmental matters OJ L 124, 17.5.2005, pp. 1–3.

20 The areas of the nuclear field covered by the Aarhus Convention are further discussed *infra* in the present section and the ensuing sections of the chapter.

21 See, the Annex to Council Decision 2005/370/EC, *Declaration by the European Community in accordance with Article 19 of the Convention on access to information, public participation in decision-making and access to justice in environmental matters.*

22 For this and a critique of the lack of clarity/precision of the declaration of competence with regard to the Aarhus Convention, see, A.D. Casteleiro, EU Declarations of Competence to Multilateral Agreements: A Useful Reference Base?, *European Foreign Affairs Review*, 2012, Vol. 17, No. 4, p. 501.

23 *Idem.*

virtue of Art.2(2) TFEU the Member States can exercise their competence only to the extent that the Union has not previously exercised its competence in the matter. In fact, the only indication for third parties to be able to discern the matters for which the Union is solely responsible is found in the statement that the European Union is to be considered responsible for the performance of those obligations resulting from the Convention which are covered by Union law in force.[24]

Within the EU legal order, the Aarhus Convention enjoys the status of a mixed international agreement binding on both the EU institutions and the Member States which in the hierarchical order of norms takes precedence over secondary legislation,[25] while at the same time it does not enjoy the status of primary law. Prior to EU's accession to the Aarhus Convention, two directives covering a large part of the subject matter of the Convention had already been in existence (Directive 90/313/EEC on the freedom of access to information on the environment[26] and Directive 85/337/EEC of 27 June 1985 on the assessment of the effects of certain public and private projects on the environment[27]). Therefore, EU's conclusion of the Aarhus Convention was, in a certain way, seen as a transposition of already existing EU legal rules into an international legal instrument.[28] Nevertheless, in order to match the improved level of procedural protection under the regime of the Convention, it was necessary to amend or replace the existent EU rules. Thus, in anticipation of EU's conclusion of the Aarhus Convention,[29] two new directives were adopted in 2003 aligning the existent Union legislation with the access-to-information and the participation-in-decision-making requirements of the Convention: *Directive 2003/4/EC of the European Parliament and of the Council of 28 January 2003 on*

---

24 *Idem.*

25 Compliance Committee, ACCC/C/17 (European Community), para. 35.

26 Council Directive 90/313/EEC on the freedom of access to information on the environment OJ L 158, 23.6.1990, p. 56.

27 Council Directive 85/337/EEC of 27 June 1985 on the assessment of the effects of certain public and private projects on the environment *OJ L 175, 5.7.1985, pp. 40–48.*

28 J. Jendroska, Public Information and Participation in EC Environmental Law: Origins, Milestones and Trends, in R. Macrory (ed.), *Reflections on 30 Years of European Environmental Law: A High Level of Protection*, The Avosetta Series: Proceedings of the Avosetta Group of European Environmental Lawyers, 2006, Europa Law Publishing, Part IV.2.

29 Both the Union (then, Community) and the Member States signed the Convention in 1998, whereas the ratification occurred at different dates/years for different MS (See, http://treaties.un.org/Pages/ViewDetails.aspx?src=TREATY&mtdsg_no=XXVII-13&chapter=27&lang=en).

public access to environmental information and repealing Council Directive 90/313/EEC[30] and *Directive 2003/35/EC of the European Parliament and of the Council of 26 May 2003 providing for public participation in respect of the drawing up of certain plans and programmes relating to the environment and amending with regard to public participation and access to justice Council Directives 85/337/EEC and 96/61/EC.*[31] However, the initial 'package deal' proposed by the Commission in October 2003 contained three legislative proposals: proposal for a regulation on the application of the Aarhus obligations with relation to the Union institutions,[32] proposal for a directive implementing the requirements under the Convention 'access to justice' pillar,[33] and a proposal for a Council decision for the ratification of the Convention.[34] Hence, it was only the first and the third proposal of the package deal that were successful, while the second proposal fell through, the reasons for which will be further elaborated in the last section of this chapter which concerns the 'access to justice' pillar of the Aarhus Convention.

In view of the foregoing, the process of transposing the Aarhus Convention's provisions into the domestic legal orders of the Member States can be characterized as a two-fold legal harmonization process, occurring at two levels: harmonization occurring at the *EU level* (the EU transposes the Aarhus obligations into EU law by adopting implementing legislation), followed by harmonization

30 OJ L 41, 14.2.2003, pp. 26–32.

31 OJ L 156, 25.6.2003, pp. 17–25 (referred to as the Public Participation Directive).

Provisions on public participation in environmental matters can also be found in *Directive 2001/42/EC of 27 June 2001 on the assessment of certain plans and programmes on the environment* (OJ L 197, 21.7.2001, pp. 30–37), also known as the Strategic Environmental Assessment directive. The former directive complements the Council Directive 85/337/EEC of 27 June 1985 on the assessment of the effects of certain public and private projects on the environment (OJ L 175, 5.7.1985, pp. 40–48) (known as the Environmental Impact Assessment Directive). The codified version of the EIA directive is Directive *2011/92/EU of 13 December* 2011 on the assessment of the effects of certain public and private projects on the environment (codification), *OJ L 26 p. 1–21.*

32 Subsequently adopted as *Regulation (EC) N° 1367/2006 of the European Parliament and of the Council on the application of the provisions of the Aarhus Convention on Access to Information, Public Participation in Decision-making and Access to Justice in Environmental Matters to Community institutions and bodies* (OJ L 264, 25.9.2006 p. 13).

33 Proposal for a Directive of the European Parliament and of the Council on access to justice in environmental matters, COM (2003) 624 final.

34 Subsequently adopted by the Council on 17 February 2005 as *Council Decision of 17 February 2005 on the conclusion, on behalf of the European Community, of the Convention on access to information, public participation in decision-making and access to justice in environmental matters,* OJ L 124, 17.5.2005, pp. 1–3.

at the *national level* (Member States transposing EU implementing legislation into national law). As can be inferred from the *Declaration of competence* annexed to the Council Decision regarding EU's conclusion of the Aarhus Convention, there still remain areas covered by the Aarhus Convention which the EU has failed to transpose, leaving it open for Member States to legislate independently and directly transpose the Convention rules into national law, in the absence of Union implementing legislation. Although the former inevitably creates certain discrepancies between the national legal systems, such a phenomenon is intrinsic to the EU legal system and cannot be circumvented.[35]

Arriving at the issue of detecting the degree of 'environmental democracy' within the Euratom system, it is to be stated from the outset that on account of the intrinsic nature of the management of nuclear energy as a 'top-down' rather than 'bottom-up' venture, nuclear energy remains to be perceived as a domain which is predominantly *dirigiste*, carrying a strong confidentiality imprint. Nuclear policy-makers do not always enjoy a reputation of being in close touch with the demands of the public, especially in the earlier days of nuclear power when nuclear policy and law were more commonly associated

35 See on this, J. Jendroska, Citizen's Rights in European Environmental Law: Stock-Taking of Key Challenges and Current Developments in Relation to Public Access to Information, Participation and Access to Justice, *Journal of European Environmental and Planning Law*, 2012 Vol. 9 Issue 1, p.79.

In light of the foregoing, a definite answer cannot be offered as to whether *all* matters which are subject to the binding provisions of the Convention must also have a corresponding EU law provision to that effect (see, J. Jendroska, Public Participation in Environmental Decision-making, Interactions Between the Convention and EU Law and Other Key Legal Issues in its Implementation in the Light of the Opinions of the Aarhus Convention Compliance Committee, in, M. Pallemaerts (ed.), *The Aarhus Convention at Ten: Interactions and Tensions between Convenional International Law and EU Environmental Law*, 2011, Europa Law Publishing, p. 112).

Thus, in the absence of Union implementing measures for particular requirements of the Aarhus Convention, the Member States have the choice to either adopt national implementing legislation or resort to directly apply the Convention provisions (See, Jendroska, *supra* n. 35, p. 79). Peter Faross (ex-Head of Commission Department General for Transport and Energy) has indicated that in the absence of EU implementing legislation Member States have resorted to direct application of the Aarhus Convention requirements which in some cases has proven to be more stringent than application performed via the implementing directives (Proceedings of the European workshop on practical implementation of the Aarhus Convention in the nuclear field (24–25 June 2009, Luxembourg) organized by the Belgian Nuclear Research Center, http://www.sckcen.be/en/Events/AARHUS , p. 19).

with the military uses of nuclear energy. The area of civil uses of nuclear energy grew in salience subsequently in the 1950s, having been considered as an unexplored domain with an uncertain future. Although the roles between civil and military application today have been reversed, we are witnessing an 'era of civil nuclear energy' in which nuclear stakeholders continue to escape a full transparency grasp. With the global political and legal discourse being dominated by the green language of 'environmental democracy' and 'environmental justice', it becomes indispensable (if not, highly desirable) to apply the standards of environmental democracy to the nuclear realm and bring the citizens in closer touch with matters of nuclear safety through securing an effective access of the public to information and to reliable expertise on nuclear safety as a crucial condition for the involvement of civil society.[36]

The European Commission has insisted that information and public participation in the nuclear sector remain insufficiently developed in the EU, which demands a further elaboration of processes and vehicles that can enable a continuous integration of these procedural democratic rights both into the EU and the national contexts.[37] It has stressed that the public opinion and the public perception of nuclear power are paramount to the future of nuclear policy making it essential for the public to be provided access to reliable information and participation in a transparent decision-making process.[38] Moreover, the potential for the public acceptance of any project or activity associated with the nuclear industry increases in direct proportion to the extent to which the stakeholders have been involved in the initial appraisal of the justifiability thereof.[39] The Commission has further indicated that European citizens do

36 Summary of a Working paper circulated by the Association Nationale des Comités et Commissions Locales d'Information (ANCCLI). The Working paper was prepared in the framework of the conference on public participation in decision making in the nuclear domain (Luxembourg 12–13 March 2013), accessible at http://www.anccli.fr/Europe-International/ACN-Aarhus-Convention-Nuclear/European-round-tables-Tables-rondes-europeennes/Quatrieme-Table-Ronde-Europeenne-surete-nucleaire, p.2.

37 Summary of ANCCLI Working paper, *supra*, p. 2.

38 Communication from the Commission to the Council and the European Parliament: Nuclear Illustrative Programme (Presented under Article 40 of the Euratom Treaty for the opinion of the European Economic and Social Committee), COM(2006) 844 final, Brussels, 10.1.2007, p. 16.

39 S. Gadbois et al., Final Report: Situation concerning public information about and involvement in the decision-making processes in the nuclear sector, May 2007, commissioned by the Commission's DG TREN, Contract Number: TREN_04_NUCL_S07-39556, available at http://ec.europa.eu/energy/nuclear/doc/governance/2007_05_summary_en.pdf, p.14.

not feel appropriately and sufficiently informed about nuclear energy and radioactivity given the significant degree of misinformation and lack of knowledge where yet another problem persists to be the quality and reliability of the received information.[40] Overcoming the former is critical to the reinforcement of the existent European legal framework in the direction of enhancing the transparency of nuclear activities by requiring that factual, timely and easily understandable information is provided to the public.[41]

The European Parliament has also urged for transparency in the nuclear field. Namely, MEPs from different political groups recently launched a call to the European institutions and to the Member States for increasing the transparency of nuclear activities and the involvement of civil society in order to achieve and preserve a high level of nuclear safety in the EU in the aftermath of the Fukushima accident.[42] In this respect, the Parliament has failed to see the legitimacy in the assumption that Euratom issues are of such a technical nature that they can circumvent effective political oversight and public scrutiny, demanding that appropriate mechanisms of accountability to which the public can relate are put into place.[43]

Furthermore, the Council of Europe has, on its own part, taken an interest in matters of transparency in the nuclear sector. The Parliamentary Assembly of the Council of Europe has picked up on the seriousness and the crucial role

---

40 Gadbois, *supra*, p. 9; According to the Report, polls indicate that physicians, independent scientists and environmental groups are the most trusted groups (together with university and school teachers), while authorities and operators are the least trusted categories of actors.

41 Communication from the Commission to the European Parliament, the Council and the Economic and Social Committee: Update of the Nuclear Illustrative Programme in the context of the Second Strategic Energy Review, COM (2008) 776 final, Brussels 13.11.2008, p. 6.

42 European Parliament Call for a 'Nuclear Transparency Watch' issued on 4 December 2012 (available at http://www.anccli.fr/Europe-International/Nuclear-Transparency-Watch), p. 1. See also, Resolution of the European Parliament of 14 March 2013 on risk and safety assessments ('stress tests') of nuclear power plants in the European Union and related activities (2012/2830(RSP)) (available at http://www.europarl.europa.eu/sides/getDoc.do?type=TA&language=EN&reference=P7-TA-2013-89). In point 31 of the Resolution the Parliament appeals to the EU and the Member States, in the interests of democracy, involvement of the European Parliament, transparency and full public access to information, to treat nuclear power in the same manner as any other energy source under the TFEU.

43 European Parliament – Directorate-General for Research, Working paper: The European Parliament and the Euratom Treaty: past, present and future (*Energy and Research* Series) ENER 114 EN 2–2002 (accessible at http://www.uni-mannheim.de/edz/pdf/dg4/ENER114_EN.pdf), pp. xvi–xvii.

of exchange of information in matters of radiation protection. Namely, in a 1996 *Resolution on the consequences of the Chernobyl disaster,*[44] aimed at coping with the consequences of the nuclear disaster and motivated by the irreparable consequences brought on by the tragic Chernobyl incident, the Parliamentary Assembly underscored the importance of the public's access to clear and full information on the subject of preventing and coping with nuclear accidents and went as far as viewing the right to access to clear and full information as a basic human right.[45]

The relationship between the Aarhus Convention and the nuclear field is not in the least an issue sufficiently covered in the political or legal discourse – in fact, the forums where the issue has been covered are quite scarce.[46] In this sense, there have been certain misapprehensions as to whether the Euratom Community can be considered to be bound by the provisions of the Aarhus Convention, given that only the Union (at the time, Community) appears as a contracting party thereto. Nonetheless, the fact that the Convention provisions cover an important range of nuclear activities and given that all the parties to the Euratom Community Treaty are equally parties to the Aarhus Convention, implies that the Convention is indeed applicable to the Euratom domain.[47] Namely, the obligations that the Convention establishes with regard to access to environmental information (Arts.4 and 5) clearly extend to the nuclear field

44 Parliamentary Assembly Resolution 1087 (1996) on the consequences of the Chernobyl disaster, adopted on 26 April 1996 (available at: http://assembly.coe.int//Main.asp?link=http://assembly.coe.int/Documents/AdoptedText/ta96/eres1087.htm#1.).

45 Point 4 of the Resolution.

46 See, Proceedings of the European workshop on practical implementation of the Aarhus Convention in the nuclear field (24–25 June 2009, Luxembourg) http://www.sckcen.be/en/Events/AARHUS organized by the Belgian Nuclear Research Center; Proceedings of the Round table discussion 'Aarhus Convention and Nuclear: Joint Event on Public Participation in Decision-Making in the Nuclear Domain' (12–13 March 2013, Luxemburg, organised under the auspices of the Aarhus Convention's Task Force on Public Participation in Decision-making, the Directorate-General Energy of the European Commission and the Association Nationale des Comités et Commissions Locales d' Information (ANCCLI), available at http://www.anccli.fr/Europe-International/2013-ACN-Aarhus-Convention-Nuclear).

47 It has even been proposed that an attempt is made for the Euratom Community to accede to the Convention (See J. Haverkamp in, Proceedings of the European workshop on practical implementation of the Aarhus Convention in the nuclear field, *supra*, p. 31). *Contra* to this, a future accession of the Euratom Community to the Convention could conceivably achieve the opposite effect – that of undermining all environmental transparency efforts (political and legal) in the nuclear field that have been undertaken under the *Union* purview preceding such accession.

(thus, Euratom's purview) – the definition of environmental information provided therein comprises information on '[f]actors, such as substances, energy, noise and *radiation* (...) affecting or likely to affect the elements of the environment'.[48] Furthermore, Annex I of the Aarhus Convention enumerates the activities covered by the requirements regarding public participation in the decision-making process (Art.6.1(a)), among which the following are included:

> Annex I of the Aarhus Convention
> (...)1. Energy sector:
> (...)
> – Nuclear power stations and other nuclear reactors including the dismantling or decommissioning of such power stations or reactors 1/ (except research installations for the production and conversion of fissionable and fertile materials whose maximum power does not exceed 1 kW continuous thermal load);
> – Installations for the reprocessing of irradiated nuclear fuel;
> – Installations designed:
> – For the production or enrichment of nuclear fuel;
> – For the processing of irradiated nuclear fuel or high-level radioactive waste;
> – For the final disposal of irradiated nuclear fuel;
> – Solely for the final disposal of radioactive waste;
> – Solely for the storage (planned for more than 10 years) of irradiated nuclear fuels or radioactive waste in a different site than the production site;
> (...);

Nevertheless, it is vital to note that the Union has transposed the provisions of the Aarhus Convention relevant to nuclear activities through the use of *Union* instruments (directives and regulations) with legal bases found in the *'Union'* treaties, which however apply both to the Union and to the Euratom framework.[49] The former has been accomplished through the practice of extension (extrapolation) of Union rules to the Euratom domain which was deftly elaborated in Chapter 2.

48 Art.2(3)(b); Emphasis added.

49 These instruments and their relevance to the nuclear domain will be covered *infra*, in Sections III.1 and IV.4.

II The Aarhus Convention Pillars – Key Aspects

As indicated *supra*, the Aarhus Convention establishes three main groups of obligations for the State parties representing the three Convention 'pillars': *access to information, participation in decision-making* and *access to justice* by citizens. The 'access to information' and 'participation in decision making' pillars shall be covered in two separate sections of this chapter, in function to their relevance to the nuclear domain.

Before going into a more in-depth analysis of the Convention's provisions, several clarifications need to be made regarding the nature and scope of the procedural standards endorsed by the Convention. These procedural standards represent a *floor*, rather than a ceiling in the sense that Parties may introduce higher standards by granting wider access to information and participation in decision-making procedures, including wider access to courts to their citizens,[50] thus unhinging a process of so-called 'upward harmonization'.[51] The Convention inroduces rights for '*the public*' and '*the public concerned*'[52] where the definition of '*public*' follows the 'any person' principle according to which there are no pre-set conditions to be met by a particular member of the public in order for them to avail themselves of a particular right under the Convention (for ex., such as that of 'being affected' or 'having an interest').[53]

> Article 2 – Definitions
>
> (...)
>
> 4. 'The public' means one or more natural or legal persons, and, in accordance with national legislation or practice, their associations, organizations or groups. (...);
>
> 5. 'The public concerned' means the public affected or likely to be affected by, or having an interest in, the environmental decision-making; for the purposes of this definition, non-governmental organizations promoting environmental protection and meeting any requirements under national law shall be deemed to have an interest.(...);

---

50 United Nations Economic Commission for Europe (UN ECE), *The Aarhus Convention: An Implementation Guide*, ECE/CEP/72 (prepared by S. Stec and S. Casey- Lefkowitz in collaboration with J. Jendroska (Editorial Adviser)), December 2000 (available at http://www.unece.org/fileadmin/DAM/env/pp/acig.pdf), p. 5.

51 *Idem*, p. 31.

52 *Idem*, p. 5.

53 *Idem*, p. 39.

The term '*public concerned*', on the other hand, is less broad in scope and only covers the public which is affected or likely to be affected by environmental decision-making, *or,* the public having either a factual or legal interest therein.[54] Moreover, in keeping with the overall tenor of the Convention of promoting a more advantageous treatment to non-governmental organizations (NGOs),[55] those NGOs active in the field of environmental protection that satisfy the national law requirements are regarded as having an *a priori,* presumed interest under the Convention. However, while it has been argued that the Convention enhances the participatory rights of NGOs, it has failed to broaden participation outside of the NGO sphere to other interest groups belonging to the civil society by entitling them to a facilitated access to public participation under Arts.6, 7 and 8 thereof.[56] This point is especially valid being that certain NGOs could be reputed to solely cater to their own specific agendas and interests rather than the interests of the public.[57]

The obligations set out under the Convention are directed at the States' *public authorities*, to the exclusion of bodies and institutions that perform a judicial or legislative function.[58] This exception further extends to the executive branch authorities acting in a legislative or judicial capacity.[59] According to Art.2(2), for the purposes of the Convention, 'public authority' denotes:

> (…) (a)Government at national, regional and other level;
>
> (b)Natural or legal persons performing public administrative functions under national law, I ncluding specific duties, activities or services in relation to the environment;
>
> (c)Any other natural or legal persons having public responsibilities or functions, or providing public services, in relation to the environment, under the control of a body or person falling within subparagraphs (a) or (b) above;
>
> (d)The institutions of any regional economic integration organization referred to in Article 17 which is a Party to this Convention (…);

54 *Idem*, p.40.

55 *Idem*, p.39.

56 See, Pedersen, *supra* n. 12, p. 99; Similarly, see, Lee and Abbot, M. Lee and C. Abbot, The Usual Suspects? Public Participation Under the Aarhus Convention, *Modern Law Review*, 2003, Vol 66 Issue 1 2003, p. 108.

57 Lee and Abbot, *supra*, p. 86, 87.

58 Art.2 of the Conventon.

59 *The Aarhus Convention Implementation Guide*, p. 35.

The Convention is not applicable to the legislative process, but nonetheless, for the purpose of achieveing transparency in all branches of government, legislative bodies are *invited* to implement the principles of the Convention in their work.[60] Furthermore, the EU institutions are covered under the definition of 'public authority' of Art.2(2)(d) of the Convention[61] which, however, is not to be taken to mean that the Convention provisions apply solely to those EU organs enjoying the status of 'institutions'. Actually, the term 'institutions' used in the context of the application of the Convention is considered to encompass all the Union bodies and agencies.[62]

In addition, a strong non-discrimination *ratio* has been embedded in the Convention's legal regime where Art.3(9) stipulates that:

> Within the scope of the relevant provisions of this Convention, the public shall have access to information, have the possibility to participate in decision- making and have access to justice in environmental matters *without discrimination as to citizenship, nationality or domicile* and, in the case of a legal person, without *discrimination as to where it has its registered seat or an effective centre of its activities.*;[63]

The former non-discrimination clause provides that citizens and non-citizens of the States Parties alike enjoy equal rights under the Convention, irrespective of their citizenship, nationality or domicile. With respect to legal persons, any sort of discrimination based on their place of registration or their effective centre of activities is prohibited. The non-discrimination clause has served to delineate the scope of both the notions of '*public*' and '*public concerned*' of the Convention and thus safeguard the rights belonging to the persons who are not citizens of the States Parties, counteracting the tendency of public authorities to sometimes disregard the legitimate interests of non-citizens when applying the Convention principles.[64]

The language of the Convention is not always consistently prescriptive as to establish precise and unconditional obligations, thus leaving additional room

60 Para. 11 of the Preamble.

61 '(...) (d) The institutions of any regional economic integration organization referred to in Article 17 which is a Party to this Convention (...)'.

62 *The Aarhus Convention: An Implementation Guide*, p. 34. See also, Art.1 of *Regulation* (EC) *No 1367/2006 on the application of the provisions of the Aarhus Convention on Access to Information, Public Participation in Decision-making and Access to Justice in Environmental Matters to Community institutions and bodies.*

63 Emphasis added.

64 *The Aarhus Convention Implementation Guide*, p. 48.

for legislative action to be further taken at national level (or the EU level) via the adoption of implementing measures intended to give effect to the Convention's provisions. It must be noted that the text of the Convention abounds with terms such as '*within the framework of national legislation*' and '*in accordance with national legislation*'[65] which, in turn, have not been defined anywhere in the Convention. Such lack of stringency of the Convention's provisions could be justified by the need for flexibility in accommodating to the variety of approaches embedded in national legal systems. Flexibility is mainly observed regarding the means that a State has at its disposal in meeting the obligations flowing from the Convention, framed by the obligation of the State to refrain from adopting new or keeping in force national rules that contradict the Convention obligations.[66] The breadth of the Convention's flexibility has been considered by some to comprise both the *choice* of the means used to implement the obligations and the discretion in interpreting the scope and/or content of the obligations[67] which potentially bears the effect of undermining the uniformity of the procedural protection system of the Aarhus Convention. At the same time, it is this very flexibility which articulates the intrinsic value of the Convention as an instrument that regulates a cross-cutting domain joining aspects of administrative and governmental practice together with environment protection and procedural aspects.[68]

Furthermore, the obligations set out by the Aarhus Convention are reviewable before national courts (irrespective of whether they have directly become part of national law or via implementing national or EU legislative acts). The Convention itself has provided for the establishment of a mechanism for the review of compliance[69] discharged by the Aarhus Convention Compliance Committee which was established by *Decision 1/7* of the Meeting of the Parties[70] as the main governing body of the Convention. The Compliance Committee is comprised of independent experts who are nationals of the Parties and Signatories to the Convention, elected upon their personal capacity rather than nationality.[71] The Convention compliance mechanism can be activated in the

65 Found in Arts.2,4,5,6 and 9.

66 *The Aarhus Convention Implementation Guide*, p. 30.

67 *Idem*, p. 30, 31.

68 *Idem*, p. 31.

69 See Art.15 of the Convention.

70 United Nations Economic and Social Council, ECE/MP.PP/2/Add.8, at http://www.unece.org/fileadmin/DAM/env/pp/documents/mop1/ece.mp.pp.2.add.8.e.pdf.

71 J. Jendroska, Aarhus Convention Compliance Committee: Origins, Status and Activities, *Journal of European Environmental and Planning Law*, 2011, Vol 8 Issue 4, p. 302.

following ways:[72] through a submission from a Party concerning compliance by another Party, a submission from a Party concerning its own compliance, a referral from the Secretariat, and through communications proceeded by members of the public concerning a Party's compliance with the Convention. The third avenue has been most frequently used since any member of the public (natural or legal person), regardless of their country of citizenship, is entitled to file a communication regarding the non-compliance of a Party.[73]

The Convention compliance mechanism is non-confrontational, non-judicial and consultative in nature[74] with the Compliance Committee's findings being non-binding on the Parties given that the former was not intended to serve as a forum for redress of violations of individual rights.[75] The main task of the Compliance Committee consists of adopting findings and addressing recommendations to the Meeting of the Parties, or, sometimes, to individual States.[76] Once the Meeting of the Parties has received the findings and the accompanying recommendations from the Compliance Committee, it proceeds with deciding on the adequate measures to be taken to tackle the non-compliance. These measures include: issuing recommendations to the Parties on specific measures, requesting the Party concerned to submit a strategy (together with a time schedule which involves the duty of the Party to report back to the Compliance Committee regarding the implementation of the strategy), issuing declarations of non-compliance, issuing cautions or, *in extremis*, suspend the special rights and privileges a Party enjoys under the Convention.[77]

Finally, in the event of a dispute arising between the Parties to the Convention concerning the interpretation or application of the Convention, the former have the choice to either submit their dispute for arbitration or to the International Court of Justice as the *ultima ratio*.[78] Given that only States are eligible to appear before the ICJ in contentious cases, with respect to the EU it is only the former alternative that would apply.

---

72 http://www.unece.org/env/pp/ccbackground.html.

73 Jendroska , *supra* n. 71, p. 311.

74 V. Koester, Review of Compliance under the Aarhus Convention: A Rather Unique Compliance Mechanism, *Journal of European Environmental and Planning Law*, 2005, Issue 1, p. 42.

75 Jendorska, *supra* n. 71, p. 311.

76 *Idem*, p. 312; Since its establishment in 2002, the Committee has issued a number of findings: for an overview of the meetings of the Committee and the findings adopted with respect to individual Parties (see at, http://www.unece.org/env/pp/cc.html).

77 See Decision 1/7, point 37.

78 Art.16(2) of the Convention.

III The 'Access to Information' Pillar of the Aarhus Convention

In comparison to similar access-to-environmental-information provisions which can be found in various international legal instruments with a narrower scope than the Aarhus Convention,[79] the 'access-to-environmental information' provisions of the Convention are unique in that they are *general* in scope i.e. relate to all types of environmental information. Principally, the 'access-to-environmental-information' pillar of the Aarhus Convention covers two main types of access to information. The first one concerns the right of the public to seek information from public authorities, entailing the mirroring obligation on the part of public authorities to provide information in response to such a request. This is the 'passive' type of access to information, covered by Art.4 of the Convention which grants all the members of the *public* the right to address requests for provision of environmental information to public authorities without having to state an interest.[80] The second type of access to information, prescribed by Art.5 of the Convention, is known as the 'active' access to information whereby the authorities have the duty to collect and disseminate information of public interest to the public, which is not contingent on any specific request from the public.[81] The term 'environmental information' is defined in Art.2(3) as:

> (...) any information in written, visual, aural, electronic or any other material form on:
>
> (a) *The state of elements of the environment*, such as air and atmosphere, water, soil, land, landscape and natural sites, biological diversity and its components, including genetically modified organisms, and the interaction among these elements;
>
> (b) *Factors*, such as substances, energy, noise and *radiation*, and

79 Such instruments are, the *Convention on Civil Liabilities for Damage Resulting from Activities Dangerous to the Environment* (1993), the *United Nations Framework Convention on Climate Change* (1992), the *Convention on the Protection and Use of Trans-boundary Watercourses and International Lakes* (1992), etc. (see, *The Aarhus Convention Implementation Guide, supra*, p. 50). The obligation to collect and disseminate environmental information (as prescribed in Art.5 of the Aarhus Convention) is also found in many other environmental treaties of the past 15 years (that is, environmental information respective to the nature of the subject matter of those treaties) – e.g., the 1992 *Convention on the Trans-boundary Effects of Industrial Accidents* (see for this, *The Aarhus Convention Implementation Guide*, p. 50).

80 See, Art.4(1)a.

81 *The Aarhus Convention Implementation Guide*, p. 6.

activities or measures, including administrative measures, environmental agreements, policies, legislation, plans and programmes, affecting or likely to affect the elements of the environment within the scope of subparagraph (a)above, and cost-benefit and other economic analyses and assumptions used in environmental decision-making;

(c) *The state of human health and safety, conditions of human life,*[82] cultural sites and built structures, inasmuch as they are or may be affected by the state of the elements of the environment or, through these elements, by the factors, activities or measures referred to in subparagraph (b) above;

Pursuant to the former article, the 'environmental information' does not need to be in any specified form (apart from, obviously, material form),[83] the scope

82 *The Aarhus Convention Implementation Guide*, p. 38. The notion 'conditions of human life' correlates to the notion of a 'right to healthy environment' since only in conditions of a healthy environment can human existence be imaginable. The Convention reference's to 'conditions of human life' therefore seems to reflect the intention to promote a right to healthy environment (*The Aarhus Convention Implementation Guide*, p. 38). The Preamble of the Convention reads to this effect:

> (…)Recognizing that adequate protection of the environment is essential to human well-being and the enjoyment of basic human rights, including the right to life itself,
>
> Recognizing also that every person has the right to live in an environment adequate to his or her health and well-being (…).

83 Compare with the term 'documents' used in the Council of Europe *Convention on Access to Official Documents* (*Tromso Convention*) – the terms 'access to information' as considered within the framework of the Aarhus Convention and the term 'access to documents' under the Tromso Convention cannot be presumed to be essentially different, the Aarhus Convention Implementation Guide suggesting that the main difference between the former terms is that *document* implies a 'finished product' making the scope of the Aarhus Convention somewhat larger, additionally including information which is in raw and unprocessed form (p. 35 of the Implementation Guide);

The Tromso Convention was adopted by the Committee of Ministers of the Council of Europe on 27 November 2008 of the *Convention on Access to Official Documents* (*Tromsø Convention*) and is open for signature as of 18 June 2009; for the text of the Convention (http://conventions.coe.int/Treaty/EN/Treaties/Html/205.htm). Being the first binding international legal instrument to recognize a general right of access to official documents held by public authorities, the Tromso Convention lays down the minimum standards to be applied in the processing of requests for access to official documents (forms of and charges for access to official documents), review procedure and complementary measures and it has the flexibility required to allow national laws to build on this foundation and provide even greater access to official documents (http://conventions.coe.int/Treaty/

of the term encompassing the information on the *state of elements of the environment*, information on various factors *affecting or likely to affect the elements of the environment*, as well as information regarding the state of human health and safety and the conditions of human life provided the former are affected or may be affected by the state of the elements of the environment (or, alternatively, through these elements, by the factors, activities and measures that Art.2(3)(b) enumerates). The scope of the term 'environmental information' is rather comprehensive and serves to convey the approach taken by the Convention drafters towards defining the notion of 'environment' being that

---

EN/Summaries/Html/205.htm.). To date, only seven EU Member States of the Union have signed the Tromso Convention, with only three of them having ratified it while it is required that the ratification threshold of minimum ten Council of Europe Member States is reached in order for the Convention to take effect (http://conventions.coe.int/Treaty/Commun/ChercheSig.asp?NT=205&CM=&DF=&CL=ENG.).

In certain respects, the Tromso Convention signifies a progressive step forward from the Aarhus Convention regime. More particularly, under Art.1(a)(i) of the Tromso Convention, the notion of public authority comprises: (i) the government and administration bodies (at national, regional and local level); (ii) legislative bodies and judicial authorities insofar as they perform administrative functions according to national law; as well as (iii) natural or legal persons insofar as they exercise administrative authority. In comparison, Art.2.2 of the Aarhus Convention explicitly excludes bodies or institutions acting in a *judicial or legislative capacity,* failing to specify whether such an exemption applies to legislative and judicial bodies with relation to their entire activity or solely to the exercise of their legislative or judicial functions. In addition, the Tromso Convention invites the Convention parties to extend, on their own motion, the definition of 'public authorities' so as to supplementary cover legislative bodies in performance of their *other,* non-legislative activities; and/or judicial authorities regarding their *other* activities (primarily, adjucatory activites) (Art.1(a)(ii));

The future ratification of the Tromso Convention by all or by the majority of EU Member States as Council of Europe States would eventually lead to the existence of multiple legal frameworks potentially covering the access to environmental information in the EU Member States. The former consideration would, *per extensiam,* apply to the general access to documents, not only those pertaining to environmental information. In the event of such a development, the potential applicants, having the choice of multiple legal avenues for their legal claims, would most probably rely on the more favorable legal regime. For a discussion on the Tromso Convention and how it relates to the Union's legal regime on access to information, see, Jendroska (2012), *supra*, pp. 80–82; Also, F. Schram, From a General Right of Access to Environmental Information in the Aarhus Convention to a General Right of Access to All Information in Official Documents: The Council of Europe's Tromsø Convention, in, M. Pallemaerts (ed.), *The Aarhus Convention at Ten: Interactions and Tensions between Convenional International Law and EU Environmental Law*, 2011, Europa Law Publishing.

the definition of 'environmental information' is the closest that the Convention comes to defining the scope of the former notion.[84] Consequently, it implies that, by virtue of Art 2.3(a), the Convention considers the notion of environment as consisting of (...) *elements of the environment, such as*[85] *air and atmosphere, water, soil, land, landscape and natural sites, biological diversity and its components, including genetically modified organisms, and the interaction among these elements* (...). The former list of 'elements of the environment' is non-exhaustive and leaves room for other elements of the environment to be included in the definition[86] affording a latitude to the Convention Parties to broaden the scope of the definition of environmental information in their national laws implementing the Convention.[87] The aforementioned definition of 'environmental information', which includes factors such as, inter alia, substances, energy, noise and *radiation*, clearly points to a link between the field of nuclear energy and the scope of the Convention, further developed in EU's implementing legislation covering the access to environmental information in the civil nuclear domain.

The 'active' access to environmental information is broad in scope and follows the 'any person' principle for the requests for information directed at public authorities. In addition, Art.4(2) foresees that the requested environmental information is to be made available as soon as possible and at the latest within *one month after the submission of the request*, except for those instances where the volume and the complexity of the information require an extension of this period up to two months after the request has been made.[88] Apart from the usual deficiencies on the grounds of which the request may be refused (if the public authority to which the request is addressed does not hold the environmental information requested; the request is manifestly unreasonable or too generally formulated; or, if the request concerns material in the course of completion or concerns internal communications of public authorities (where such an exemption is provided for in national law or customary practice)),[89] the public authorities are allowed to derogate from the obligation of disclosure

84 *The Aarhus Convention: An Implementation Guide*, p. 36.

85 Emphasis added.

86 *The Aarhus Convention: An Implementation Guide*, p. 30.

87 *The Aarhus Convention: An Implementation Guide*, p. 35.

88 In comparison, the Tromso Convention provides no strict time limits for the handling of requests: 'A request for access to an official document shall be dealt with promptly. The decision shall be reached, communicated and executed as soon as possible or within a reasonable time limit which has been specified beforehand'. (Art.5(4) of the Convention).

89 Art.4(3).

of information and may refuse to disclose a particular information on the condition that such disclosure would jeopardise (Art.4(4)):

> (...) (a) The confidentiality of the proceedings of public authorities, where such confidentiality is provided for under national law;
> (b) International relations, national defence or public security;
> (d) The confidentiality of commercial and industrial information, where such confidentiality is protected by law in order to protect a legitimate economic interest. Within this framework, information on emissions which is relevant for the protection of the environment shall be disclosed;
> (...)
> The aforementioned grounds for refusal shall be interpreted in a *restrictive way*, taking into account the *public interest* served by disclosure and taking into account whether the information requested relates to emissions into the environment.;[90]

The breadth of the former derogations is curtailed by the last subparagraph of Art.4(4) which sets a limit upon the public authorities' discretion when invoking the grounds for refusal to respond to a request. The public authorities are under the obligation to interpret the derogations restrictively, by taking into account the public interest served by the disclosure and ensuring that the requested information relates to emissions into the environment. The two cumulative requirements raise the bar of 'contingency' for the effective provision of the requested information. A purely literal reading of the latter requirement may indicate that it would not be applicable to emissions which are *not* relevant to the protection of the environment. The fact that Convention fails to delineate the scope of the term 'emissions into the environment' creates a potentially unwarranted latitude for the public authorities in interpreting the foregoing exemptions.[91] Attempting to adequately construe the term 'emissions', the Aarhus Convention Implementation Guide has referred to *Directive 96/61/EC of 24 September 1996 concerning integrated pollution prevention and control* which defines the former term as the 'direct or indirect release of substances, vibrations, heat or noise from individual or diffuse sources in the installation into the air, water or land'.[92] Given that the Convention has previously made a specific mention to 'radiation' (Art.2(3)(b)), it is difficult to assume

90 Emphasis added.

91 See, *The Aarhus Convention: An Implementation Guide,* p. 60.

92 *Idem.*

that it was intended for 'radiation' to be fitted under the scope of the term 'emissions' as used in the last paragraph of Art.4(4). Substantiating its broad construction of the former provision, the Aarhus Convention Implementation Guide sides with the view that *any information* on emissions that *may* affect the quality of the environment is to be considered relevant for the protection of the environment, irrespective of the extent of the actual or potential effect thereto.[93]

The attention now turns to the Art.5 'active' access to environmental information regarding the obligation of public authorities to collect and disseminate information of public interest without the need for a specific request to that effect coming from the public or the public concerned.

Article 5 – Collection and Dissemination of Environmental Information

1. Each Party shall ensure that:
   (a) Public authorities possess and update environmental information which is relevant to their functions;
   (b) Mandatory systems are established so that there is an adequate flow of information to public authorities about proposed and existing activities which *may significantly affect the environment*;
   (c) In the event of *any imminent threat to human health or the environment*, whether caused by human activities or due to natural causes, all information which could enable *the public* to take measures to prevent or mitigate harm arising from the threat and is held by a public authority is disseminated immediately and without delay *to members of the public who may be affected.*
2. Each Party shall ensure that, within the framework of national legislation, the way in which public authorities make environmental information available *to the public* is transparent and that environmental information is effectively accessible, inter alia, by:
   (a) Providing sufficient information *to the public* about the type and scope of environmental information held by the relevant

93 *Idem.*; Another similar problem of interpretation arises in the appraisal of the 'public interest' within the meaning of Art.4(4), which is again a term that the Convention does not define the scope or content of, or provide any guidance to that effect (*The Aarhus Convention: An Implementation Guide,* p. 58, 62).

> public authorities, the basic terms and conditions under which such information is made available
> and accessible, and the process by which it can be obtained. (…);[94]

Corresponding to the obligation of States to ensure that public authorities possess and update the environmental information relevant to their functions (Art.5(1)(a)), mandatory systems are to be established to ensure an adequate flow of information to public authorities with regard to activities that *may significantly affect the environment* (Art.5(1)(b)).[95] There is a notable discrepancy regarding the scope of application of the former and the latter provision: while the former applies to all environmental information as defined under Art.2(3)(b), the latter only concerns information on proposed and existing activities which may significantly affect the environment. In this sense, the threshold for the nature of the information that the public authorities are under a duty to impart has been set higher in comparison to the Art.4 reference to *activities affecting or likely to affect the elements of the environment*. Furthermore, Art.5(1)(c) provides that in the event of *an imminent threat to human health or the environment*, all information that the public authorities are in possession of and which could enable *the public* to take measures to prevent or mitigate harm arising from such a threat, is to be immediately disseminated *to members of the public who may be affected*.[96] The existence of an imminent threat to human health or the environment presupposes that actual harm does not have to exist in order to trigger the application of the provision,[97] but the public authority's action must nonetheless be driven by 'urgency' concerns. In this way, only once the public authority is satisfied with the imminent character of the threat would the positive obligations arising from Art.5 be triggered.[98] *Grosso modo*, the foregoing evidences that the type of information covered by Art.5 only involves *specific categories* of environmental information which is to be made available to the public, underpinning the requirement for active collection and

94 Emphasis added.

95 For a discussion on the 'significance' of the effect, see, *The Aarhus Convention: An Implementation Guide*, p. 67.

96 Emphasis in text.

97 *The Aarhus Convention: An Implementation Guide*, p. 70.

98 On the practical ways in which sates can execute the task of dissemination and collection of information, see, *The Aarhus Convention: An Implementation Guide*, p. 69, 70.

dissemination of information with a certain demand of 'urgency' and 'importance' for those types of information to reach the public domain.[99]

As to the specific category of 'people' targeted by the obligation to disseminate environmental information, it is only Art.5(1)(c) which makes an express mention of '*members of the public who may be affected*'. The Implementation Guide interprets the former use of the word 'may' to the effect that there should exist a reasonable possibility that members of the public could be affected in order for the public authority to act.[100] However, the parameters for determining the existence of a 'reasonable possibility' for the population to be affected depends on the individual finding of the public authority seized with the matter. To the difference of Art.5(1)(c), all the other provisions of Art.5 introduce a myriad of tasks to be undertaken by the Parties in order for an adequate flow of information to be provided to the *public*. Regrettably, these provisions lack any precision that would help determine the exact scope and content of the requirements incumbent on the Parties and therefore fall short of creating actual and concrete obligations.[101]

The options for the public authorities to derogate from the obligation 'to collect and disseminate' the environmental information are the same exemptions provided under Art.4(4) *supra*[102] while the exact time frames for the execution of the Art.5 obligations have not been specified, save for the occurence of imminent threat to human health or the environment where the public that may be affected should *immediately and without delay* be imparted all information that would further enable them to take measures aimed at preventing or mitigating the harm arising from such threat.[103]

III.1 *The Access-to-information Pillar Transposed in Union/Euratom Law*

The access-to-information and participation-in-decision-making requirements endorsed under the Aarhus Convention seize Euratom's purview, more particularly, with regard to the domain of radiation protection (and to a certain extent, environmental protection). The scope of the former transparency obligations applicable to Euratom's purview will be examined through an analysis of the relevant primary law and secondary law instruments adopted within the Union and the Euratom legal framework. From a more general

99 *The Aarhus Convention: An Implementation Guide*, p. 67.

100 *The Aarhus Convention: An Implementation Guide*, p. 71.

101 Art.5(2) – (10).

102 Art.5(10): 'Nothing in this article may prejudice the right of Parties to refuse to disclose certain environmental information in accordance with Article 4, paragraphs 3 and 4. (…)'.

103 Art.5(1)c.

perspective, the transparency under the Euratom system will be examined starting out from the standards and principles concerning transparency devised at the level of the Union's and Euratom's primary law, relative to the general access to information as a wider notion, going beyond strictly the fields of radiation protection and environmental protection.

The access-to-information principles applicable to the work of the EU institutions were initially introduced by the Amsterdam Treaty and extended to the sphere of application to the Euratom Treaty by way of *Declaration no.41 on the provisions relating to transparency, access to documents and the fight against fraud* (*attached to the Treaty of Amsterdam*).[104] The former principles have now been translated into Art.15 TFEU which refers to the duty of transparency and good governance on the part of the institutions, guaranteeing a right of access to documents to every citizen of the Union.[105] Art.15 TFEU has been extended, through the bridging provisions of Art.106(a)(1) Euratom, to the purview of the Euratom Treaty. According to the article, all citizens of the Union and all natural or legal person residing or having its registered office in a Member State are

---

104 Indicated by P. Faross, in, *Practical implementation of the Aarhus Convention in the nuclear field…*, *supra* n. 46, p. 19;

The text of Declaration no.41 on the provisions relating to transparency, access to documents and the fight against fraud (OJ C 340, 10 November 1997) reads:

The Conference considers that the European Parliament, the Council and the Commission, when they act in pursuance of the Treaty establishing the European Coal and Steel Community and the Treaty establishing the European Atomic Energy Community, should draw guidance from the provisions relating to transparency, access to documents and the fight against fraud in force within the framework of the Treaty establishing the European Community, Treaty of Amsterdam amending the Treaty on European Union, the Treaties establishing the European Communities and related acts.

105 Art.15 TFEU (ex. Art.255 TEC):

1. In order to promote good governance and ensure the participation of civil society, the Union's institutions, bodies, offices and agencies shall conduct their work as openly as possible.

2. The European Parliament shall meet in public, as shall the Council when considering and voting on a draft legislative act.

3. Any citizen of the Union, and any natural or legal person residing or having its registered office in a Member State, shall have a right of access to documents of the Union's institutions, bodies, offices and agencies, whatever their medium, subject to the principles and the conditions to be defined in accordance with this paragraph.

Each institution, body, office or agency shall ensure that its proceedings are transparent and shall elaborate in its own Rules of Procedure specific provisions regarding access to its documents, in accordance with the regulations referred to in the second subparagraph.

granted a right of access to documents of the Union's institutions, bodies, offices and agencies where the general principles that govern this right of access to documents are to be determined by the European Parliament and the Council.[106] As a corollary to the former right, a duty is established for each institution, body, office or agency to ensure that their proceedings are transparent where the details for the execution of which duty is to be additionally devised in their respective Rules of Procedure by including specific provisions regarding the access to documents .[107]

The text of the Euratom Treaty itself contains provisions relating to access to and exchange of information among the EU institutions and the Member States, with the noticeably influential role of the Commission as the intermediary in the process of provision and exchange of information.[108] The Chapter on *Dissemination of information* (Arts.12–29) is divided into a section on information over which the Community has the power of disposal and a section covering other types of information, complemented by corresponding security provisions serving to safeguard the flow of the information. The nature of the former type of information is highly technical and does not concern (at least not in any direct way) the protection of human health or the environment. The Commission enjoys the dominant authority for the disposal over this information: the information acquired as a result of the Community's research programme the disclosure of which is capable of harming Member States' interests is subject to a security grading system established via security regulations adopted by the Council which introduce a panoply of security gradings and corresponding security measures applicable to those gradings.[109] The Commission thereafter applies a particular security grading to the information it considers liable to harm Member States' defense interests, in accordance with the applicable security regulation.[110]

In addition, under Art.187, the Commission has been vested with the general prerogative, exercised within the limitations posed by the Council in accordance with the provisions of the Euratom Treaty, to '*collect any information* and carry out any checks required for the performance of the tasks entrusted to it [the Commission]'.[111] However, the Treaty does not prescribe the modalities in which the Commission is to discharge of this important

106 Art.15(3) TFEU.

107 Art.15(3) TFEU.

108 See, Arts.12–29; Art.187, Art.194, Arts.35–38; Arts.41–44.

109 Art.24(1).

110 Art.24(2).

111 Art.187; Emphasis added.

prerogative, nor does it offer the possibility for individual undertakings or natural persons to request the information that the Commission has acquired in the former way.

Furthermore, Art.194 Euratom, acting as a safeguard clause, introduces a *duty of non-disclosure* regarding any persons, whether they be members of the EU institutions or persons who, in the course of their duties or their public or private relations with the institutions/installations of the Community/Joint Undertakings, have had access to any facts, information, knowledge, documents or objects that are subject to a security system. Pursuant to the duty of non-disclosure, these persons are required, upon the discharge of their duties or termination of their relations, to keep the former material secret from the general public.[112] Moreover, Member States are asked to communicate to the Commission all national rules that apply to the classification and secrecy of information, knowledge, documents or objects covered by the Treaty, upon which the Commission ensures that the respective provisions are then further communicated to the other Member States.[113]

Being that, for the most part, the types of information covered by the Euratom Treaty concern the technical aspects of nuclear energy production, the former cannot be subsumed under the definition of 'environmental information' pursuant to the Aarhus Convention. Actually, it is only the Health and Safety Chapter of the Treaty, dealing with the human and environmental effects of radiation and the disposal of radioactive waste, which is of direct relevance to the provision and exchange of environmental information. Here, again, the Commission plays a crucial role in managing the information on radiation-related nuisances which calls for interaction between the Commission and the Member States' authorities. While there is no possibility for any direct involvement of natural or legal persons, under Arts.35 and 36 Euratom, Member States are obliged to perform continuous checks of the level of radioactivity in the air, water and soil and periodically communicate information to the Commission regarding the performed checks in order that the latter is kept informed of the level of radioactivity to which the public is exposed.[114] Furthermore, the Member States are to furnish the Commission with the general data relating to any plan for the disposal of radioactive waste

112 Art.194(1).

113 Art.194(2).

114 Art.36; See for the application of Art.35 Euratom, Commission Communication, Application of Article 35 of the Euratom Treaty: Verification of the operation and efficiency of facilities for continuous monitoring of the level of radioactivity in the air, water and soil, Report 1990–2007, Brussels, 20.12.2007 COM(2007) 847 final.

(a particular form for the data has not been prescribed), enabling the latter to estimate whether the implementation of the disposal plan is liable to result in radioactive contamination of the water, soil or airspace of another Member State.[115]

Proceeding down to the secondary law instruments relevant to the access to information in the environmental field and pertaining to Euratom's scope of application, the discussion will further focus on the two Union instruments implementing the first pillar of the Aarhus Convention at Union level: *Directive 2003/4/EC on public access to environmental information* and *Regulation No 1367/2006 on the application of the provisions of the Aarhus Convention on Access to Information, Public Participation in Decision-making and Access to Justice in Environmental Matters to Community institutions and bodies* (the Aarhus Regulation). *Directive 2003/4/EC on public access to environmental information*[116] establishes the legal regime for access to information regarding environmental matters in the EU while the Directive's pre-cursor, *Directive 90/313/EC on freedom of access to information on the environment*[117] which was already in place at the time of signature of the Aarhus Convention on the part of the European Community, served as the starting ground for the negotiations on the 'access to information' regime to be established under the Convention.[118] The 1990 Directive was, understandably, somewhat more restrictive in scope than the subsequent access-to-information provisions of the Convention.[119]

In order to cater to the reinforced procedural protection regime of the Aarhus Convention, it was imminent that a new directive be adopted, improving

115 Art.37. On the modalities of application of the article, see, Commission Recommendation on the application of Article 37 of the Euratom Treaty (2010/635/Euratom) L 279/36-67.

116 OJ L 41, 14.2.2003, pp. 26–32.

117 OJ L 158, 23.6.1990, pp. 56–58.

118 *The Aarhus Convention: An Implementation Guide*, p. 65.

119 See, *The Aarhus Convention: An Implementation Guide*, p. 65, for a comparison of the texts of the Convention and the Directive, especially regarding the definition of the terms 'environmental information' and 'public authority' (which appears to be broader in the Convention) and the requirement for the applicant to state their interest (which is absent from the Directive which does not foresee any requirement for the applicant to prove the existence of an interest).

Nevertheless, the EU Court of Justice contributed for the former restrictive scope of the *Directive 90/313/EEC on the freedom of access to information on the environment* to be overcome by extending the scope of the term 'environmental information' in the *Mecklenburg* case (C-321/96 ECR 1998 Page I-03809) by deciding to treat a statement of views given by a public authority in development consent proceedings as 'information relating to the environment', in accordance with the language of the Directive.

the regime on access to information in the environmental domain. With respect to the nuclear realm, the 2003 Access-to-information Directive, extends the scope of the term 'environmental information' circumscribed in the Convention by including 'substances, energy, noise, *radiation* or waste, including *radioactive waste*, emissions, discharges and other releases into the environment' among the factors that influence the state of the environment (Art.2(1)(b)).[120] Effectively, with regard to the factors linked to nuclear energy, the Directive goes further from the Convention's sole reference to 'radiation', complementing it with an express reference to 'radioactive waste'. The EU Court of Justice has, in its own right, accepted to offer a broad construction of the former definition of 'environmental information' of Art.2(1) of the Access-to-Information Directive.[121]

---

120 Emphasis added; Article 2 of the Directive states:

Definitions

For the purposes of this Directive:

1. 'Environmental information' shall mean any information in written, visual, aural, electronic or any other material form on:

(a) the state of the elements of the environment, such as air and atmosphere, water, soil, land, landscape and natural sites including wetlands, coastal and marine areas, biological diversity and its components, including genetically modified organisms, and the interaction among these elements;

(b) factors, such as substances, energy, noise, radiation or waste, including radioactive waste, emissions, discharges and other releases into the environment, affecting or likely to affect the elements of the environment referred to in (a);

(c) measures (including administrative measures), such as policies, legislation, plans, programmes, environmental agreements, and activities affecting or likely to affect the elements and factors referred to in (a) and (b) as well as measures or activities designed to protect those elements; (…).

121 The CJEU set an important precedent by interpreting the definition of 'environmental information' of Article 2(1) of the Access-to-Information Directive extensively in the case C-266/09 *Stichting Natuur en Milieu v College voor de toelating van gewasbeschermingsmiddelen en biociden* (*ECR 2010 p. I-13119*) which dealt with the refusal of a German administrative body to disclose certain studies and reports concerning the effectiveness of a plant protection product. The Court was asked to inquire into whether the information submitted within the framework of a national procedure for the authorisation of a plant protection product could be subsumed under the part of the definition for 'environmental information' of Art.2(1)(c) of the Directive relative to *measures (including administrative measures), such as policies, legislation, plans, programmes, environmental agreements, and activities affecting or likely to affect the elements and factors* (…)(Para. 25 of judgment);. The requested information did not directly involve any assessment of the consequences on human health and was relevant to elements of the environment which *may* affect human health (should excess levels of the residues be present) so that it was considered

While the 2003 Access-to-Information Directive lays down access-to-information obligations incumbent on public authorities in the Member States, as concerns the environmental information obtainable from the EU institutions and/or bodies, there appears that a dual legal regime is in place borne by, on the one hand, *Regulation No 1367/2006 on the application of the provisions of the Aarhus Convention on Access to Information, Public Participation in Decision-making and Access to Justice in Environmental Matters to Community institutions and bodies* (the Aarhus Regulation)[122] and *Regulation 1049/2001*

to fall within the ambit of the term 'environmental information'. However, another issue was whether the refusal to disclose could be saved under the derogation relating to the confidentiality of commercial or industrial information provided in Art.4(2) of the Directive (Para.42). The Court pointed out that the grounds for refusal to provide information were to be interpreted in a restrictive way and taking into account the public interest served by the disclosure to the extent that the former interest appeared to outweigh the interest served by the refusal to disclose (Para. 53).

Subsequently, in *C-204/09 Flachglas Torgau GmbH* (*ECR 2012 I-0000*), however, the Court interpreted the exemption regarding 'bodies or institutions when acting in a judicial or legislative capacity' of the second subparagraph of Art.2(2) of the 2003 Directive in a broad manner, opining that government ministries participating in the legislative process were caught under the former exemption for the duration of the legislative process. The case concerned a request addressed to the German Federal Ministry for the Environment, Protection of Nature and Reactor Safety for information regarding the legislative process leading to the adoption of a 2007 law and its subsequent implementation (more specifically, internal memoranda of the Ministry and its correspondence with the Federal Office for the Environment) (Para. 22, 23 of judgment). The German Ministry had refused the request considering the information to be part of the legislative process that the ministry had been involved in and thereby exempt from the duty to provide the requested information (Para.24). The CJEU conceded that the former derogation could extend to government ministries to the extent that they participate in the legislative process, in particular by tabling draft laws or giving opinions (Para. 51). However, the Court reminded that once the legislative process was finished, the bodies or institutions of the former kind were no longer to be regarded as 'acting in legislative capacity' and the option for the Member States to consider them in this sense had been precluded (Para. 58);

The CJEU's has produced ample case law on access to information in the environmental field, for more commentary on the more recent case law, see, *Report from the Commission to the Council and the European Parliament on the experience gained in the application of Directive 2003/4/EC on Public Access to Environmental Information;* COM(2012) 774 final; Brussels, 17.12.2012.

122 OJ L 264, 25.9.2006 p.13; In order to further implement the 2006 Aarhus Regulation, the Commission has adopted two decisions: Commission Decision 2008/50/EC of 13 December 2007 laying down detailed rules for the application of Regulation (EC) No 1367/2006 of the European Parliament and of the Council on the Aarhus Convention

regarding public access to European Parliament, Council and Commission documents, on the other.[123] The former instrument is specific to the access to environmental information obtainable by private and legal persons from the EU institutions and bodies while the latter is a general 'access to information' bill for the EU institutions and bodies, irrespective of the type of information requested. The duality of applicable legal regimes has resulted in certain inconsistencies concerning their respective scope of application[124] with a number of the provisions of the 2006 Regulation specifically being aimed at evening out the potential conflict of norms that may arise between the two regulations.[125] In so far as the access to environmental information is concerned, Regulation 1367/2006 practically extends the scope of the term 'environmental information' to the purview of Regulation 1049/2001.[126]

---

as regards requests for the internal review of administrative acts (OJ 2008 L 13/24); and Commission Decision 2008/401/EC, Euratom of 30 April 2008 amending its Rules of Procedure as regards detailed rules for the application of Regulation (EC) No 1367/2006 of the European Parliament and of the Council on the application of the provisions of the Aarhus Convention on Access to Information, Public Participation in Decision-making and Access to Justice in Environmental Matters to Community institution and bodies (OJ 2008 L 140/22).

123 OJ L 145/43, 31.5.2001; The Regulation draws from ex-Art.255(2) TEC (presently Art.15(3)TFEU) concerning the right of access to documents of the Union's institutions, bodies, offices and agencies, equally applicable to the Euratom scope.

124 J. Jendroska, Citizen's Rights in European Environmental Law: Stock-Taking of Key Challenges and Current Developments in Relation to Public Access to Information, Participation and Access to Justice, *Journal of European Environmental and Planning Law*, 2012, Vol. 9 Issue 1, p. 81.

125 Points 7,8,12,13,15 of the Preamble; Arts.3,4,6 of the 2006 Regulation.

126 Article 3 of the 2006 Regulation determines the scope of application of Regulation (EC) No 1049/2001 with respect to access to environmental information:

> Application of Regulation (EC) No 1049/2001
>
> Regulation (EC) No 1049/2001 shall apply to any request by an applicant *for access to environmental information* held by Community institutions and bodies without discrimination as to citizenship, nationality or domicile and, in the case of a legal person, without discrimination as to where it has its registered seat or an effective centre of its activities.
>
> For the purposes of this Regulation, the word 'institution' in Regulation (EC) No 1049/2001 *shall be read as 'Community institution or body'*;[Emphasis added]
>
> On the other hand, the 2006 Regulation espouses the following definition for environmental information in Art.2(1)(d):
>
> (...) (d) '*environmental information*' means any information in written, visual, aural, electronic or any other material form on:

The provisions of the 2006 Aarhus Regulation regarding access to information have a direct bearing on the Euratom field since the scope of the environmental information covered by the Regulation, extends to, *inter alia*, factors (such as substances, energy, noise, *radiation or waste, including radioactive waste*, emissions, discharges and other releases into the environment) that affect or are likely to affect the elements of the environment (comprising of air and atmosphere, water, soil, land, biological diversity and its components etc.).[127] The former inclusion of 'radiation' and 'radioactive waste' aligns with the definition for 'environmental information' provided in the Access-to-information Directive *supra*, thus making both of these acts applicable to access to information on the state of the environment affected or likely to be affected by radiation and/or radioactive waste.

The Aarhus Regulation does not only adopt an inclusive approach towards the subject matter covered, it is equally progressive in terms of the subjects of the obligations provided therein. Namely, the Regulation applies equally to the EU institutions and bodies acting in an administrative capacity and in a legislative capacity[128] which seems to be a revolutionary legal enterprise for the Union legislators having in view the optional character of the former demand under the Aarhus Convention.[129] Lastly, the Aarhus Regulation further builds up from the Convention's requirements by adopting the 'any person' principle both in the context of submission of requests for information and the collection and dissemination of environmental information.[130] The former progressive

(i) the state of the elements of the environment, such as air and atmosphere, water, soil, land, landscape and natural sites including wetlands, coastal and marine areas, biological diversity and its components, including genetically modified organisms, and the interaction among these elements;

(ii) *factors, such as substances, energy, noise, radiation or waste, including radioactive waste*, emissions, discharges and other releases into the environment, *affecting or likely to affect the elements of the environment* referred to in point (i);[Emphasis added].

127 Emphasis added; Art.2(1)(d) of the 2006 Regulation.

128 Art.2(1)(c).

129 The Preamble to the Aarhus Convention recognizes the '(…) the desirability of transparency in all branches of government and inviting legislative bodies to implement the principles of this Convention in their proceedings (…)'.

130 Arts.3 and 4.

The EU General Court narrowly defined the scope of the information to be requested from the Union institutions and bodies in terms of form (information contained in a document) in a case concerning the duty to record information T-264/04 *WWF European Policy Programme v. Council* (ECR 2007 II-00911), where the center of gravity was the 2001 Regulation, whereas the Aarhus Regulation failed to apply *ratione temporae* even though the applicants had also relied on it. For an analysis of the case, see, S. De Abreu

features of the Regulation are a demonstration of deference on the part of the Union legislators towards the general tenor of inclusiveness of the Preamble to the Aarhus Convention.

Having in mind the Commission's dominant prerogatives in the exercise of control over the flow of information under Arts.35 and 36 Euratom, referred to *supra*, reliance on the access-to-information mechanisms available under the Aarhus Regulation can be used to offset the potentially arbitrary behavior of the Commission in this respect – that is, to the extent that information related to radiation and/or radioactive waste is at issue.

In turn, there are also several Euratom measures that have directly or marginally (incidentally) covered the aspect of access to information in the field of nuclear health and safety, the Fukushima nuclear accident serving as a reminder of the importance attached to enhancing the transparency on nuclear safety matters and promoting independence in regulatory decision-making.[131] In this vein, the 2014 amendments to *Directive 2009/71/Euratom of 25 June 2009 establishing a Community framework for the nuclear safety of nuclear installations*[132] establish an obligation for Member States to ensure that

---

Ferreira, The Fundamental Right of Access to Environmental Information: a Critical Analysis of WWF-EPO v. Council, *Journal of Environmental Law* 2007 Vol 19, Issue 3;

Further on, in *Joined cases C-514/11 P and C-605/11 P Liga para a Protecção da Natureza (LPN) and Republic of Finland v European Commission (not yet published)*, both the 2001 Regulation and the Aarhus Regulation were at issue, the cases centering on a request for access to information from the Commission concerning documents relating to an infringement procedure at the prelitigation stage where the applicants had invoked, *inter alia*, Art.6(1) of 2006 Regulation referring to the overriding public interest in disclosure which must exist where the information requested relates to emissions into the environment (para. 80 of the judgment). For a case note, see J. Dupont-Lassalle, Accès aux documents et confidentialité des enquêtes de la Commission, Europe 2014 janvier Comm. n° 1 pp. 19–20.

In general, for a more thorough coverage of the intersection between the 2001 Regulation and the 2006 Aarhus Regulation and related case law, see, S. De Abreu Ferreira, Passive Access to Environmental Information in the EU: An Analysis of Recent Legal Developments, *European Energy and Environmental Law Review*, August 2008; and, P. Leino, Just a Little Sunshine in the Rain: The 2010 Case Law of the European Court of Justice on Access to Documents, *Common Market Law Review*, Issue 48, 2011.

131 See, point 12 of the Preamble to Directive 2014/87/Euratom of 8 July 2014 amending Directive 2009/71/Euratom establishing a Community framework for the nuclear safety of nuclear installations OJ 2014 L 219/42.

132 OJ 2009 L 172/18; amended by Directive 2014/87/Euratom of 8 July 2014 amending Directive 2009/71/Euratom establishing a Community framework for the nuclear safety of nuclear installations OJ 2014 L 219/42.

necessary information in relation to the nuclear safety of nuclear installations and its regulation is made available to workers and the general public, with specific consideration to local authorities, population and stakeholders in the vicinity of a nuclear installation.[133] That obligation entails that the competent regulatory authority and the licence holders are to provide in the framework of their communication policy: '(a) information on normal operating conditions of nuclear installations to workers and the general public, and (b) prompt information in case of incidents and accidents to workers and the general public and to the competent regulatory authorities of other Member States in the vicinity of a nuclear installation'.[134] Under Art.8(2) of the Directive, information is to be made available to the public in accordance with *relevant legislation* and *international instruments*, provided that this does not jeopardise other overriding interests, such as security, which are recognised in relevant legislation or international instruments.[135] In comparison to the treatment of the access to information under the former version of the directive, the amended directive is much more elaborate and underpinned by overriding transparency concerns.

In the field of spent fuel and radioactive waste management, the availability of relevant information to the public is also of pivotal significance. Under Art.10(1) of the *Directive 2011/70/Euratom of 19 July 2011 establishing a Community framework for the responsible and safe management of spent fuel and radioactive waste,*[136] Member States are to ensure that *necessary information* on the management of spent fuel and radioactive waste be made available to workers and the general public, which is corollary to the obligation of ensuring that the competent regulatory authority informs the public in the fields of its competence. Information is to be made available to the public in accordance with national legislation and international obligations, provided that this does not jeopardise other interests such as, inter alia, security, recognised in national legislation or international obligations.[137] The language of the Directive, especially in comparison to the above mentioned Nuclear Safety Directive, is sketchy as to the type of information to be imparted with the general public since it only refers to 'necessary information' while offering no guidance as to how the necessity for making the information available is to be established.

---

133 Art.8(1) of the 2014 Directive.

134 *Idem.*

135 Emphasis added.

136 OJ L 199, 02/08/2011 PP. 0048–0056.

137 Art.10(1).

The provisions concerning the supply of information of *Directive 2013/59/Euratom laying down basic safety standards for protection against the dangers arising from exposure to ionising radiation,*[138] which establishes a comprehensive legal regime in the matter of human health protection against (potentially or actually) dangerous ionizing radiaton, gravitate around the duty of Member States to ensure that information related to the justification of classes or types of practices, the regulation of radiation sources and of radiation protection is made available to undertakings, workers, members of the public, as well as patients and other individuals subject to medical exposure.[139] Similarly to the foregoing Euratom instruments, it envisages that information be made available in accordance with national legislation and international obligations, provided that this does not jeopardise other interests such as, inter alia, security, recognised in national legislation or international obligations.[140] Furthermore, given that the new 2013 Basic Safety Standards Directive has repealed the former *Directive 89/618/Euratom of 27 November 1989 on informing the general public about health protection measures to be applied and steps to be taken in the event of a radiological emergency,*[141] it has incorporated and further developed the rules applicable to the exchange of information in the event of radiological emergency belonging to the latter directive, based on a regime applicable to members of the public *likely to be affected* in the event of an emergency or members of the public *actually affected* in the event of an emergency. Thus, Member States are under an obligation to provide members of the public likely to be affected in the event of an emergency with information about the health protection measures applicable to them and about the action they should take in the event of such an emergency, ensuring that the information is updated and distributed at regular intervals and whenever significant changes take place (the former information is to be permanently available to the public).[142] For members of the public actually affected when an emergency occurs, Member States are to make sure that the former are informed

138 OJ 2014 L 13/1.

139 Art.77.

140 *Idem.*

141 OJ L 357, 07/12/1989 PP. 0031–0034; The standards introduced by the original 1989 Directive have been considered to represent what is known as the 'first phase' in the evolution of the EU/Euratom legislation on public information and participation (Gadbois et al., *supra* n. 39, p. 9).

142 Art.70.

without delay about the facts of the emergency, the steps to be taken and, as appropriate, the health protection measures applicable to them.[143]

The foregoing regime regarding the exchange of information in the event of radiological emergency complements the regime established pursuant to *Council Decision 87/600/Euratom of 14 December 1987 on Community arrangements for the early exchange of information in the event of a radiological emergency,*[144] the scope of which does not cover the aspect of provision of information to the general public. Namely, the Council Decision deals with the arrangements that apply with regard to the notification and provision of information whenever a Member State decides to take measures of a wide-spread nature in order to protect the general public in case of a radiological emergency, centering on the urgent exchange of information between the Member States and the Commission in the event of such emergency.[145]

A salient feature of the foregoing Euratom instruments is their fairly permissive language and, consequently, the large discretion they afford to Member States and national authorities in the discharge of their duties regarding the provision of necessary information to the workers or/and the general public. The above discussed Euratom instruments as well as the Euratom Treaty, unfortunately, do not foresee any immediate involvement for the public/public concerned to address specific requests for access to information to the respective national authorities and, thus, only cover the 'active' type of access to environmental information. The former lack of sufficient public involvement in the access to information within the Euratom construct pertaining to the field of nuclear health and safety indicates a serious lack of environmental democracy which can (only partially and sporadically) be extenuated through the application of the *Union* instruments transposing the Aarhus Convention obligations which equally cover the Euratom remit.

---

143 Art.71; The detailed arrangements for the execution of the tasks laid down in Arts.70 and 71 have been produced in Annex XII of the Directive.

144 OJ L 371, 30.12.1987, p. 76.

145 See Arts.1, 2 and 3 of the Council Decision.

For more references on provision of information in specific nuclear energy contexts, see the following Euratom acts: 2005/844/EURATOM Commission Decision of 25 November 2005 concerning the accession of the European Atomic Energy Community to the Convention on Early Notification of a Nuclear Accident (OJ L-314 of 30/11/2005 pp. 21–22); 2005/845/EURATOM Commission Decision of 25 November 2005 concerning the accession of the European Atomic Energy Community to the Convention on Assistance in the case of Nuclear Accident or Radiological Emergency (OJ L314 of 30/11/2005 pp. 27–34).

IV The Participation-in-decision-making Pillar of the Aarhus Convention

The objective corollary to that of achieving a satisfactory and effective access to environmental information is the inclusion of the public in the decision-making processes for matters pertaining to environmental protection which is, in a certain way, the flip side of the 'environmental democracy' medal. The public's involvement in the decision-making (in general) is instrumental to the accomplishment of 'good governance', denoting the work of the public administration which is efficient and effective[146] as well as transparent, accountable and accessible. The ultimate goal of introducing the public participation mechanisms has been seen as not only challenging the administrative decision-making, but also, in the wider spectrum, challenging the very legitimacy of representative democracy.[147]

The idea of including the public in the decision-making process in the environmental field is not an invention peculiar to the Aarhus Convention regime, it is a concept also found in other international instruments pre-dating the Aarhus Convention. In this sense, the 1991 *Convention on Environmental Impact Assessment in a Transboundary Context* (*Espoo Convention*) which provides that the assessment of proposed activities having a potentially significant transboundary environmental impact is to be carried out with the participation of the public in the areas likely to be affected, is considered as containing one of the most developed set of public participation provisions.[148] In a similar vein, the 1992 Rio Declaration on Environment and Development, adopted by the United Nations Conference on Environment and Development, instituted the requirement for public participation in Principle 10 which expresses that environmental issues are best handled with the participation of all concerned citizens, at the relevant level, demanding of the Parties to facilitate and encourage public awareness and participation by making information widely available.

The Aarhus Convention 'participation in decision-making' requirements are three-fold, encompassing the public participation in decisions on specific activities (Art.6), the public participation concerning plans, programmes and policies relating to the environment (Art.7) and the public participation in the

146 Jendroska, *supra* n. 28, Part. II.3.

147 Lee and Abbot, *supra* n. 56, p. 106.

148 *The Aarhus Convention: An Implementation Guide*, p. 87; See, Art.2(2) and (6), and Art.4(2) of the Espoo Convention. The text of the Convention is available at: http://www.unece.org/fileadmin/DAM/env/eia/documents/legaltexts/conventiontextenglish.pdf.

preparation of executive regulations and/or generally applicable legally binding normative instruments (Art.8). In a manner similar to the preceding sections of the chapter which dealt with the 'access to information' pillar, firstly, the general features of the participation in decision-making regime under the Aarhus Convention will be elaborated, followed by a look at the relevant Union and Euratom instruments transposing the Convention requirements to the EU level or independently drawing on the matter of public participation.

In terms of their level of stringency, the requirements prescribed under Arts.7 and 8 of the Aarhus Convention have been phrased in more dispositive terms thus offering the Parties greater flexibility in fulfilling their obligations pertaining to public participation,[149] while the Art.6 provisions are more concrete regarding the scope and content of the set obligations and the degree of compulsion to be borne by the Parties. Establishing these more precise obligations ensures greater public involvement in the decision-making on specific activities and reflects the consideration that the public that is (significantly) affected is fully entitled to influence the decision-making process.[150]

IV.1 *Public Participation in Decisions on Specific Activities (Article 6)*

The requirements of Article 6 regarding public participation in decisions on specific activities apply to permitting decisions on the proposed activities listed in Annex I of the Convention, which mainly concern specific administrative decisions (i.e. decisions adopted to permit a proposed project, activity or action to go forward with an activity).[151] The proposed activities in Annex I include, *inter alia*, activities that concern various aspects of the production of nuclear energy[152] and are thus directly relevant to Euratom's scope of activities.

---

149 See, *The Aarhus Convention: An Implementation Guide*, p. 86.

150 *Idem.*

151 *Idem*, p. 90; The acts adopted by the relevant national authorities pursuant to Art.6 of the Convention are, typically, permits, permissions, consents, licenses – usually in fields such as siting and construction of installations, use of resources, pollution control etc. (See, Jendroska, *The Aarhus Convention at Ten...*, *supra* n. 35, p. 117).

152 Annex I – List of Activities Referred To in Article 6, Paragraph 1 (a)

1. (...)

- Nuclear power stations and other nuclear reactors including the dismantling or decommissioning of such power stations or reactors 1/ (except research installations for the production and conversion of fissionable and fertile materials whose maximum power does not exceed 1 kW continuous thermal load);
- Installations for the reprocessing of irradiated nuclear fuel;
- Installations designed:
- For the production or enrichment of nuclear fuel;

Moreover, in accordance with their national law, Parties are allowed to extend the application of Art.6 to other, non-listed activities which may potentially bear a *significant* effect on the environment.[153]

All of the Art.6 provisions are targeted at the 'public concerned' (except for Art.6(7) and Art.6(9) which grant participatory rights to the 'public'[154]): the 'public concerned' is to be informed early in the environmental decision-making procedure, in an adequate, timely and effective manner of, among other, the proposed activity and the application upon which the decision is to be taken, the nature of the possible decisions or the draft decision, the public authority responsible of adopting the decision as well as the envisaged procedure for the adoption of the former.[155] The information concerning the procedure should include (as long as available): the start of the procedure, the opportunities for public participation, the time and venue of any envisaged public hearing, designation of the public authority from which relevant information can be obtained (as well as where the relevant information had been

– For the processing of irradiated nuclear fuel or high-level radioactive waste;
– For the final disposal of irradiated nuclear fuel;
– Solely for the final disposal of radioactive waste;
– Solely for the storage (planned for more than 10 years) of irradiated nuclear fuels or radioactive waste in a different site than the production site (…);

153 Art.6(1)b; The Implementation Guide of the Aarhus Convention suggests that the *significance* of the effect should be measured as the function of the usefulness and the necessity of the public participation process where the quality of 'significance' is what separates the ordinary decision-making from environmental decision-making (*The Aarhus Convention: An Implementation Guide*, p. 93). Therefore, in order to adequately judge the 'significance' of the effect to the environment, example can be taken from the Appendix III to the Espoo Convention which sets out the relevant criteria to be taken into account in examining whether an activity is likely to have a significant adverse transboundary impact: the size of the proposed activities, the location for the proposed activities and the effects (i.e. proposed activities with particularly complex and potentially adverse effects), etc. (See, *The Aarhus Convention: An Implementation Guide*, p.93,94).

154 Article 6

(…) 7. Procedures for public participation shall allow the public to submit, in writing or, as appropriate, at a public hearing or inquiry with the applicant, any comments, information, analyses or opinions that it considers relevant to the proposed activity. (…)

9. Each Party shall ensure that, when the decision has been taken by the public authority, the public is promptly informed of the decision in accordance with the appropriate procedures. Each Party shall make accessible to the public the text of the decision along with the reasons and considerations on which the decision is based. (…);

155 Art.6(2).

subjected to examination by the public), an indication of the relevant public authority/official body to which comments or questions can be addressed along with a time schedule for delivering comments or questions as well as an indication of what environmental information relevant to the proposed activity is available.[156] The former mechanisms are to be put into place within reasonable time-frames allowing sufficient time for the public to effectively participate.[157]

Concomitantly, the competent public authorities must be able to ensure free-of-charge access for examination of all information relevant to the decision-making (referred to *supra*) which is available at the time of the public participation procedure to the public concerned.[158] Such information is to include, at a minimum: a description of the site and the physical and technical characteristics of the proposed activity (including an estimate of the expected residues and emissions), a description of the significant effects of the proposed activity on the environment, a description of the measures envisaged to prevent and/or reduce the effects, a non-technical summary of the former, an outline of the main alternatives to the proposed activity, and (in accordance with national legislation) the main reports and advice provided to the public authority at the time the public concerned was to be informed in accordance with Art.6(2).[159] It is to be gathered that, under Art.6, the 'public concerned' subset has the preferential role regarding notification and examination of the proposed activities as opposed to the 'public' which is entitled to submit (in writing or, at a public hearing or inquiry with the applicant) comments, information, analyses or opinions which it considers relevant to the proposed activity.[160]

In terms of the end result of the participative role of the public, Parties have the duty to provide that in reaching the final decision *due account* is taken of the outcome of the public participation.[161] The concerned term is rather evasive in view of what it is presumed to encompass as well as the pertinent parameters which are to be applied in estimating the former. In this sense, the requirement of taking 'due account' is to be construed as relative to the duty of the public authority to seriously consider the substance of all the comments received from the public (regardless of their source) and include the substance of these comments into the motivation/statement of reasons of the final

156 Art.6(2).
157 Art.6(3).
158 Art.6(6).
159 Art.6(6).
160 Art.6(7).
161 Art.6(8).

decision (the relevant authority is however not required to *accept* the substance of all the received comments and modify its decision pursuant thereto).[162] Failure to respect the procedural requirement of taking due account of the contribution originating from public participation may be seen as a procedural violation and give rise to legal challenges by the members of the public whose comments were not duly taken into consideration.[163] Upon reaching its decision, the public authority is responsible to promptly inform the public of the decision and make the text of the decision accessible to the public along with a statement of reasons.[164] Moreover, it should be noted that even where the applicant's original proposal does not undergo any significant changes, the successful implementation thereof is nonetheless often times largely dependent on the active public participation during the decision-making process.[165] Pursuant to the national defence derogation, however, all the former procedural obligations will fail to apply in the event that a Contracting Party considers that the application of these provisions would adversely affect certain activities that serve national defence purposes.[166]

With respect to the nature of the Art.6 requirements, it is necessary to clarify that the former do not have the purpose of imposing an obligation for a licensing or permitting procedure to be put into place at the national level[167] so that they only become applicable provided that such a procedure has already been envisaged under national law. Another caveat lies in the frequent (however, faulted) understanding that Art.6 serves to incorporate EIA (Environmental Impact Assessment) requirements to the public participation process.[168] Actually, the EIA should not be seen as an end in itself given that it does not represent a permitting process, but it is essentially one of the means used in the decision-making process.[169] The application of the Art.6 requirements to a particular decision-making procedure is not determined by whether the procedure in question requires an EIA (or is labelled as 'environmental decision-making', for that matter), but rather by whether the decision-making as such is deemed liable to produce a significant impact on the environment.[170] Although the Aarhus Convention does not establish an EIA regime *per se*, its provisions

162 *The Aarhus Convention: An Implementation Guide*, p. 109.

163 As provided under Art.9(2) of the Convention.

164 Art.6(9).

165 *The Aarhus Convention: An Implementation Guide*, p. 85.

166 Art.6(1)(c).

167 *The Aarhus Convention: An Implementation Guide*, p. 89.

168 *Idem*, p. 90.

169 *Idem*.

170 *Idem*.

do ultimately establish a kind of an obligatory review of the environmental effects of particular activities which is to be undertaken in the course of the relevant decision-making process.[171] Thus, the Convention does not make environment assessment compulsory to all public participation procedures being that environmental impact assessment is not necessarily part of all the public participation procedures potentially covered by the former – the reverse is nevertheless true: public participation represents a constitutive part of the environmental assessment procedure.[172] More particularly, in addition to decision-making procedures that include an EIA, Art.6 covers other types of decision-making where the EIA is not applicable or suitable as a mechanism (for example, regulatory decisions on rate-setting, approvals for the introduction of new products into commerce, etc.).[173] In this sense, the notion of public participation is intrinsically linked with the EIA as a procedural mechanism given that the public will often not be able to form a valid science-based opinion in the course of its participation in the decision-making process in the absence of adequate environmental reports and related documents which concern the actual or potential environmental and health risks of the planned activities.[174]

IV.2 *Public Participation Concerning Plans, Programmes and Policies Relating to the Environment (Article 7)*

The duties concerning public participation in the drafting of plans, programmes and policies relating to the environment are covered by Article 7 which, in turn, fails to define either of the former terms for which reason one is led to rely on their habitual, common-sense legal meanings in the national legal systems of the UN/ECE countries.[175] The regime applicable to plans and programmes is different from that on policies, the latter being less elaborate

171 *Idem*, p.91.

172 Jendroska, *The Aarhus Convention at Ten...*, *supra* n. 35, p. 101.

173 *The Aarhus Convention: An Implementation Guide*, p. 91.

174 Jendroska, *The Aarhus Convention at Ten...*, *supra* n. 35, p. 99; See also, Communication ACCC/C/24 (Spain), para. 55.

175 *The Aarhus Convention: An Implementation Guide*, p. 113; The Convention introduces a comparatively higher standard in that it covers all plans and programmes 'relating to the environment' rather than only those having a potential effect or a potentially harmful effect thereupon (see, *The Aarhus Convention: An Implementation Guide*, p. 115); The acts typically adopted pursuant to the Art.7 rules are plans, programmes and strategies, while the fields they habitually apply to are zoning, spatial planning, resource management, water management, waste management and nature conservation (Jendroska, *The Aarhus Convention at Ten*, *supra* n. 35, p. 117).

and more flexible in nature. Thus, while it is required that Parties 'make appropriate practical and/or other provisions for the public to participate during the preparation of plans and programmes relating to the environment', with relation to policies, Parties are required to 'endeavor to provide opportunities for public participation in the preparation of policies relating to the environment'.[176] In addition, in the preparation of plans and programmes relating to the environment, public authorities are instructed to offer reasonable time-frames for the different phases of the decision-making, provide for early public participation and ensure that in adopting the decision due account is taken of the outcome of the public participation.[177]

Due to the lack of prescription as to the manner in which the Parties should implement the foregoing obligations, the former are lead to revert to the applicable national rules in assessing the relevance of particular plans, programmes and policies to the environment.[178] In this sense, the use of the 'strategic environmental assessment (SEA)' has been suggested as a suitable mechanism that enables the public authorities to integrate environmental considerations into the development of plans, programmes and policies.[179] One can conceivably make an analogy between the way in which the EIA mechanism vehicles the decision-making process under Art.6 with the role of the SEA mechanism in appraising the potential environmental effects of the proposed plans, programmes and policies.[180]

As concerns the category of people encompassed by the requirements, the first sentence of Art.7 employs the 'any person' principle referring to the duty of the Parties to make appropriate practical and/or other provisions for the *public* to participate during the preparation of plans and programmes, within a transparent and fair framework and by having provided the necessary information to the public.[181] However, the second sentence of the article restricts the scope of the former duty to the *public which may participate*, leaving to the discretion of the relevant public authorities to identify this section of the public by taking into account the objectives of the Convention. The way in which the evident difference in scopes has been explained is that the first sentence

176 Art.7.

177 Art.7.

178 *The Aarhus Convention: An Implementation Guide*, p. 114.

179 *Idem.*

180 *Idem.*; For more on the 'strategic environmental assessment' process and the Sofia Initiative on Environmental Impact Assessment, see, *The Aarhus Convention: An Implementation Guide*, p. 115.

181 Art.7.

concerns the obligation to provide necessary information to the public which would thereupon enable it to participate in the preparation of plans and programmes relating to the environment (as a general responsibility for notification), while the second sentence would presumably apply strictly to the process of participation *per se*.[182] Therefore, in determining the scope of the 'public which may participate' the public authorities should take guidance from the provisions of the Convention's Preamble which insists that an inclusive approach is adopted in identifying the interested members of the public.[183] In this vein, the public authorities should employ a methodology that is verifiable and transparent which would itself be most effectively accomplished by introducing a uniform definition in the national implementing law/s for the category of the 'public that may participate'.[184]

IV.3 *Public Participation in the Preparation of Executive Regulations and/or Generally Applicable Legally Binding Normative Instruments (Article 8)*

With the legislative branch of government being excluded from scrutiny under the Aarhus Convention regime, the legislative prerogatives of the executive branch in environmental decision-making are nevertheless caught under the scope of Article 8 of the Convention. The former article introduces a rather negligible degree of compulsion, aiming to provide guidance rather than lay down binding rules for the public authorities. Pursuant to Art.8, public authorities should *strive* to promote effective public participation at an appropriate stage (while options are still open) during the preparation of executive regulations or other generally applicable legally binding rules that *may have a significant effect on the environment*. Hence, to the difference of the provisions concerning plans, programmes and policies relating to the environment, the threshold for the application of Art.8 has been set higher so as to only cover legally binding rules that may have a significant effect on the environment. The legal acts that Art.8 applies to are not solely those which are immediately executable (as the title of the acts may suggest), and can include various decrees, regulations, ordinances, instructions, normative orders, etc.[185] For the purpose

182 *The Aarhus Convention: An Implementation Guide*, p. 118.

183 *Idem.*

184 *Idem.*; The Implementation Guide suggests the drafting of standing lists of interested individuals and NGOs in which persons express their interest in being informed of and in participating in planning and policymaking in specific areas or on specific subjects, as a feasible solution.

185 *The Aarhus Convention: An Implementation Guide*, p. 120.

of allowing the public to participate, appropriate time-frames should be set whereas the draft rules should be published (or otherwise be made publicly available) providing *the public* with the opportunity to comment, directly or through representative consultative bodies.[186] At the stage of the final drafting of the act to be adopted, the public authority ought to attempt to note all the public involvement that has previously taken place and omitting to do so could plausibly be considered to be a breach of the Convention procedural requirements.[187] Unfortunately, though, the need for the result of the public participation to be taken into account as far as possible often times succumbs to the 'politics' involved in the legislative process which is liable to hinder any thorough examination of the possible procedural defects of the decision-making process and, as a result, deny the possibility to challenge the outcome of the decision-making in any substantive manner.[188]

A controversy that surrounds the correct implementation of the Art.8 requirements is the issue of whether the scope of these requirements should extend to the public authorities' participation in the legislative process which concludes with the passing of the acts drafted by the executive on to the legislative organs. The Implementation Guide offers an affirmative stance, considering that in this way the Convention rules ensure the public participation in the legislative process through the medium of public authorities rather than directly interacting with the legislative branch.[189] *A fortiori*, the stage of preparation of draft legislation can not be qualified as acting in a legislative capacity (within the meaning of the Convention) to the effect that the public's involvement in the course of the preparation of the legal acts by public authorities signifies 'participation at an early stage'.[190] Such public participation at an appropriate stage prevents that any problems regarding the adopted text emerge

186 Art.8.

187 *The Aarhus Convention: An Implementation Guide*, p. 122.

188 *Idem.;* In support to this claim, observe the requirement that 'due account' is taken of the outcome of public participation (under Art.6) as opposed to the requirement that the former is taken into account 'as far as possible' (under Art.8). the latter sets a slightly higher standard which can be accounted for by the fact that the specific activities subsumed under Art.6 directly affect the rights and interests of particular members of the public, unlike the legislative process which is played out at the government level and is therefore not as tenable and immediate as the former (*The Aarhus Convention: An Implementation Guide*, p. 109).

189 *The Aarhus Convention: An Implementation Guide*, p. 120.

190 *Idem.*

in the future so that once the draft legislation is finally passed on to the legislature it no longer belongs to the remit of Art.8.[191]

The former progressive reading of the Convention's provisions cannot be (without difficulty) reconciled with the reality of the law-making process especially in the absence of an express provision extending the application of the Convention rules to the preparatory stage of the legislative process.[192] Being that Art.8 is concerned with legal acts adopted by the public authorities which are 'final' rather than preparatory, the former way of interepreting the Art.8 provisions is potentially conducive to an unwarranted extension of the scope of application of the former article and the Convention as a whole.

The general conclusion to be drawn from the foregoing discussion is that law-making at the domestic level remains to be a sensitive and delicate domain for the Parties, which is bourne out by the permissive character of the Art.8 provisions and the employment of a 'best efforts' approach[193] to a field which potentially creates the most far-reaching effects for the ordinary citizen.

IV.4 *The Participation-in-decision-making Pillar Transposed in Union/ Euratom Law*

Completing the previously raised discourse regarding the scope of the transparency obligations belonging to Euratom's purview, the breadth of the participation-in-decision-making requirements pertaining to the environmental field and applicable to the former purview shall be examined through an analysis of the relevant primary law and secondary law instruments adopted under the Union and the Euratom legal framework.

First and foremost, it is essential to indicate that the Union Treaties contain provisions of a participatory nature relative to the closer involvement of the Union citizen in the work of the Union's instiutions, bodies, offices and

191 *Idem*; Were the situation reverse, namely, should a public authority adopt a law drafted by a legislative body which has acted in full legislative capacity, Art.8 would consequently fail to apply as the activity in question cannot be qualified as 'preparation' within the meaning of the Convention (*The Aarhus Convention: An Implementation Guide*, p. 120).

192 See, on this, J. Ebbesson, Public Participation and Privatisation in Environmental Matters: An Assessment of the Aarhus Convention, *Erasmus Law Review*, 2011, Vol 4 Issue 2, p. 75; The author argues that the preparation of generally applicable regulations and normative instruments is not to be mixed with legislation as the Aarhus Convention, according to Art.2(2), does not apply to bodies and institutions acting in a legislative or judicial capacity.

193 *The Aarhus Convention: An Implementation Guide*, p. 119.

agencies (Art.15(1) TFEU)[194] and, on a more general note, the participation in the democratic life of the Union (Art.10(3) TEU).[195] Furthermore, Art.10(3) requires that decisions are taken as openly and closely as possible to the citizen (whereby it has not been specified whether the former only concerns the Union's decisions or additionally includes the decisions adopted at the national level). While Art.15 TFEU has been extended to the Euratom framework via the bridging provisions of Art.106a Euratom, the Art.10 TEU requirements are however not applicable to the Euratom Treaty's scope of application. Moreover, the Euratom Treaty itself fails to include any (even incidental) references to the participation of the public in Euratom's decision-making process. It would seem that, for a treaty which is relatively 'old' and has not yielded to any substantial changes since its adoption, it could not be expected of the Euratom Treaty drafters to have allowed themselves the luxury of endorsing active public participation mechanisms at the expense of the dominant promotional character of the Treaty with respect to a budding new industry which was nuclear energy at the time.

As concerns the secondary law instruments, the provisions of the Aarhus Convention covering the participation in the decision-making have been transposed into EU law via the 1985 *Environmental Impact Assessment* (*EIA*) *Directive* 85/337/EEC[196] (codified by Directive 2011/92/EU[197]) (concerning specific projects), Directive 2001/42/EC[198] known as the *Strategic Environmental Assessment* (*SEA*) *Directive* (concerning public plans and programmes that are likely to have a significant effect on the environment)[199] and the 2003 *Public*

194 Article 15 TFEU:

1. In order to promote good governance and ensure the participation of civil society, the Union institutions, bodies, offices and agencies shall conduct their work as openly as possible. (…);

195 Article 10 TEU:

(…) 3. Every citizen shall have the right to participate in the democratic life of the Union. Decisions shall be taken as openly and as closely as possible to the citizen;

196 Council Directive 85/337/EEC of 27 June 1985 on the assessment of the effects of certain public and private projects on the environment *OJ L 175, 5.7.1985, pp. 40–48*. The Directive has been amended three times, in 1997, 2003 and 2009.

197 Directive 2011/92/EU of the European Parliament and of the Council of 13 December 2011 on the assessment of the effects of certain public and private projects on the environment (codification) OJ L 26, pp. 1–21.

198 Directive 2001/42/EC of the European Parliament and of the Council of 27 June 2001 on the assessment of the effects of certain plans and programmes on the environment *OJ L 197, 21.7.2001, pp. 30–37*.

199 See http://ec.europa.eu/environment/eia/home.htm.

Participation Directive 2003/35/EC[200] (with respect to the drawing up of certain plans and programmes relating to the environment). The former directives, together with the 2003 Public Information Directive, have been succinctly described as largely completing the European regulatory framework on public information and participation in the decision-making process on nuclear matters.[201] To the extent that the activity of the EU institutions and bodies is concerned, the second pillar requirements of the Aarhus Convention have been transposed to the EU level via the *Regulation No 1367/2006 on the application of the provisions of the Aarhus Convention on Access to Information, Public Participation in Decision-making and Access to Justice in Environmental Matters to Community institutions and bodies* (the Aarhus Regulation).

In this sense it is to be reminded that only the Art.6 and Art.7 (the provisions relating to the participation in the preparation of plans and programmes) of the Aarhus Convention have their corresponding implementing Union rules while the provisions regarding involvement in the policy-making as well as the adoption of executive regulations and generally applicable legally binding measures, have not been covered by Union implementing rules. Admittedly, EU legislators are not under an obligation to adopt the former implementing rules given that the Convention provisions in question merely require legal or policy adjustments at the domestic level[202] and, in view of their pervasively dispositive character, do not intend to institute any strict regulatory regime.

The *EIA Directive* applies to the assessment of the environmental effects of public and private projects that have a significant impact on the environment, where the term 'project' presupposes the execution of construction works, installations, schemes and other interventions in the natural surroundings and landscape.[203] Member States bear the responsibility to adopt all necessary measures to ensure that prior to giving a consent on a proposed project likely to have a significant impact on the environment, such a project is made subject to an assessment with respect to its potential effects on the environment (by taking account of the nature, size and location of the project as well as other determinative characteristics etc.).[204] Employing the mechanism of environmental impact assessment (EIA) involves the identification, description and

200 Directive 2003/35/EC of 26 May 2003 providing for public participation in respect of the drawing up of certain plans and programmes relating to the environment, OJ L 156, 25/06/2003 PP. 0017–0025.

201 See, Gadbois et al., *supra* n. 39, p. 14.

202 Jendroska, *The Aarhus Convention at Ten…*, *supra* n. 35, p. 102.

203 Art.1(1) and (2).

204 Art.2(1).

assessment of the direct and indirect effects of a project on the following factors of environment: '(a) human beings, fauna and flora; (b) soil, water, air, climate and the landscape; (c) material assets and the cultural heritage; and, (d) the interaction between the factors referred to in points (a), (b) and (c)'.[205]

The Directive covers two types of projects: projects that are subject to an EIA *ipso jure* (listed in Annex I) and projects which can be optionally included for an EIA upon the decision of Member States (listed in Annex II).[206] With respect to the latter, Member States make their decision based on a case-by-case examination or by laying down various applicable thresholds or criteria.[207] Thus, while the Directive follows the enumeration included in Annex I of the Aarhus Convention, it further allows for an extension of the scope of the public participation obligations by enlisting additional projects with respect to which the Member States enjoy the discretion in deciding on their inclusion under the Directive's public participation procedures. *Viz.* nuclear energy projects, Annex I of the Directive copies the enumeration of Annex I of the Convention while Annex II thereof introduces an addition with regard to projects involving deep drillings for the storage of nuclear waste material.[208]

---

205 Art.3.

206 Art.4.

207 Art.4(1) and 4(2); On how the process develops from the application stage to the adoption of the development consent, see Arts.5–10.

208 *Annex I* – Projects Referred To in Article 4(1)

2. (...)

(b) *Nuclear power stations and other nuclear reactors* including the dismantling or decommissioning of such power stations or reactors (1) (except research installations for the production and conversion of fissionable and fertile materials, whose maximum power does not exceed 1 kilowatt continuous thermal load).

3. (a) Installations for the reprocessing of irradiated nuclear fuel;

(b) Installations designed:

(i) for the production or enrichment of nuclear fuel;

(ii) for the processing of irradiated nuclear fuel or high-level radioactive waste;

(iii) for the final disposal of irradiated nuclear fuel;

(iv) solely for the final disposal of radioactive waste;

(v) solely for the storage (planned for more than 10 years) of irradiated nuclear fuels or radioactive waste in a different site than the production site.

Annex II – Projects Referred To in Article 4(2)

(...) 2. EXTRACTIVE INDUSTRY

(...) (d) Deep drillings, in particular:

(...) (ii) *drilling for the storage of nuclear waste material* [...] with the exception of drillings for investigating the stability of the soil (...) [Emphasis added];

The EIA Directive prescribes different responsibilities towards the 'public' and the 'public concerned', defining the 'public concerned' as the 'public affected or likely to be affected by, or having an interest in, the environmental decision-making procedures [dealt with under the Directive]'.[209] Under Art.6(2) of the EIA Directive, early in the environmental decision-making procedures or, at the latest, as soon as information can reasonably be provided, *the public* is to be informed, *inter alia*, of the following : '(a) the existence of the request for development consent; (b) the fact that the project is subject to an environmental impact assessment procedure; (c) the public authorities responsible for taking the decision (those from which relevant information can be obtained, those to which comments or questions can be submitted, as well as details on the time schedule for delivering comments or questions); (d) the nature of the possible decisions or the draft decision; (f) an indication of the times and places at which, and the means by which, the relevant information will be made available;(…) [etc]'.

Furthermore, Member States are responsible to ensure that within reasonable time-frames the *public concerned* is granted access to any information gathered from the developer in the process and (in accordance with national legislation) the main reports and advice issued to the competent authorities.[210] The public concerned is to be given early and effective opportunities to participate in the environmental decision-making procedures and is for that purpose entitled to give comments and opinions before the decision on the request for development consent is taken.[211]

The practical arrangements for making the information available to the public (usually by bill posting within a certain radius or via publications in local newspapers) and for consulting the public concerned (e.g., by written submissions or by launching a public inquiry), are to be determined by the Member States along with the requirement for reasonable time-frames for the different stages of the procedure allowing sufficient time for the public to have access to the relevant information and for the public concerned to prepare and effectively participate in the decision-making.[212] The development consent procedure should take stock of the results of the public consultations[213] with

209 Art.1(2)(e); Further on, in Art.1(2)(e): '(…) For the purposes of this definition, non-governmental organisations promoting environmental protection and meeting any requirements under national law shall be deemed to have an interest'.;

210 Art.6(3)(a) and (b).

211 Art.6(4).

212 Art.6(5) and (6).

213 Art.8.

the duty that once a decision to grant or refuse development consent has been taken by the authorities, the latter shall inform the public of the existence of such a decision and provide the public with the following information: (a) the content of the decision; (b) the main reasons and considerations on which the decision is based (including information about the public participation process); (c) a description (where necessary) of the main measures to be used to avoid, reduce and, if possible, counteract the major adverse effects.[214]

The *Strategic Environmental Assessment* (SEA) Directive covers plans and programmes that are in the process of preparation and/or adoption by a national, regional or local authority or which are prepared by an authority for the subsequent adoption, through a legislative procedure, by Parliament or Government.[215] Under the Directive, the environmental assessment is understood as the process comprising the preparation of an environmental report, the carrying out of consultations, the taking into account of the environmental report and the results of the consultations in the decision-making and the provision of information on the final decision.[216] The environmental assessment is to be conducted during the preparation of a plan or programme, prior to the adoption of the latter or its submission to the legislative procedure.[217] The environmental report that is to be prepared within the scope of the assessment should identify, describe and evaluate the likely significant effects that the implementation of the plan or programme may cause to the environment, coupled with a choice of reasonable alternatives and taking the objectives and the geographical scope of the plan or programme into consideration.[218]

214 Art.9(1).

215 Art.2(a).

216 Art.2(b).

217 Art.4(1).

218 Art.5(1). Annex I outlines the type of information the environmental report is expected to contain, pursuant to the reference in Art.5(1):

> Annex I – Information Referred to in Article 5(1)
>
> The information to be provided under Article 5(1), subject to Article 5(2) and (3), is the following:
>
> (a) an outline of the contents, main objectives of the plan or programme and relationship with other relevant plans and programmes;
>
> (b) the relevant aspects of the current state of the environment and the likely evolution thereof without implementation of the plan or programme;
>
> (c) the environmental characteristics of areas likely to be significantly affected;
>
> (d) any existing environmental problems which are relevant to the plan or programme including, in particular, those relating to any areas of a particular environmental importance, such as areas designated pursuant to Directives 79/409/EEC and 92/43/EEC;

The former environmental assessment is specific to plans and programmes that are likely to have significant environmental effects,[219] namely those prepared in the fields of agriculture, forestry, fisheries, energy, industry, transport, waste management, water management, telecommunications, tourism, town and country planning or land use, which set the framework for future development consent of projects listed in Annexes I and II to Directive 85/337/EEC'[220]. To the extent that concerns the nuclear field, Annexes I and II of Directive 85/337/EEC cover a wide range of activities in the field of nuclear energy (referred to *supra*) which indicates that the EIA and the SEA directives cover the identical range of nuclear activities. The SEA Directive does not apply to plans and programmes that deal with the use of small areas at local level, nor to minor modifications to plans and programmes which, in turn, require an environmental assessment (provided the Member States have not classified the former as likely to have significant environmental effects).[221] Furthermore, plans and programmes the sole purpose of which is to serve the national defence or civil emergency as well as financial or budget plans and programmes have been categorically excluded from the scope of the SEA Directive.[222]

Given that both the EIA and the SEA Directives precede the entry into force of the Aarhus Convention at the EU level, the *Public Participation Directive* had been specifically targeted at transposing the Aarhus Convention

(e) the environmental protection objectives, established at international, Community or Member State level, which are relevant to the plan or programme and the way those objectives and any environmental considerations have been taken into account during its preparation;

(f) the likely significant effects(1) on the environment, including on issues such as biodiversity, population, human health, fauna, flora, soil, water, air, climatic factors, material assets, cultural heritage including architectural and archaeological heritage, landscape and the interrelationship between the above factors;

(g) the measures envisaged to prevent, reduce and as fully as possible offset any significant adverse effects on the environment of implementing the plan or programme;

(h) an outline of the reasons for selecting the alternatives dealt with, and a description of how the assessment was undertaken including any difficulties (such as technical deficiencies or lack of know-how) encountered in compiling the required information;

(i) a description of the measures envisaged concerning monitoring in accordance with Article 10;

(j) a non-technical summary of the information provided under the above headings. (...);

219 Art.3(1).

220 Art.3(2)(a).

221 Art.3(3).

222 Art.3(8).

requirements on participation in decision-making in environmental matters to the EU legal framework.[223] The Directive lays down the procedural arrangements for Members States to allow the public to early and effectively participate in the preparation and modification or review of plans and programmes relating to the environment, falling within the scope of six pre-existing environmental directives.[224] There has been doubt expressed as to whether the Directive effectively covers all the relevant plans and programmes relating to the environment since the scope of the six directives it makes express reference to is fairly narrow – the reasons for such a restrictive approach on the part of the Union legislators remaining unclear.[225] On the positive side, there is a possibility for this impending *lacuna* to be counteracted by way of including provisions on public participation in environmental decision-making in all future Union legislative proposals that relate to environmental plans and programmes, which as a general intention has been expressed by the relevant EU institutions.[226] Moreover, plans and programmes for which a public participation procedure is carried out under the SEA Directive are excluded from the scope of the Public Participation Directive.[227] Hence, the applicable regime for plans and programmes on nuclear energy is the one postulated

223 Jendroska explains why the 2003 Directive has not supplemented the pre-existing regime on plans and programmes in any substantial manner (See, Jendroska, *The Aarhus Convention at Ten, supra* n. 35, pp. 99–105); In addition, the Directive restricts the right to participate in environmental decision-making to those 'affected by or with an interest in the decision' (i.e. 'the public concerned'), rather than 'any member of the public' (as foreseen in the Aarhus Convention) (see, also, Mason, *supra* n. 3, p. 22). Jendroska has observed that the difference in scope will have significant consequences since it restricts the range of subjects enjoying rights prescribed under the Convention which is a failure on the part of the EU legislature which has not been addressed – in spite of the fact that it concerns only one aspect of public participation which is the Art.6 possibility to submit comments and opinions (see, Jendroska, *The Aarhus Convention at Ten, supra*, p. 132).

224 Art.2(2); The Directives have been listed in Annex I of the Public Participation: Council Directive 75/442/EEC of 15 July 1975 on waste, Council Directive 91/157/EEC of 18 March 1991 on batteries and accumulators containing certain dangerous substances, Council Directive 91/676/EEC of 12 December 1991 concerning the protection of waters against pollution caused by nitrates from agricultural sources, Council Directive 91/689/EEC of 12 December 1991 on hazardous waste, Directive 94/62/EC of the European Parliament and of the Council of 20 December 1994 on packaging and packaging waste; and Council Directive 96/62/EC of 27 September 1996 on ambient air quality assessment and management.

225 Jendroska, *The Aarhus Convention at Ten, supra* n. 35, p. 104.

226 Jendroska, *The Aarhus Convention at Ten, supra* n. 35, p. 103.

227 Art.2(5).

under the SEA Directive, eliminating the necessity for the two separate regimes of the SEA and the Public Participation Directives to be reconciled concerning the former field.

The discrepancy is further reflected in the existent inconsistencies in the relationship between the SEA Directive and the Public Participation Directive primarily due to the fact that the remit of the former is manifestly narrower as it only applies to plans and programmes that are 'likely to have a significant effect on the environment' while the latter covers plans and programmes 'relating to the environment' (in keeping with the letter of Art.7 of the Aarhus Convention).[228] Such a shortcoming rules out the possibility to apply the more inclusive obligations of Art.8 of the Convention (translated in the Public Participation Directive) to the plans and programmes already covered by the remit of the SEA Directive, given that the two regimes are mutually exclusive.

In comparison to the language of the directives discussed *supra*, the corresponding duties devolving on the EU institutions and bodies under the *2006 Aarhus Regulation* are not as prescriptive and detailed, but the core principles have nevertheless been preserved. Namely, the institutions are entrusted with the task of providing early and effective opportunities for the public to participate during the preparation, modification or review of plans or programmes relating to the environment when all the options are still open.[229] The Aarhus Regulation does not provide a list of the particular plans and programmes under its scope, although, given that it transposes the Aarhus Convention provisions on the matter, the silence of the Regulation's text implies that the former covers the identical range of plans and programmes as the Aarhus Convention.

As the initiator of legislation, the Commission is under the duty to ensure public participation in the preparatory stage for a proposal on a plan or programme relating to the environment which it subsequently submits to other institutions or bodies for decision.[230] The institutions and bodies are obligated to take due account of the outcome of the public participation and inform the public of the plan or programme that has been adopted by furnishing the former with the text of the plan or programme together with a statement on the reasons for the adoption thereof.[231] It is significant to note that, unlike the access-to-information provisions, the provisions on participation in decision making of the Aarhus Regulation only apply to the Union institutions and

228 See, also, Jendroska, *The Aarhus Convention at Ten*, *supra* n. 35, p. 100.

229 Art.9(1).

230 Art.9(1).

231 Art.9(5).

bodies when in performance of an executive or administrative function, *excluding* the legislative process.[232]

232 The CJEU was asked to delimit the scope of the notion of 'legislative act' with respect to the public participation process in cases such as *Solvay* (C-182/10 Marie-Noëlle Solvay and Others, ECLI:EU:C:2012:82) and *Boxus C (134/09 and C 135/09 Antoine Boxus and Others, ECR 2011 p. I-9711)*. Namely, Art.1(5) of EIA Directive 85/337 (present Art.1(4) of the 2011/92/EU Directive) translates the Aarhus Convention Art.2(2) exemption regarding bodies/institutions acting in a legislative capacity and enables the disapplication of the Directive to projects the details of which are adopted by a specific act of national legislation on the condition that the objectives of the Directive together with the objective of supplying information are achieved through the legislative process that lead to its adoption. The Court made the application of the former exemption contingent on two conditions, namely that the details of the project must form part of a specific act of legislation, where the Directive's objectives (including that of supplying information) are capable of being achieved through the legislative process (Para. 31 of the *Solvay* judgment; the CJEU had already established the former in the *Boxus* judgment (Para. 37) and even earlier, in C-435/97 *WWF and Others* [1999] ECR I-5613, para. 57). Furthermore, the legislative act adopting the project needs to be specific and own the same characteristics as consent of the same kind, and, in particular, it must grant upon the developer the right to execute the project (Para. 32 of *Solvay* judgment). The Court held that where a legislative act merely 'ratifies' a pre-existing administrative act, by solely referring to overriding reasons in the public interest without there be prior commencement of a substantive legislative process enabling those conditions to be fulfilled, it is not be regarded as a specific legislative act and is therefore not sufficient grounds to exclude the project at issue from the scope of Directive 85/337 (Para.39 of *Solvay* judgment, Para. 45 of the *Boxus* judgment). Hence, the national court was entrusted with the duty to verify whether the two conditions are met by taking due account of the content of the legislative act as well as the entire legislative process that led to its adoption (with particular consideration of the preparatory documents and parliamentary debates) (Para. 43 of *Solvay*); For a case note on the *Solvay* judgment, see, C. Poncelet, Évaluation des incidences sur l'environnement. L'arrêt Solvay C/ Région Wallonne: la technique de ratification législative des permis devant la Cour de justice, *Revue juridique de l'environnement* 2013 pp. 95–102; Also, for commentary on the *Boxus* judgment, see, M. Hedemann-Robinson, EU Enforcement of International Environmental Agreements: The Role of the European Commission, European Energy and Environmental Law Review, February 2012, p. 24.

Other recent public participation cases decided by the CJEU include C-115/09 *Bund fur Umwelt und Naturschutz Deutschland, Landesverband Nordrhein-Westfalen eV* on German restrictions on NGO court access considered to be in breach of the EIA Directive; *C-275/09 Brussels Hoofdstedelijk Gewest* et al. on the possibility for the renewal of an existing permit to operate an airport to be considered a 'project' under the EIA Directive and thus subject to assessment; *C-416/10 Jozef Križan and others* on the right to access urban planning decisions in competition with the confidentiality of industrial secrets, etc; For a comprehensive account of all the public participation cases of the CJEU involving the

In consequence to the foregoing, it seems adequate to round off the discussion by referring to the Euratom acts which have a certain bearing on the notion of participation in decision-making and create obligations for Member States in this regard. The common approach to be observed under the Euratom framework is that of a striking deficiency of mechanisms for public involvement in the decision-making procedures provided under the Euratom Treaty and the Euratom secondary legislation – a far cry from the full blown transparency and participatory mechanisms fostered under the *Union* framework. For instance, the Preamble to *Directive 2011/70/Euratom establishing a Community framework for the responsible and safe management of spent fuel and radioactive waste*[233] makes a reference to the Public Participation Directive,[234] emphasizing the importance of transparency in the area of management of spent fuel and radioactive waste that is to be accomplished by providing adequate opportunities for effective public participation in the decision-making processes for the public and the rest of the stakeholders.[235] The Directive attempts to reconcile the public participation concerns in the domain of spent fuel and radioactive waste management with the security and management-of-proprietary-information concerns.[236] Thus, the Member States are under the obligation to provide *the public* with the necessary opportunities to participate effectively in the decision-making process regarding the spent fuel and radioactive waste management, in accordance with national legislation and international obligations.[237] Unfortunately, the former duty seems to lack any binding effect and rather acts declaratory statement since it omits to foresee any concrete binding mechanisms for Member States to discharge of their duty to ensure effective public participation.

Furthermore, it appears that the improved transparency regime endorsed under *Directive 2014/87/Euratom of 8 July 2014 amending Directive 2009/71/Euratom establishing a Community framework for the nuclear safety of nuclear installations*[238] has equally found an expression in the public participation

mechanism of environmental impact assessment, see, European Commission, Environmental Impact Assessment of Projects: Rulings of the Court of Justice, *European Union*, 2013.

233 Council Directive 2011/70/Euratom of 19 July 2011 establishing a Community framework for the responsible and safe management of spent fuel and radioactive waste OJ L 199, 02/08/2011 PP. 0048–0056.

234 Point 11 of Preamble.

235 Point 31 of Preamble.

236 Art.1(3).

237 Art.10(2).

238 OJ L 219, 25.7.2014, pp. 42–52.

domain. The Directive draws on the importance of giving the general public opportunities to participate in the relevant phases of the decision-making process related to nuclear installations in accordance with the national framework for nuclear safety,[239] creating an obligation for Member States to ensure that the general public is given 'the appropriate opportunities to participate effectively in the decision-making process relating to the licensing of nuclear installations, in accordance with relevant legislation and international instruments'.[240] Similarly to the preceding example, the duty to enable the general public to participate effectively in the decision-making established thereby lacks any sufficiently prescriptive character and affords a large margin of appreciation to Member States.

V The Implementation of the Aarhus Convention Obligations

The preceding sections elaborated the nature and scope of the Aarhus Convention obligations, bringing about the necessity to shed light on the aspect of the actual implementation of the former obligations at the EU and the Member State level. The monitorning of the access-to-information and public participation requirements at the EU level is performed by the Commission which, to date, has issued two implementation reports that were thereupon submitted to the Aarhus Convention bodies (in 2008 and 2011).[241] The 2011 Implementation report (which for the time being is the most recent one issued by the Commission)[242] notes the most significant developments in the application of the Aarhus Convention requirements (mostly, the regulatory activity of the institutions and the relevant case law of the EU Court of Justice[243]), but, curiously enough, does not indicate any obstacles encountered therein. To the contrary, it is found there had been none, apart from those related to meeting the Convention's access-to-justice requirements[244] (dealt with in the last section of this chapter). Given its fairly laconic style and lack of

239 Point 12 of Preamble.

240 Art.8(4).

241 Although the reporting cycle of the implementation reports is three years, the 2014 Aarhus Convention Implementation Report has not yet been published (http://ec.europa.eu/environment/aarhus/reporting.htm).

242 European Commission, *Aarhus Convention Implementation Report*, Brussels 14 April 2011, COM (2011) 208 final.

243 Dealt with in the following section of this chapter.

244 European Commission, *Aarhus Convention Implementation Report*, *supra* n. 242, pp. 28–33.

thoroughness the Implementation report does not offer much insight into the *actual* effects of the implementation of the Aarhus Convention at the EU level.

Generally speaking, in the context of implementing the aforementioned obligations and the enforcement of the rights for the public stemming therefrom, practices and modalities have varied from one Member State to the other. Specifically concerning the nuclear sector, it has been reported that in some Member States information centres have been established that allow the local population access to nuclear installations and easy access to information; the relevant authorities' have been involved in educational activities in schools with the goal of increasing the awareness and knowledge of nuclear issues; the engagement of certain nuclear plant operators in issuing regular bulletins to local communities or providing information through the Internet; as well as the establishment of local committees as the focal point bringing together different stakeholders.[245] Pursuant to the requirements of the EIA Directive regarding public involvement, the holding of mandatory public hearings has been observed in some countries as well as organizing public meetings at the request of a certain number of local politicians or local residents and launching local opinion polls.[246]

In this respect, it is indispensable to note that the European Commission, on its part, contributes to empowering the nuclear stakeholders at the national level role by setting the example for applying the Aarhus Convention standards on access to information and public participation in the decision-making to its own regulatory activity pertaining to the nuclear field.[247] In this sense, it has been insisted that the Commission involve the different stakeholders together with the local and regional governments in the preparatory process for the future legislation.[248] Thereby, the role of the European Parliament as an equally concerned institutional actor would be to counterbalance the weight of the Commission and the Council and strive to uphold the transparent and democratic approach in nuclear matters by adopting a non-provocative and non-threatening attitude toward national governments and other stakeholders, relying on its signature political weapon which is 'the instrument of embarrassment'.[249]

In spite of the above mentioned implementation efforts, there exists a prevalent impression that the EU citizens, on the whole, do not feel well informed

245 Gadbois et al., *supra* n. 39, p. 26.

246 *Idem.*

247 *Idem*, p. 14.

248 *Idem.*

249 European Parliament Working Paper, *supra* n. 43, p. xvii.

on nuclear issues. However, according to recent Eurobarometer reports scanning the European public opinion on nuclear safety issues[250] there has nevertheless been a marked improvement in the attitude of European citizens towards nuclear energy. More particularly, a link has been discerned between public acceptance of nuclear energy and the availability of safe solutions for management of radioactive waste where the former grows in direct proportionality to the latter.[251]

A 2007 Eurobarometer Report on Europeans and Nuclear Safety indicated that the citizens were not familiar with safety issues regarding nuclear power plants.[252] The notion of being informed was mainly in direct correlation to whether the surveyed citizens came from a nuclear country or non-nuclear country, where the former usually do not feel sufficiently informed about the safety of nuclear power plants.[253] According to the Report, although the main source of information for the EU citizens was the mass media, the very particular nature of the nuclear safety information prevented it from being fully and adequately conveyed via the mass media.[254] Almost half of the Europeans considered the information provided by scientists to be most trustworthy (48%), followed by the information coming from non-governmental organisations (30%) and national nuclear safety authorities (28%).[255] As concerns the citizens' involvement in the making of national energy strategies, only around 1 in 5 Europeans expressed the preference to be directly consulted in the decision

250 See the following Eurobarometer reports:
Special Eurobarometer Report 271: Europeans and Nuclear Safety (Fieldwork October – November 2006), February 2007 http://ec.europa.eu/public_opinion/archives/ebs/ebs_271_en.pdf ;
Special Eurobarometer Report 297: Attitudes to radioactive waste, published July 2008 http://ec.europa.eu/public_opinion/archives/ebs/ebs_297_en.pdf.
Special Eurobarometer Report 324: Europeans and Nuclear Safety, March 2010, http://ec.europa.eu/public_opinion/archives/ebs/ebs_324_en.pdf;

251 Commission Communication: Update of the Nuclear Illustrative Programme in the context of the Second Strategic Energy, Update for the nuclear illustrative programme, *supra*, p. 7.

252 Special Eurobarometer Report 271: Europeans and Nuclear Safety (Fieldwork October – November 2006), February 2007 http://ec.europa.eu/public_opinion/archives/ebs/ebs_271_en.pdf, p.43; A quarter of the respondents felt completely uninformed about nuclear safety issues (26%) and a further 50% considered themselves not very well informed.

253 p. 44 of Report.

254 p. 46 of Report.

255 p. 51 of Report; Followed by journalists (26%) and international organisations working on uses of nuclear technology (26%) which have a similar confidence level of slightly over a quarter.

making process (21%), with most respondents feeling more at ease with having their democratically elected representatives stepping in in their place and a considerable number of them (39%) preferring for nongovernmental organisations to be consulted instead.[256] Regarding the decision-making process *per se*, a majority of the respondents would rather leave the decision-making exclusively to the authorities responsible for nuclear safety in their country or to NGOs involved in the field.[257]

By comparison, a 2010 Eurobarometer report (which, curiously, is the most recent report commissioned and published by the EU regarding nuclear safety)[258] revealed that Europeans continue to be mostly unfamiliar with nuclear safety issues related to nuclear power plants where only a quarter of citizens feel 'very well' or 'fairly well' informed, compared with three in four people who feel 'not very well', or 'not at all' informed about the safety of nuclear power plants. The former statistic is almost identical to the one showcased in the previous report.[259] Nonetheless, the connection between the feeling of being uninformed and the presence/absence of nuclear powers plants in a country appears to be less evident than in the past,[260] while respondents in countries with active nuclear power plants have expressed slightly more favorable opinions than citizens in countries where domestic electricity comes from other sources.[261] The mass media remains to be the dominant source of information; however, neither the amount nor the quality of the information is considered sufficient by a majority of the respondents to be able to have an informed opinion on the risks and the benefits of nuclear energy choices.[262] Curiously, even though the mass media has been cited as the primary information source for information on nuclear energy, almost half of the Europeans consider the information provided by scientists to be most trustworthy (46%)[263] (followed by national nuclear safety authorities (30%), international

256 p. 55.

257 p. 55.

258 Special Eurobarometer Report 324: Europeans and Nuclear Safety, March 2010, http://ec.europa.eu/public_opinion/archives/ebs/ebs_324_en.pdf.

259 p. 119 of Report.

260 p. 88.

261 p. 92.

262 p. 91. Television ranks first (72%), ahead of all other information sources, followed by newspapers (40%), the Internet which is cited as the third most used source for information on nuclear energy (27%) and the radio (23%). Below the level of 20%, respondents cite magazines (18%) or friends and family (12%). Only 7% mention schools and universities (p. 99 of Report).

263 p. 101.

organisations working on uses of nuclear technology (24%) and journalists (23%)[264]).

According to the 2010 Report, only around a quarter of the EU citizens preferred to be directly consulted in the decision-making process (24%), while most respondents would like non-governmental organisations to be consulted (25%) and 24% of them would choose to place their trust in the responsible authorities in the field.[265] Manifestly, the preference for personal and direct involvement in the decision-making process has remained stable with a notable decline in the trust in NGOs, the results of the reports suggesting that as far as decisions on energy issues in general and the use of nuclear energy in particular are concerned citizens favour discussion and debate. Therefore, it remains to be considered a priority that the responsible authorities in the Member States include the different stakeholders (and the civil society, in particular) when taking decisions on nuclear energy-related issues.[266]

VI The Access-to-information and Participation-in-decision-making Requirements in Environmental and Nuclear Matters before International and Regional Judicial Fora

On the point of the actual enforcement of the right of access to information and the right to participate in decision-making processes as corollary rights, what needs to be emhpasized is that the two rights are intrinsically linked both in terms of their respective scope and content, which commonly renders them intertwined in the jurisprudence of international and regional courts. Cases that relate to access to information would frequently also involve participation issues and *vice versa*, since it is not always possible to draw a stark line between *information* and *participation*: one needs to have access to information in order to be able to participate and, conversely, the key of the participation process lies in obtaining information. Thus, the participation requirement should be perceived as not only complementing the information requirement but rather

264 p.102; Fewer than 20% of the sample mention non-governmental organisations (19%), national governments (18%) and the European Union (15%). Energy companies that operate nuclear power plants and regional and local authorities have a similar confidence level (12% and 10%, accordingly).

265 p. 114. A further fifth would prefer national parliaments to be consulted and to participate in the decision-making process (18%).

266 p. 115.

being the essential motivation thereof.[267] The respective remits of the right of access to information and the right to participation in decision-making differ depending on the particular international legal instrumentaria they have been covered under. Since these are rights of a relatively recent coinage, their exact scope and content are still currently modelled by the hands of the judges so that, in the absence of a more stringent international legal regime in this respect, courts can be seen as acting at the same time both as creators and defenders of the right of access to information and the right to participate in decision-making processes.

Being that to date only few cases involving access to information and public participation in the nuclear field have arisen before international and regional judicial forums, the present section will deal with the relevant cases in this regard that have appeared before the European Court of Human Rights and certain international tribunals and bodies. While the EU Court of Justice has thus far not dealt with cases pertaining to aplication of the Aarhus obligations to the nuclear field, the issue of access to information in the nuclear field has indeed arisen before the ECtHR concerning the health protection in the nuclear field. Even though it has comparatively been less favourably placed than the CJEU whose adjudicatory role has been enabled by a panoply of primary and secondary legal instruments covering the fields of access to information and participation in decision-making in the environmental protection domain, the ECtHR has made its own contribution in the development of the participatory concepts in the field of environmental protection.[268] In the absence of an expressly prescribed right of access to information under the European Convention on Human Rights, the ECtHR habitually decides to rely on Art.8 (right to private and family life)[269] as the suitable proxy for the safeguarding of the procedural rights in the environmental realm. Thus, surprisingly

267 The latter has been pointed out in, Gadbois et al., *supra* n. 39, p. 8.

268 For a more general discussion on the European Court of Human Rights's stake in the environmental protection equation, see, M. Fitzmaurice, The European Convention of Human Rights and the Human Right to a Clean Environment, in, M. Fitzmaurice, *Contemporary Issues of International Environmental Law*, Edward Elgar Publishing, 2009, pp. 170–206; O.W. Pedersen, The Ties that Bind: The Environment, the European Convention on Human Rights and the Rule of Law, *European Public Law*, 2010, Vol. 16 Issue 4; and, O.W. Pedersen, European Environmental Human Rights and Environmental Rights: A Long Time Coming?, *Georgetown International Environmental Law Review*, 2008–2009, Vol. 21 No. 1.

269 Article 8 of the European Convention on Human Rights:

> Everyone has the right to respect for his private and family life, his home and his correspondence.

enough, despite of the former shortcoming, the case-law of the ECtHR in the field has proven to be similarly or even just as authoritative as that of the CJEU.[270]

There shall be no interference by a public authority with the exercise of this right except such as is in accordance with the law and is necessary in a democratic society in the interests of national security, public safety or the economic well-being of the country, for the prevention of disorder or crime, for the protection of health or morals, or for the protection of the rights and freedoms of others.;
Nevertheless, the text of the ECHR does offer a reference to the 'freedom to hold opinions and to receive and impart information and ideas without interference by public authority and regardless of frontiers' (Art.10(1)) as one constitutive of the *right to freedom of expression*. However, the wording of the former provision reveals that the intent of the drafters was not to lay down an independent right to information, but the freedom to receive and impart information in the context of the ECHR is rather conceived as ancillary and therefore in service to the fulfilment of the right to freedom of expression. The former has also been reflected in the extensive scope of the derogation belonging to states in upholding these freedoms Art.10(2)(Art.10(2) states: 'The exercise of these freedoms, since it carries with it duties and responsibilities, may be subject to such formalities, conditions, restrictions or penalties as are prescribed by law and are necessary in a democratic society, in the interests of national security, territorial integrity or public safety, for the prevention of disorder or crime, for the protection of health or morals, for the protection of the reputation or rights of others, for preventing the disclosure of information received in confidence, or for maintaining the authority and impartiality of the judiciary';

270 Two of the more recent access-to-information judgments deserve a mention as they represent the current approach of the ECtHR in the matter. The reasoning offered by the ECtHR in the recent *Di Sarno* judgment (*Di Sarno et autres c. Italie* , no. 30765/08, ECHR 2012) is consistent with all similar access to information cases that have appeared before the Court. The case deals with the state of emergency in the Campania region of Italy and the related failure of the system for waste collection, treatment and disposal. The Court held that by virtue of Art.8 ECHR states were under a duty to establish a pertinent regulatory framework applicable to hazardous activities so that in the instant case it was Italy's obligation to impart information to the public enabling it to assess the degree of the danger it had been exposed to. Namely, considering that the collection, treatment and disposal of waste are hazardous activities, the state was responsible to adopt appropriate measures in order to uphold the right of the persons concerned to respect for their private life and home, and in a more general manner, their right to a healthy and safe environment (Para. 110 of judgment). The Italian authorities had for a relatively long period failed to assure the proper functioning of the waste collection, treatment and disposal service which directly affected the former rights of the applicants (Para. 111 et seq.). Inter alia, specific reference was made to Art.5(1)(c) of the Aarhus Convention which has been ratified by Italy (Para. 107). However, the Court only found a breach of the material component of Art.8, being satisfied that the procedural component of the article had been met,

mainly on account of the involvement of the Italian authorities in conducting and publishing of the impact studies in 2005 and 2008 which the Court considered as demonstrative of the authorities having fulfilled their duty to inform the persons concerned on the potential risks to which they had been exposed (Para. 113).

A case much in line with the last is *Tatar* (*Tatar c. Roumanie*, Requête no. 67021/01, ECHR 2009) concerning applicants that lived in the vicinity of a gold mine the extraction process for which involved the use of the hazardous chemical compound sodium cyanide. In the *Tatar* judgment the Court refers to the Aarhus Convention in its elaboration on the particular situation of the interested parties who attempt to challenge the result of the impact studies and thus have access to documents relative to the decision-making process considering themselves a subset of the 'population potentially affected' category (Para. 119), considering the Aarhus Convention to be relevant to the case (Para. 118). The Court observed that the existence of a serious and material risk for the applicants' health and well-being triggered the duty of the State to conduct an assessment of the risks and take appropriate measures, both at the time the operating permit was granted and once the accident had occurred (Para. 118 et seq.). It was noted that in spite of the preliminary impact assessment conducted by the Romanian Ministry of the Environment, the Romanian authorities did not take sufficient account of the risks caused by the extraction activity to the environment and human health when laying down the operating conditions (Paras. 118–124). The Court further stressed that it fell upon the national authorities to ensure public access to the conclusions of the available investigations and studies and to guarantee the right of members of the public to participate in the decision-making process regarding environmental issues (Paras. 118–124). In this regard, it found that the Romanian Government had neglected its obligation to inform the public, especially by failing to publicize the 1993 impact assessment on the basis of which the operating licence had initially been granted and thus making it virtually impossible for members of the public to challenge the results of that assessment (Para. 122). In addition, the Court observed that this state of unavailability of information persisted in spite of the probable anxiety experienced by the local people (Para.). Finally, the Romanian authorities were found to be in breach of their duty to assess the potential risks of the extractive activity and accordingly take appropriate measures to protect the concerned population's right to respect for their private life and home and, more generally, their right to have a healthy and safe environment (Para. 112 of judgment); For a case note on the Tatar judgment, see, D. Shelton, International Decision: *Tatar c. Roumanie*, App. No. 67021/01 European Court of Human Rights, Jan. 27, 2009, American Journal of International Law (2010) Issue 104;

Both the *Tatar* and *Di Sarno* judgments are marked by strong environmental considerations, prioritizing the applicants' right to a safe and healthy environment. In terms of the actual legal outcome, while in *Tatar* a breach of Art.8 ECHR was found in its 'entirety', in *di Sarno* the Court was only satisfied with the existence of a material rather than a procedural breach of the said article. From a 'bottom line' point of view, making a split between the procedural and the material violation of the duty to respect the right to respect of family life and home in the context of human health and environmental protection seems both artificial and superfluous given that the procedural aspect of the former right is intrinsically linked to its material aspect. In fact, one could not speak of an adequate and satisfactory fulfilment of the right to a safe and healthy living environment in any

The ECtHR has decided two cases involving the access to information in the nuclear field, examining the application of Art.6 (right to a fair trial) and Art.8 (right to respect for family and private life) of the ECHR. Both cases concern the nuclear weapons atmospheric tests performed by the UK in the Christmas Island in the Pacific Ocean in the period between 1952 and 1967 involving around 20 000 servicemen. *McGinley and Eagan v. United Kingdom*[271] relate to the pension claims of two UK citizens involved in the Christmas Island tests whose appeals before the Pensions Appeal Tribunal (PAT) had been dismissed by reason of their lacking the required documents proving deterioration in their health attributable to the carrying out of the nuclear tests. The UK's defense relied on the applicants' failure to avail themselves of the opportunity to request the production of the relevant documents in accordance with the procedure available under Rule 6 of the national PAT Rules,[272] claiming that the applicants had not exhausted all the legal avenues available under national law.

Viz. the alleged breach of Art.6(1) ECHR, the Court was not convinced that the UK government possessed the documents which the applicants claimed were central to their pension appeals and inferred that since no individual monitoring of servicemen was performed during the nuclear testing it followed that there were no personal medical records in existence (the applicants had acknowledged that the records relative to the environmental radiation on Christmas Island would not have assisted them in their claims).[273] To the extent that it could hypothetically be established that the State was in possession of the relevant documents at the time the applicants had deposited their appeals, the Court noted that the latter had the possibility to make use of the Rule 6 procedure of the PAT Rules in order to request the material containing radiation levels records (along with the impending guarantee that no security derogation for withholding the records would apply).[274] Since that the applicants did not avail themselves of such an option, the Court did not find it conclusive that they had been denied effective access to or a fair hearing before the PAT which would point to a violation of Art.6(1).[275]

---

substantial manner where the procedural safeguards for that right have not been met, and *vice versa*.

271 Application no.21825/93 and 23414/94, ECHR 1998-III; See, for a commentary on the case, Chapter 2, Section II.1.2.

272 Para. 31.

273 Para. 88.

274 Para. 89.

275 Para. 90.

Furthermore, the European Commission of Human Rights (at the time) observed that the applicants' pension claims notwithstanding, the State had not aligned with its Art.8 positive obligation to provide to the applicants '(…) on an individual basis any explanation or information as to the nature and impact of their participation in the test programme'.[276] The Court conceded that the applicants had an interest under Art.8 to obtain such records assessing the radiation levels they had been exposed to, but noted that the existence of such records had not been confirmed or proven.[277] It reiterated that where states engage in hazardous activities with potentially adverse consequences on those involved in the activities, they are required under Art.8 to set up an effective and accessible procedure through which these persons could obtain access to all the relevant information.[278] Finally, the Court did not find that the evidence adduced before it indicated that the procedure laid down in Rule 6 would prove ineffective for the provision of the documents sought by the applicants.[279]

According to the Joint Dissenting Opinion of Judges De Meyer, Valticos and Morenilla, the mere existence of the Rule 6 procedure was not sufficient to conclude that the State had exhausted its positive obligations under Arts.6 and 8 of the Convention. According to the former judges, the applicants had the right to be informed of all the actual consequences their presence during the testing could have borne on their health, even *without* them having to specifically ask for such information. In addition, Judge Pekkanen in his Dissenting Opinion suggested that the applicants had a *general interest* in obtaining access to information relating to the harmful levels of radiation, independent of their particular interest to be awarded pension entitlement.[280] The former argument stands valid especially in light of the fact that the rights obtainable under the PAT rules were of a strictly procedural nature whereas what was essentially (if only, implicitly) at issue in the case was the *material breach* of Art.8 i.e. the positive obligation of the State to have produced, kept and made available records on the actual health effects caused by the nuclear tests on the nuclear servicemen concerned (regardless of the nature or intensity of the effects).[281]

276 Para. 95.

277 Para. 99.

278 Para. 101.

279 Para. 103.

280 Point 3.

281 This argument would have been further reinforced had the Court brought the precautionary principle into play.

The Christmas Island tests saga did not end there. The European Commission of Human Rights lodged a request for revision of the judgment of 9 June 1998 in the McGinley and Egan case[282] to the ECtHR. The revision request reflected on the inadequate character and lack of effectiveness of the Rule 6 procedure which had been proven through another person's unsuccessful application under the same procedure which itself was cited as a fact that had been discovered but which the applicants could not reasonably have known before the delivery of the judgment in the original case.[283] The applicants claimed that the newly found correspondence arguing against the Government's written and oral submissions to the Court 'would have had a decisive influence on the original judgment of the Court'.[284] The Court responded by offering a purely textual reading of the revision criteria of the Rules of the Court which require that the fact which might have a decisive influence be unknown to the Court and to the party demanding the revision, at the time when the judgment was delivered.[285] It was gathered that the applicants had sufficiently detailed knowledge about the developments in the other person's case to the effect that they had undoubtedly been aware of the existence of the correspondence prior to the commencement of the proceedings in the original case.[286] While the Court conceded that the copies of the correspondence on which the revision request was based could not have been effectively obtained by the applicants until after the delivery of the original judgment, it found that it was manifest that the applicants had prior knowledge of the existence of such correspondence[287] therefore rejecting the request for revision. In spite of the failure to meet the procedural criteria, the substantive issue of the existence of an ineffective and inadequate national procedure for the award of certain types of pension claims in the UK remained unaddressed by the Court. Furthermore, the Court failed to acknowledge the overriding concern over the existence of a *substantive* breach of the right to information of the applicants as one taking priority over the procedural issue of pension claims compensation.[288]

282 Decision pursuant to Rule 58 of former Rules of Court, Reports of Judgments and Decisions 2000-I.

283 Para. 25.

284 Para. 26.

285 Para. 24.

286 Para. 35.

287 Para. 36.

288 Some have argued that the outcome of the case might have been different had the case been decided after the coming into force of the Aarhus Convention given that in a subsequent case related to requests for information in connection with military activities (*Roche v. United Kingdom*, Application no. 32555/96 ECHR 2005) the ECtHR had found a

The lack of contemporaneous health records from the time of the Christmas Island tests further gave rise to the *L.C.B. v. United Kingdom* case[289] over UK Government's alleged failure to take preventive measures regarding the health of the child of a serviceman (the applicant in the case) who took part in the aforementioned nuclear tests. The Court examined the applicability of Art.2 (right to life) and Art.8 of the ECHR deducing that the records of contemporaneous measurements of radiation on the Christmas Island submitted to it did not indicate that radiation had reached dangerous levels.[290] It considered that the state would only have been required to provide advice to the applicant's parents and monitor her health had it appeared likely at the time that any such radiation exposure of her father might have engendered a genuine risk to the applicant's health.[291] In view of the body of information it was presented with, the Court could not discern a causal link between the father's radiation exposure and the subsequent illness of the applicant.[292] It unanimously held there had been no violation of Art.2, considering it unnecessary to further examine the alleged failure of the state under Art.8, to take preventive measures with respect to the applicant's health, in the absence of a causal link between the two. Nevertheless, the case remains to be authority for the States' obligation under Art.2 to take preventative measures to protect life on the condition that a causal link is proven whereby the former obligation is to be considered in the light of the scientific knowledge available at the time and the evidence made available to the Court.[293]

There are two additional cases that have appeared before the ECtHR (*Balmer-Schafroth* and *Athanassoglou*),[294] concerning with the health effects of nuclear energy projects, where the applicants claimed a material breach of Art.8 ECHR. The facts of both of the cases did touch upon issues of access to information and public participation as they dealt with the granting of operating licenses

---

breach of Art.8 ECHR (See, O.W. Pedersen, The Ties that Bind: The Environment, the European Convention on Human Rights and the Rule of Law, *European Public Law* (2010) Vol. 16 Issue 4, p. 580).

289 *L.C.B. v United Kingdom* (1998) 27 EHRR 212; For more on this case, see Chapter 2, Section II.1.2.

290 Para. 37.

291 Para. 38.

292 Para. 39.

293 *United Nations Environment Program (UNEP) Compendium on Human Rights and the Environment: Selected International Legal Materials and Cases*, UNEP, 2013, (http://www.unep.org/environmentalgovernance/Portals/8/publications/UNEP_Compendium_HRE.pdf), p. 60.

294 The two cases have been discussed in greater detail *supra* in Chapter 2, Section II.1.2.

for nuclear installations in Switzerland. However, the Court failed to establish the existence of a causal link between the effects of the activities in question and the health of the applicants, finding the link to be too remote so as to trigger any substantive assessment on its part.

The case law analysis will proceed with two cases dealing with certain aspects of public involvement in the preparation and execution of nuclear projects, one appearing before an OSPAR Convention Arbitral Tribunal and the other before the Aarhus Convention Compliance Committee. The first case elucidates one aspect of the cumbersome *Sellafield MOX plant* legal saga which comprised of several different litigations before different tribunals. The issue related to the radioactive discharges into the Irish Sea stemming from the mixed oxide (MOX) fuel plant at the Sellafield nuclear facility in the UK.[295] Ireland instituted proceeding against the UK relying on the Art.9(2) of the *Convention for the Protection of the Marine Environment of the North-East Atlantic* (*OSPAR*) regarding the Contracting Parties' obligation to provide access to any available information on activities or measures *adversely affecting* or *likely to affect* the maritime area.[296]

The application before the OSPAR Arbitral Tribunal gravitated around the matter of provision of the information requested by Ireland and additionally raised other issues which were not confined to the interpretation of the OSPAR Convention provisions on the scope of the term 'environmental information' but extended to placing the nature and scope of the former term in a wider, more general context. Namely, Ireland had relied on the access-to-information provisions of Art.9 of the 1992 OSPAR Convention in order to request access to information which had been redacted from certain reports commissioned by

295 Also, on the MOX case, see *supra* Chapter 1, Section III.3.5 and Chapter 2, Section II.1.2.

296 Emphasis added; Final Award of 2 July 2003, Ireland v UK, Dispute concerning access to information under Article 9 of the Ospar Convention (http://pca-cpa.org/upload/files/OSPAR%20Award.pdf);

Concomitantly, Ireland raised proceedings against the UK before a *UNCLOS* (*United Nations Convention on the Law of the Sea*) Arbitral Tribunal. Pending the constitution of the arbitral tribunal, Ireland requested the International Tribunal for the Law of the Sea (ITLOS) to adopt a decision on provisional measures ordering the UK to immediately suspend the authorisation of the operating license of the Sellafield MOX plant or alternatively, take appropriate measures to prevent the operation of the MOX plant. The proceedings before the UNCLOS Arbitral Tribunal were suspended due to uncertainties regarding the division of competences between the European Union (Community) and the Member States with respect to the scope of the UNCLOS Convention, implicating the ambit of the jurisdiction of the Court of Justice of the EU in these matters (para 43 Case C-459/03 Commission v Ireland ECR 2006 p. I-4635).

the UK government as part of the approval process for the commissioning of the Mox Plant at Sellafield.[297] The UK had refused to provide the requested information, considering the Art.9 OSPAR requirements to be inapplicable to the case, and, in any event, caught under the Art.9(3) OSPAR exceptions.[298] Thus, Ireland demanded full disclosure of two reports (referred to in the proceedings as the 'PA' and the 'ADL' reports) for the purpose of being able to fully envisage the impacts that the commissioning of the MOX plant would or might have on the marine environment of the Irish Sea.[299]

The background to the dispute reveals complex administrative procedures that preceded the final decision to approve the operation of the MOX plant to process spent nuclear fuels. Originally, British Nuclear Fuels, plc ('BNFL'), a public limited company wholly owned by the United Kingdom, applied for a permission to build the MOX plant. The consents to build the plant were given in 1994, the construction was completed by 1996[300] and the UK Department of the Environment, Food and Rural Affairs finally approved the manufacture of

---

297 Article 9 of the OSPAR Convention:

ACCESS TO INFORMATION

1. The Contracting Parties shall ensure that their competent authorities are required to make available the information described in paragraph 2 of this Article to any natural or legal person, in response to any reasonable request, without that person's having to prove an interest, without unreasonable charges, as soon as possible and at the latest within two months.

2. The information referred to in paragraph 1 of this Article is any available information in written, visual, aural or data base form on the state of the maritime area, on activities or measures adversely affecting or likely to affect it and on activities or measures introduced in accordance with the Convention.

3. The provisions of this Article shall not affect the right of Contracting Parties, in accordance with their national legal systems and applicable international regulations, to provide for a request for such information to be refused where it affects: (a) the confidentiality of the proceedings of public authorities, international relations and national defence; (b)public security; (c) matters which are, or have been, sub judice , or under enquiry (including disciplinary enquiries), or which are the subject of preliminary investigation proceedings;

(d) commercial and industrial confidentiality, including intellectual property; (e) the confidentiality of personal data and/or files; (f) material supplied by a third party without that party being under a legal obligation to do so; (g) material, the disclosure of which would make it more likely that the environment to which such material related would be damaged.

4. The reasons for a refusal to provide the information requested must be given;

298 Para. 1 et seq. of the Final Award.

299 Para. 41.

300 Para. 15.

Mox fuel at Sellafield in 2001.[301] Ireland asked for the Tribunal to find the UK to be in breach of its obligation for disclosure under Art.9 of the OSPAR Convention and order the UK to provide Ireland with a complete copy of both the PA and ADL reports (or, alternatively, provide a copy of the reports which contains all information the release of which the arbitration tribunal decides would not affect the commercial confidentiality within the meaning of Art.9(3)(d) of the Convention).[302] The UK refused the disclosure purporting that Ireland had failed to show that the requested information fell within the scope of Art.9(2) given that the former could not be qualified as information sufficiently linked to 'the state of the maritime area or to measures or activities affecting or likely to affect it'.[303] Ireland had identified fourteen categories of information that had been redacted or removed from the pubic version of the reports.[304] Looking at the nature of the information, the Tribunal considered that none of these categories of information could plausibly be characterized as 'information on the state of the maritime area' and therefore none of the material contained therein could be presumed to fall within the definition of information of Art.9(2).[305]

Furthermore, the Tribunal referred to the concept of 'inclusive causality' which was invoked by Ireland, pursuant to which '(...) anything, no matter how remote, which facilitated the performance of an activity is to be deemed part of that activity'.[306] In this vein, Ireland argued that in the absence of the two reports there would not be any discharges from the MOX plant into the Irish Sea[307] urging the Tribunal to examine whether the drafters of the OSPAR Convention had intended to endorse the interpretative theory of inclusive

301 Para. 37.

302 Para. 42.

303 Para. 43.

304 Para. 161 ; These categories concern information related to:

(...) (A) Estimated annual production capacity of the MOX facility; (B) Time taken to reach this capacity;

(C) Sales volumes; (D)Probability of achieving higher sales volumes; (E) Probability of being able to win contracts for recycling fuel in 'significant quantities'; (F) Estimated sales demand; (G) Percentage of plutonium already on site; (H) Maximum throughput figures; (I) Life span of the MOX facility; (J) Number of employees; (K) Price of MOX fuel; (L) Whether, and to what extent, there are firm contracts to purchase MOX from Sellafield; (M) Arrangements for transport of plutonium to, and MOX from, Sellafield; (N) Likely number of such transports.(...);

305 Para. 163.

306 Para. 164.

307 Para. 164.

causality, which was finally concluded in the negative.[308] The Tribunal held that Ireland had not succeeded to prove the existence of *adverse* effect given that its argumentation had largely been focused on the *directness* of the effect and the environmental character of the information sought.[309] The decision of the Tribunal dismissed Ireland's claims regarding the applicability of Art.9(2), *inter alia*, taking note of Ireland's reliance on treaties that were, at the material time, not yet ratified and not in force (among which, the Aarhus Convention) and observing that it was '(…) arguable – but in the view of the Tribunal not conclusive – that Ireland's claim might have succeeded under some of these instruments' (such a task exceeding the competence of the Tribunal which was not empowered to apply 'legally unperfected instruments').[310]

Evidently, the decisive element in the decision to dismiss Ireland's claims under Art.9(2) was that of Ireland's failure to provide sufficient proof that the measures in question 'affect adversely' rather than simply 'affect' the maritime area.[311] Nevertheless, the Tribunal's literal reading of the OSPAR Convention does not sit well with a reader knowledgeable in international environmental law. Looking at the attached dissenting opinion of one of the three members of the tribunal, Gavan Griffith QC, one gains insight into quite a different angle to the dispute (the decision of the Tribunal was not unanimous). Griffith considers that the Tribunal should have applied the letter of the Convention in accordance with the broadly-defined concept of 'international law', in the place of being confined strictly to the international law in force binding on the Parties.[312] His view departs from the majority's view to reject the normative value and applicability of the unratified international instruments relied on by Ireland and, in this sense, dismissing the relevance of the Aarhus Convention.[313] He concurs that the Aarhus Convention- which both the UK and Ireland had only signed but not yet ratified at the material time- could not act as binding international law for either of the parties,[314] but the former could not in itself discount reliance on the Aarhus Convention for the purpose of arriving at a proper construction of Art.9 of the OSPAR Convention.[315] The Aarhus Convention can be seen as providing a 'relevant normative and evidentiary value'[316]

308 Para. 164.

309 Para. 180; Emphasis added.

310 Para. 180; Ireland ratified the Aarhus Convention as late as in 2012.

311 Para. 180.

312 Point 5.

313 Point 7.

314 Pont 9.

315 Point 10.

316 Point 10.

to the MOX case, serving to 'inform and confirm the content of the definition of information contained in Art.9(2) of the OSPAR Convention'.[317] Griffith argued against the majority's view that the Aarhus Convention was unperfected law especially since it had entered into force on 30 October 2001 with the majority of the signatory parties having already ratified it so that it should have been treated as *lex lata*.[318] Moreover, it could be argued that although the UK was not directly bound by the Aarhus Convention, under the letter of Art.18 of the Vienna Convention on the Law of Treaties,[319] as a signatory to the Aarhus Convention the UK was nonetheless under the obligation to refrain from any act that would undermine the objectives of the Aarhus Convention provisions.[320]

Given that the essential issue in the dispute concerned the breadth of the Art.9(2) reference to 'information on *activities or measures adversely affecting or likely to affect* the state of the maritime area' and the extent to which the commercial nature of the redacted parts of the reports could preclude them from falling within the scope of the former term,[321] Griffith suggested employing an approach similar to the one previously endorsed by the CJEU in the *Mecklenburg* case where the CJEU decided to treat a 'statement of views' as a 'measure' by establishing the existence of a causal link between the document and the hazardous activity in question.[322] The UK had stressed the fact that the nature of the reports was decidedly commercial which makes the balancing exercise between the potentially harmful effects and the operation of the facility 'broadly neutral', precluding the information contained in the reports to be treated as 'environmental'.[323] In sum, it was the economic effect of authorizing the operation of the facility that outweighed the environmental considerations,

317 Point 19.

318 Point 11.

319 Article 18: *Obligation not to defeat the object and purpose of a treaty prior to its entry into force*

> A State is obliged to refrain from acts which would defeat the object and purpose of a treaty when:
>
> (*a*) it has signed the treaty or has exchanged instruments constituting the treaty subject to ratification, acceptance or approval, until it shall have made its intention clear not to become a party to the treaty; or
>
> (*b*) it has expressed its consent to be bound by the treaty, pending the entry into force of the treaty and provided that such entry into force is not unduly delayed.(…);

320 Point 13.

321 Point 41.

322 Point 48.

323 Point 60.

in spite of both the parties having agreed that the manufacture of Mox fuel *may* affect the maritime area.[324]

Regarding the 'likely adverse effect' requirement, Griffith suggests that the former could have plausibly been extensively interpreted so as to be equated with the notion of 'potentially adverse effect' as conceived under Art.9(2).[325] The former article could have been constructed in such a way that the requirement to establish a direct and proximate link between the harmful activity and its effect on the state of the maritime area is dispensed with and replaced by the possibility to merely prove the existence of *any* link between the potential harmful effects of the MOX plant operation and the information contained in the reports.[326] Furthermore, although the application of the precautionary principle to this case could have changed the inequality of arms in the procedure,[327] the Tribunal failed to examine the applicability of the former principle thus putting the burden of proof on Ireland to show that the radioactive discharges from the Mox facility were capable to potentially significantly harm the marine environment of the Irish Sea.[328]

---

324 Point 69; Emphasis added.

325 Point 79.

326 Point 97.

327 Article 2(2) of the OSPAR Convention:

General obligations:

2.The Contracting Parties shall apply:

a. the precautionary principle, by virtue of which preventive measures are to be taken when there are reasonable grounds for concern that substances or energy introduced, directly or indirectly, into the marine environment may bring about hazards to human health, harm living resources and marine ecosystems, damage amenities or interfere with other legitimate uses of the sea, even where there is no conclusive evidence of a causal relationship between the inputs and the effects (...);

The application of the precautionary principle (enshrined in Article 2(2)(a) of the OSPAR Convention) to the present case would result in the responsibility to provide scientific evidence being transferred to the producer of potentially hazardous substances rather than the potential victim (see, point 73 of Griffith's Opinion). Furthermore, it is possible that the outcome of the proceedings may have been different had the Tribunal deferred to take into consideration Article 2(3)(b) of the Aarhus Convention which refers to '(...) cost-benefit and other economic analyses and assumptions used in environmental decision-making' as part of the definition of environmental information (point 115 of Opinion) enabling for the proximity of the link between the contents of the reports and the effects from the operation of the MOX plant to be automatically presumed.

328 Points 70 and 72.

Having in mind the substantive aspects of the *MOX* case, Ireland arguably stood a better chance at winning the case had it brought its claim before the CJEU, given that the Union offered a satisfactory access-to-information and decision-making regime. Even though the Environmental Information Directive and EIA Directive were still in their original versions at the time, they provided for more detailed procedural obligations than the OSPAR and the UNCLOS Conventions.[329] Nevertheless, the CJEU gave its own imprint on the MOX saga, even if only marginally since the case before the CJEU (*Commission v. Ireland*[330]) only related to Ireland's failure to respect its obligations as a Member State by having submitted a dispute concerning the interpretation and/or application of a Convention signed by the Union before a jurisdiction different from that of the Union's. Thus, the CJEU was not called upon to adjudicate on the substantive issues of the dispute – that is, the possible violation of the Union environmental rules on the part of the UK. The foregoing produced a situation where different judicial bodies (each of them for different reasons) circumvented addressing the substantive issues of the *MOX* case, leaving Ireland's right to justice clearly violated[331] and its essential claim unresolved. While the CJEU's judgment confirms the Union court's exclusive jurisdiction in such type of cases and strengthens the uniformity and consistency of the Union legal order, the issue of protection of the Irish Sea marine environment and the related health concerns of the population of the surrounding area remains unaccounted for.[332]

Lastly, a case which is illustrative of the Aarhus Convention Compliance Committee's practice in handling the breaches of the public's participatory rights under the Convention which concerned the extension permits for the Mochovce nuclear power plant in Slovakia.[333] Namely, the original construction permit for Mochovce NPP was issued in 1986 (Slovakia acceded to the

329 R. Churchill and J. Scott, The MOX Plant Litigation: The FirstHalf-Life, *International and Comparative Law Quarterly*, 2004, Vol 53, pp. 674–675; See, also, N. Lavranos, The Epilogue in the MOX Plant Dispute: An End Without Findings, *European Energy and Environmental Law Review*, June 2009, p. 182.

330 C-459/03 *Commission v Ireland* ECR 2006 p. I-4635; For more on this case, see Chapter 1, Section III.3.5.

331 See, Lavranos, *supra* n. 329, pp. 180–182.

332 See also, S. Marsden, MOX Plant and the Espoo Convention: Can Member State Disputes Concerning Mixed Environmental Agreements be Resolved Outside EC Law?, *Review of European Community and International Environmental Law*, 2009, Vol 18 Issue 3, p. 313; Also, Lavranos, *supra*, p. 184.

333 Communication ACCC/C/2009/41 concerning compliance by Slovakia, adopted on 17 December 2010 ECE/MP.PP/2011/11/Add.3.

Aarhus Convention in 2005)[334] while the case before the Compliance Committee concerned the extension permits adopted by the Slovak Nuclear Regulatory Authority subsequently in 2008. After confirming that permitting activities for civil nuclear power plants such as the Mochovce NPP are activities covered by Art.6(1) and Annex I.1 of the Aarhus Convention which require public participation,[335] the Compliance Committee focused on examining whether the 2008 decisions of the nuclear authority could be qualified as 'reconsideration or an update of the operating conditions' within the meaning of Art.6.10 of the Convention.[336] By establishing a breach of the provisions on public participation of Art.6 of the Convention, the Compliance Committee concluded that the decision of the nuclear regulatory authority, regardless of whether it resulted in any significant change or extension of the activity, was to be considered as a 'reconsideration and update of the operating conditions by a public authority' in accordance with Art.6.10 of the Convention, Slovakia having failed to ensure that the provisions of Art.6(2)-(9) were applied 'mutatis mutandis, and where appropriate'.[337]

In this sense, the terms 'mutatis mutandis', and 'where appropriate' are not to be construed as bestowing upon states an absolute discretionary power in subsuming potential situations within the remit of these terms,[338] and are to be considered as representing an 'objective criterion to be seen in the context of the goals of the Convention'.[339] In view of the potential impact the permitting of the nuclear installation would have on the public and the environment, the Compliance Committee found that public participation would have been appropriate[340] so that by neglecting to provide for public participation as foreseen in Art.6(2)-(9) during the decision-making process resulting in the 2008 decisions, Slovakia failed to comply with Art.6(10) of the Convention.[341]

Further on, the Committee went on to verify whether the criterion contained in Art.6(4) for ensuring public participation in decisions on specific activities at an early stage 'when all options are open and effective public

334 Para. 43.

335 Para. 43.

336 Para. 50.

337 Para. 55; Art.6 para.10 reads : 'Each Party shall ensure that, when a public authority reconsiders or updates the operating conditions for an activity referred to in paragraph 1, the provisions of paragraphs 2 to 9 of this article are applied mutatis mutandis, and where appropriate'.

338 Para. 55.

339 Para. 56.

340 Para. 57.

341 Paras. 57 and 59.

participation can take place' had been satisfied.[342] It was noted that an EIA procedure under Slovak law had been put in place in 2009 *before* the adoption of the operating permit for the Mochovce plant but however *after* the issuing of the construction permit.[343] The Committee observed that once the installation was constructed there was considerable risk that it would be no longer politically realistic to expect the public authority to block the operation on the basis of issues relating to the construction, technology or infrastructure which have been discovered or revealed subsequently.[344] Consequently, it was concluded that the former was incompliant with Art.6(4) of the Convention.[345]

The Committee did not articulate whether the detected deficiency in the Mochovce NPP decision-making process was indicative of a general failure of the Slovak legal framework on public participation – namely, whether the current Slovak legislation on reconsideration and updating of old permits complies with the Aarhus Convention's public participation requirements. What was emphasized was that the legal framework of the state concerned should ensure early and effective public participation in accordance with Art.6(4) of the Convention[346] and, in this vein, it was recommended that the former undergoes a revision to this effect.[347] In conclusion, the Compliance Committee decided that by omitting to ensure early and effective public participation in the decision-making leading to the 2008 decisions concerning Mochovce NPP, Slovakia failed to meet the requirements of Art.6(4)-(10) of the Convention.[348]

The foregoing case law analysis has demonstrated a tendency of the courts to address the issues regarding access to information and public participation in the nuclear arena in a less straightforward manner than the 'regular' environmental cases where the courts seem better accustomed to the subject matter and therefore felt better placed to proceed. What is manifest is a 'lingering' deference towards the vested prerogatives belonging to the states coupled with an impending wariness on the part of the courts not to trample thereupon,

342 Para. 61.
343 Para. 61.
344 Para. 64.
345 Para. 64.
346 Para. 67.
347 Para. 70(a).
348 Para.69; For an insight into the back and forth correspondence between the Aarhus Convention Compliance Committee and Slovakia on the progress of the implementation of the findings and recommendations of the Compliance Committee, see at: http://www.unece.org/environmental-policy/treaties/public-participation/aarhus-convention/envpptfwg/envppcc/envppccimplementation/fourth-meeting-of-the-parties-2011/slovakia-decision-iv9e.html.

which thickens the shroud of confidentiality typically vitiating the nuclear field. Therefore, *pro futuro*, it is indispensable that international and regional courts exhibit a more activist approach when interpreting and applying the legal rules pertaining to access to information and public participation in the nuclear domain thus empowering the national courts to follow suit. It is highly unlikely that in the absence of an activist international and regional jurisprudence in the matter, the Member States' judicial organs will have the courage to independently take a more open and flexible stance towards applying the Aarhus Convention's standards for environmental democracy to matters in the nuclear domain.

VII The Aarhus Convention Access-to-justice Regime in EU Law – An 'Accomplished' Failure

The issue of fully transposing the access-to-justice requirements of Art.9 of the Aarhus Convention to the EU level, as was indicated at the outset, remains to be contentious especially in view of the Union's already well established regimes on access to information and public participation in decision making in the field of environment. At this point it would be pertinent to make a reference to EU's Declaration of competence made to the Aarhus Convention[349] where the European Community (at the time) affirmed that while it has adopted several legal instruments binding on the Member States which implement provisions of the Aarhus Convention, the legal instruments in force did not fully cover the implementation of the obligations resulting from Art.9(3) of the Aarhus Convention which concerns the administrative and judicial procedures to challenge acts and omissions by private persons and public authorities other than the Community institutions. Consequently, according to the Declaration of competence, the Member States are considered responsible for the performance of the former obligations until the Community adopts provisions of Community law covering the implementation of those obligations. Therefore, given that almost a decade later the requirements of Art.9(3) of the Aarhus Convention have not been fully transposed to the EU level[350] (the proposal for a directive on access-to-justice in environmental matters in 2003

349 *Declaration by the European Community in accordance with Article 19 of the Convention on access to information, public participation in decision-making and access to justice in environmental matters*, Annex to Council Decision 2005/370/EC, cited *supra*.

350 Relevant parts of the text of Art.9 of the Aarhus Convention will be reproduced in full:
Access to justice

being unsuccessful, having remained at the proposal stage[351]), in the absence of Union regulation it has fallen upon the Member States to independently align their national legal regimes with the Convention's provisions. The modalities in which the Conventions' provisions become binding national law for the Member States as Contracting Parties are determined by the particularities of

---

1. Each Party shall, within the framework of its national legislation, ensure that any person who considers that his or her request for information under article 4 has been ignored, wrongfully refused, whether in part or in full, inadequately answered, or otherwise not dealt with in accordance with the provisions of that article, has access to a review procedure before a court of law or another independent and impartial body established by law.

In the circumstances where a Party provides for such a review by a court of law, it shall ensure that such a person also has access to an expeditious procedure established by law that is free of charge or inexpensive for reconsideration by a public authority or review by an independent and impartial body other than a court of law.

Final decisions under this paragraph 1 shall be binding on the public authority holding the information. Reasons shall be stated in writing, at least where access to information is refused under this paragraph.

2. Each Party shall, within the framework of its national legislation, ensure that members of the public concerned

(a) Having a sufficient interest or, alternatively,

(b) Maintaining impairment of a right, where the administrative procedural law of a Party requires this as a precondition, have access to a review procedure before a court of law and/or another

independent and impartial body established by law, to challenge the substantive and procedural legality of any decision, act or omission subject to the provisions of article 6 and, where so provided for under national law and without prejudice to paragraph 3 below, of other relevant provisions of this Convention.

What constitutes a sufficient interest and impairment of a right shall be determined in accordance with the requirements of national law and consistently with the objective of giving the public concerned wide access to justice within the scope of this Convention. To this end, the interest of any non-governmental organization meeting the requirements referred to in article 2, paragraph 5, shall be deemed sufficient for the purpose of subparagraph (a) above. Such organizations shall also be deemed to have rights capable of being impaired for the purpose of subparagraph (b) above.(…)

3. In addition and without prejudice to the review procedures referred to in paragraphs 1 and 2 above, each Party shall ensure that, where they meet the criteria, if any, laid down in its national law, members of the public have access to administrative or judicial procedures to challenge acts and omissions by private persons and public authorities which contravene provisions of its national law relating to the environment.;

351 Commission Proposal for a Directive of the European Parliament and the Council on access to justice in environmental matters, Brussels, 24.10.2003, COM (2003) 624 final, 2003/0246 (COD).

their domestic legal systems (monist v. dualist approach): in most of the Western European countries national implementing legislation must be passed in order for the Convention to become part of domestic law (dualist approach), while in most East European countries international legal instruments as sources of law are presumed to be directly applicable and do not require any transposing legislation (monist approach).[352] However, in the case of the Aarhus Convention such general 'rule of thumb' is not always fully applicable, primarily because of the manner in which the Convention provisions are drafted.[353] A predominant number of the articles of the Convention entrust the States with a duty to legislate in order to conform to the rules of the Convention, which indicates that the former is not essentially conceived to be a self-executing treaty, at least not to a full extent.[354]

Concerning the possibility for the provisions of international agreements concluded by the Union, such as the Aarhus Convention, to produce direct effect, the EU Court of Justice confirmed the former possibility in the *Lesoochranárske zoskupenie* case[355] provided that the criteria applicable to examining the direct effect of international agreements concluded by the Union have been satisfied: namely, that the provision the direct effect of which is being appraised must be put into the context of the purpose and the nature of the international agreement and therefore must contain a clear and precise obligation which is not further subject to the adoption of any subsequent implementing measure.[356] The case concerned the issue of direct applicability

352 Wates, *supra* n. 1, p. 9.

353 *Idem.*

354 For example, note the language of the following articles: Art.3(1) ('Each Party shall take the necessary [...] measures' (...)'), Art 3(2) ('Each Party shall endeavour to ensure that (...)'), Art.5 ('Each Party shall ensure that (...)'), Art.6 ('Each party shall (...)'), etc.

355 C-240/09 *Lesoochranárske zoskupenie VLK v Ministerstvo životného prostredia Slovenskej republiky*, ECR *2011 p. I-1255*.

356 Para.44 of the judgment; The criteria to be applied in the appraisal of the direct effect are the following: '(...)[A] *provision in an agreement concluded by the European Union with a non-member country must be regarded as being directly applicable when, regard being had to its wording and to the purpose and nature of the agreement, the provision contains a clear and precise obligation which is not subject, in its implementation or effects, to the adoption of any subsequent measure* (...)' (para.44 of judgment);

The former attempt for inclusiveness toward the legal standing of applicants is difficult to be reconciled with the governing national practices in Member States such as France. The French Conseil D'Etat had on one occasion rejected the claims made by French environmental NGOs attacking the validity of the Decree licensing the construction of the nuclear installation 'Flamanville 3' purporting that the former violates Art.6(4) and Art.8 of the Aarhus Convention considering that the Convention did not have direct

of Art.9(3) of the Aarhus Convention before national courts, more precisely, the issue of access to courts for national non-governmental organizations in cases of breaches of national environmental laws. Notwithstanding that the provisions the direct effect of which the CJEU was called upon to appraise (Art.9(3) of the Aarhus Convention) had not previously been subject to EU regulation, the Court noted that an issue addressed in an international agreement concluded by the EU but not yet subject to specific EU legislation was nevertheless to be considered as part of EU law where the issue concerns a field to a large extent covered by EU law.[357]

While concluding that the provisions of Art.9(3) of the Aarhus Convention failed to satisfy the criteria for producing direct effect, the Court considered that the former provisions, although drafted in broad terms, were nonetheless intended to ensure effective environmental protection.[358] It thereby emphasized the importance of ensuring effective judicial protection in the fields covered by EU environmental law which required that national courts interpret national law in a way which, to the fullest extent possible, is consistent with the objectives laid down in Art.9(3) of the Aarhus Convention.[359] In this way, the CJEU instructed the referring national court to interpret, to the fullest extent possible, the national procedural rules relating to the conditions to be met in order to bring administrative or judicial proceedings in accordance with the objectives of Art.9(3) of the Aarhus Convention and the objective of effective judicial protection of the rights conferred by EU law thus enabling an environmental protection organisation, such as the non-governmental

---

effect in the domestic legal system (Case-law Digest: France, *Nuclear Law Bulletin*, Vol. 2009/1, p. 92, 93).

357 Paras.40–42 of judgment.

It has been suggested that by making this pronouncement the CJEU failed to offer a proper reading of the EU's Declaration of competence or rather, ran counter to the wording of the declaration, potentially creating problems as far as the participation of the EU and its Member States in the Aarhus Convention. Namely, by stating that Article 9(3) of the Aarhus Convention falls within the scope of EU law since it relates to a field covered in large measure covered by it, the Court seemed to argue that Article 9(3) of the Aarhus Convention falls within EU's exclusive competence even though the declaration of competence provides that unless the Union has adopted legislation on that specific issue Member States retain their competence on Article 9(3). The foregoing goes to the extent of interpreting the Court's approach as that, according to the Court, Member States seem to even be no longer competent on issues covered by Article 9(3) (See, Casteleiro, *supra*, n. 22, p. 507).

358 Paras. 45, 46.

359 Para. 50.

organization in question, to challenge before a national court a decision taken following administrative proceedings which is liable to be contrary to Union environmental law.[360] The CJEU's findings recognized the provisions of the Aarhus Convention as source of EU law containing binding obligations for national courts to take into account for the purpose of interpreting national rules concerning the rights of access to justice of the public relying on EU environmental legislation (in the instant case the EU 'Habitats Directive'[361])[362] thus superseding restrictive national rules regarding legal standing of non-governamental organizations. Finally, in consequence to the ruling the Slovak referring court, by way of interpretation, had admitted the appellant non-governmental organization as party to the proceedings.[363]

The lacuna that the absence of an access-to-justice directive creates in the Union environmental transparency regime has been offset to a certain degree by the insertion of access-to justice provisions in the existing Union legal instruments implementing the Aarhus Convention which corresponding to the first and the second pillar of the Convention (the Public Information Directive and the EIA Directive). The Union legislators' inconsistency in approach regarding the Convention's first and second pillar requirements, on the one hand, as opposed to the third pillar requirements, on the other, seriously jeopardizes the uniformity of legal effect of the Convention at Union level and further allows for different national courts to potentially give diverse

360 Para. 51.

361 Council Directive 92/43/EEC of 21 May 1992 on the conservation of natural habitats and of wild fauna and flora OJ 1992 L 206/7.

362 See, M. Hedemann-Robinson, EU Implementation of the Aarhus Convention's Third Pillar: Back to the Future over Access to Environmental Justice? (Part 1), *European Energy and Environmental Law Review*, June 2014, p. 113.

363 See, E. Mariolina, Collective Redress in Environmental Matters in the EU: A Role Model or a 'Problem Child'?, *Legal Issues of Economic Integration,* 2014, Vol.41 Issue 3, p. 269.

According to Mariolina, the Court of Justice did not merely point to the duty of consistent interpretation, but, somewhat 'directed' the results of the exercise of interpretation to be performed by the national court, since it sort of directs that the interpretation is to enable environmental protection organizations such as the Slovak NGO, to challenge before a court a decision taken following administrative proceedings liable to be contrary to EU environmental law'. Mariolina considers this pronouncement of the Court as remarkable as the CJEU effectively broadens the scope of indirect effect quite significantly thus inevitably overstepping the competences of the EU legislature, which has, as mentioned above, not yet legislated on Article 9(3). The question which arises is then how national courts would have to go about their interpretative duty if national procedural law did not allow for such an interpretation, or if there was no national law to be interpreted (see, Mariolina, p. 268).

interpretations and therefore distinctly apply the Convention's access-to-justice provisions (however, the latitude given to national courts has been significantly reduced in light of the CJEU's pronouncement in *Lesoochranárske zoskupenie* establishing a duty for national courts to interpret national rules consistently with the provisions of the Aarhus Conventions which have not yet been covered by EU regulation).

Therefore, Union regulatory action is imperative primarily due to the existing shortcomings regarding the control over the application of environmental law in the Union[364] which derive from the notable difference in the level of environmental protection offered by and the procedural safeguards for environmental law enforcement applied by different Member States.[365] Such disparities in the application of environmental law may generate conflicts among Member States, especially in the areas of international watercourse and air quality protection, and cross border emissions of polluting substances thus contributing to the weakening of the overall impact of the Aarhus Convention.[366] However, the perceptible lack of urgency for adopting a directive of the former kind can be plausibly accounted for by the fact that at the time the Aarhus Convention was negotiated most Member States had already well-established legal traditions in the application of the Art.9(3) requirements regarding breaches of national environmental laws, some of which were much more liberal than those envisaged by the proposed access-to-justice Directive.[367]

With the benefit of hindsight, the (unsuccessful) proposal for a Directive on access to justice in environmental matters will be looked at in order to gain insight into what was initially envisaged for the Union access-to-justice regime to be. Firstly, laying down obligations aiming to ensure access to justice in environmental proceedings to members of the public and to qualified entities in the Union, the provisions of the proposed Directive did not intend to prejudice the existing Community provisions concerning access to justice in environmental matters (included in the Public Information Directive and the EIA Directive). Secondly, the term 'environmental proceedings' under the proposed Directive encompassed the administrative or judicial review proceedings in environmental matters (excluding the proceedings in criminal matters) before a court or other independent body established by law which are concluded by

364 p. 6 of the Proposal for the Access-to-justice Directive, cited *supra*.

365 p. 6 of the Proposal.

366 p. 6 of the Proposal.

367 M. Bar, Towards Implementation of the Aarhus Convention Third Pillar: Draft EU Access Directive Compared with the Situation in Poland, *Environmental Liability*, 2004, Vol. 12 Issue 2, p. 68.

a binding decision.[368] Member States were to ensure that members of the public and qualified entities who have legal standing and '(...) who consider that an administrative act or administrative omission is *in breach of environmental law*, are entitled to make a request for internal review to the public authority that has been designated in accordance with national law'.[369] Furthermore, the proposal foresaw the holding of an internal review as a preliminary step which entails strict time limits to be respected and requires that the decision of the authorities performing the review to be sufficient as to ensure compliance with environmental law.[370] Failing this, the applicant would be entitled to further institute environmental proceedings whereby it devolves on the Member States to provide adequate and effective proceedings which are objective, equitable, expeditious and not prohibitively expensive.[371]

368 Art.2 of the proposed Directive.

369 Art.3 of the proposed Directive; Under Art.2 of the proposed Directive, the scope of the term 'environmental law' included Union legislation and legislation adopted to implement EU legislation which 'have as their objective the protection or the improvement of the environment, including human health and the protection or the rational use of natural resources, in areas such as:
(i) water protection
(ii) noise protection
(iii) soil protection
(iv) atmospheric pollution
(v) town and country planning and land use
(vi) nature conservation and biological diversity
(vii) waste management
(viii) chemicals including biocides and pesticides
(ix) biotechnology
(x) other emissions, discharges and releases in the environment.
(xi) environmental impact assessment
(xii) access to environmental information and public participation in decision-making';
The proposed Directive offers an inclusive definition for the term 'environmental law' by introducing a catch-all enumeration in determining the scope of the term in that the former lack of prescription makes way for a greater discretion to be exercised on the part of the Member States in assessing the scope of the term 'environmental law'. If the same inclusiveness is maintained in a future directive, nuclear emissions as well as radioactive waste would presumably be caught under the ambit of that directive. One cannot claim with certainty whether the inclusiveness in the proposed directive's approach constitutes one of the reasons why the adoption of the text has been so objectionable.

370 Arts. 9 and 10.

371 Art.10 of proposed Directive; Emphasis added.

The failure to adopt the access-to-justice directive notwithstanding, the observance of the public participation and access-to-information rights of the EU citizens has been secured via the corresponding access-to-justice provisions inserted in the Access-to-information and the EIA directives, however only to a limited degree. According to the Aarhus Convention, in granting the access to information each Party is to ensure that *any person* who considers that their request for information made pursuant to Art.4 of the Convention has been ignored, wrongfully refused, inadequately answered, or in any other way not dealt with in accordance with the provisions of Art.4, is entitled to a review procedure before a court of law (or another independent and impartial body established by law).[372] While the former requirement has been mirrored in Art.6 of the 2003 Access-to-information Directive, the access-to-justice provisions of the Directive further provide an added value by extending the breadth of the procedural protection espoused under Art.9(1) and (2) so as to include the Art.5 and Art.6 access-to-information requirements in addition to the Art.4 requirements which the Convention foresees as the 'minimum standard'.[373] The 'enhanced' scope of the judicial protection under the Directive evidences an implementation effort which has exceeded the minimum standard by setting a higher threshold of protection.

With regard to participation in decision-making, the Aarhus Convention endorses the participatory rights under Art.6 as a kind of 'threshold', allowing national legislators to further extend the scope of judicial protection with respect to, *inter alia*, Arts.7 and 8, or even Art.5.[374] Thus, each Party should,

---

372 Art.9(1).

373 Art.6(1) (Access to justice) of *Directive 2003/4/EC on public access to environmental information*: 'Member States shall ensure that any applicant who considers that his request for information has been ignored, wrongfully refused (whether in full or in part), inadequately answered or otherwise not dealt with in accordance with the provisions of Articles 3, 4 or 5, has access to a procedure in which the acts or omissions of the public authority concerned can be reconsidered by that or another public authority or reviewed administratively by an independent and impartial body established by law. Any such procedure shall be expeditious and either free of charge or inexpensive'.

374 Art.9(2) of the Aarhus Convention reads:

> Each Party shall, within the framework of its national legislation, ensure that members of the public concerned
>
> (a) Having a sufficient interest or, alternatively,
>
> (b) Maintaining impairment of a right, where the administrative procedural law of a Party requires this as a precondition,
>
> have access to a review procedure before a court of law and/or another independent and impartial body established by law, to challenge the substantive and procedural legality of any decision, act or omission subject to the provisions of article 6 and,

within the framework of its national legislation, ensure that members of the *public concerned* that have a sufficient interest or, alternatively, maintain the impairment of a right, have access to a review procedure before a court of law (and/or another independent and impartial body established by law) to challenge the substantive and procedural legality of any decision, act or omission subject to the provisions of Art.6 or, *where provided by national law* – other relevant provisions of the Convention.[375] The frame of reference used for appraising 'sufficient interest' and 'impairment of a right' is also to be foreseen under national law, in accordance with the general objective of providing wide access to justice to the public concerned.[376] Furthermore, any non-governmental organization meeting the requirements referred to in Art.2(5) of the Convention is presumed as having 'sufficient interest'.[377] These requirements have found an adequate expression in the EIA Directive (more particularly, through the amendments introduced by the 2003 Public Participation Directive which have enhanced the EIA Directive's public participation regime by adding adequate access-to-justice provisions[378]). While a satisfactory judicial review regime has been established with respect to public participation in *specific projects*

where so provided for under national law and without prejudice to paragraph 3 below, of other relevant provisions of this Convention.;

For further reading, see, *The Aarhus Convention: An Implementation Guide,* p.128; In the context of the application Art.9(3) there does exist a possibility for the provisions of Arts.7 and 8 of the Convention to be justiciable. However, being that Art.9(2) and (3) of the Convention contain certain provisions which are to be implemented only at the discretion of national legislators, it cannot be claimed that Arts. 7 and 8 create legally binding obligations (see, Jendroska, *Aarhus Convention at Ten, supra* n. 35, p. 96).

375 Art.9(2).

376 Art.9(2).

377 Under Art.2(5) of the Aarhus Convention, 'the public concerned' means the public affected or likely to be affected by, or having an interest in, the environmental decision-making; for the purposes of this definition, *non-governmental organizations promoting environmental protection and meeting any requirements under national law shall be deemed to have an interest.* [Emphasis added].

378 Article 1

Objective

The objective of this Directive is to contribute to the implementation of the obligations arising under the Aarhus Convention, in particular by:

(a) providing for public participation in respect of the drawing up of certain plans and programmes relating to the environment;

(b) improving the public participation and providing for provisions on access to justice within Council Directives 85/337/EEC and 96/61/EC. (…);

on the environment, a similar regime has not been envisaged in the context of public participation in the drafting of *plans and programmes* relating to the environment. Failing to extend the application of the access-to-justice provisions to the process of preparation of plans and programmes relating to the environment represents a serious drawback to the Union's public participation regime that has not been sufficiently well addressed.[379]

With respect to the justiciability of the administrative acts and omissions of the Union institutions and bodies regarding environmental matters, the former are (to a certain extent) reviewable under Art.10 of the 2006 Aarhus Regulation. Nonetheless, the scope of persons entitled to require the judicial review is highly restrictive, if not poor. More particularly, under the Regulation only non-governmental organizations have the legal standing to challenge the administrative acts and omissions of the Union institutions and bodies,[380] by lodging a request for internal review before the concerned EU institution or body allegedly at fault followed by the option to further initiate a procedure before the CJEU.[381] The generous procedural entitlement given to non-governmental organizations closely follows the language of Art.9(2)(2) of the Aarhus Convention whereby non-governmental organizations are presumed to have sufficient interest to initiate proceedings before courts or other relevant bodies. All the while, the Regulation makes a clear retreat from the Convention's liberal approach of prescribing the 'any person' requirement for cases of denied or unsatisfactory access to environmental information (Art.9(1)), equally failing to foresee legal standing for 'members of the public concerned having a sufficient interest' or 'maintaining impairment of a right' by reason of their Art.6 entitlements (pursuant to Art. 9(2)(1) of the Convention).

The Aarhus Convention Compliance Committee addressed the forementioned lacuna in the access-to-justice regime established under the 2006 Aarhus Regulation in its findings adopted pursuant to a communication proceded by the non-governmental organization ClientEarth which brought attention to EU's failure to comply with Art.9(2) of the Convention concerning access to

379 The decision on the part of the Union legislators to maintain such a restrictive approach was not preceded by any significant debate within the EU (for this, see, Jendroska, *supra* n. 28, Part VII. 1).

380 Article 10(1) of the Aarhus Regulation:

> Request for internal review of administrative acts
>
> 1. Any non-governmental organisation which meets the criteria set out in Article 11 is entitled to make a request for internal review to the Community institution or body that has adopted an administrative act under environmental law or, in case of an alleged administrative omission, should have adopted such an act. (...);

381 Art.12 of the Regulation.

justice of members of the public concerned.[382] More specifically, the Communication attacked the Union's restrictive rules regarding standing in matters related to the environment which impede the NGOs as well as the individuals from having full access to justice in challenging the decisions of the Union institutions. *Grosso modo*, the communicant observed a general failure on the part of the EU to comply with the provisions of the Convention on access to justice in environmental matters.[383] In addition, the communicant claimed that should the jurisprudence of the EU courts not be altered, the EU would fail to comply with Art.9(2)-(5) of the Convention. In response to the communication, the Compliance Committee expressed the need for a new direction in the jurisprudence of the EU Courts to be established in order to ensure compliance with the Convention and recommended that '(...) all relevant EU institutions within their competences take the steps to overcome the shortcomings reflected in the jurisprudence of the EU Courts in providing the public concerned with access to justice in environmental matters'.[384] Nevertheless, it is difficult to claim with certainty whether the former recommendation voiced by the Compliance Committee intimates at the need for revision of the existent EU access-to-justice regime for environmental matters.

The restrictive approach exhibited by the EU legislator in the 2006 Aarhus Regulation can be explained with the caution not to tramle upon the established rules on legal standing of the TFEU[385] and the related case law of the CJEU in the matter combined with the fear of potentially opening the 'floodgates' for natural or legal persons (other than NGOs) to challenge all administrative acts and omissions of EU institutions coming within the scope of the Regulation (certainly, provided the concerned persons are at the outset able to prove direct and individual concern). *Arguendo*, such a state of affairs points to the existence of a democratic deficit (reflected in the difficulty to challenge the acts and omissions of the EU institutions before the EU courts) which invariably engenders an 'implementation deficit' for the Union environmental rules.[386] Such implementation deficit is to be attributed both to the Member States and the EU institutions given that the acts and omissions

382 Findings and recommendations with regard to communication ACCC/C/2008/32 (Part I) concerning compliance by the European Union, Adopted on 14 April 2011 ECE/MP.PP/C.1/2011/4/Add.1.

383 Para. 3 of the Findings.

384 Paras. 97 and 98 of the Findings.

385 On the criteria regarding legal standing, see Art.263(4) TFEU.

386 J. Ebbesson, Chapter 2: European Community, in, J. Ebbesson (ed.), *Access to justice in environmental matters in the EU*, Kluwer Law International, 2002, p. 52.

of the latter determine the degree and quality of the implementation efforts of the former.[387]

Concerning the nuclear field (and thus the scope of Euratom), pending the adoption of an access-to-justice directive, the potential legal avenues for safeguarding the access-to-information and public participation rights in environmental matters will be those provided under the Public Information and the EIA directives, to the extent applicable to nuclear projects and activities. It follows that until a directive on access to justice is adopted, the scope of the judicial protection of the Aarhus Convention rights in the nuclear sector will be questionable in terms of determining the 'minimum' standard for procedural protection in view of the lack of comprehensive codification. Given the delicate nature of the judicial protection of procedural environmental rights, it is insufficient to presume the existence of a standard – it is indispensable to have one ink on paper.

387 *Idem.*

CHAPTER 4

Euratom and Non-Proliferation of Nuclear Weapons

The present chapter covers the field of non-proliferation of nuclear weapons as covered under the purview of the Euratom Community and the nuclear safeguards mechanisms devised thereunder as well as the policy of non-proliferation of nuclear weapons as a policy inaugaurated under the Union framework *stricto sensu*. The former two areas of focus are approached from the perspective of the legal and political instruments that Euratom and the Union, respectively, have at their disposal in the achievement of the non-proliferation objective.

The global nuclear non-proliferation discourse is as old as the proliferation of nuclear weapons itself, the latter being arguably the only weapons which best achieve their goal when not used, given their potentially far-reaching devastating effects.[1] Matters are made more complex by the delicate nature of nuclear technology as inherently *dual* give that the possibility for diversion from peaceful to non-peaceful uses of nuclear energy is technically a straightforward exercise, making the two types of uses of nuclear energy difficult to always fully differentiate one from the other.[2] It is for this reason that the legal regimes applicable to both civil and military uses of nuclear energy, although clearly distinct, are functionally intertwined and inter-dependent. In addition, there have been certain 'grey zone' issues (e.g. the issue of radioactive waste from military nuclear installations) which implicate the two legal regimes, but nevertheless necessitate that only one regime is applied. Thus, the struggle to find the pertinent legal rule to apply proves to be a weighty and a potentially perilous exercise, directly implicating the states' sovereignty and security concerns.

The term 'nuclear weapons proliferation' has been defined as the multiplication of nuclear arms without distinguishing the number of states that possess them.[3] While the subject of non-proliferation of nuclear weapons pertains

1 N. Pélopidas, Non-proliferation through International Norms: A European Preference? *Cahiers Europeens N°02/2006* (http://www.portedeurope.org/IMG/pdf/Cahier_norme_1_Pelopidas.pdf), p. 2.

2 L. Scheinmann, Euratom: Nuclear Integration in Europe, *International Concilliation*, May 1967, No. 563, Carnegie Endowment for International Peace, p. 12.

3 G. Fischer, *The Non-Proliferation of Nuclear Weapons*, Europa Publications, 1971, p. 21.

 | DOI 10.1163/9789004310414_006

to both civil and military uses of nuclear energy, the former, understandably, has a predominant bearing on the latter. The subject has been deeply rooted in the history of European integration: looking at the very beginnings of the Euratom Community, one of the conceptual questions that spurred harsh disagreement among the Member States at the time was the question of whether the future Euratom member states should forswear the use of nuclear energy for military purposes[4] and whether the Euratom Treaty should cover the realm of military uses of nuclear energy.

In parallel to the nuclear non-proliferation objective furthered under the Euratom purview through the application of the nuclear safeguards arrangements, the Union *stricto sensu* participates in the non-prolferation equation through the development of the Union's non-proliferation policy, a subset of which is the policy regarding the non-proliferation of nuclear weapons. Indeed, the Union has been equipped with both the adequate resources and legal mechanisms to contribute to the global non-proliferation dialogue and claim its role as a serious actor in the field. Thus, both Euratom and the Union having remained to exist as separate legal entities after the entry into force of the Lisbon Treaty (2009), has left them with an important stake in the non-proliferation field, functioned upon their respective competences in the field.[5]

The chapter deals both with the *legal* dimension of non-proliferation devised at the EU level, assumed by Euratom and represented by the Euratom safeguards regime, and the *policy* dimension, belonging to the scope of the *Union* framework and known as the Union's non-proliferation policy – the former two being intrinsically linked and, thus, co-existent. It starts out by looking at the global legal regime on non-proliferation, exploring the principles and mechanisms endorsed under the 1968 Treaty on the Non-proliferation of Nulcear Weapons (NPT)) (in force since 1970) and, more specifically, the nuclear safeguards component which is further implemented through the International Atomic Energy Agency (IAEA) safeguards agreements. Nuclear safeguards, as technical measures aimed at deterring the proliferation of nuclear weapons,[6] represent a crucial component of the NPT regime and thus an essential asset for achieving the non-proliferation objective. The analysis puts the non-proliferation obligations established at the international level are subsequently into the context of the Euratom safeguards framework devised

4 M. Camps, *Britain and the European Community 1955–1963*, Princeton University Press, 1964, p. 54.

5 For practical reasons, throughout the text the term 'non-proliferation' will sometimes be used interchangeably with the term 'non-proliferation of nuclear weapons', certainly, bearing in mind that the scope of the latter term belongs to the much larger scope of the former.

6 http://www.iaea.org/safeguards/.

pursuant to the Euratom Treaty and the Euratom secondary legislation, inquiring into the relationship between the corresponding NPT/IAEA and Euratom safeguards regimes.

With the intent to comprehensively delimit Euratom's portion of competence in the field of non-proliferation of nuclear weapons, the analysis further addresses the controversial issue of the existence of any (if only marginal) Euratom competence in the field of military uses of nuclear energy. In this vein, it is to be reminded that, typically, military uses of nuclear energy are presumed to be 'vested' Member State competence[7] (depending on the nature of the issue, implicating the EU Foreign and Security policy) whereas civil uses have traditionally been seen as 'trademark' Euratom competence. Furthermore, the exercise of delimiting the competence of Member State as opposed to Euratom competence regarding the civil and military applications of nuclear energy is significant not solely from the perspective of those Member States which are nuclear weapons states (France and the United Kingdom) as well as those Member States that host NATO tactical nuclear weapons on their territory under the nuclear weapons sharing arrangements (Belgium, Germany, Italy, etc.), but equally for those Member States that have developed purely civil nuclear programmes primarily due to the national security risks involved therein[8] (along with the impending difficulty to precisely separate the purely peaceful from the purely military uses of nuclear energy[9]).

The former delimitation of scopes cannot be accomplished by simply looking at the text of the Euratom Treaty since the former fails to provide any express or blanket exemption regarding military uses so that, in the absence of an explicit exemption, an attempt to find a tacit one will be undertaken. For the purpose of giving an answer on whether certain Euratom Treaty provisions can be presumed to apply to the nuclear defence sector, the discussion begins by elucidating the original intentions of the Union's founding fathers and employing a historical and teleological approach by reviewing the relevant historical projects and documents that pre-date the adoption of the Euratom Treaty (the 1956 Spaak Report, the Draft Minutes of the 1956 Venice Conference, etc.). The inquiry further focuses on particular provisions of the current text of the Euratom Treaty (the chapters on Nuclear Supplies, Nuclear Safeguards and Property Ownership) which can be considered as pertaining (directly or indirectly) to the Member States' defence interests. Being that the issue of the

7 See, Case Commission v UK, C-61/03, *ECR 2005 p. I-2477*, para. 44.

8 R. Kobia, The EU and Non-Proliferation: Need for a Quantum Leap? *Nuclear Law Bulletin*, June 2008, No. 81, p. 39.

9 D.A. Howlett, *Euratom and Nuclear safeguards*, Macmillan Press, 1990, p. 8.

relationship between Euratom and military applications of nuclear energy remains to be labeled as a legal 'grey area', the chapter concludes with a section elaborating the EU Court of Justice's pronouncements in several cases that touch upon the issue of applying the Euratom Treaty or the Euratom secondary legislation to matters related to the national nuclear defense of Member States.

1 Non-proliferation and Disarmament – Two Concomitant Objectives of the Treaty on the Non-Proliferation of Nuclear Weapons (The NPT)

> The unleashed power of the atom has changed everything except our way of thinking.
>
> ALBERT EINSTEIN

The devastating effects of the atomic bombs in Hiroshima and Nagasaki heralded the advancement of a clear and unshakeable non-proliferation objective pursued by the entire international community. The idea to put the control of manufacturing of nuclear weapons under the umbrella of one international treaty is one of the greatest enterprises in human history especially since it is one thing to advocate non-proliferation through policy mechanisms, but quite another to establish an international legally binding instrument in the area of non-proliferation such as the Treaty on the Non-Proliferation of Nuclear Weapons (NPT).[10]

The *Treaty on the Non-Proliferation of Nuclear Weapons* (Non-Proliferation Treaty – NPT) is the key international legal instrument that regulates the field of non-proliferation on a global and all-encompassing scale. So far a total of 190 parties have joined the Treaty (including the five nuclear weapons states: USA, Russia, China, France and the United Kingdom) which was opened for signature on 1 July 1968 and entered into force on 5 March 1970.[11] All the countries of the famous EU 'Six',[12] except for France, signed the NPT in August 1968

10 *Treaty on the Non-Proliferation of Nuclear Weapons*, United Nations Treaty Series, Vol. 729, I-10485.

11 See, the website of the United Nations Office for Disarmament Affairs (http://www.un.org/disarmament/WMD/Nuclear/NPT.shtml).

12 The 'Six' reference relates to the six founding members of the then, European Community: France, Germany, Italy, Belgium, the Netherlands and Luxembourg.

and ratified it as late as in May 1975.[13] France was the last of the EU founding member states and Security Council permanent members to accede to the NPT as late as in August 1992, the French government having stated on several occasions that although not a party to the Treaty, France considered itself bound by its provisions.[14] The principal reason why France abstained from becoming part of the NPT was because it did not perceive the NPT as an effective disarmament mechanism.[15] The United Kingdom, on the other hand, which became a Member State in 1973, was one of the original signatories to the NPT and had deposited the instrument of ratification already in November 1968.[16] Since the entry into force of the NPT, regular review (and extension) conferences have been held every year while at the 1995 NPT Review and Extension conference it had been decided that the NPT be extended indefinitely.[17]

The NPT pursues three fundamental objectives: *non-proliferation* as a focal objective, *disarmament* as a secondary, more remote objective (the two being inherently intertwined) and lastly, the objective of ensuring the transfer of nuclear technology in the *pursuance of peaceful uses of nuclear energy*.[18] Within the term proliferation, distinction is to be made between *vertical* and *horizontal* proliferation. Vertical proliferation refers to quantitative and qualitative increases in weapons held by states that have already declared themselves as nuclear weapon states and is to be differentiated from horizontal proliferation covered by the NPT and related to the increase in the number of countries that

---

13 Consult the site of the United Nations Office for Disarmament Affairs for an overview of the States that have signed and ratified the Treaty (http://unhq-appspub-01.un.org/UNODA/TreatyStatus.nsf/NPT%20%28in%20alphabetical%20order%29?OpenView).

14 B. Goldschmidt, Proliferation and Non-proliferation in Western Europe: A Historical Survey, in H. Muller (ed.), *A European Non-Proliferation Policy: Prospects and Problems*, Clarendon Press, 1987, p. 24.

Fischer reports a statement from a French delegate at the UN General Assembly: 'No country that has the terrifying responsibilities resulting from the possession of these [nuclear] weapons will ever agree to share them with others. For its part, France will not sign the Treaty but will behave in future in this field exactly like the states which do decide to adhere'. (see, Fischer, *supra* n. 3, p. 62).

15 V. Lamm, The Utilization of Nuclear Energy and International Law, Akademia Kiado, Budapest, 1984, p. 93.

16 See at http://www.un.org/disarmament/WMD/Nuclear/NPT.shtml.

17 Final Document, 1995 Non-Proliferation Treaty Review and Extension Conference, NPT/CONF.1995/32 (Part I), p. 13.

18 Mölling, *The Grand Bargain in the NPT: Challenges for the EU beyond 2010*, in, J.P. Zanders, (ed.), Chaillot Papers (April 2010), European Union Institute for Security Studies, accessible at http://www.iss.europa.eu/uploads/media/cp120.pdf, p. 51.

have nuclear weapons.[19] Non-proliferation, as endorsed by the NPT, seeks to prevent the acquisition of nuclear weapons by states other than the five Nuclear Weapon States (NWS) recognized by the Treaty.[20] Pursuant to the letter of the NPT, possession and acquisition of nuclear weapons is prohibited for all states considered to be non-nuclear weapon states (NNWS). Concomitantly, the NPT does not oblige the NWS to disarm their nuclear arsenals, but guides them, together with the NNWS, in the direction of disarmament as a long-term perspective: 'Each of the Parties to the Treaty undertakes to pursue negotiations in good faith on effective measures relating to cessation of the nuclear arms race at an early date and to nuclear disarmament, and on a treaty *on general and complete disarmament* under strict and effective international control'.[21] It follows that the NPT has a pervasive non-proliferation objective which is distinguishable from its subsidiary, but equally important disarmament objective and is therefore not a disarmament treaty *per se*.[22]

According to the letter of the NPT, a nuclear weapon State is one which has manufactured and exploded a nuclear weapon or other nuclear explosive device prior to 1 January 1967 (Art. IX).[23] This means that the Treaty allows for the NWS to maintain their nuclear weapons arsenal and indeed increase it if they so wish, at the same time prohibiting horizontal proliferation i.e. any future rise in the number of nuclear weapon states. In this respect the NPT

19 Fischer, *supra* n. 3, p. 21.

20 Mölling, *supra* n. 18, p. 51.

21 Art.VI of the NPT; Emphasis added.

22 B. Tertrais, Summary of the meeting of the Committee on Foreign Affairs (AFET) and the Subcommittee on Security and Defence (SEDE), Public hearing: '*The Future of the Nuclear Non-Proliferation Treaty* (*NPT*)', Brussels, 12 July 2006 Brussels, 13157/06 PE 294, p. 2; Compare the foregoing statement with the clear disarmament character of the *Tlatelolco Treaty on the Prohibition of Nuclear Weapons in Latin America* which establishes a nuclear weapons-free area among the contracting parties (United Nations, Treaty Series, Vol. 634, I-9068); The NPT, unlike the Tlatelolco Treaty, by making the distinction between NWS and NNWS actually recognizes the right of NWS to manufacture nuclear weapons.

23 Something which has caused disagreements among nuclear scientists over the years is the parameter to be used to determine whether a state qualifies as a nuclear weapons state. According to the conventionally accepted parameter, a state that has conducted a nuclear test is automatically presumed to have the nuclear capacity to produce nuclear weapons (i.e. the *nuclear test/no nuclear test* criterion)(see, J.E.C. Hymans, When Does a State Become a 'Nuclear Weapon State'?: An Exercise in Measurement Validation, *Non Proliferation Review*, March 2010, Vol. 17 Issue 1, p. 176); There are also those who favor the test which examines whether a state has accumulated sufficient fissile material to produce a nuclear bomb (*significant quantity* (*SQ*) *test*) in order to establish the military nuclear readiness of a particular state (See, Hymans, p. 176).

provisions are overtly discriminatory in their letter and effect- the NNWS that would have aimed to test-explode a nuclear weapon after the designated date are put in an unfavorable position while the 'nuclear weapons state' status of the other five is being preserved. The Treaty in a certain way treats nuclear weapons as a 'necessary evil', something one is compelled to condone on the condition that the *status quo* in the number of nuclear weapons states is complied with. However, such a *status quo* requirement regarding the augmentation of the NWS' nuclear weapons arsenals is absent from the Treaty. Admittedly, this sort of 'endorsed discrimination' in law and fact is redeemed through the inclusion of the Art.VI disarmament objective.

In furtherance of the disarmament objective, the NPT endows the signatory parties with a long-term mandate to draft a treaty on general and complete nuclear disarmament that fosters the objective for a complete cessation of the nuclear arms race (Article VI of the NPT). It is common knowledge that a large majority of the international community[24] subscribes to a world free of nuclear weapons, however, in realistic terms, complete nuclear disarmament is a gradual process dependent on many factors (political, economic, social and cultural) which themselves cannot be artificially influenced. The task of complete nuclear disarmament may well take several decades, even centuries or, ultimately, may never happen,[25] putting into perspective all the challenge the

---

24 There are certain controversies surrounding the nuclear programs of the Islamic Republic of Iran (a contracting party to the NPT), the Democratic People's Republic of Korea (which withdrew from the NPT in 1993 and conducted a nuclear weapons test in 2009 (see on that the Security Council Press Release SC/9679 12 June 2009, http://www.un.org/News/Press/docs/2009/sc9679.doc.htm. For a chronology of the relations between IAEA and DPRK, see, http://www.iaea.org/NewsCenter/Focus/IaeaDprk/chrono_pre2002.shtml; The IAEA has also expressed concern about the Israeli nuclear capabilities, having called upon Israel to accede to the Non-Proliferation Treaty and place all its nuclear facilities under comprehensive IAEA safeguards (IAEA, General Conference, Israeli nuclear capabilities: Resolution adopted on 18 September 2009 during the tenth plenary meeting (http://www.iaea.org/About/Policy/GC/GC53/GC53Resolutions/English/gc53res-17_en.pdf).

25 Robert Oppenheimer, an American theoretical physicist, has expressed a very radical view on the future possibility of adopting a convention that would ban nuclear weapons. He envisioned such a nuclear-weapons-free world as a world laden with an ever present climate of distrust among states where states would only maintain civil nuclear facilities, but at the same time the design of these facilities would be such that would enable an easy and straightforward conversion to the production of nuclear weapons. ('We know very well what we would do if we signed such a convention: We would not make atomic weapons, at least not to start with, but we would build enormous plants, and we would design these plants in such a way that they could be converted with the maximum ease and the minimum time delay to the production of atomic weapons saying, this is just in

global community is currently facing regarding the untimely ratification of certain international instruments in the field of non-proliferation (see, for instance, the ratification status of the Comprehensive Nuclear Test Ban Treaty[26]).

The disarmament process should be seen as an important corollary to the non-proliferation process whereby the two should rather be perceived as complementing rather than contradicting each other. The Conference on Disarmament (CD), established in 1979 under the auspices of the United Nations Office in Geneva (UNOG), is the key multilateral disarmament negotiating forum of the international community[27] which focuses on managing projects and activities related to the cessation of the nuclear arms race, nuclear disarmament, prevention of nuclear war and all related matters.[28] Currently, the negotiations for the conclusion of the future Fissile Material Cut-Off Treaty,[29] which is expected to ban any further production of fissile material for nuclear weapons or other explosive devices, have been underway under the auspices of the Conference on Disarmament.

It has been argued that a complete achievement of *all* three of NPT's objectives outlined *supra* would be a most difficult if not an impossible task since certain of these objectives are to a certain degree and in certain instances mutually exclusive (e.g., the non-proliferation and the disarmament objective) so that it is possible that the strengthening of one can have a *detrimental* effect on the other objective.[30] In fact, sanctioning the differentiation between NWS and NNWS, on the one hand, and working at attaining a fully nuclear-weapons-free world, on the other, is, at least on the face of it, a contradictory exercise intrinsic to the system created by the NPT which should nevertheless not be exaggerated

case somebody two-times us; we would stockpile uranium; we would keep as many of our developments secret as possible; we would locate our plants, not where they would do the most good for the production of power, but where they would do the most good for protection against enemy attack.') (http://www.fissilematerials.org/ipfm/pages_us_en/fissile/production/production.php).

26 http://treaties.un.org/doc/Publication/MTDSG/Volume%20II/Chapter%20XXVI/XXVI-4.en.pdf.

27 The Conference on Disarmament presently counts 65 Member States, including all of the world's nuclear-weapons states. For a complete membership list, see, http://www.unog.ch/80256EE600585943/%28httpPages%29/6286395D9F8DABA380256EF70073A846?OpenDocument.

28 http://www.unog.ch/80256EE600585943/%28httpPages%29/2D415EE45C5FAE07C12571800055232B?OpenDocument.

29 The term 'fissile material' relates to high enriched uranium and plutonium. On the current status of the negotiations for the conclusion of the Fissile Material Cut-Off Treaty, see, http://www.nti.org/treaties-and-regimes/proposed-fissile-material-cut-off-reaty/.

30 Mölling, *supra* n. 18, p. 51.

given that it is a 'workable' contradiction, not affecting in any way the overall functioning of the non-proliferation regime.

Ultimately, the fact that the NPT text has endorsed the existence of nuclear weapons and has thus made it 'legal', inevitably raises the question of the legitimacy of the maintenance of national nuclear weapons arsenals. In this vein, the International Court of Justice was asked by the UN General Assembly to give an Advisory Opinion on whether the threat or use of nuclear weapons in any circumstance is permitted under international law[31] where the Court's response was that of failing to find a specific authorization of the threat or use of nuclear weapons in neither customary nor conventional international law,[32] or, any comprehensive and universal prohibition thereof.[33] It opined that '(...) the threat or use of nuclear weapons would *generally be contrary* to the rules of international law applicable in armed conflict, and in particular the principles and rules of humanitarian law (...)'.[34] However, taking stock of the current state of international law, the Court could not conclude '(...) definitively whether the threat or use of nuclear weapons would be lawful or unlawful in an extreme circumstance of self-defence, in which the very survival of a State would be at stake'.[35] More importantly, the Court closed with a very important *dictum* urging the states to pursue negotiations that would lead to nuclear disarmament '(...) in all its aspects under strict and effective international control'.[36] Effectively, having in mind the political sensitivity of the issue and the highly conflicting opinions shared by different states, the Court did not opt for an unequivocal solution and chose not to completely criminalize the threat or use of nuclear weapons, pulling the 'self-defence' trump card and allowing for the threat or use of nuclear weapons to be exercised only in extreme instances necessitating the dire need for the survival of a state to be preserved.

II The Architecture of the NPT Regime and the IAEA Safeguards Arrangements

As mentioned supra, the NPT regime is grounded upon a basic differentiation between Nuclear Weapons States (NWS) and Non-Nuclear Weapons States (NNWS) to which the Treaty accords different rights and obligations. Primarily,

31 *Legality of the Threat or Use of Nuclear Weapons*, Advisory Opinion, I.C.J. Reports 1996, p. 226.

32 Para. 105(2)A.

33 Para. 105(2)B.

34 Emphasis added; Para. 105(2)E(1).

35 Para. 105(2)E(2).

36 Para. 105(2)F.

the Treaty foresees a passive obligation for the Nuclear Weapon states i) not to transfer to any recipient whatsoever nuclear weapons or other explosive devices or control over such weapons or devices, directly or indirectly; and ii) not to assist, encourage or induce any NNWS to manufacture or otherwise acquire nuclear weapons or other n-explosive devices or control over such (Art. I). The mirroring obligation on the part of Non- Nuclear Weapons States is not to receive transfer, not to manufacture and not to seek or receive any assistance in the manufacture of nuclear weapons (Art. I).

Secondly, it is incumbent on *both NWS and NNWS* not to provide to any non nuclear weapon state source or special fissionable material[37] or equipment or material especially designed or prepared for the processing, use or production of special fissionable material for peaceful purposes, *unless* the source or special fissionable material is subject to the safeguards arrangements required by the same Article III (Art. III(2)). The latter provision vehicles the commitment of NNWS to conclude safeguards agreements with the IAEA for the purpose of verifying the fulfillment of their NPT obligations regarding prevention from diversion from peaceful uses (Art. II). These verification procedures are to be applied to source or special fissionable material that is being produced, processed or used in any principal nuclear facility or is outside any such facility (i.e. all source or special fissionable material in all peaceful nuclear activities within the territory of the NNWS, under its jurisdiction, or carried out under its control anywhere else)(Art. III(1)).

Nevertheless, the established NPT non-proliferation regime is certainly not flawless: for instance, on a simple reading of the provisions regarding the obligation for NWS not '[..] to assist, encourage, or induce any non-nuclear-weapon State to manufacture or otherwise acquire nuclear weapons or other nuclear explosive devices, or control over such weapons or explosive devices' (Art I), it can be observed that the Treaty fails to foresee such a prohibition for the NNWS. The former lacuna potentially opens way for NNWS that are effectively prepared for the manufacture of nuclear weapons[38] to act as the go-between in

37 Regarding the terms 'source and special fissile material', the definition provided in Art. XX of the IAEA Statute is followed:

1. The term 'special fissionable material' means plutonium-239; uranium- 233; uranium enriched in the isotopes 235 or 233; any material containing one or more of the foregoing; (...)

3. The term 'source material' means uranium containing the mixture of isotopes occurring in nature; uranium depleted in the isotope 235; thorium; any of the foregoing in the form of metal, alloy, chemical compound, or concentrate; (...).

38 Lamm, *supra* n. 15, p. 96.

practices of 'assisted' or 'encouraged' acquiring of nuclear weapons. Evidently, this is a grey area that the NPT has omitted to address.

Additionally, in order to further reinforce the non-proliferation role of the NWS, the *UN Security Council Resolution 984*[39] has introduced the mechanism of *security assurances* which are essentially statements or declarations issued by NWS in which they undertake not to use nuclear weapons against NNWS, parties to the NPT, carrying a passive obligation for NWS and therefore qualifying as negative security assurances.[40] Furthermore, it is also possible to offer a positive security assurance where the NWS pledges to NNWS that it 'will act immediately in accordance with the relevant provisions of the Charter of the United Nations, in the event that such States [NNWS] are the victim of an act of, or object of a threat of aggression in which nuclear weapons are used'.[41] While it is clear from the text of *UN Security Council Resolution 984* is that all the NWS have offered negative security assurances whereas in the case of positive security assurances the Security Council merely '[w]elcomes the intention expressed by *certain States*[42] that they will provide or support immediate assistance, in accordance with the [UN] Charter, to any non-nuclear-weapon State Party to the Treaty on the Non-Proliferation of Nuclear Weapons that is a victim of an act of, or an object of a threat of aggression in which nuclear weapons are used'.[43] A comparison between the corresponding passages of all the NWS statements on security assurances given to the Security Council and the General Assembly reveals a variance in the extent of the assistance that NWS are ready to offer in the event of nuclear attack of a NNWS.[44] Four of the NWS

39 S/RES/984 (1995), UN Security Council Resolution 984.

40 Point 1.

41 Point 2.

42 Emphasis added.

43 Point 7.

44 For comparison, relevant parts of different statements on security assurances have been reproduced:

'[...] China, as a permanent member of the Security Council of the United Nations, *undertakes to take action within the Council to ensure that the Council takes appropriate measures* to provide, in accordance with the Charter of the United Nations, necessary assistance to any non-nuclear-weapon State that comes under attack with nuclear weapons, and imposes strict and effective sanctions on the attacking State'. (Emphasis added), Statement on security assurances of the People's Republic of China S/1995/265;

'[...] France, as a Permanent Member of the Security Council, pledges that, in the event of attack with nuclear weapons or the threat of such attack against a non-nuclear-weapon State party to the Treaty on the Non-Proliferation of Nuclear Weapons, France will immediately inform the Security Council and *act within the Council to ensure that the latter takes immediate steps to provide, in accordance with the Charter*, necessary

(China, France, the United Kingdom and the Russian Federation) consider the positive security assurances through the medium of taking action within the Security Council by urging the former to take appropriate measures in the event of attack, while the United States are the only NWS which is itself ready to '[…] provide or support immediate assistance, in accordance with the Charter, to any non-nuclear-weapon State Party to the Treaty on the Non-Proliferation of Nuclear Weapons that is a victim of an act of, or an object of a threat of, aggression in which nuclear weapons are used'.[45]

Before proceeding with an elaboration of the international safeguards arrangements devised pursuant to Art. III(2) NPT, it is useful to note that all the EU Member States have signed and ratified the NPT and are thus fully bound by the Treaty's provisions. In this sense, a pattern can be discerned in the treaty accession practice within the EU whereby international conventions/treaties with non-proliferation relevance are customarily signed by the Member States[46] while for the conventions/treaties dealing exclusively with the

---

assistance to any State which is the victim of such an act or threat of aggression' (Emphasis added), Statement of France S/1995/264;

'[…] The United States affirms *its intention to provide or support immediate assistance, in accordance with the Charter, to any non-nuclear-weapon* State Party to the Treaty on the Non-Proliferation of Nuclear Weapons that is a victim of an act of, or an object of a threat of, aggression in which nuclear weapons are used'. (Emphasis added), Statement of the United States of America S/1995/263;

'[…] I, therefore, recall and reaffirm the intention of the United Kingdom, as a Permanent Member of the United Nations Security Council, *to seek immediate Security Council action to provide assistance*, in accordance with the Charter, to any non-nuclear-weapon State, party to the Treaty on the Non-Proliferation of Nuclear Weapons, that is a victim of an act of aggression or an object of a threat of aggression in which nuclear weapons are used.' (Emphasis added; Statement of the United Kingdom of Great Britain and Northern Ireland, S/1995/262);

'[…] In the event of aggression involving the use of nuclear weapons or the threat of such aggression against a non-nuclear-weapon State party to the Treaty on the Non-Proliferation of Nuclear Weapons, the nuclear Powers which are permanent members of the Security Council *will immediately bring the matter to the attention of the Council* and will seek to ensure that they provide, in accordance with the Charter, necessary assistance to the State that is a victim of such an act of aggression or that is threatened by such aggression' (Emphasis added; Statement of the Russian Federation Russia S/1995/261);

45 Emphasis added; Statement of the United States of America S/1995/263.

46 See, the Partial Nuclear-test-ban Treaty (UN Treaty Series, vol. 480, I-6964) and the Comprehensive Nuclear-Test-Ban Treaty (not yet in force) at: http://treaties.un.org/pages/ViewDetails.aspx?src=UNTSONLINE&tabid=2&mtdsg_no=XXVI-4&chapter=26&lang=en#Participants.

peaceful uses of nuclear energy, it is either Euratom or the Union that appear as signatory parties.[47] The fact that neither Euratom nor the Union have acceded to the NPT signifies that non-proliferation of nuclear weapons persists to be predominantly Member State competence which, nevertheless, does not rule out a complementary or shared Euratom/Union involvement in the area.

The pervasive non-proliferation objective of the NPT cannot be separated from the objective of promoting and safeguarding the peaceful uses of nuclear energy as the former cannot be accomplished without the use of nuclear safeguards as the essential tool in countering the diversion of nuclear material to non-peaceful uses. Thus, even though nuclear safeguards are instruments aimed at furthering the civil uses of nuclear energy, they are at the same time considered to be an integral part of the non-proliferation equation.[48] Arguably, nuclear safeguards are a manifestation of the overlap between the two concurring objectives – the promotion of civil uses of nuclear energy and the non-proliferation of nuclear weapons. Nuclear safeguards are not conceived as a nuclear weapon deterrent and are therefore specifically concerned with the non-diversion of the civil uses of nuclear energy to military ends.

In order to arrive at a precise and exhaustive definition for nuclear safeguards, academic literature first had to deal with semantically delimiting '*peaceful uses*' from '*military uses*' of nuclear energy. The language used in international treaties indicates a noteworthy difference between the Statute of the International Atomic Energy Agency[49] and the NPT regarding the approach the two instruments have towards 'military uses'. Namely the scope of the IAEA Statute is different from that of the NPT in that it is confined to civil uses of nuclear energy while the NPT covers both civil and military uses (in function to the status of a contracting party as a NWS or a NNWS). Moreover, to the difference of the IAEA's Statute, the objectives of the NPT are not anti-military *per se* given that the Treaty sanctions the maintenance and production of nuclear weapons by NWS. The purely peaceful character of IAEA's objectives has been articulated in such a way that the Agency is to '(…) ensure, so far as it is able, that assistance provided by it or at its request or

47 See, the *Convention on Nuclear Safety* (United Nations Treaty Series, Vol. 1963, I-33545), acceded to by the Euratom Community in April 2000. Further, see the *Joint Convention on the Safety of Spent Fuel Management and on the Safety of Radioactive Waste management* and the *Convention on the Physical Protection of Nuclear Material*, where the Euratom Community also appears as a signatory party.

48 Howlett, *supra* n. 9, p. 4.

49 The IAEA Statute was approved on 23 October 1956 by the Conference on the Statute of the International Atomic Energy Agency and came into force on 29 July 1957 (http://www.iaea.org/About/statute.html).

under its supervision or control is *not used in such a way as to further any military purpose*'.[50] The IAEA is vested with the responsibility '(t)o establish and administer safeguards designed to ensure that special fissionable and other materials, services, equipment, facilities, and information made available by the Agency or at its request or under its supervision or control are *not used in such a way as to further any military purpose*'.[51] It has been suggested that the reference to military purposes employed thereby is very broad and, in addition to encompassing the production and use of nuclear weapons and nuclear explosive devices, further extends to materials and activities potentially related therewith.[52] By comparison, the NPT precludes the involvement of NNWS in the acquisition of 'any nuclear weapons or other nuclear explosive devices' (Art. II NPT), Art. III(1) NPT stipulating that the 'purpose of the IAEA verification is preventing diversion of nuclear energy from peaceful uses to *nuclear weapons or other nuclear explosive devices*'. The language employed here could suggest that under the NPT regime the utilization of nuclear energy for *certain* military purposes is to be considered permitted – namely, for military applications *other than* the acquisition of nuclear weapons or nuclear explosive devices.[53]

The foregoing variance of approaches leads to a difference in the scope of application between the NPT and the IAEA regimes, primarily determined by the category of safeguards each of them applies to: *material* or *personal safeguards*.[54] *Material safeguards* are those applied to *specified* materials and installations, presupposing a limited scope of control and usually used when a state receives nuclear material, equipment or facilities subject to IAEA safeguards either from the IAEA or from another state through the IAEA as intermediary.[55] *Safeguards* are carried out on *personal* grounds on account of a state's status vis-à-vis the IAEA, so that the state is bound, under previously assumed international obligations, to submit *all* of its peaceful nuclear activities to IAEA safeguards control.[56] With regard to the former distinction, the scope of 'military uses' provided under the IAEA Statute would be presumed to

50 Emphasis added; Art. II of the IAEA Statute. For a downloadable version of the IAEA Statute, see http://www.iaea.org/About/statute_text.html.

51 Emphasis added; Art. III A(5) of the Statute.

52 Lamm, *supra* n. 15, p. 64.

53 *Idem*, p. 65.

54 *Idem*, p. 69.

55 *Idem*.

56 *Idem*, p. 70.

apply to material safeguards while for the personal safeguards arrangements the NPT formula is to be followed.[57]

The ensuing discussion will focus on the category of *personal safeguards* applied by virtue of Art. III(4) NPT, according to which NNWS-parties to the NPT undertake to conclude agreements with the IAEA in order to meet the NPT safeguards requirements thereby allows for the safeguards to be applied on *all source or special fissionable material in all peaceful nuclear activities* within the territory of the State in question, under its jurisdiction, or carried out under its control anywhere.[58]

II.1 *The IAEA Safeguards Agreements*

The safeguards agreements the IAEA has the authority to conclude with NNWS can be generally divided into three categories: comprehensive, item specific and voluntary offer safeguards agreements.[59] The comprehensive type agreements[60] are concluded by NNWS who undertake to accept the Agency safeguards on all source or special fissionable material in all peaceful nuclear activities within their territory, under their jurisdiction, or carried out under their control anywhere.[61] In order to strengthen the IAEA safeguards system, in particular the Agency's ability to detect undeclared nuclear material and activities in States with comprehensive safeguards agreements, as from 1991, the Agency fundamentally modified its safeguards system aiming to increase the information available regarding States' nuclear activities, broaden the Agency inspectors' access to relevant locations and improve technical verification measures.[62] The further reinforcement of the safeguards efforts culminated with the approval by the IAEA Board of Governors of a model Protocol[63] accompanying the safeguards agreements which provides the Agency with more extensive and elaborate tools in the verification process. The added value

---

57 *Idem*, p. 69.

58 Emphasis added; Art. III(1).

59 http://www.iaea.org/OurWork/SV/Safeguards/safeg_system.pdf, p. 1.

60 The template for the IAEA safeguards agreements, INFCIRC/153(Corrected).

61 http://www.iaea.org/OurWork/SV/Safeguards/safeg_system.pdf, p. 2.

62 http://www.iaea.org/OurWork/SV/Safeguards/safeg_system.pdf, p. 4.
By concluding a safeguards agreement with the IAEA under the INFCIRC/153 format, States undertake to establish a State System of Accounting and Control (SSAC), the reports from which serve as a basis for independent verification by the IAEA (See, L. Scheinmann, Transcending Sovereignty in the management and control of nuclear material, *IAEA Bulletin*, 2001, Vol.43 Issue 4, p. 34);

63 IAEA, Model Protocol Additional to Agreement(s) between State(s) and the IAEA for the Application of Safeguards (INFCIRC/540 (Corrected)).

of the modified system is that it introduces a safeguards system that verifies *not only the correctness* of States' declarations of nuclear material, but also the *completeness* thereof.[64] Consequently, it is only with relation to States that have both a comprehensive safeguards agreement and an additional protocol in force that the Agency has the complete requisite machinery to verify the existence of any undeclared nuclear material and activities.[65]

As was indicated *supra*, the NPT requires all the NNWS to have signed safeguards agreements while the same is not foreseen with respect to the NWS (Art. III NPT); however, for legitimacy and confidence-building reasons, all five NWS have concluded safeguards agreements with the IAEA, *voluntarily* offering the nuclear material and/or facilities on which the Agency may *selectively* apply the safeguards measures. These voluntary offer safeguards agreements (VOAs) generally follow the format of the comprehensive safeguards agreements, but vary in the scope of materials and facilities covered (materials and facilities with national security significance are excluded from the scope). Moreover, the VOAs envisage the possibility for withdrawal of materials and facilities from the scope of application of the voluntary safeguards, at the discretion of the NWS concerned.[66]

Presently, 122 out of a total of 190 State Parties to the NPT[67] have both comprehensive safeguards agreements and additional protocols in force.[68] The incomplete coverage with comprehensive safeguards agreements and additional protocols not only leaves gaps in the system, it also undermines the normative strength of the international safeguards regime. Only once *all* NPT States[69] For the status of all the signed Additional Protocols with the Agency, see, http://www.iaea.org/OurWork/SV/Safeguards/protocol.html. with comprehensive safeguards agreements equally have an Additional Protocol in place, will the desired success for a massive compliance with the IAEA principles materialize.[70] Hence, the ultimate goal for the future would be a timely completion of the IAEA safeguards agreements and protocols with all NPT States (including the nuclear weapon States in accordance with their voluntary

64 http://www.iaea.org/OurWork/SV/Safeguards/safeg_system.pdf, p. 4.

65 *Idem*, p. 2.

66 *Idem*, p. 3.

67 According to the latest status of the Treaty (http://disarmament.un.org/treaties/t/npt).

68 For the status of the Additional Protocols, see http://www.iaea.org/safeguards/documents/AP_status_list.pdf; The Euratom Community signed the Additional Protocol in September 1998, which entered into effect in April 2004.

69 States like India and the Islamic Republic of Iran have not yet brought their Additional Protocols into force.

70 Scheinmann, *supra* n. 2, p. 34.

safeguards arrangements with the IAEA).[71] Enforcing compliance with the NPT obligations through the medium of safeguards is vital to the sustainability of the overall global safeguards system. The former goes to the extent that, if need be, the UN Security Council would be called upon to act as the 'last instance' forum in the event that all IAEA compliance mechanisms have previously been exhausted.[72]

II.2 *The Safeguards Agreement between the IAEA, Euratom and the Member States*

While Art. III(4) NPT provides the legal basis for the conclusion of safeguards agreements between the NPT countries and the IAEA, in the particular case of the Euratom states a certain confusion existed from the outset regarding the potential 'duplicity' between the IAEA and Euratom safeguards regimes since a fully devised nuclear safeguards framework had already been established under the Euratom Treaty prior to the adoption of the NPT. There was thus a potential danger for collision or mutual exclusion between the safeguards competences exercised under the IAEA and the Euratom systems, respectively. In order for this to be averted, on the occasion of the signature of the NPT, the Euratom states made a declaration to the effect that the former would only ratify the NPT after having concluded a safeguards agreement with the IAEA.[73] It was for this reason that the period of ratification of the NPT for the five Euratom countries (Germany, Italy, Belgium, the Netherlands and Luxembourg, with the exception of France) took longer than expected, thereby exceeding the time limit for the start of negotiations for the conclusion of safeguards agreements imposed by Article III(4) NPT.[74]

71 *Idem.*

72 *Idem*, p. 34, 35.

73 See the Preamble of the *Agreement between the Kingdom of Belgium, the Kingdom of Denmark, the Federal Republic of Germany, Ireland, the Italian Republic, the Grand Duchy of Luxembourg, the Kingdom of the Netherlands, the European Atomic Energy Community and the International Atomic Energy Agency in implementation of Article III (1) and (4) of the Treaty on the non-proliferation of nuclear weapons* (78/164/Euratom, OJ L 051, 22/02/1978 P. 0001–0026):

> (...) NOTING that the States, which were members of the Community when they signed the [NPT] Treaty, made it known on that occasion that safeguards provided for in Article III (1) of the [NPT] Treaty would have to be set out in a verification agreement between the Community, the States and the Agency and defined in such a way that the rights and obligations of the States and the Community would not be affected (...);

74 Article III(4) NPT: 'Negotiation of such agreements shall commence within 180 days from the original entry into force of this Treaty. For States depositing their instruments of

It was indispensable that Euratom and the IAEA secure their future relationship of cooperation for the purpose of enabling a smooth co-existence between the two safeguards regimes, prior to the conclusion of the trilateral safeguards agreement between the IAEA, Euratom and the Member States. To this end, the 1975 *Cooperation Agreement between the Euratom Community and the IAEA*[75] was concluded under which the IAEA and Euratom agreed to act in close cooperation and '[...] consult each other regularly on matters of mutual interest with a view to harmonizing their efforts as far as possible, *having due regard to their respective characters and objectives*'.[76] The entry into force of the Cooperation Agreement facilitated the coming into effect of the *Safeguards Agreement between the Euratom Member States, the Euratom and the IAEA implementing Article III (1) and (4) of the Treaty on the non-proliferation of nuclear weapons*,[77] signed in September 1973 and coming into effect in February 1977.[78] The primary objective of the Safeguards Agreement was to delimit the respective competences of the Euratom Community and the IAEA by laying down the modalities in which both safeguards systems are to be implemented. The definition for nuclear safeguards that the Agreement espouses follows the NPT formula discussed *supra*, extending to all source or special fissionable material which can potentially be diverted to nuclear weapons or other nuclear explosive devices.[79] Following the terms of the Agreement, Euratom has the authority to apply the safeguards while the IAEA assumes the role of a supervisory authority which verifies the accuracy of the conducted safeguards checks.[80] Therefore, Euratom is under the responsibility to regularly submit

ratification or accession after the 180-day period, negotiation of such agreements shall commence not later than the date of such deposit. Such agreements shall enter into force not later than eighteen months after the date of initiation of negotiations'.

75 Cooperation Agreement between the EURATOM and the IAEA, OJ L 329, 23/12/1975 p. 0028–0029.

76 Emphasis added; Art.1 of the Cooperation Agreement.

77 See IAEA, INFCIRC/193.

78 http://www.iaea.org/OurWork/SV/Safeguards/sir_table.pdf.

79 Art.1 of the Safeguards Agreement: 'The States undertake, pursuant to Article III (1) of the Treaty, to accept safeguards, in accordance with the terms of this Agreement, on all source or special fissionable material in all peaceful nuclear activities within their territories, under their jurisdiction or carried out under their control anywhere, *for the exclusive purpose of verifying that such material is not diverted to nuclear weapons or other nuclear explosive devices*'. [Emphasis added].

80 Art.3(b) of the Agreement states that:

The Agency shall apply its safeguards, in accordance with the terms of this Agreement, in such a manner as to enable it to verify, in ascertaining that there has been no diversion of nuclear material from peaceful uses to nuclear weapons or other nuclear explosive

reports to the IAEA in accordance with the requirement that the exchange of information between the two organizations is frequent.[81] Furthermore, the IAEA is entitled to conduct additional checks on its own discretion by gaining direct access to nuclear sites, in a way that would be least disruptive to the effectiveness of the established Euratom system of safeguards.[82]

11.3 *The Voluntary Offer Agreements with France and the United Kingdom*

The voluntary offer agreements (VOAs) are confidence and transparency building measures applied to the relationship between the nuclear-weapon states and the IAEA, underpinned by the benevolence of NWS to make *part* of their civil nuclear programme subject to safeguards arrangements which the former are not legally obligated to do. By concluding the voluntary offer agreements, which are to some extent modeled on the safeguards agreements between the NNWS and the IAEA, the NWS put their civil production of nuclear energy under IAEA safeguards, however, with the *caveat* that this type of agreements (to the difference of the IAEA comprehensive safeguards agreements with the NNWS) do not extend to the *entire* civil nuclear sector in the state. Instead, a selective, *numeris clausus* approach is employed by specifying the type and scope of nuclear material the safeguards are to be applied to – thus, the NWS themselves select the exact civil nuclear facilities and materials that will be subject to the VOA's safeguards requirements.

While all of the NNWS of Euratom currently have comprehensive safeguards agreements with the IAEA in place, the NWS of Euratom (France and the United Kingdom), alongside Euratom, have concluded Voluntary Offer Agreements with the IAEA which entered into force in 1978 (the UK) and 1981 (France). For France the conclusion of the VOA created a 'pre-emptive' effect to its relationship with the NPT regime as it officially became a party to the Treaty in 1996. Thus, by concluding the VOA prior to becoming a party to the NPT, France became impliedly bound by the NPT rules, at least as far as the material scope of the VOA was concerned.

devices, findings of the Community's system of safeguards. The Agency's verification shall include inter alia independent measurements and observations conducted by the Agency in accordance with the procedures specified in this Agreement. The Agency, in its verification, shall take due account of the effectiveness of the Community's system of safeguards in accordance with the terms of this Agreement;

81 Art.8(a) of the Agreement.

82 Art.3(b) of the Agreement.

The texts of the VOAs signed with France and the UK are almost identical; there is, however, a noticeable difference in the way *certain* articles are phrased. Namely, the French VOA misses the reference to the NPT, and instead foresees that the IAEA is to apply safeguards at the request of the State, to any of that State's activities in the field of nuclear energy, pursuant to Art. III(5) of the IAEA Statute.[83] In this way, by endorsing the IAEA Statute as the legal basis for the application of safeguards, an indirect link is established between France and the NPT framework in this respect given that the IAEA safeguards system is the main facet through which the NPT regime is sustained.[84] In turn, the UK's VOA cites the relevant NPT articles as the basis for the application of safeguards, according to which the UK, by virtue of its status as NPT party, undertakes to co-operate in facilitating the application of the IAEA safeguards to peaceful nuclear activities.[85] Furthermore, both Agreements make a reference to Euratom's respective competence in the area of nuclear safeguards.[86]

The objective of UK's VOA is to 'encourage widespread adherence to the Treaty [the NPT] by demonstrating to non-nuclear-weapon States that they would not be placed at a commercial disadvantage by reason of the application of safeguards pursuant to the Treaty'.[87] In order to meet this objective, the UK offers its readiness for the Agency safeguards to be applied on its territory '[...] subject to exclusions for national security reasons only'.[88] Hence, the scope of application of the safeguards extends to *all source or special fissionable material in facilities or parts thereof within the United Kingdom, subject to exclusions for national security reasons* (Art.1(a)) whereby the UK is to provide the Euratom Community and the IAEA with a list of the facilities or parts thereof which contain the types of nuclear material indicated *supra* (Art.1(b)). For national security reasons, the UK is entitled to make deletions from the list by notifying the Euratom Community and the Agency to this effect (Art.1(b)).

83 IAEA, INFCIRC/290, December 1981, Agreement of 27 July 1978 between France, the European Atomic Energy Community and the International Atomic Energy Agency for the application of safeguards in France (http://www.iaea.org/Publications/Documents/Infcircs/Others/infcirc290.pdf, point 1 of the Preamble).

84 Art.III NPT.

85 IAEA, INFCIRC/263, October 1978, Agreement of 6 September 1976 between the United Kingdom Of Great Britain and Northern Ireland, the European Atomic Energy Community and the Agency in connection with the Treaty on the Non-Proliferation of Nuclear Weapons, point 1 et seq. of Preamble; The Agreement entered into force on 14 August 1978 (http://www.iaea.org/Publications/Documents/Infcircs/Others/infcirc263.pdf).

86 See, paras. 5–8 of the French VOA and paras. 6–9 of the UK VOA.

87 Preamble of the VOA, Point 4.

88 Preamble of the VOA, Point 5.

The UK is also entitled to reintroduce the material previously removed from safeguards control by notifying the Euratom Community and the Agency of the termination of the national security requirement (Art.14).

The VOA with *France* covers the *source or special fissionable material which is to be designated by France* (Art.1(a)), whereby France provides the Community and the Agency with a list of facilities or parts thereof which contain the said material (Art.1(b)). Concerning the option for removal of certain materials or facilities from the scope of the safeguards, the same conditions *mutatis mutandis* as the ones provided for in the UK VOA apply (Art.14). The difference is that France, unlike the UK, is not under any obligation to state the *reasons* for which a removal of from the list is made.[89]

A verbatim reading of the cited passages of the French and the UK voluntary offer agreements, points to a difference in the scope of application of the safeguards. While for the UK the safeguards apply to *all source or special fissile material* subject to exclusions for *national security reasons*, according to the French VOA, safeguards apply on *source and special fissionable material which is to be designated by France*. In the latter instance, national security reasons (or any other reasons, for that matter) have not been foreseen as derogation from the safeguards obligations. Nevertheless, the foregoing does not entail that France is given any advantageous treatment. In fact, being that the UK's VOA does not define the scope of the 'national security reasons' derogation, the UK possesses a large *margin of appreciation* in construing the elusive 'national security' category. Such a generous discretion amounts to very much the same effect as the one produced via the application of the corresponding derogation of the French VOA. Evidently, there is no possibility to exert any control over a nuclear-weapon state's discretion in selecting the facilities to be subjected to the IAEA safeguards and it is this very latitude of discretion afforded to NWS that belies the *quid pro quo* rationale of the IAEA safeguards arrangements with the NWS and serves as the ultimate guarantee fending off any potential encroachment upon the national security interests of NWS.

89 Additional Protocols to France and UK's Voluntary Offer Agreements were signed on 22 September 1998 and have been in effect since April 2004. Admittedly, the importance and the effectiveness of these Protocols has been largely reduced as a result of the limited mandate given to the IAEA and the Euratom Community by virtue of the limited scope of the original VOAs (Additional Protocol with France, INFCIRC/290/Add.1, Date: 24 February 2005; and Additional Protocol with the UK, INFCIRC/263/Add.1, Date: 24 February 2005).

III The Euratom Safeguards Framework

The Euratom safeguards system forms part of what can be viewed as a four-tier nuclear safeguards system devised at i) *the international level* (IAEA safeguards instruments and mechanisms adopted pursuant to the provisions of the IAEA Statute and the NPT; ii) *the primary EU level* (safeguards mechanisms established under the Euratom Treaty as primary source of EU law); iii) *the secondary EU level* (acts adopted by the EU institutions, implementing the Euratom Treaty safeguards provisions); and lastly, iv) *the Member State level* (the implementation of the Member States' international and regional obligations in the field of safeguards).

Having covered the interaction between the IAEA, NPT and Euratom safeguards regimes occurring at the international level in what can be described as a relationship of 'controlled deference', the discussion will now focus on how the Euratom safeguards regime has been devised internally, at the primary and the secondary EU level.

III.1 *The Euratom Treaty Safeguards Provisions*

The *Safeguards* Chapter of the Euratom Treaty (Arts.77–85) establishes the legal framework for the application of nuclear safeguards in the territory of the Union at the level of primary law. The institution entrusted with the authority to comprehensively control and overview the application of the Euratom safeguards requirements is the European Commission, its chief responsibility being to ensure that in the Member States' territories ores, source materials and special fissile materials[90] are *not diverted from their intended uses* as declared by the users (Art.77 Euratom). The Euratom Treaty only employs the term '*intended uses declared by the users*' without specifying whether the former strictly covers peaceful uses, which, in turn, reveals an important difference in the way in which the concept of safeguards has been construed under the IAEA and the Euratom regimes. Namely, Art.1 of the *Safeguards Agreement between the IAEA, the Euratom and the Member States* provides that IAEA safeguards are applied on all source or special fissionable material in all peaceful nuclear activities within the states' territories, under their jurisdiction or carried out under their control anywhere, for the exclusive purpose of verifying that such material is *not diverted to nuclear weapons or other nuclear explosive devices*. Manifestly, in difference to the language of the Euratom Treaty, the prohibition of diversion to military uses is mentioned *expressis verbis* in the

90 For the definition of ores, source materials and special fissile materials, see Art.197 Euratom, reproduced *supra*, n. 125.

Safeguards Agreement. The former lack of precision of the Euratom Treaty has been somewhat compensated by the Art.84(3) Euratom derogation regarding the Member States defence requirements, according to which '[t]he safeguards may not extend to materials intended to meet defence requirements which are in the course of being specially processed for this purpose or which, after being so processed, are, in accordance with an operational plan, placed or stored in a military establishment'.

However, there have been objections expressed with respect to the former 'complementary' paragraph completing the Euratom Treaty definition of nuclear safeguards due to its ambiguous character. For instance, AG Geelhoed's Opinion in C-61/03 *Commission v UK* suggested that Art.84(3) Euratom may be interpreted in a way that the Euratom safeguards should not be considered as inapplicable to *all* the nuclear materials intended to meet defence requirements, but rather, only to those materials which are 'in the course of being specially processed for [defence purposes] or which, after being so processed are, in accordance with an operational plan, placed or stored in a military establishment'.[91]

In order for the safeguards requirements to be correctly implemented, anyone setting up or operating an installation for the production, separation or other use of source materials or special fissile materials or for the processing of irradiated nuclear fuels is required *to declare* to the Commission the basic technical characteristics of the former installations (Art.78(1)). Additionally, the Commission *approves the techniques to be used for the chemical processing of irradiated materials* to the extent necessary for the attainment of the objectives set out in Art.77 (Art.78(2)). In function to the supervision exercised by the Commission, it is required that *operating records are kept and produced* so as to enable accounting for ores, source materials and special fissile materials used or produced (which equally applies to the transport of source and special fissile materials) (Art.79(1)). The subjects coming within the scope of the foregoing obligations have to notify the national authorities of the respective Member State of any communications made to the Commission pursuant to the foregoing obligations (Art.79(2)).

Furthermore, the Commission is entitled *to send on-site inspectors to the Member States*, and consult the Member State concerned regarding the first assignment of an inspector in its territory (the consultation covers the current and all the future assignments of the inspector (Art.81(1)). The Euratom

91 See the AG Geelhoed Opinion in C-61/03 *Commission v. UK*, para. 52; In addition, the 2005 Euratom Safeguards Regulation further clarifies the scope of application of the Euratom safeguards (see, *infra* in this section).

inspectors, upon presenting a document establishing their authority, are to have access at all times to all places and data and to all persons who, by reason of their occupation, deal with materials, equipment or installations subject to the safeguards, to the extent necessary to apply the safeguards to ores, source materials and special fissile materials and to ensure compliance with the provisions of Art.77 (Art.81(1)). In the event of opposition to the carrying out of an inspection, the President of the EU Court of Justice or the Commission can issue a decision to the effect that the inspection on the territory proceeds (Art.81(2)). The Euratom inspectors are recruited by the Commission and are responsible for obtaining and verifying the records outlined in Art.79 (Art.82(2)) as well as reporting any sort of infringement to the Commission (Art.82(2)). Once an infringement on the part of a Member State has been found, the Commission may issue a directive calling upon the Member State to rectify the infringement (Art.82(3)). In the event of persistent non-compliance, the matter can be directly referred to the EU Court of Justice thus circumventing all the steps foreseen for the conventional enforcement procedure of Art.258 and 259 TFEU (Art.82(4)). Moreover, if the infringement has been committed by persons or undertakings, the Commission has the authority to impose sanctions which can vary from issuing a warning to ordering a total or partial withdrawal of source or special fissile materials (Art.83(1)). The Commission decisions imposing these sanctions are fully enforceable in the territories of the Member States) (Art.83(2)).[92]

92 The following two Commission decisions can serve as an illustration of the manner in which the Commission disposes of its prerogative to impose the sanctions:

Commission Decision 90/413/Euratom of 1 August 1990 relating to a procedure in application of Article 83 of the Euratom (OJ L 209/8) was related to the undeclared export of nuclear material from the Federal Republic of Germany to the United States of America by *Advanced Nuclear Fuels GmbH* ('ANF Lingen') which ran a fabrication plant which regularly received nuclear material from Advanced Nuclear Fuels of Richland (USA). The sanctions that the Commission imposed on the undertaking in question via the Decision was the placing of the former under the administration of a person or board appointed by common accord of the Commission and the Federal Republic of Germany for a period of four months;

In comparison to the previous Decision which concerned a material breach of the Euratom safeguards obligations, the Commission *Decision of 15 February 2006 pursuant to Article 83 of the Treaty establishing the European Atomic Energy Community* (2006/626/Euratom OJ L 255/5) addressed to the British Nuclear Group Sellafield (BNG SL) was only limited to issues of adequacy of the accounting and the reporting procedures in place at Sellafield and did not find any material to be actually lost or diverted from its intended purpose. The Commission issued a warning to BNG SL with the understanding that,

III.2 *Commission Regulation (Euratom) No 302/2005*

Commission Regulation (Euratom) No 302/2005 on the application of Euratom safeguards[93] complements the safeguards arrangements set out under the Euratom Treaty by precisely defining the nature and scope of the safeguards requirements of Arts. 78 and 79 Euratom and providing for a more detailed and comprehensive regime for the application of the Euratom safeguards requirements. The Regulation is highly technical in nature and therefore only those provisions which contribute to the enhancement of the non-proliferation component of the Euratom safeguards system shall be examined.

Firstly, Art.34(1) of the Regulation clarifies the dilemma raised *supra* regarding the correct interpretation of the Art.84(3) Euratom derogation on the Member States' defence requirements by stipulating that materials, installations and parts of installations that have been *assigned to meet defence requirements* by nuclear-weapon Member States have been excluded from the ambit of the Regulation. In comparison to the above cited Art.84(3) Euratom which did not confine itself to the notion of '*materials or installations intended to meet defence requirements*' and went on to enumerate the types of nuclear material that the 'defence requirements' exemption applies to (that is '(...) materials intended to meet defence requirements which are in the course of being specially processed for this purpose or which, after being so processed, are, in accordance with an operational plan, placed or stored in a military establishment'), conversely, Art.34(1) of the Regulation does without the reference to the specific kinds of nuclear material which are to be excluded from the safeguards' remit and adopts a simpler, catch-all formula ('materials/installations assigned to meet defence requirements').[94]

Further on, the Regulation addresses certain grey areas concerning the use of nuclear energy as is the case with installations and materials that can potentially be assigned to meet defense requirements or, indeed, with installations which *at certain times* operate with nuclear materials for strictly civil purposes and *other times* operate with materials liable to be assigned to meet defence

within a specified period, the undertaking implements adequate remedies against the failures and sources of infringement identified.

93 Commission Regulation (Euratom) No 302/2005 on the application of Euratom safeguards of 8 February 2005, OJ L 54/1 (replacing Regulation (Euratom) No 3227/76 of 19 October 1976 concerning the application of the provisions on Euratom safeguards).

94 Provisions specific to nuclear-weapon Member States: '1. This Regulation shall not apply: (a) to installations or parts of installations which have been assigned to meet defence requirements and which are situated in the territory of a nuclear-weapon Member State; or (b) to nuclear materials which have been assigned to meet defence requirements by that nuclear-weapon Member State (...)' (Art.34(1)).

requirements. Thus, Art.34(2) of the Regulation covers installations and materials that are situated in the territory of a Member State which is a nuclear-weapons state and are *liable* to be assigned to meet defence requirements. The breadth of application of the former provisions of the Regulation is to be defined by the Commission in consultation and in agreement with the Member States concerned, whereby *the objectives* of the Euratom safeguards regime need to be taken into account.[95]

It follows from the foregoing Euratom primary and secondary law safeguards arrangements that the Commission has been mandated with developing and implementing the Euratom safeguards system which covers all civil nuclear installations in the Union[96] which is a task consisting of two parts: the first part which concerns the nuclear material accountancy system implemented by the nuclear operators of the EU (and their related accountancy declarations made to the Commission as prescribed by Commission Regulation (Euratom) 302/2005); and the second part which is relative to the activities of the Commission to verify the completeness, correctness and coherence of the former nuclear operator accountancy declarations.[97] As was indicated *supra*, in the performance of the latter, the Commission is assisted by the Euratom on-site inspectors that are sent to do accountancy as well as physical and other verifications on the nuclear material present at the installations in order to verify the correctness and coherence of the nuclear operators' declarations.[98]

In order to monitor the progress of the implementation of the safeguards obligations, the Commission issues regular yearly reports taking note of the progress in the implementation of the Euratom safeguards, the most recent of which covers the time period of the year 2013. The Report shows that a total of 1300 inspections were carried out by the Commisison's Department-General for Energy in 2013, 626 of which were joint inspections executed together with the IAEA[99]

95 For the applicable regime to installations which are at times operated exclusively with nuclear materials liable to be assigned to meet *defence requirements* and at times operated exclusively with *civil* nuclear materials (Art.34(3)(a)); while for installations which produce, treat, separate, reprocess or use in any other way, simultaneously, *both civil nuclear materials and nuclear materials assigned or liable to be assigned to meet defence requirements* (Art.34(3)(b)).

96 European Commission (Directorate-General for Energy), Report on the Implementation of Euratom Safeguards in 2013, Ref. Ares(2014)1534607 – 14/05/2014, April 2014, p. 3.

97 Report on the Implementation of Euratom Safeguards, p. 4.

98 *Idem.*

99 *Idem*, p. 5.

whereby no cases of nuclear material diversion have been found nor any irregularities have been reported for the EU by the IAEA.[100]

To complete the foregoing discussion regarding the NPT/IAEA and the Euratom safeguards systems, when speaking of the coexistence of the legal orders created under the Euratom Treaty and the Non-Proliferation Treaty, one speaks of two distinct but at the same time intrinsically linked regulatory frameworks that complement each other. In spite of there being no superiority of one legal order over the other, it is arguably the Euratom safeguards system which can be said to derive its legitimacy from the NPT regime (even though the former regime pre-dates the latter as such).[101]

There are nevertheless certain inherent conceptual differences that underlie the relationship between the Euratom and the NPT regimes which need to be pointed out. These differences are especially pronounced with regard to the application of the non-discrimination principle and the scope of the objectives fostered under each of the two legal frameworks. Namely, by establishing

100 *Idem*, p. 4.

101 There exists a legal *curiosum* as to whether, formally speaking, the Euratom is to be presumed bound by the Non-Proliferation Treaty as such. Among the Member States, France had in the past adopted a clear stance on the issue, the background of which comes from a heated dispute between France and the Euratom Commission occurring over the application of nuclear safeguards to the French plutionum producing plant at Marcoule, France (See, Howlett, *supra* n. 9, p. 108). The European Commission considered that it was entitled to perform safeguards controls on all nuclear materials on the Community territory up to the point where the former have been turned into weapons or stored in military establishments thus extending the scope of the control also to the previous production stages. To the contrary, France claimed that nuclear military establishments fell outside of the scope of Euratom safeguards (See, J.G. Polach, *EURATOM: Its Background, Issues and Economic Implications*, Oceana Publications inc., 1964, p. 129.);

France reiterated its resolute stance once again on the occasion of Spain's accession negotiations in the course of the discussion as to whether Spain's accession to the NPT should be imposed as a pre-requisite for the country's accession to the European Community. France took the view that no link could be established between the NPT and the Euratom Treaty since it regarded non-proliferation as a purely political issue which did not concern the Euratom in any way (See, J.R. Goens, The opportunities and Limits of European Co-operation in the Area of Non-proliferation, in, H. Muller (ed.), *A European Non-Proliferation Policy: Prospects and Problems*, Clarendon Press, 1987, p. 41); Nevertheless, it seems fairly difficult to support the claim that the the Euratom is not to be considered (at least, impliedly) bound by the NPT in view of the existent elaborate Euratom safeguards framework and the Safeguards Agreement between the Euratom Member States, the Euratom and the IAEA which provide the legal mechanisms for the furtherance of the goal of non-proliferation of nuclear weapons at the EU level.

the NNWS/NWS division the NPT endorsed a sort of an 'implied' discrimination between those states which are allowed to produce and maintain nuclear weapons on their territory and those that are not. By contrast, the principle of non-discrimination is an essential part of the European Union's *raison d'etre* and is therefore deeply embedded in the Euratom legal and political construct. The fact that all of the Euratom states have become parties to the NPT effectively creates a difference in treatment between those Member States that are NWS and those that are NNWS, in light of the application of the NPT rules.[102] Given that the maintenance of such a 'warranted' discrimination between the NPT countries is critical to the attainment of the global non-proliferation objective, the difference in treatment thus occurring is more of a *prima faciae* type of incompatibility between the NPT and the Euratom regimes rather than a substantive one.

In view of the objectives pursued, apart from the non-proliferation objective, the scopes of the NPT and the Euratom legal frameworks also coincide with regard to the objective for the development of the civil nuclear industry. However, unlike the NPT framework where the objective concerning the development of the civil nuclear industry has remained rather rudimentary and has not been elaborately articulated, the Euratom framework takes the former objective further from a purely policy level to a fully fledged regulatory level by establishing a comprehensive legal regime for the civil nuclear industry.

IV Euratom and EU's Policy on the Non-proliferation of Nuclear Weapons

IV.1 *The Raison d'être of EU's Non-proliferation Policy*

The competence of the European Union in the field of non-proliferation of nuclear weapons can be said to have assumed two intrinsically linked dimensions, a legal and a policy dimension. While the former has been embodied by the Euratom safeguards regime and has been devised through the application of nuclear safeguards, health and safety and physical protection measures as well as measures linked to export controls and countering illicit trafficking,[103] the latter has been assumed by the Union *stricto sensu* and exists as a subset of the Common Foreign and Security Policy (CFSP) as a much wider, over-arching

102 Fischer, *supra* n. 3, p. 96.

103 *Communication from the Commission to the Council and the European Parliament, Communication on nuclear non-proliferation*, Brussels, 26.3.2009, COM (2009) 143 final, Section 3.

policy. The Union's policy on non-proliferation, being intergovernmental in character,[104] has been devised on a confederal rather than a federal level[105] and can be described as a joint effort among the Union, the Euratom Community and the Member States, which coordinate their actions in accordance with their respective competences under the CFSP and the Euratom frameworks.[106]

EU's policy regarding the non-proliferation of nuclear weapons represents only one aspect of the larger EU policy against the proliferation of Weapons of Mass Destruction (WMD) which covers the proliferation of nuclear, chemical and biological weapons.[107] The Union's adherence to the promotion of the non-proliferation of nuclear weapons is seen as a clear and straightforward objective and, thus, a non-issue – however, this does not eliminate the competition of competences which subsists in the non-proliferation arena among the Union institutional actors, most notably, the European Commission (serving as the 'guardian' of the Union's interests) and the European Council (representing the 'voice' of the Member States).[108] Such competition is habitually resolved in favor of the European Council, the Commission being regarded as competent to decide only on issues that strictly concern the Euratom scope.[109] The European Council, pursuant to the Lisbon Treaty amendments, has been placed as the highest decision-making organ under the CFSP which works in close co-relation with the Council of the EU and the High Representative for Foreign Affairs and Security Policy as the key exponent of EU's external action.[110] As regards the involvement of the European Parliament, even though the Treaties have accorded it a relatively marginal role within the scope of the CFSP,[111] and, more particularly in the context of the non-proliferation policy,

104 Mölling, *supra* n. 18, p. 61.

105 H. Müller, Non-proliferation Policy in Western Europe: Structural Aspects, in, H. Müller (ed.), *A European Non-Proliferation Policy: Prospects and Problems*, Clarendon Press, 1987, p. 92.

106 Commission Communication (2009), *supra*, Section I.

107 See, Council of the European Union, *EU Strategy against proliferation of weapons of mass destruction*, 15708/03, 10 December 2003, p. 3.

108 T. Sauer, How 'common' is European nuclear non-proliferation policy, Joint Session of Workshops of the European Consortium for Political Research, Edinburgh, 2003, p. 18.

109 *Idem.*

110 On the respective prerogatives of the European Council, the Council of the EU and the High Representative for Foreign Affairs and Security Policy in the framing and the implementation of the CFSP, see, Arts.24–31 TFEU.

111 The Parliament is regularly consulted by the High Representative on the main aspects and the basic choices of the common foreign and security policy and the common security and defence policy and is informed of how these policies evolve. The High Representative is to ensure that the views of the Parliament are duly taken into consideration (Art.36 TFEU).

the latter has nonetheless attempted to be ever more closely associated to the matter of non-proliferation, mostly by issuing a number of resolutions pertaining to the field.[112]

In retrospect, the initial step marking the conception of a singular EU approach toward the issue of non-proliferation of nuclear weapons was the creation of a Working group on nuclear questions within the context of the European Political Co-operation (EPC) in 1981.[113] Ever since, the non-proliferation policy has been undergoing an active consolidation mainly on account of the new strategic environment created after the end of the Cold War which lead to the creation of a separate CFSP pillar under the 1992 Maastricht Treaty thus facilitating a more intense and more immediate cooperation in foreign and security matters among the Member States (including in the area of WMD non-proliferation).[114] The WMD non-proliferation policy of the EU gained greater momentum on a global scale in the past decade, mostly as a result of the aftermath of the September 11th 2001 terrorist attacks on the USA and the US-led invasion of Iraq in March 2003.[115]

EU's involvement in the field non-proliferation of WMD has been succinctly described as being developed on *three levels:* the *first* level is designated for the political dialogue the EU conducts with third countries concerning the non-proliferation agenda, the most prominent feature here being the introduction of the requirement for a '*non-proliferation clause*' to be included in EU agreements

112 On this, see, P. Van Ham, The European Union's WMD Strategy and the CFSP: A Critical Analysis, *Non-Proliferation Papers*, September 2011, p. 6; Further reading: European Parliament, *Resolution on measures to safeguard the Non-Proliferation Treaty*, OJ C262, 14 October 1985, p. 84; European Parliament, *Resolution on the importance of the Non-Proliferation Treaty Review Conference*, OJ C262, 14 October 1985, p. 85; European Parliament, Report on Non-Proliferation of Weapons of Mass Destruction: A Role for the European Parliament, Committee on Foreign Afairs, 2005/2139, FINAL A6-0297/2005, 12 Oct. 2005.

113 C. Portela, *The Role of the EU in the Non-Proliferation of Nuclear Weapons: The Way to Thessaloniki and Beyond* (Research Report no.65), Peace Research Institute – Frankfurt, 2003, p. 2.The activities of the Working group were confidential, its existence being formalized in 1986 with the Singe European Act (see, P. Van Ham, *supra*, p. 1). For a recent account on the external dimension of EU's non-proliferation policy, consult, P.J. Cardwell (ed.), *EU External relations law and policy in the post-Lisbon era*, Springer, 2012.

114 Van Ham, *supra*, p. 2. An additional enabling factor for the reinforcement of the EU non-proliferation policy was France's long-awaited accession to the Non-Proliferation Treaty in 1992 as the last EU Member State to accede to the Treaty (see, Van Ham, *supra*, p. 2).

115 Van Ham, *supra*, p. 3.

with third countries.[116] The requirement was introduced with the adoption of the *Basic Principles for an EU Strategy against Proliferation* at the European Council Summit in Thessaloniki in 2003.[117] The *second* level comprises activities pertaining to the implementation of the safeguards systems and the commitments undertaken by the Member States in the context of the export controls and non-proliferation regimes,[118] and the *third* level being concerned with strategizing and implementing assistance programmes for third countries.[119]

The *European Security Strategy*[120] and the *EU Strategy against Proliferation of weapons of mass destruction*,[121] adopted in 2003, are the key policy documents that provide the structural framework for conducting the EU's non-proliferation policy which equally serve as the basis for the future adoption of all EU documents concerning non-proliferation. Furthermore, the EU is equipped with a satisfactory institutional capacity and manpower put at disposal for the realization of the non-proliferation goals. EU's *WMD monitoring centre*, founded in 2003 and attached to the Council Secretariat, serves to enhance the consistent implementation of the *EU Strategy against Proliferation of weapons of mass destruction*, ensuring a joint collaboration among the High Representative for Foreign Affairs and Security Policy, the Commission and the Member States.[122] One of the chief tasks of the centre is to oversee the collection of information and intelligence regarding the flow of WMD-related materials and provide for a permanent channel of communication with the relevant

116 A. Wetter, *Enforcing European Union Law on Exports of Dual-use Goods*, Stockholm International Peace Research Institute Research Report No.24, Oxford University Press, 2009, p. 23,24.

117 The 'Basic Principles for an EU Strategy against Proliferation' were drafted in parallel to the EU's first-ever security strategy, both having been presented at the Thessaloniki European Council in June 2003. See, Council of the European Union, Action Plan for the Implementation of the Basic Principles for an EU Strategy against Proliferation of Weapons of Mass Destruction, 10354/1/03 Rev 1, 13 June 2003.

118 Wetter, *supra* n. 116, p. 24.

119 *Idem*, p. 25.

120 European Council, A Secure Europe in a Better World: European Security Strategy, Brussels, 12 December 2003.

121 Council of the European Union, *EU Strategy against proliferation of weapons of mass destruction*, 15708/03, 10 December 2003; Both the *European Security Strategy* and the *EU Strategy against proliferation of weapons of mass destruction* identify the WMD proliferation as potentially the greatest threat to EU security.

122 General Secretariat of the Council of the EU, *EU Strategy against the proliferation of WMD: Effective multiaterlaism, prevention and international cooperation*, November 2008, (www.consilium.europa.eu/uedocs/cms_data/librairie/PDF/EN), p. 12.

international bodies.[123] The Centre is the focal point bringing together the work of the Council (i.e. the Member States) and the Commission.[124] Rather than monitoring WMD-related developments around the world as its name suggests, the centre acts more as a coordination mechanism aimed at streamlining the non-proliferation policies of EU institutions.[125]

Upon the entry into force of the Lisbon Treaty, the responsibility for providing consistency in EU's action in the field of WMD non-proliferation had been principally taken over by the European External Action Service (EEAS), headed by the High Representative of the Union for Foreign Affairs and Security Policy, and more specifically, under the auspices of the Directorate for Non-Proliferation and Disarmament.[126] In this respect, it is important to mention the work of the European Council Working Group on Global Disarmament and Arms Control,[127] as well as the Council of the EU's Working Party on Non-Proliferation (CONOP) and the Working Party on Global Disarmament and Arms Control (CODUN) which are now permanently chaired by EEAS officials.[128]

With the adoption of *Council Decision 2010/430/CFSP establishing a European network of independent non-proliferation think tanks in support of the implementation of the EU Strategy against Proliferation of Weapons of Mass Destruction,*[129] the WMD non-proliferation role of the EU further evolved through the establishment of a network assembling foreign policy institutions and research centres from across the EU in order to encourage political discussion and exploration of measures to combat the proliferation of weapons of mass destruction and their delivery systems.[130] The EU Non-Proliferation

---

123 Action Plan for the Implementation of the Basic Principles, *supra*, part B point 14; See also, Council of the EU, EU Strategy against the proliferation of WMD: Monitoring and enhancing consistent implementation, 16694/06.

124 *Idem.*

125 Van Ham, *supra* n. 112, p. 6; In 2003 the former High Representative for Foreign Affairs and Security Policy, Mr. Javier Solana, even appointed a Personal Representative for Non-Proliferation of WMD (See, http://www.consilium.europa.eu/uedocs/cmsUpload/09-06-22_speech_Sopot_AG.pdf).

126 http://www.consilium.europa.eu/eeas/foreign-policy/non-proliferation,-disarmament-and-export-control-/wmd?lang=en.

127 http://www.consilium.europa.eu/eeas/foreign-policy/non-proliferation,-disarmament-and-export-control-/ms-clara-ganslandt?lang=en.

128 Van Ham, *supra* n. 112, p. 6.

129 Council Decision 2010/430/CFSP of 26 July establishing a European network of independent non-proliferation think tanks in support of the implementation of the EU Strategy against Proliferation of Weapons of Mass Destruction OJ L 202/5.

130 For more on the operational structure and mechanisms involved in the promotion of the causes of non-proliferation and disarmament, consult the website of the EEAS: http://www.eeas.europa.eu/non-proliferation-and-disarmament/index_en.htm.

Consortium, introduced by virtue of the former Council Decision, counts over 60 think-tanks from all over Europe and has assumed a large part of the technical operation and responsibilities, working in close cooperation with the European External Action Service.

IV. 2 *EU's Policy on the Non-proliferation of Nuclear Weapons and the Treaty on the Non-Proliferation of Nuclear Weapons (NPT)*

In light of the objectives fostered by the NPT (*non-proliferation, nuclear disarmament* and *development of civil uses of nuclear energy*), the Union has attempted a cautious approach to not favor any one objective in particular and thus afford equal importance to all three objectives.[131] However, the former has not always been feasible given that the objectives of *non-proliferation* and *disarmament* are often found inter-twined in EU's non-proliferation practice. The difficulty to precisely separate the Union's non-proliferation objective from its disarmament objective is mainly due to two factors that characterise EU's nuclear reality: on the one hand, the diversity of nuclear attitudes in the Union (ranging from Member States that are nuclear weapon states (France and the UK), nuclear states that only subscribe to peaceful uses of nuclear energy (Germany, Italy, Finland, Slovenia, Lithuania, Bulgaria etc.) to countries that champion the foregoing of the use of nuclear energy altogether (Austria, Ireland, Sweden)[132]), and, on the other hand, the ongoing plans for the future creation of a common *European nuclear deterrent* (also known as a *dissuasion concertée*) to be headed by France and the UK as EU's only two nuclear weapon states.

Marked skepticism has been expressed with regard to the nuclear deterrence arrangements as they are seen as liable to compromise Member States' non-proliferation commitments under the NPT. It has been argued that the existence of a common nuclear deterrent would produce quite the contrary effect of encouraging states outside the EU to acquire nuclear weapons in order to counterbalance the common nuclear deterrent shared by France and the UK.[133] Therefore, in the long run, it would prove imminent to address the issue of the role played by nuclear weapons in EU's security in the sense of whether they constitute both a guarantee and a threat to security.[134] The issue becomes increasingly topical in view of the new-and-improved Union defense

131 L. Kulesa, Global Zero: Implications for Europe, in, Jean Pascal Zanders (ed.), European Union Institute for Security Studies Chaillot Papers, 2010, p. 96,97.

132 Van Ham, *supra* n. 112, p. 5,6.

133 C. Portela, and U. Jasper, EU Defense Integration and Nuclear Weapons: A Common Deterrent for Europe? *Security Dialogue*, 2010, p. 163.

134 Mölling, *supra* n. 18, p. 64.

policy which is to be put into place under the Lisbon Treaty amendments[135] in that the success of the concept of a common European nuclear defense has been conditioned upon the accomplishment of a fully developed and implemented European Security and Defense Policy.[136]

The legal repercussions from the operation of a European *dissuasion concertée* in the nuclear domain are, arguably, prone to jeopardize or even outright contradict the NPT-established non-proliferation regime. Namely, a system of concerted dissuasion of the former kind may potentially trigger the participation of non-nuclear weapon Member States that have, pursuant to Arts. I and II of the NPT, committed not to develop nuclear weapons or be involved in transfer thereof or transfer of materials linked thereto. The former practice is to be regarded as contrary both to the letter[137] and spirit of the NPT regime,[138] the main logic of the NPT being for states to *eventually* completely cease the production and use of nuclear weapons and devote solely to furthering the development of the civil nuclear industry.[139] Furthermore, on account of the EU's

135 *Idem.*

136 B. Ribeiro, Le role de l'arme nucleaire dans la mise en oeuvre d'une PESCD, in, P. Buffotot et N. Vilboux (dirs.), *Vers une politique europeenne de securite et de defense: Defis et opportunites*, Economica, 2003, p. 168.

137 The three main NPT objectives have been outlined in Arts. I, II and VI of the Treaty:
'Article I
Each nuclear-weapon State Party to the Treaty undertakes not to transfer to any recipient whatsoever nuclear weapons or other nuclear explosive devices or control over such weapons or explosive devices directly, or indirectly; and not in any way to assist, encourage, or induce any non-nuclear-weapon State to manufacture or otherwise acquire nuclear weapons or other nuclear explosive devices, or control over such weapons or explosive devices.
Article II
Each non-nuclear-weapon State Party to the Treaty undertakes not to receive the transfer from any transferor whatsoever of nuclear weapons or other nuclear explosive devices or of control over such weapons or explosive devices directly, or indirectly; not to manufacture or otherwise acquire nuclear weapons or other nuclear explosive devices; and not to seek or receive any assistance in the manufacture of nuclear weapons or other nuclear explosive devices.(...)
Article VI
Each of the Parties to the Treaty undertakes to pursue negotiations in good faith on effective measures relating to cessation of the nuclear arms race at an early date and to nuclear disarmament, and on a treaty on general and complete disarmament under strict and effective international control. (...)' (*Treaty on the Non-Proliferation of Nuclear Weapons*, United Nations Treaty Series, Vol.729, I-10485);

138 Ribeiro, *supra* n. 136, p. 166; See also, Portela and Jasper, *supra* n. 133, p. 162.

139 Portela and Jasper, *supra*, p. 163.

non-proliferation policy being based on the concept of 'lowest common denominator' for states with divergent attitudes towards the use of nuclear weapons, in reality the objective of nuclear disarmament has been overshadowed by and appears secondary to pursuing the objective of non-proliferation of nuclear weapons.[140] For instance, while the text of the NPT clearly recognizes the link between disarmament and non-proliferation, EU's policy documents in the field have not adequately addressed the issue of EU's own disarmament so that the accent is put largely on the enforcement of the disarmament obligations of third countries rather than the EU Member States.[141]

Irrespective of the lack of an unequivocal stance on the part of the EU with regard to important nuclear proliferation issues which comes as a result of the divergent domestic nuclear attitudes,[142] the Member States have nonetheless managed to accumulate a solid track-record of concerted actions within the NPT forum. The EU has brought a prolific contribution to the NPT deliberation forum through the preparation of working papers and issuing statements addressed at the Non-Proliferation Treaty review conferences which have been the result of an achieved consensus between the Member States that takes into careful consideration the individual states' prerogative to issue workings papers and statements in their national capacity.[143] EU's ambitious diplomatic campaign for the indefinite extension of the NPT is one exceptional proof of EU's vigorous involvement in the global non-proliferation cause.[144] In the one year period preceding the 1995 NPT Review and Extension Conference which was to decide whether the NPT would be renewed for a limited period of time or extended indefinitely, the EU adopted a Joint action in support of the option of indefinite extension of the NPT.[145] Finally, the goal was met, among other, due to the contribution of EU's relentless diplomatic activity, at the 1995

140 *Idem*, p. 155.

141 *Idem.*

142 See, Summary of the meeting of the Committee on Foreign Affairs (AFET) and the Subcommittee on Security and Defence (SEDE), Public hearing 'The Future of the Nuclear Non-Proliferation Treaty (NPT)' Brussels, 12 July 2006 Brussels, 22 September 2006, 13157/06 PE 294 – ANNEX: The future of the Nuclear Non-Proliferation Treaty: The approach of the EU to nuclear non-proliferation and disarmament, Annalisa Giannella, Personal Representative of the High Representative – Non-Proliferation of Weapons of Mass Destruction, Brussels, 14 IX 2006, p. 8.

143 Portela, *supra* n. 113, p. 7.

144 *Idem.*

145 As reported in, Portela, *supra* n. 113, p. 7.; See, Presidency Conclusions, Corfu European Council, 24–25 June 1994. The text of the Joint Action was also reprinted in: Europe no. 6277, 20 July 1994, p. 6.

Conference[146] where it was decided for the NPT to be extended for an indefinite period of time. It has thus become common practice that prior to each NPT Review Conference the Council of the EU adopts *common positions* through which the Member States outline the priorities to be discussed among the participants to a given NPT conference.[147]

Subsequently, in the run up to the 2000 NPT Review Conference, the Member States again successfully aligned their positions by adopting the 1999 and the 2000 Common Positions, where the emphasis was put on further strengthening of the international non-proliferation legal instruments through the promotion of their timely signature and/or implementation (particularly with respect to the NPT and the Comprehensive Test Ban Treaty).[148] The former produced a tangible impact on to the outcome of the Review Conference, given that at least three provisions in the 2000 NPT Conference Final Document are recorded as having been inspired by EU's Common Positions, most notably, the reference to the principles of 'irreversibility' and 'transparency'.[149] Another important point thereby raised by the Member States was urging the NPT states to reduce the number of non-strategic nuclear weapons which was the first time that an appeal for the reduction of non-strategic nuclear weapons[150] had appeared in an NPT Conference Final Document.[151] The EU also engaged tremendous efforts in anticipation of and during the 2010 NPT Review Conference

146 Portela, *supra*, p. 7.

147 See the following documents: Council Decision of 25 July 1994 (OJ L 205/0001-0002) regarding the preparation for the 1995 Conference of the States parties to the NPT; Council Common Position of 29 July 1999 (OJ L 204/1–2) relating to EU's contribution to the promotion of the early entry into force of the CTBT; Council Common Position 2000/297/CFSP of 13 April 2000 relating to the 2000 Review Conference of the Parties to the NPT (L 97/1–3); Council Common Position of 25 April 2005 relating to the 2005 Review Conference for the NPT (OJ L 106/32–35).

148 See, Council Common Position of 29 July 1999 (OJ L 204/1–2) relating to EU's contribution to the promotion of the early entry into force of the CTBT; and, Council Common Position 2000/297/CFSP of 13 April 2000 relating to the 2000 Review Conference of the Parties to the NPT (L 97/1–3).

149 Noted in, Portela, *supra* n. 113, p. 7. For this purpose, also see, *Final Document of the NPT Review Conference 2000*, Art. VI(15)(5) and (9).

150 Strategic nuclear weapons are to be contrasted to non-strategic or tactical nuclear weapons in that the former relate to a strategic plan for attack and are usually targeted at military bases or highly populated civilian areas. They have longer or inter-continental ranges while the non-strategic weapons have shorter ranges (Hans M. Kristensen, Non-Strategic Nuclear Weapons, Federation of American Scientists, Special Report No. 3 May 2012 (http://www.fas.org/_docs/Non_Strategic_Nuclear_Weapons.pdf)), p. 9.

151 Portela, *supra* n. 113, p. 8.

where action taken by the Union consisted of issuing demarches regarding states parties or states non-parties to the NPT urging their alignment with the NPT objectives;[152] working on draft proposals to be submitted by individual Member States on behalf of the Union as potential basis for adoption of the final decisions at the 2010 Review Conference;[153] releasing various statements in the framework of the debates organized at the Review Conference;[154] etc.

While it cannot be denied that the EU recognizes the NPT as 'a unique and irreplaceable multilateral instrument for maintaining and reinforcing international peace, security and stability',[155] a comparison of the texts of EU's common positions adopted on the occasion of the 2005 and the 2010 Review Conferences points to a departure in approach. In the latter document, the EU positions itself more boldly as a non-proliferation actor by being more vocal about the pressing problems surrounding the global non-proliferation and disarmament regime. The 2010 Common Position is much more detailed and concrete and less declaratory in nature[156] whereas the 2005 Common Position mostly contained declaratory statements drawing attention to the potential implications borne to international peace and security by the withdrawal from the NPT and calling for the adoption of measures aimed to discourage such withdrawal.[157] Furthermore, while the 2005 Common Position simply took notice of 'serious nuclear proliferation events [that] have occurred since the end of the 2000 Review Conference',[158] the 2010 Common Position did some finger-pointing by specifically referring to the major proliferation challenges encountered in the case of the Democratic People's Republic of Korea and the Islamic Republic of Iran. The former statements do not simply figure as dead letter on paper as they reflect EU's practical on-the-field efforts in advocating non-proliferation throughout the globe.[159]

152 See, Council Decision 2010/212/CFSP of 29 March 2010 relating to the position of the European Union for the 2010 Review Conference of the Parties to the Treaty on the Non-Proliferation of Nuclear Weapons, OJ L 90/8, Art.4(a).

153 Art.4(b) of Council Decision.

154 Art.4(c).

155 Art.3(b)(2).

156 Art.3(b)(28).

157 Art.2(b)(8).

158 Art.2(b)(6).

159 For this, see NPT/CONF.2010/PC.III/WP.26 Preparatory Committee for the 2010 Review, Conference of the Parties to the Treaty on the Non-Proliferation of Nuclear Weapons 6 May 2009: Working paper on forward-looking proposals of the European Union on all three pillars of the Treaty on the Non-Proliferation of Nuclear Weapons to be part of an action plan adopted by the 2010 Review Conference.

In anticipation of the upcoming 2015 NPT Review Conference, the Preparatory Committee for the conference held three sessions, the most recent of which was held in April/May 2014. At the occasion, the EU reiterated the formerly voiced concerns regarding the nuclear programs of the Democratic People's Republic of Korea and the Islamic Republic of Iran, and, additionally, addressed the issue of the deployed nuclear weapons on the territory of Europe. Namely, the Union welcomed the proposals made by US President Obama in June 2013 in Berlin to reduce deployed strategic nuclear weapons by one-third and to seek bold reductions on US and Russian non-strategic weapons in Europe, considering such further bilateral voluntary reduction to be a contribution to the goal of complete nuclear disarmament.[160] At the occasion, the priority attached to the immediate commencement and early conclusion of the negotiation for a Treaty banning the production of fissile materials for nuclear weapons or other nuclear explosive devices had been emphasized, in accordance with the nuclear disarmament objective of the NPT.[161] Additionally, in keeping with the goal of non-proliferation of nuclear weapons, the Union has also been fervent in advocating for the timely entry into force of the *Comprehensive Test Ban Treaty*[162] – the universalisation of which remains to be one of the top priorities of the Union's non-proliferation agenda.[163] Many of the former proposals were subsequently

160 EU Statement By Mr. Jacek Bylica, Principal Adviser and Special Envoy for Non-Proliferation and Disarmament European External Action Service, Third Session of the Preparatory Committee for the 2015 Review Conference of the States Parties to the Treaty on the Non-Proliferation of Nuclear Weapons (Cluster 1), United Nations, New York, 2 May 2014(http://eeas.europa.eu/delegations/un_geneva/documents/eu_statments/conference_disarmament/2014_05_02_npt_prepcom_cluster_1_eu_statement_final.pdf), point 6.

161 *Idem*, at point 14; Supporting the work of the Conference on Disarmament for the expected conclusion of a Treaty banning the production of fissile material for nuclear weapons the EU has encouraged all States to uphold a moratorium on the production of fissile material for nuclear weapons or other nuclear explosive devices (See, Council Common Position of 13 April 2000 relating to the 2000 Review Conference of the Parties to the NPT (L 97/1–3); Common Position of 25 April 2005 relating to the 2005 Review Conference for the NPT (OJ L 106/32–35)).

162 Council Common Position of 29 July 1999 relating to the EU's contribution to the promotion of the early entry into force of the Comprehensive Test Ban Treaty OJ L 204/1–2.

163 See, supra, EU Statement, Third Session of the Preparatory Committee for the 2015 Review Conference of the States Parties to the Treaty on the Non-Proliferation of Nuclear Weapons (Cluster 1), at point 12.

See, also, the following statements the EU has issued at the Third Session of the Preparatory Committee for the 2015 NPT Review Conference: EU Statement By Mr. Jacek Bylica Principal Adviser and Special Envoy for Non-Proliferation and Disarmament

incorporated in the Council Conclusions on the Ninth Review Conference of the Parties to the Treaty on the Non-Proliferation of Nuclear Weapons,[164] adopted in April 2015, shortly pre-dating the 2015 NPT Review Conference.

IV.3 *The 'Weapons of Mass Destruction (WMD)' Clause in Agreements with Third Countries*

The EU has been actively involved and has exhibited a serious commitment to implement its agenda in the field of non-proliferation of weapons of mass destruction[165] and one of the most tangible manifestations of the Union's commitment to further the non-proliferation cause, or as one author phrases it, the 'only coercive policy used by the EU to promote non-proliferation'[166] is the endorsement of a non proliferation conditionality applied to its co-operation agreements and assistance programmes concluded with third countries.[167] To this end, since 2003 the Council of the EU has urged for the insertion of a 'non-proliferation of WMD' clause to agreements with third countries thus making non-proliferation an important – if not essential – component of EU's

European External Action Service Third Session of the Preparatory Committee for the 2015 Review Conference of the States Parties to the Treaty on the Non-Proliferation of Nuclear Weapons (Cluster 2), United Nations, New York, 1 May 2014 (http://eeas.europa.eu/delegations/un_geneva/documents/eu_statments/conference_disarmament/2014_05_01_eu_statement_cluster_2_final.pdf); EU Statement By Mr. Jacek Bylica Principal Adviser and Special Envoy for Non-Proliferation and Disarmament European External Action Service, Third Session of the Preparatory Committee for the 2015 Review Conference of the States Parties to the Treaty on the Non-Proliferation of Nuclear Weapons (General Debate), United Nations, New York, 29 April 2014 (http://eeas.europa.eu/delegations/un_geneva/documents/eu_statments/conference_disarmament/2014-04-29-npt-2014-prepcom-eu-general-statement_final.pdf).

164 *Council Conclusions on the Ninth Review Conference of the Parties to the Treaty on the Non-Proliferation of Nuclear Weapons*, 20 April 2015, CONOP 29 CODUN 9 CFSP/PESC 61.

165 The Council of the EU issues regular six-monthly reports noting the progress in the implementation of the 2003 *EU Strategy against the Proliferation of Weapons of Mass Destruction*. For the more recent of these reports, see Council Six-Monthly Progress Report on the Implementation of the EU Strategy Against the Proliferation of Weapons of Mass Desctruction (2013/I), *OJ 2013/C 228/05*; Council Six-Monthly Progress Report on the Implementation of the EU Strategy Against the Proliferation of Weapons of Mass Desctruction (2013/II) OJ 2014/C 54/01.

166 Van Ham, *supra* n. 112, p. 4.

167 Council of the European Union, Action Plan for the Implementation of the Basic Principles for an EU Strategy against Proliferation of Weapons of Mass Destruction, 10354/1/03 Rev 1, 13 June 2003, part B, point 8.

relations with its partners throughout the world.[168] The Council defines the non-proliferation clause as part of 'an effective stick and carrot policy linked to non-proliferation commitments in [EU's] relations with third countries',[169] and thus, an enterprise of 'mainstreaming non-proliferation policies into the EU's wider relations with third countries'.[170] The standard non-proliferation clause is based on the mutual understanding between the EU and the other country 'to cooperate and to contribute to countering the proliferation of weapons of mass destruction and their means of delivery through full compliance with and national implementation of their existing obligations under *international disarmament and non-proliferation treaties and agreements and other relevant international obligations*'.[171]

In addition to requiring compliance with *existing* non-proliferation obligations under international non-proliferation instruments, the WMD clause requires cooperation aimed at taking part in *all other relevant international instruments* the country has not yet acceded to, for the purpose of countering

168 Pursuant to the Action Plan for the Implementation of the Basic Principles for an EU Strategy against Proliferation of Weapons of Mass Destruction (See, on this, Council of the EU General Secretariat Brussels, Note on the implementation of the WMD clause 5503/09 (2003–2008 period) of 19 January 2009, p. 2).

169 Action Plan for the Implementation of the Basic Principles, part B, point 8.

170 Action Plan for the Implementation of the Basic Principles, part B, point 8.

171 Emphasis added; For the text of the standard WMD clause, see, Stabilisation and Association Agreement between the European Communities and their Member States, of the one part, and the Republic of Montenegro, of the other part (OJ L 108/3):

'(...) 3. The Parties consider that the proliferation of weapons of mass destruction (WMD) and their means of delivery, both to state and non-state actors, represents one of the most serious threats to international stability and security. The Parties therefore agree to cooperate and to contribute to countering the proliferation of weapons of mass destruction and their means of delivery through full compliance with and national implementation of their existing obligations under international disarmament and non-proliferation Treaties and Agreements and other relevant international obligations. The Parties agree that this provision constitutes an essential element of this Agreement and will be part of the political dialogue that will accompany and consolidate these elements. The Parties furthermore agree to cooperate and to contribute to countering the proliferation of weapons of mass destruction and their means of delivery by:

(a) taking steps to sign, ratify, or accede to, as appropriate, and fully implement all other relevant international instruments;(b) establishing an effective system of national export controls, controlling the export as well as the transit of WMD-related goods, including a WMD end-use control on dual use technologies and containing effective sanctions for breaches of export controls; (...)

(c) Political dialogue on this matter may take place on a regional basis. (...)';

the proliferation of weapons of mass destruction and their means of delivery.[172] Furthermore, under the terms of the WMD clause, the contracting party undertakes to establish an effective system of national export controls for the export and transit of WMD-related goods (including WMD end-use control on dual-use technologies[173]) and to provide effective sanctions for breaches of export controls.[174]

Technically, the WMD clause can be split into two parts: under the first part, the parties commit themselves to fully comply with and implement their

172 Observe the text of the standard WMD clause reproduced in, *Note on the implementation of the WMD clause, supra*, p. 4.

173 Once on the non-proliferation arena, another issue that cannot be neglected is EU's export controls regime for dual-use items and technology. It is a matter which is hybrid in nature as it follows two concomitant objectives: a commercial and a non-proliferation objective whereby the former takes priority. The predominance of the commercial aspect of the dual-use items regime has been rubberstamped by the CJEU in the *Werner* (C-70/94 *Fritz Werner Industrie-Ausrüstungen GmbH v Federal Republic of Germany*) and *Leifer* (C-83/94 *Criminal proceedings against Peter Leifer, Reinhold Otto Krauskopf and Otto Holzer*) judgments where the Court pronounced the dual-use items export controls to be a facet of EU's common commercial policy. The dominant commercial aspect has been further substantiated by the choice of former Art.133 TEC (presently, Art.207 TFEU) on the EU common commercial policy as legal basis for *Council Regulation* (*EC*) *No 428/2009 L 134/1 setting up a Community regime for the control of exports, transfer, brokering and transit of dual-use items*. The ratio behind the passing of the Regulation is to establish a common system of export controls that is in accordance with international non-proliferation commitments and responsibilities of the Member States and the EU (point 3 of Preamble). The Regulation sets up a Union-wide regime for the control of exports, transfer, brokering and transit of dual-use items, aiming to eliminate national differences in the treatment of exports of dual use items, thus unifying and strengthening Member States' export control policies and practices concerning dual-use items. Article 2 of the Regulation defines 'dual-use items' as 'items, including software and technology, which can be used for both civil and military purposes, and shall include all goods which can be used for both non-explosive uses and assisting in any way in the manufacture of nuclear weapons or other nuclear explosive devices'. Therefore, nuclear materials, facilities and equipment are caught by the provisions of the Regulation as dual-use items (Listed in Annex 1, under Category 0).

For an overview of the dual-use export control system of the European Union, see, European Commission Green Paper, The dual-use export control system of the European Union: ensuring security and competitiveness in a changing world, COM (2011) 393 final.); For a look at the CJEU's reasoning in the *Leifer* and *Werner*, see, I. Govaere, Case commentary, cases C-70/94 and C-83/94 (Leifer and Werner) of the European Court of Justice concerning dual use goods, *Common Market Law Review*, 1997 Vol.34, pp. 1019–1037.

174 *Note on the implementation of the WMD clause, supra*, p. 4.

already existing obligations in the fields of non proliferation and disarmament whereas the second part is more generally phrased urging the parties to a mutual cooperation which is expected to result in the country's becoming member of international instruments it has not yet participated to.[175] The obligations covered by the first part of the WMD clause are usually interpreted as pertaining to the Non-Proliferation Treaty (including IAEA Comprehensive Safeguards Agreement and Additional Protocols), the Chemical Weapons Convention, the Biological and Toxic Weapons Convention and the relevant UN Security Council Resolutions, in particular Security Council Resolution 1540 (2004)[176] and the Resolutions dealing with nuclear crises.[177] The former types of obligations are what is effectively considered as an essential element of the agreement whereby failure to comply therewith may, in extreme cases, lead to the suspension of the concerned agreement.[178] However, depending on the particularities of each case, at its own discretion, the EU may also decide to regard the *second* part of the WMD clause as an essential element to the agreement.[179]

Manifestly, the aim of the WMD clause is to factor the WMD non-proliferation concerns into EU's external diplomatic and economic activities and programmes[180] in a way that EU's declared political principles can be translated into concrete EU actions.[181] The conditionality approach is similar to the kind of conditionality the EU applies in promoting human rights and democracy in third countries[182] – the notorious 'human rights clause' which represents an essential element to EU's trade and cooperation agreements with third countries. According to the Council's WMD strategy progress reports, the EU has concluded negotiations with (a rough estimate of around) 100 countries for agreements containing a clause which is adequate to the spirit and the content

175 *Note on the implementation of the WMD clause, supra*, p. 4.

176 The UN Security Council Resolution 1540 describes the proliferation of WMD and their means of delivery as a threat to international peace and security and is most commonly cited as one of the legal bases for the decisions adopted within the official NPT forums as well as EU's common positions regarding non-proliferation (for example, see, point 4 of the preamble of 2010 Decision on the NPT; point 3 of the preamble of 2005 Decision on the NPT, etc.).

177 *Note on the implementation of the WMD clause, supra*, p. 5.

178 *Note on the implementation of the WMD clause, supra*, p. 5.

179 *Note on the implementation of the WMD clause, supra*, p. 4.

180 *EU Strategy against Proliferation of Weapons of Mass Destruction, supra*, p. 13.

181 *Note on the implementation of the WMD clause, supra*, p. 4.

182 Van Ham, *supra* n. 112, p. 7.

of the standard WMD standard clause.[183] However, with regard to the entry into force of EU agreements incorporating a WMD clause, the situation has been rather complicated for mixed agreements as the former additionally require the ratification by all the EU Member States appearing as signatory parties.[184]

Although the effectiveness of the WMD clause as EU's non-proliferation tool has had a solid track-record,[185] it is nonetheless difficult to measure the extent to which the increasingly wider coverage of the international non-proliferation instruments is to be attributed to EU's direct or indirect involvement. In fact,

183 Council, Six-monthly progress report on the implementation of the EU Strategy against the Proliferation of Weapons of Mass Destruction (2009/I) 11490/09, 26 june 2009, p. 36; See also, General Secretariat of the Council of the EU, The EU Strategy against the proliferation of WMD: Effective multiateralism, prevention and international cooperation, November 2008, www.consilium.europa.eu/uedocs/cms_data/librairie/PDF/EN, p. 11; The site of the EU External Action Service which contains all the EU official documents and publications on non-proliferation does not provide a more recent official estimate of the number of EU agreements covered by a WMD non-proliferation clause.

184 L.Grip, The EU Non-proliferation Clause: A Preliminary Assessment, Stockholm International Peace Research Instiute Background Paper, November 2009 (http://books.sipri.org/files/misc/SIPRIBP0911.pdf), p. 6; As reported in the former paper, an interview with a European Commission official has confirmed that it is the general impression that the WMD clause has met resistance from third countries in most negotiations.

185 The *Note on the implementation of the WMD clause* recorded the accomplishments in the implementation of the WMD clause for the time period between 2003 and 2008, reporting on the countries that have been assisted by the EU in signing and ratifying the relevant international non-proliferation instruments after the adoption of the WMD strategy in December 2003. Since the former date, 34 countries have joined the Comprehensive Nuclear Test Ban Treaty (CNTBT) although EU's actions in this respect did not target any country in particular, whereas since the same referring time period, 16 new countries have signed a Comprehensive Safeguards Agreement with the IAEA and 29 countries signed the Additional Protocol to the IAEA Agreement, while 15 of them have benefitted from EU's assistance in concluding the final act of signature (*Note on the implementation of the WMD clause, supra*, p. 9). The EU has been involved in providing legislative assistance for the implementation of State's obligations under IAEA safeguards agreements and additional protocols, with regard to the following countries: Angola, Azerbaijan, Armenia, Botswana, Burundi, Cameroon, Cape Verde, Comoros, Congo, Côte d'Ivoire, Croatia, Former Yugoslav Republic of Macedonia, Gabon, Georgia, Kazakhstan, Madagascar, Mauritius, Niger, Namibia, Sierra Leone, Swaziland, Turkey, Ukraine and Uzbekistan; Furthermore, the EU has been active in strengthening States' capabilities for detection of and response to illicit trafficking: Albania, Algeria, Azerbaijan, Bosnia and Herzegovina, Ghana, Jordan, Lebanon, Morocco, Serbia & Montenegro, South Africa, Sudan, Tanzania, Tunisia, Uganda and Zambia (*Note on the implementation of the WMD clause, supra*, p. 9).

the wider impact of the WMD clause has been regarded as very limited and highly political,[186] or even somewhat questionable.[187] For instance, while EU's important trade partners such as China, India, and certain Central American states have been reluctant to accede to agreements containing a WMD clause, countries where the conclusion of such agreements has been successful and unproblematic are predominantly countries with fairly marginal stake in the field of non-proliferation[188] (e.g., the revised Cotonou Agreement with most of the African, Carribean and Pacific Group of States, the Association Agreement with Albania, The Stabilisation and Association Agreement with Montenegro, the Partnership and Cooperation Agreement with Tajikistan, etc.).

IV.4 *The Nuclear Sharing Arrangements under NATO*

The NATO nuclear sharing arrangements on the territory of the EU have not been devised under either the Euratom or the Union framework – these arrangements have been entered into independently by certain (non-nuclear-weapon) Member States of the EU and the North-Atlantic Treaty Organization (NATO). The existence of the NATO nuclear sharing arrangements has been a controversial issue that has raised many eyebrows both in political and legal terms as the former have been considered liable to prejudice the relationship between the EU and the NPT framework.

The practice of certain Member States storing NATO nuclear weapons on their territory dates back to the period of the Cold War (Belgium- 1962, Italy-1960, Germany-1959, Netherlands-1959).[189] The nuclear sharing arrangements are part of NATO's security concept of 'extended nuclear deterrence' in Europe,[190] the original reason for their putting into place being to secure the peace and stability on the European continent. In this sense, the chief objective of NATO's nuclear forces in Europe (headed by the U.S.) is purely political and centers on the maintenance of peace and prevention of war.[191] Views on the nuclear sharing concept vary from those perceiving it as a valuable nuclear

186 See, Van Ham, *supra* n. 112, p. 7.

187 Mölling, *supra* n. 18, p. 59.

188 Van Ham, *supra* n. 112, p. 7.

189 L. Spagnuolo, *NATO nuclear burden sharing and NPT obligations*, BASIC Getting to Zero Papers Number 13, April 2009 (accessible at http://www.basicint.org/sites/default/files/gtz13.pdf), p. 3.

190 For more on this concept, see, M. Chalmers, NATO's Nuclear Weapons: An Introduction to the Debate, in, M. Chalmers and S. Lunn (eds.), NATO's Tactical Nuclear Dilemma, March 2010, Royal United Services Institute (downloadable at http://www.rusi.org/downloads/assets/NATOs_Nuclear_Dilemma.pdf), p. 1 et seq.

191 http://www.nato.int/issues/nuclear/sec-environment.html.

deterrence and non-proliferation instrument[192] to those that regard the deployed NATO nuclear weapons as '"political" weapons, [where] appearances matter as much, if not more, than what might, or might not, happen in the event of war'.[193]

Although the exact numbers for the NATO-stored weapons on the European continent have very often been kept in strict confidentiality, estimates show that weapons available to NATO's sub-strategic forces in Europe today amount to approximately 180 nuclear weapons[194] which is a notable reduction by from the the peak reached at the height of the Cold War[195] and the 2500 nuclear warheads that were reportedly in place in 1991.[196] Presently, a secure and well organized weapon-storage system has been devised consisting of the remaining gravity bombs delivered by Dual-Capable Aircraft (DCA) that have been stored safely in storage sites under highly secure conditions.[197] NATO has not neglected to assure that its present nuclear forces in Europe are not aimed at targeting any particular country indicating that their future putting to use is a highly unlikely possibility.[198]

The 'nuclear weapons sharing' is put into place through the conclusion of bilateral agreements between the host states and the US (or NATO).[199] These

192 M. Ruhle, NATO and Extended Deterrence in a Multinuclear World,, *Comparative Strategy*, Vol. 28 No. 1, January 2009, p. 10.

193 Chalmers, *supra* n. 190, p. 2.

194 Originally reported by the US mission to NATO (U.S. Mission to NATO: PDUSDP MILLER CONSULTS WITH ALLIES ON NUCLEAR POSTURE REVIEW, Cable 09USNATO0378, Brussels, 4.9.2009), reproduced in, O. Nassauer, Die Nuklearwaffen der USA in Europa – Doch kein Ende in Sicht?, *Wissenschaft und Frieden*, August 2012, No.3/12, p. 1 (downloadable from the website of the Berlin Information center for Transatlantic Security http://www.bits.de/frames/publib.htm); As a comparison, 240 NATO nuclear weapons were reported to be in existence in Europe in 2010 (reported in, *Le Soir*, 22 April 2010, 'Arme nucléaire en Europe: pas de retrait sans accord de l'Otan', http://archives.lesoir.be/arme-nucleaire-en-europe-pas-de-retrait-sans-accord_t-20100422-00VYHQ.html?query=armes+atomiques&queryand=armes+atomiques,+OTAN&queryor=armes+atomiques&firstHit=0&by=10&when=-1&sort=datedesc&pos=1&all=65&nav=1).

195 See,http://www.nato.int/nato_static/assets/pdf/pdf_topics/20091022_NATO_Position_on_nuclear_nonproliferation-eng.pdf.

196 Chalmers, *supra* n. 190, p. 1; There are also reports of 1400 nuclear bombs in existence at the end of the cold war (see, Nassauer, *supra* n. 194, p. 1).

197 http://www.nato.int/issues/nuclear/sec-environment.html.

198 http://www.nato.int/issues/nuclear/sec-environment.html.

199 J. Burroughs, *Two Legal Issues Confronting NATO And The Non-Proliferation Regime: US Presidential Decision Directive 60 Versus Pledges of Non-Use of Nuclear Weapons Made to*

agreements are part of a meticulously elaborated legal framework[200] comprising of i) agreements governing the use of the territorial state military bases (entered into by the US (or NATO) and the host state) which are general in nature and scope and often referred to as 'umbrella agreements'; on to ii) agreements for cooperation on the use of atomic energy for mutual defense purposes (between the US and a host state) which are unclassified agreements determining the rules by which US nuclear weapons are deployed in NATO countries; and lastly, ii) technical agreements implementing the former two.

The nuclear sharing arrangements are carried out in a way that in peacetime the stored NATO nuclear weapons are under full control and possession of the US[201] whereas in time of war the US passes the control of the nuclear weapons over to the host states' pilots for use with aircrafts belonging to these states. Thus, once the aircraft has started its mission, control over the respective weapon(s) is presumed to have been transferred to the state hosting the weapons.[202] In peace time, the weapons are controlled by US Munitions Support Squadrons (MUNSS) and can only be released for use through an allied Dual-Capable Aircraft (DCA) upon NATO command, securing the authorization of both of the governments involved.[203] The air forces of Belgium, Germany, Italy and the Netherlands continue to organise and train for such missions and their aircraft are prepared for the use of nuclear munitions.[204]

Legality and Legitimacy Issues Linked to the Practice of Nuclear Weapons Sharing

Bearing in mind the non-proliferations obligations incumbent on nuclear-weapon states and non-nuclear-weapon states, the NATO nuclear weapons sharing arrangements elaborated above seem to be patently in breach of Art. I and II of the NPT as the key premise of the overall NPT regime which is the obligation for NWS not to transfer nuclear weapons or control thereof and the

Non-Nuclear Weapon States and NATO Nuclear Sharing versus the Nuclear Non-Proliferation Treaty, Lawyers' Committee on Nuclear Policy, 1999, p. 9.

200 Spagnuolo, *supra* n. 189, p. 2.

201 http://www.nato.int/nato_static/assets/pdf/pdf_topics/20091022_NATO_Position_on_nuclear_nonproliferation-eng.pdf.

202 O. Nassauer, Nuclear Sharing in NATO: Is it Legal?, Newsletter of the Institute for Energy and Environmental Research: *Science for Democratic Action* Vol. 9 No.3, May 2001 (accessible at http://www.ieer.org/sdafiles/vol_9/9-3/nato.html).

203 M. Chalmers, NATO Dual-Capable Aircraft: A Stocktake, in, M. Chalmers and S. Lunn (eds.), *NATO's Tactical Nuclear Dilemma*, 2010, Royal United Services Institute, accessible at http://www.rusi.org/downloads/assets/NATOs_Nuclear_Dilemma.pdf, p. 21.

204 For a table of the current capabilities in each of the four states, see Chalmers, *supra*, p. 22.

corresponding obligation for NNWS not to receive such transfers. The act of deployment of US nuclear weapons on foreign territory can be regarded as a kind of 'transfer' of nuclear weapons or transfer of 'control' thereof to non-nuclear weapons states which is what the US is basically performing when assisting non-nuclear weapon states in possibly acquiring such control.[205]

Not surprisingly, the issue was raised in the run-up to the adoption of the Non-Proliferation Treaty when the US asserted its steadfast conviction that the NPT '[...] does not deal with arrangements for deployment of nuclear weapons within allied territory as these do not involve any transfer of nuclear weapons or control over them *unless and until a decision were made to go to war, at which time the treaty would no longer be controlling*'.[206] The main reason why the US presumes the NPT to be inapplicable in times of outbreak of a general war is because from that point further there would be no possibility to prevent the spread of nuclear weapons thus making the purpose of the Treaty obsolete.[207] Another argument the US has used to support its controversial position is a temporal one – which is the fact that the NATO nuclear sharing arrangements had been put in place *prior to* the signature of the NPT in consequence to which they do not '[...] represent proliferation *subsequent* to the establishment of the NPT regime'.[208]

Provided that the arguments offered by the US in this regard lean on a purely 'legalist' understanding of the implementation of the NPT non-proliferation commitments, it has been suggested that the former can quite plausibly be discounted in light of the standpoint of the NPT contracting parties taken in

---

205 Burroughs, *supra* n. 199, p. 11.

206 Emphasis added; *Questions on the Draft Non-Proliferation Treaty Asked by U.S. Allies Together With Answers Given by the United States*" in, NPT Hearings, US Senate 90–92, p. 262.

207 The key reason why the US presumes the NPT to be inapplicable in war time is given in the following statement extracted from a secret US memorandum:

'(...)The purpose of such a treaty [NPT], as the preamble could be expected to express it, would be to prevent the spread of nuclear weapons and, by this measure among others, to avoid the outbreak of nuclear war anywhere in the world. Thus, the treaty has its application in time and in a situation when no conflict has broken out and when it continues to be possible to prevent such a conflict. Once general hostilities involving nuclear weapons have occurred, however, the point of prevention has been long passed, and the purpose of the treaty can no longer be served. In such circumstances the treaty would not apply, and a nuclear power would be free to transfer nuclear weapons to an ally for use in the conflict (...)' (as reproduced in M. Butcher, O. Nassauer, T. Padberg and Dan Plesch, *Questions of Command and Control: NATO, Nuclear Sharing and the NPT*, British American Security Information Council Research Report, PENN Research Report vol.1 2000, http://www.basicint.org/pubs/Research/2000nuclearsharing3.htm, Section 2.5.);

208 Burroughs, *supra* n. 199, p. 12.

the Final Document of the 1995 Review Conference[209] according to which '[t]he Conference agrees that the strict observance of the terms of Articles I and II [NPT] remains central to achieving the shared objectives of preventing *under any circumstances* further proliferation of nuclear weapons and preserving the Treaty's vital contribution to peace and security (…)'. It is evident that the participating parties to the Conference have esteemed the NPT's provisions to be binding *under any circumstances* – that is, including in wartime.[210] Moreover, the former claim stands valid bearing in mind the consideration that the NPT is a treaty that deals with nuclear weapons so that the obligations stemming therefrom should *a fortiori* be regarded as all the more prominent during wartime.[211] Ultimately, upon weighing in on all the pros and cons regarding the existence of the NATO nuclear sharing arrangements, it is fair to point out that a practice such as nuclear sharing, if not against the letter of the NPT *per se*, is nevertheless in open contradiction with the spirit and the objectives of this Treaty as it effectively turns the NNWS into '"surrogates" on behalf of the nuclear powers',[212] serving as a covert extension of the NWS' military nuclear power.

The issue of the compatibility between the NATO nuclear sharing and the NPT is not merely an issue of *legality*, but also an issue of *legitimacy* since enhancing the legitimacy of these arrangements reinforces their legality and ultimately – their justifiability.[213] Despite the apprehensions expressed with

209 Part II, NPT/CONF.1995/MC.II/1, p. 307.

210 On the applicability of the NPT regime in war time, see, Burroughs, *supra*, p. 11,12; and, Spagnuolo, *supra*, p. 3, 4.

211 See, Burroughs, *supra*, p. 11.

212 H.M. Kristensen, *U.S. Nuclear Weapons in Europe: A Review of Post-Cold War Policy, Force Levels, and War Planning*, Natural Resources Defense Council, February 2005 (accessible at http://www.nrdc.org/nuclear/euro/euro.pdf), p. 71.

213 Reports show that public opinion in certain European countries has been increasingly favorable of a reduction that would lead to a complete elimination of NATO nuclear weapons from the territories of the Member States (See S. Lunn, A Crucial Decision: NATO's Nuclear Weapons in the Twenty-First Century, in, M. Chalmers and S. Lunn (eds.), NATO's Tactical Nuclear Dilemma, 2010, Royal United Services Institute, p. 12). The EU Member States' national governments have articulated different responses to the issue, with views ranging from German Chancellor Merkel fully supporting the NATO nuclear sharing, having stated on one occasion that hosting American nuclear weapons secures Berlin's influence in NATO as a defense alliance (SpiegelOnLine, 4 October 2009, '*Foreign Minister Wants US Nukes out of Germany*' http://www.spiegel.de/international/germany/0,1518,druck-618550,00.html.), to the view taken by the former Belgian Senator Phillipe-Mahoux who proposed a bill in October 2009 before the Belgian Senate to constitutionally ban nuclear weapons on Belgian territory (http://www.nti.org/gsn/article/belgian-senate-to-consider-nuclear-weapon-ban/).

regard to the legitimacy of the practice of nuclear weapons sharing, NATO remains fully ascribed to maintaining all of the nuclear capacities that form part of its deterrence strategy'.[214] Furthermore, a change in NATO's nuclear policy cannot be done unilaterally and requires a common accord of all the NATO allies,[215] and, judging by the rhetoric used in the new NATO Strategic Concept adopted in November 2010, any further reduction of the number of deployed NATO nuclear weapons is to be directly conditioned upon Russia's cooperativeness in relocating its own nuclear weapons in Europe away from the territory of NATO member states.[216] The former equally stands valid in light of the present day circumstances.[217]

The implications stemming from the view that nuclear (or any other kind) weapons can serve as a deterrent from further weapons proliferation cuts both ways, especially since the mere fact of maintaining a nuclear arsenal (however small or insignificant) on one's territory sends the message of potential readiness to go to war. In this way, the practice of nuclear sharing inadvertently

214 See, O. Meier, 'NATO Sticks With Nuclear Policy', *Arms Control Today*, June 2012, (https://www.armscontrol.org/act/2012_06/NATO_Sticks_With_Nuclear_Policy).

215 *Le Soir*, 22 April 2010, '*Arme nucléaire en Europe: pas de retrait sans accord de l'Otan*', at: http://archives.lesoir.be/arme-nucleaire-en-europe-pas-de-retrait-sans-accord_t-20100422-00VYHQ.html?query=armes+atomiques&queryand=armes+atomiques,+OTAN&queryor=armes+atomiques&firstHit=0&by=10&when=-1&sort=datedesc&pos=1&all=65&nav=1.

216 NATO, *Strategic Concept For the Defence and Security of The Members of the North Atlantic Treaty Organisation* (adopted by Heads of State and Government in Lisbon) (at: http://www.nato.int/lisbon2010/strategic-concept-2010-eng.pdf), point 26:'(...) In any future reductions, our aim should be to seek Russian agreement to increase transparency on its nuclear weapons in Europe and relocate these weapons away from the territory of NATO members. Any further steps must take into account the disparity with the greater Russian stockpiles of short-range nuclear weapons'.

217 See, *New York Post*, 10 September 2014, Russia developing new nuclear weapons to counter US, NATO (http://nypost.com/2014/09/10/russia-developing-new-nuclear-weapons-to-counter-us-nato/); NATO nuclear weapons do not merely represent a military force, but, also, and possibly more importantly, they are to be perceived as political weapons. The deployment of US nuclear weapons in foreign territories has served as a visible symbol of the U.S. commitment to defend NATO countries with all of the military power it possesses which carries the concern that withdrawing the weapons would symbolize lessening of the U.S. commitment to defend the former (see, B. Scowcroft, S.J. Hadley and F. Miller, 'NATO-based nuclear weapons are an advantage in a dangerous world', *The Washigton Post*, 17 August 2014 (http://www.washingtonpost.com/opinions/nato-based-nuclear-weapons-are-an-advantage-in-a-dangerous-world/2014/08/17/059d0ddc-23ba-11e4-8593-da634b334390_story.html)).

contributes to the possibility of a nuclear war outbreak as whilst providing deterrence, it also potentially serves as a provocation to other nuclear weapon states.[218] This is an issue the EU institutions have not been very vocal about, but which is of direct relevance to EU's non-proliferation policy and one liable to affect (if not tarnish) EU's non-proliferation 'image'. In this respect, it is important to re-evaluate the message the Union sends to the world by condoning the existence of a deterrence mechanism on its territory which is liable to promote nuclear weapons proliferation. Therefore, the EU is running the risk of possibly being labeled as violator of the letter and spirit of the NPT[219] which, in turn, would need to be reconciled with the pacifist and value-oriented approach assumed in the conduct of its external policy.

IV.5 *Concluding Observations*

Decidedly, the EU places immense importance on portraying itself as a serious global and regional non-proliferation actor. However, it is a different matter whether this self-projected image matches the political reality. Advocating the non-proliferation of WMD – nuclear weapons in particular – is not a cause liable to be easily or ever fully achieved, mainly since it involves the joining together of extensive resources (human and other). Nevertheless, in spite of the elaborate framework of EU organs and bodies working on non-proliferation, it appears that in reality the EU persists to experience a large capabilities–expectations gap in the field.[220]

For the time being, the greatest obstacle to a coherent and effective Union WMD non-proliferation policy is the variance of nuclear attitudes among the Member States, encompassing both of Member States which are nuclear weapon and non-nuclear weapon states as well as Member States which are members of the North Atlantic Treaty Organization (NATO) and those that are non-NATO states.[221] Hence, despite EU's sincere efforts, its non-proliferation policy remains largely dependent on the willpower and the extent of the involvement of national experts and representatives from Member States.[222] Having assumed a somewhat supporting rather than leading role in the global non-proliferation campaign, EU's status as independent actor – especially with respect to nuclear disarmament – has become highly questionable.[223] It seems

218 Burroughs, *supra* n. 199, p. 13.

219 Nassauer, *supra* n. 194, p. 4.

220 Van Ham, *supra* n. 112, p. 5.

221 *Idem*, p. 5,6.

222 *Idem*, p. 6.

223 Kulesa, *supra* n. 131, p. 96,97.

that the Union is more at ease with the 'road more traveled by', predominantly relying on multilateral diplomacy skills and the use of 'soft power' mechanisms[224] as the *modus operandi* it is commonly best known for. Thus, its contribution to non-proliferation on a global scale boils down to performing the role of an enabling structure i.e. an intermediary rather than a primary actor,[225] merely supporting policy decisions and providing the necessary channels of communication among various interest groups.[226] Regrettably, a realistic projection into the future indicates that a double role for the EU as both an active non-proliferation advocate and a nuclear defense force would be an untenable concept, the EU, arguably, remaining to act as a soft power rather than a bastion of nuclear defense.

V Euratom and Military Uses of Nuclear Energy – A Thundering Silence?

Being an issue that exists at the dividing line between civil and military applications of nuclear energy, non-proliferation of nuclear weapons implicates the national defence interests and thus, national sovereignty concerns. In order to round off the discussion regarding Euratom's share in the non-proliferation equation, it is pertinent to proceed by examining the ambiguous and highly controversial relationship between Euratom and the military uses of nuclear energy. The Euratom Treaty is silent on the matter – it neither provides for a complete exemption of military uses from its scope nor does it make an express reference with regard to the Euratom Community's extending its prerogatives to the former field. The foregoing begs the question whether such 'omission' comes as a consequence to the fact that at the time of the adoption of the Euratom Treaty the issue was considered to be clear and self-evident beyond reasonable doubt, or, indeed, the issue was considered so controversial that addressing it needed to be avoided.

In order to appraise, to the extent possible, the potential for Euratom Community's claim over the area of military uses of nuclear energy, the discussion starts out by providing a historical perspective on the original intentions of Europe's founding fathers with respect to the matter through the analysis of several important documents concerning the European integration which have pre-dated the Euratom Treaty, proceeding with a look at the relevant

224 *Idem*, p. 98.

225 Mölling, *supra* n. 18, p. 59.

226 *Idem*, p. 60.

chapters of the Euratom Treaty which directly or indirectly touch upon the scope of Member States' military activities in the nuclear sphere,[227] and concluding with the relevant pronouncements of the EU Court of Justice regarding the possibility for applying the Euratom Treaty provisions to the nuclear defense industry.

V.1 *Concepts and Strategies on Nuclear Energy in Europe Predating the Adoption of the Euratom Treaty*

By omitting to provide a *de integro* exemption for military applications of nuclear energy, the Euratom Treaty opens a generous leeway to the Member States and the EU institutions in the interpretation of the Treaty provisions. Another curiosum which arises in this respect is whether the 'silence' of the Euratom Treaty is accidental or, indeed deliberate. In the absence of a straightforward answer, it is appropriate to employ a historical and teleological approach to the issue and look at the original intentions that guided the treaty makers in deciding to condone such ambiguity. The historical developments that lead to the establishment of the Euratom Community showcase the diverse national perceptions on the issue whereby an insight into the historical projects of European integration with relevance to the nuclear field will help to acquire an accurate perspective on the history of European non-proliferation and, additionally, acquiring a better grasp of the current non-proliferation reality in the EU. A both textual and contextual analysis of these historical documents (draft treaties and policy documents) may help shed some light on the initial reasons that lead the drafters of the Euratom Treaty to evade addressing the issue of the relationship between Euratom and military uses of nuclear energy in a more straightforward manner – the *European Defence Community Treaty*, the *Western European Union Treaty*, the *Spaak Report* and the *Draft Minutes of the Venice Conference* shall now be examined in turn.

V.1.1 The European Defence Community (EDC)

The project for the establishment of the European Defence Community (EDC), which dates back to the 1950s, is one of the most ambitious projects in the history of the European political integration and one that was arguably the most 'supranational' in tenor. The EDC Treaty, signed in Paris on 27 May 1952 by

227 Since the current chapter deals exclusively with non-proliferation of nuclear weapons, all the references in the Treaty dealing with national defense issues bearing no relevance to the subject of non-proliferation will not be examined.

'the Six' (France, W. Germany, Italy, Benelux),[228] foresaw the establishment of a common supranational institutional framework (Council of Ministers, a Commissariat, a Common Assembly, a Court of Justice – Art.8), the constitution of a democratically elected Assembly (Art.38), common European defence forces and a unified coordination of Member States' defence strategies (Arts. 9–18; Arts. 68–79) as well as a centralized control on the production of war material by the Member States exercised by the Commissariat (Art.107).[229]

The scope of the EDC Treaty covered the following categories of war material: conventional weapons, biological, chemical weapons and atomic weapons (Annex I to Art.107) whereby the production, import and export of these weapons was to be prohibited in the Community – with the exception of the EDC Commissariat granting a special license stating otherwise (Art.107(1)). However, the Commissariat was not empowered to grant licenses regarding items (the weapons outlined in Annex I) placed in 'strategically exposed areas', except upon unanimous decision by the Council to this effect (Art.107(4)a). The Treaty did not offer a clarification on what the term 'strategically exposed areas' (régions stratégiquement exposées) covers.[230] As regards civil uses, the extent to which the EDC Treaty intended to regulate the former field is not clear – the single reference to civil uses was given in Art.107(4)f which entrusted the Commissariat with the responsibility to grant general licenses concerning certain products outlined in Annex I when these are destined for civil purposes.[231]

Unfortunately, the ambitiously articulated objectives of the EDC Treaty fell short of materializing when in August 1954 France failed to ratify it (it was the last of the 'Six' to ratify). The draft Treaty did not win the French Assembly's confidence vote, to the extent that the Assembly even refused to consider the ratification of the Treaty as a point of order, having reached a 319 to 264 vote to

228 *Traité instituant la Communauté européenne de défense*, Mémorial du Grand-Duché de Luxembourg, 05.05.1954, No 24, pp. 644–675.

229 A simple reading of the text of the EDC Treaty points to a great resemblance between the prerogatives of the EDC institutions and their subsequent EC/EU counterparts.

230 In light of the post war climate of mutual distrust among the former adversaries at the time (Germany as opposed to the other countries of the 'Six'), the term should be given the conventional definition as encompassing zones or territories that make for favourable points for the conduct of military activities.

231 *Contra* to the claims of some authors (see, G. Mallard, Can the Euratom Treaty Inspire the Middle East: The Political Promises of Regional Nuclear Communities, *Non Proliferation Review*, November 2008, Vol.15 Issue 3, p. 462), it cannot be held that the EDC Treaty had the objective of establishing an all-encompassing control over both the civil and military nuclear industry in the Member States, since according to the letter of the Treaty, the former did not have such a far-reaching objective.

proceed to other business.[232] The period immediately preceding the Assembly vote was characterized by much upheaval in the French political climate where the ratification of the EDC Treaty had been fervently debated among French parliamentarians whose objections to the draft Treaty mainly centered on the Treaty's pervasive supranational character and the modalities for the French involvement in the integrated forces that the former envisaged.[233]

V.1.2 The Western European Union (WEU)

In the wake of the unsuccesful ratification of the EDC Treaty, Europe witnessed the creation of the Western European Union (WEU) (now extinguished)[234] which came much closer to a traditional intergovernmental form of organization than a supranational entity of the type the European Defence Community was conceived to be.[235] On 17 March 1948 the UK, France and Benelux signed the Treaty of Brussels (Treaty of Economic, Social and Cultural Collaboration and Collective Self-Defense), amended by the Paris Agreements of 23 October 1954 following the failure of the EDC,[236] which made way for the establishment of the Brussels Treaty Organization i.e. the Western European Union.[237]

The WEU compensated for the defense identity the European Community was lacking while maintaining a full alignment with NATO's activities and operations thus avoiding any unnecessary duplication in their respective tasks. In defense terms, the novelty introduced by the amended WEU Treaty was the creation of a collective defense system between the contracting parties which was to be put into operation in the event a contracting party was the object of

232 Camps, *supra* n. 4, p. 16.

233 *Idem.*

234 See, the *Statement of the Presidency of the WEU* of 31 March 2010, where the Parties to the WEU Treaty confirm the termination of the Treaty and the dissolution of organization. Pursuant to the Statement issued by the Presidency of the Permanent Council of the WEU on 31 March 2010 (http://www.weu.int/), the Presidency considers that a new phase in European security and defence begins with the entry into force of the Lisbon Treaty, and that the WEU has therefore accomplished its historical role.

235 Camps, *supra* n. 4, p. 17.

236 The Modified Brussels Treaty as amended by the Protocol modifying and completing the Brussels Treaty (Paris, 23 October 1954), available at: http://www.weu.int/index.html.

237 The Federal Republic of Germany was now able to join the WEU. Article I of Protocol III on the Control of armaments takes note of the Declaration submitted by the Federal Republic of Germany whereby the country undertakes not to manufacture, *inter alia*, atomic, chemical or biological weapons on its territory. This was the *quid pro quo* Germany had to concede to in order to be included in the European 'defense club' (See, Protocol III on the Control on Armaments, Annex I).

an armed attack, alerting the other parties to offer to the attacked party all the military and other aid and assistance in their power (Art. V WEU Treaty).[238]

The main body entrusted with implementing the Brussels Treaty was the Council of the WEU which shared an important part of its duties with the Agency for the Control of Armaments (Art. VIII). The exercise of common control over the Contracting Parties' armaments was devised through the provisions of the Protocol No.III on the 'Control of armaments' and the Protocol No.IV on the 'WEU Agency for the control on armaments'. In particular, Article III of the Protocol on the Control of armaments introduced control on the level of stocks of atomic,[239] biological and chemical weapons which the contracting parties were allowed to hold on the mainland of Europe. The former type of control was to be put into effect by a majority vote decision of the Council of the WEU, which never materialized since the Council of the WEU, up until the dissolution of the WEU in 2010, did not adopt such decision.

Protocol IV to the Brussels Treaty defined the primary role of the *WEU Agency for the control of armaments* which was to ensure that the obligations undertaken by virtue of Protocol III were being observed by the contracting parties. The WEU Agency was mandated to scrutinize the statistical and budgetary information supplied by the members of the WEU and the NATO authorities, conduct test checks on the mainland of Europe, execute visits and inspections at production plants, depots and forces (other than depots or forces under NATO authority) and subsequently report to the Council of the WEU. (Art. VII(2)). For the purposes of conducting test checks, visits and inspections, the members of the Agency were accorded free access on demand to plants and depots where all relevant accounts and documents were to be made available to them (Art. XII).

A remarkable complementarity can be observed between the established Euratom safeguards system and the envisaged WEU armaments control system, the former covering the civil and the latter covering the military applications of nuclear energy, provided both of these systems had been in their full

238 With the changes introduced via the Lisbon treaty, this provision has now been mirrored in Art.42(7) TEU.

239 'Atomic weapon', pursuant to Annex II (I(a)) of the Protocol, refers to 'any weapon which contains, or is designed to contain or utilise, nuclear fuel or radioactive isotopes and which, by explosion or other uncontrolled nuclear transformation of the nuclear fuel, or by radioactivity of the nuclear fuel or radioactive isotopes, is capable of mass destruction, mass injury or mass poisoning'; while according to Annex II: '[A]ll apparatus, parts, equipment, installations, substances and organisms, which are used for civilian purposes or for scientific, medical and industrial research in the fields of pure and applied science shall be excluded from this definition'.

operational capacity. Regrettably, as ambitious as the elaborateness of the armaments control system may have seemed at first glance, the concept was never implemented mainly due to the WEU's lack of authority to be able to force the contracting parties to respect their armaments commitments.[240] Another prohibitive factor was the difficulty to obtain the consent of the WEU Council which resulted in the gradual diminishment of the role of the WEU Agency (especially with regard to atomic weapons).[241] In hindsight, the establishment of a functional WEU armaments control system could have potentially made up for the Euratom military applications *lacuna* in that once the safeguards controls to the materials entering the military facility were no longer applicable, the former were to be subsequently covered under the WEU armaments control regime.[242]

Its role having become obsolete with time, the WEU Agency for the Control of Armaments was abolished in 1997, leaving the Protocol IV of the modified Brussels Treaty without any practical effect.[243] Nevertheless, with the establishment of the Western European Armaments group (WEAG) the European armaments cooperation was still able to continue,[244] however with a less binding tenor. The inevitable dissolution of the Western European Union, which was once conceived as the future defense pillar of the European Union, was the cumulative result of a long standing practice of deference toward the NATO alliance translated in the way that the WEU mechanisms themselves had been devised and implemented. The execution of the WEU's tasks had frequently been made contingent on the prior careful coordination with the NATO forces, an attitude further confirmed by the last statement of the WEU Permanent Council Presidency issued on the occasion of the dissolution of the WEU which asserted that NATO '(…) for those States which are members of it, remains the foundation of their collective defence and the forum for its implementation'.[245]

240 D. Keohane, *The EU and Armaments Co-operation*, Centre for European Reform Working Paper (www.cer.org.uk), London, December 2002, p. 32.

241 http://www.ena.lu/collective_defence_armaments_control-2-35601.

242 Goldshmidt, *supra* n. 14, p. 12, at ft.5.

243 WEU Council of ministers, Erfurt Declaration 18 November 1997, p. 12, accessible at: http://www.weu.int.

244 WEU Council of Ministers, Rome Communique 19 May 1993, accessible at: http://www.weu.int.

245 In the statement issued following the dissolution of the WEU, the Presidency of the Permanent Council of the WEU (31 March 2010, http://www.weu.int/) outlines the novelties introduced by the Lisbon Treaty in the field of security and defense. It states that the newly framed European Security and Defense policy of the Union after Lisbon has taken on a number of the objectives and mechanisms that were already available under the

V.1.3 The Spaak Report

After the failure of the European Defence Community, the motors of the *relance* of European economic integration were set in motion by the *Messina Resolution*,[246] adopted by the Foreign Ministers of the Member States of the European Coal and Steel Community (ECSC) in June 1955. The Resolution entrusted the Spaak Committee (composed of government delegates headed by the Belgian Foreign Minister Paul-Henri Spaak) with a mandate to draft a Report which was later on to be submitted to the ECSC Foreign Ministers for discussion. As far as nuclear energy was concerned, their task focused on the civil uses of nuclear energy with the understanding that the development of civil nuclear industries will open up '(...) prospects of a new industrial revolution far beyond anything achieved during the past hundred years (...)'(Part I, A.2).

The *Spaak Report*,[247] adopted on 21 April 1956, was expected to offer an elaborate plan for the future of European economic integration and set out the priority goals for a more intensive integration among the Member States. The Intergovernmental Committee drafting the Report devoted their attention to two focal areas – the Common Market and the Atomic Energy Community projects. Wary not to overstep its prerogatives, the Committee considered the issue of military uses of nuclear energy as a political issue that surpassed the limits of its mandate for which reason the delegates felt no need to pronounce themselves on the matter (Part II). Nevertheless, the last sentence of Part II

WEU Treaty. Further on, it marks the establishment of a European Defence Agency in the field of defence capabilities development, research, acquisition and armaments which '(...) *shall identify operational requirements, shall promote measures to satisfy those requirements, shall contribute to identifying and, where appropriate, implementing any measure needed to strengthen the industrial and technological base of the defence sector, shall participate in defining a European capabilities and armaments policy, and shall assist the Council in evaluating the improvement of military capabilities* [i.e. the military capabilities that the Member States have made available to the Union for the implementation of the common security and defence policy]' (Art.42(3) TEU); In this respect, NATO's crucial role in the Union common defense policy has been confirmed in the new Art.42(7) TEU pursuant to which '[the North Atlantic Treaty Organisation] [...] *for those States which are members of it, remains the foundation of their collective defence and the forum for its implementation*'.

246 Archives historiques du Conseil de l'Union européenne, Bruxelles, Négociations des traités instituant la CEE et la CEEA (1955–1957), CM3. Réunion des ministres des affaires étrangères, Messine, 01–03.06.1955, CM3/NEGO/006 (http://www.ena.lu/resolution_adopted_foreign_ministers_ecsc_member_states_messina_june_1955-2-24617).

247 Comité intergouvernemental créé par la conférence de Messine, Rapport des chefs de délégation aux ministres des Affaires étrangères. Bruxelles: Secrétariat, 21 avril 1956, pp. 9–135. (http://www.ena.lu/report_heads_delegation_foreign_ministers_brussels_21_april_1956-2-25213).

leaves an important *caveat* and raises certain ambiguities of interpretation specifically with regard to military uses: 'This issue [...] concerns very important technical aspects, but they [the Heads of Government] believe it is possible to elaborate a solution which would preserve the efficacy of the system they propose one of the essential features of which would be a fail-proof control'.[248]

Furthermore, before the holding of the Venice Conference where the Foreign Ministers were expected to discuss the Spaak Report and the future creation of the Common Market and the Euratom Community, Paul-Henri Spaak addressed a letter on his own motion[249] to the Member States' ministers where he elaborated the possible routes to be taken in order to resolve 'one of the most difficult problems that are before the delegates'.[250] In his letter, which can be regarded as a prelude to the upcoming conference, Spaak noted that during the discussions the heads of delegation had conceded to the position that in order to provide for efficient solutions to certain problems related to the development of peaceful uses of nuclear energy, it would be indispensable for the Member States to agree on the conditions under which certain of them could eventually proceed to undertake military applications of nuclear energy.[251] Spaak reminded that the heads of delegation had been aware of the fact that the issue raised important political aspects, but, nevertheless, decided to abstain from giving any suggestions of their own thus remaining within the limits imposed by the scope of their mandate. In order not to compromise the credibility of the Intergovernmental Committee members, Spaak expressed the desire to submit his own proposition on what could serve as basis for the future discussions of the Member States' foreign ministers.

Hence, in line with the long-term objective of global disarmament, Spaak suggested a renouncement of the production of strategic nuclear weapons (of massive destruction) and tactical nuclear weapons, *for a certain period*. Upon expiration of the given time period, a Member State would only be entitled to produce nuclear weapons by way of consent given by at least two other

248 Free translation from French by the author; The original version reads: '(...) Cette question revêt des aspects techniques très importants, mais [les délégations] croient possible qu'une solution soit élaborée qui maintienne l'efficacité du système qu'ils proposent et dont un des traits essentiels est un contrôle sans fissure'.

249 Archives historiques du Conseil de l'Union européenne, Bruxelles, Négociations des traités instituant la CEE et la CEEA (1955–1957), CM3, Conférence intergouvernementale: documents divers concernant principalement l'utilisation militaire de l'énergie nucléaire, CM3/NEGO/187.

250 Last paragraph of the Spaak letter.

251 Para. 2 of the Spaak letter.

Member States. The Euratom Community would be in charge of ensuring that the supply of nuclear combustibles for the military production is carried out as agreed upon among the Member States, while the production thereof would be subject to the same rules and controls envisaged for the civil uses of nuclear energy.

Emphasizing Euratom's fundamental commitment to the development of atomic energy for peaceful aims, Spaak considered that establishing uniform conditions for eventual derogation from this commitment would make any unilateral derogations impossible thus creating a climate of confidence among the Member States and preserving the functioning of the established system. In this sense, it was considered that according an unrestricted freedom of military use of nuclear energy to the Member States would inevitably entail the danger of rendering the system proposed by the experts inefficient and useless.

Although an informal document, Spaak's letter is an indication of the importance the national delegations attached to the national military nuclear programs as the former represented one of the most delicate issues that the foreign ministers had been presented with in their deliberations on the future of European integration. Evidently, as head of the Intergovernmental Committee, Spaak was against a liberal, *laisser faire* approach to the issue and – while not completely opposing the nuclear weapon industry – he was nonetheless convinced that once the proposed 'moratorium' on nuclear weapons production expired the Member States should be accorded a *controlled discretion* in deciding on their national nuclear weapons policies. Therefore, in Spaak's opinion, the drafting of the Euratom Treaty could not have been finalized without previously clarifying whether and to what extent the future Euratom Community would be involved in the Member States' nuclear energy production for military aims.

V.1.4 The Draft Minutes of the Venice Conference

The Draft minutes of the Venice Conference held on 29 and 30 May 1956[252] shed further light on the positions taken by the participating national delegations regarding the projects of the Common market and Euratom. On this occasion, at the insistence of Mr. Spaak, the issue of *eventual* military use of nuclear energy by the Member States was examined. Namely, the French minister Pineau considered the letter addressed by Spaak as a solid starting point for the discussion between the ministers, noting however that the nature of

252 Archives historiques du Conseil de l'Union européenne, Bruxelles, Négociations des traités instituant la CEE et la CEEA (1955–1957), CM3, Conférence des ministres des affaires étrangères, Venise, 29–30.05.1956, CM3/NEGO/093.

the subject itself is more political rather than technical.[253] The German position, presented by Mr. Hallstein, was in favour of all military applications of nuclear energy being subject to the same general rules and controls that apply to the peaceful applications.[254] The Italian side considered it inopportune for continental Europe to *a priori* renounce the use of the most modern instrument of defence of the time,[255] esteeming that the production of nuclear weapons required a long period of preparation during which time the links of cooperation and confidence between the Member States, which represent the very essence of the Euratom regime, could be strongly reinforced. In that sense, it was believed that a possible solution could be negotiated by the governments only after that said period had expired.[256] In closing, it was agreed that the foreign ministers reconvene periodically in order to examine the reports drafted by the heads of delegation and, consequently, take the necessary political decisions. In this regard, a special mention was made of the fact that in the future the ministers would especially have to pronounce themselves on, *inter alia*, the *eventual* military use of nuclear energy.[257]

Ostensibly, in view of the divergent attitudes towards the possibility to include the military applications of nuclear energy within the scope of the Euratom Treaty, it was impossible for the 'Six' to reach a unanimous decision on the matter: Germany was at one of end of the spectrum, being in favor of the maintenance of a controlled nuclear weapons programme, while at the opposite end was France as a proponent of keeping the military uses outside of the scope of the Euratom Treaty and, thus, safe from any Community interference.[258] What further complicated matters was the heated debate regarding the creation of the Euratom Community before the French Assembly in July 1956 where observations were raised with regard to the supranational nature of Euratom as well as the potential for the Euratom Treaty to possibly prevent

253 Point 5.

254 Point 7.

255 Point 13.

256 Point 13.

257 Point 14.

258 It has also been reported that from the outset Jean Monnet, one of the European Community's founding fathers, was much more inclined to the Member States committing themselves solely to furthering the peaceful uses of nuclear energy. However, once it became clear that such a position could potentially rekindle many of the same French arguments used against the ratification of the European Defence Community Treaty, Monnet, being wary of risking another treaty debacle, abandoned his original position (See, Camps, *supra* n. 4, p. 55).

France from becoming the fourth nuclear power in the world[259] (the motion in support of continuing the negotiations on the Euratom Treaty was approved by a 332 to 181 vote with 70 abstentions[260]). For some, the much publicized debate on the prospects of the Euratom Treaty before the French Assembly was the 'kiss of death' for any future non-proliferation role for Euratom.[261] Nevertheless, upon receiving the green light from the French Assembly, the Euratom Treaty negotiations could finally gain momentum the end result of which is *mutatis mutandis* the version of the Euratom Treaty we have today which, save for the explicit exclusion of 'materials intended to meet defence requirements' under the Safeguards chapter, is otherwise completely mute on the issue of military uses of nuclear energy.

V.2 *The Euratom Treaty Provisions*

In spite of a lack of an express (general or specific) provision in the Euratom Treaty concerning the military applications of nuclear energy, there are scattered references in the treaty text directly or indirectly pertaining to the national defense requirements of Member States found in the *Supply, Safeguards* and *Property Ownership* chapters.

As regards the Euratom Community's nuclear supply policy (Chapter VI), the supply of ores, source materials and special nuclear materials in the Euratom Community is ensured through the instruments of the common supply policy based on the principle of equal access to sources of supply (Art.52(1)). The Euratom Supply Agency is the body charged with the execution of the policy which works under the supervision of the Commission and has the *right of option* on nuclear materials (ores, source materials and special fissile materials) produced in the territories of Member States paired with the *exclusive right to conclude contracts* relating to the supply of nuclear materials coming from inside or outside of the Community (Art.52 (2b)).

The Supply Agency exercises its right of option mainly through the conclusion of contracts with producers of ores, source materials and special fissile materials carried out in a way that the producer first offers the materials to the Agency which acts as the intermediary at the point where the available supply and demand orders meet (Art.57(2)). The potential users periodically inform

259 Camps, *supra* n. 4, p. 67.

260 *Idem*, p. 68. The negotitating parties arrived at a bargain where the French Government would undertake not to explode an atomic bomb before 1 January 1961, but after that regain complete freedom of action, on the condition that there would be no restriction on the research and development of the atomic bomb (as reported in, Camps, *supra*, p. 68).

261 See Camps, *supra*, p. 68.

the Agency of the supplies they require (Art.60(1)) upon which the Agency informs all potential users of the offers made and calls upon them to place their order (Art.60(3)). Subsequently, the Agency matches the supply offers and the demand orders while in doing so, it is not allowed to discriminate between the users on *grounds of the use* which they intend to make of the requested supplies unless *such use is unlawful* or is found to be contrary to the conditions imposed by suppliers outside the Community on the consignment concerned (Art.52(2)). The Euratom Treaty does not offer further explanation on what these 'grounds of use' encompass, opening way for the Supply Agency to be able to broaden its scrutiny to national-defence-related grounds for use of nuclear material, given the lack of a specific 'national defence requirements' derogation in the 'Supplies' chapter alike to the one regarding the application of the safeguards provisions.[262]

Another issue that has caused ambiguities in interpretation is the 'unlawful use' of supplies which the Agency has to oversee. The Euratom Treaty does not provide any referential criteria for the Agency to rely on in assessing the 'unlawful' character of the use, again leaving generous margin of interpretation that would potentially consider both the use of nuclear supplies that contravenes the Euratom safeguards criteria and the use thereof for military purposes as unlawful. The letter of the Euratom Treaty being extremely sketchy as to the extent of the Supply Agency's non-proliferation role, it was as late as in 2009 that the Commission issued a Communication on nuclear non-proliferation[263] that clarified the confusion. Namely, the Commission determined the Supply Agency's role as one of verifying that all supply contracts contain a safeguards clause and are solely concluded for peaceful end-uses[264] thus going beyond simply an extensive interpretation of the Euratom Treaty regarding the modalities of the execution of the Supply Agency's prerogatives and writing a new approach into the Treaty which itself was not evident and could not be *prima faciae* inferred from the relevant Treaty provisions.

In addition, there have been futher differences in interpretation with respect to the authorisation of export of materials outside of the Community borders where by virtue of Art.59(2) Euratom the Commission is entitled to refuse to

262 For an insight into how the Agency's tasks are performed in practice, see, Report on the annual accounts of the Euratom Supply Agency for the financial year 2009, *OJ C 338, 14/12/2010 P. 0006 – 0009*; also, Report on the annual accounts of the Euratom Supply Agency for the financial year 2008, together with the Agency's replies, OJ C 304, 15/12/2009 P.0006 – 0009.

263 Communication on nuclear non-proliferation, COM(2009) 143 final, Section 3.3.

264 Section 3.3 of Communication.

grant such authorisation should it not be convinced by the recipients of the supplies that the *general interests* of the Community will be thereby safeguarded or should the terms and conditions of the export contracts be *contrary to the objectives of the Euratom Treaty*. In this sense, the Communication on non-proliferation sets out the criteria the Commission is to rely upon in assessing the 'general interest of the Community' when granting the authorisations for export of nuclear materials produced within the Community. These criteria include, among other, verifying that the materials will be used for non-explosive purposes and ensuring that adequate IAEA guarantees are duly applied to them.[265] The Communication compensates for the lack of prescription of the Treaty provisions by clarifying that in order for the Euratom Community's interests to be preserved the nuclear supply provisions are only to be applied in conjunction with the safeguards requirements.[266] In truth, the appraisal of the 'general interest' in this regard has largely been political where practice has shown that the Commission frequently turns to the relevant provisions of the Non-Proliferation Treaty and other non-proliferation instruments as benchmarks.[267] Therefore, some view the broad discretion the Commission enjoys in applying the nuclear supply provisions as the stepping stone for the future creation of a Euratom common non-proliferation policy in its own right.[268]

As concerns the *Safeguards* chapter (Chapter VII) which covers the nuclear safeguards arrangements as the key tool in the furtherance of the non-proliferation objective, the former contains the only specific mention to Member States' defence requirements in the Euratom Treaty to the effect of excluding nuclear materials intended to meet defense requirements from the safeguards' scope of application. More particularly, pursuant to Art.84(3) Euratom, the safeguards are not to be applied to materials intended to meet defence requirements 'which are in the course of being specially processed for this purpose or which, after being so processed, are, in accordance with an operational plan, placed or stored in a military establishment'.[269]

Lastly, the chapter that deals with the Euratom Community's right of ownership (Chapter VIII-*Property Ownership*) which foresees that special fissile

265 Section 3.3 of Communication.

266 See, also, A. Bouquet, How Current are Euratom provisions on Nuclear Supply and Ownership in view of the European Union's enlargement? *Nuclear Law Bulletin*, No.6, December 2001, p. 19.

267 *Idem*, p. 18.

268 Goens, *supra* n. 4, p. 43.

269 For an elaboration on the Euratom safeguards arrangements, see, *supra*, Section III.

materials are the property of Euratom, the Community's right of ownership extending to all special fissile materials which are produced or imported by a Member State, a person or an undertaking and are subject to the safeguards provided in Chapter 7 (Art.86 Euratom). The second part of the former definition is very significant since it links the exercise of ownership by the Community with the application of safeguards to the respective nuclear material. Consequently, material imported into or produced in the Community which is intended to meet military ends is exempted from the application of the safeguards requirements (according to Art.84(3)) and therefore remains outside Community ownership.[270] Furthermore, the Commission considers that the concept of Community ownership entails the responsibility to apply nuclear safeguards as well as physical protection measures, taken in the broader sense of the term.[271] Applying the former inclusive approach suggested by the Commission results in additionally extending the scope of application of safeguards so as to accommodate the objectives linked to the physical protection of nuclear material (nuclear security objectives).

V.3 *Clearing the Waters – The CJEU on the Application of the Euratom Treaty to Military Uses of Nuclear Energy*

From the legal and contextual analysis of the foregoing chapters of the Euratom Treaty it is to be concluded that (inadvertently or not) military uses have not been completely and categorically excluded from the remit of the Treaty. However, the absence of any blanket exclusion does not *automatically* lead to the conclusion that the Euratom Treaty is not to apply to the military filed under any circumstance. The lacuna created by the Euratom Treaty's elusiveness regarding military uses of nuclear energy has engendered various interpretations, depending on the context in which they were made. This existent lacuna peculiar to the Euratom system has indeed been addressed in the case law of the EU Court of Justice: following is an elaboration of the Court's standpoint, but also the standpoint of different EU institutions and Member States which have been part of or have intervened in the procedure before the Court.

Bearing in mind the compelling legal ambiguity vitiating this issue, it was as late as in 2005 that the highest judicial authority of the Union offered its unequivocal stance on the issue, after what amounted to circa four decades of legal uncertainty. In this respect, a pattern is to be observed in the positions

270 Bouquet, *supra* n. 266, p. 28.

271 Communication from the Commission to the Council and the European Parliament: *Communication on nuclear non-proliferation*, COM (2009) 143.

assumed by, on the one hand, the Commission as a proponent for an extensive reading of the Euratom Treaty endorsing the inclusion of military uses within the Treaty remit and, on the other hand, the nuclear-weapon Member States (United Kingdom and France) as traditional opponents to the possibility of Member States' military nuclear programs being (even if only incidentally) affected by the Euratom rules. Notwithstanding the final outcome of the decade long dispute, it is the argumentation offered by the two camps that deserves special attention especially the pervasiveness of policy-oriented as opposed to strictly legal arguments used in support of their positions.

V.3.1 Ruling 1/78

In *Ruling 1/78*,[272] around three decades before finally 'sealing' the issue, the EU Court of Justice was called upon to rule on the compatibility of the provisions of the Euratom Treaty with the envisaged accession of the Euratom Community to the Convention on the Physical Protection of Nuclear Materials, Facilities and Transports.[273] Having acknowledged that the Convention excludes installations, materials or transports destined for military purposes from its scope,[274] the Court went on to state that the fields of application of the Convention and the Euratom Treaty overlap in that in substance they both cover the same type of materials and nuclear facilities, whereas '(...) *materials and facilities for military purposes are excluded from the scope of the Convention as well as from that of the Treaty*'. (Art.2 of the Convention and Arts.84 and 86 of the Euratom Treaty).[275]

Admittedly, the Court opted for a somewhat rash generalization, possibly unawares of the potential ramifications of such a statement, especially given that the issue of military uses was only discussed on the sidelines of the proceedings and the case itself being centered on a different subject matter. The Court's pronouncement provided *supra* will from then on be used as a trump card by both France and the UK in the subsequent cases dealing with the issue of military applications of the Euratom rules.[276] In this respect, it would be ill-advised to consider the former statement of the Court as one intended to establish a general rule of non-application of the Euratom Treaty to uses of

272 Ruling 1/78 of 14 November 1978, *ECR 1978 p. 2151*.

273 Ruling 1/78 has been examined *supra* in Chapter 1, Section III.3.1 in the context of the international legal personality of the Euratom and its competence to enter into international agreements.

274 Para. 8 of Ruling.

275 Para. 12; Emphasis added.

276 See, AG Geelhoed Opinion, *C-61/03 Commission v. UK*, ECR 2005 p. I-2477, para. 54.

nuclear energy for defense purposes: the statement was made specifically and explicitly with regard to Arts. 84 and 86 Euratom (the derogation referring to the exemption of the materials intended to meet national defense requirements from the application of safeguards), in the context of a general comparison between the fields of application of the Convention and the Treaty.[277]

V.3.2 T- 219/95 R Danielsson v Commission

An interesting issue arose before the General Court (formerly, the Court of First Instance) in *Danielsson and Others v Commission*[278] concerning an application for interim measures where the Court ruled that the applicants which were private persons could not be regarded as being prima faciae individually concerned by the Commission decision they attempted to challenge, declaring the action as manifestly inadmissible.[279] The applicants had requested that the legal effects of a Commission decision of 23 October 1995 allowing for the French nuclear tests in French Polynesia be suspended as well as that an order is issued empowering the Commission to take all necessary measures to protect the applicants' rights under the Euratom Treaty. The latter concerned the obligation flowing from Art.34 Euratom for the Member States in whose territories particularly dangerous experiments are to take place to apply additional health and safety measures. To the contrary, the French Government's leading argument submitted at the hearing was that the health and safety provisions of the Treaty did not apply to nuclear activities in the military sphere.[280] The Commission's essential position, as presented by Commission President Santer before the European Parliament, was that Art.34 applied to both civil and military experiments, and that an experiment was to be regarded as particularly dangerous for the purposes of that article if it were to present a perceptible risk of significant exposure of workers or the general public to ionizing radiation.[281]

The General Court considered that the applicants had failed to demonstrate to be individually concerned by the Commission decision, in accordance with

277 See, AG Geelhoed Opinion, *C-61/03 Commission v. UK*, ECR 2005 p. I-2477, para. 95. The academic commentary covering Ruling 1/78 has not dealt with the aspect of military uses of nuclear energy given that the former was minor and non-substantial to the problematic at issue (see, J.A. Usher, International Competence of Euratom, *European Law Review*, 1979 Vol 4, p. 306; D. Allen, The Euratom Treaty, Chapter VI: New Hope or False Dawn, *Common Market Law Review*, 1983 Vol. 20, Issue 3, p. 483).

278 Case T-*219/95 R*, ECR 1995 Page II-03051 (*Order of the President of the Court of First Instance of 22 December 1995*).

279 Para. 76 of judgment.

280 Para. 33.

281 Para. 12.

the ex-Art.146(4) TEC (now Art.263(4) TFEU) test for 'individual and direct concern' in order to establish the legal standing for applicants.[282] The Court decided to dismiss the application, refusing to pronounce itself on the question of military applications as a question belonging to the examination of the merits of the contested act and concluded that '[...] it is not appropriate to rule in advance, in the present interim proceedings, on the question whether, in accordance with the Commission's interpretation which was challenged by the French Government at the hearing, Chapter 3 of the Treaty, concerning health and safety measures, and Art.34 in particular, is applicable to nuclear activities of a military nature'.[283] Given that the Commission was intent on persuading the Court to endorse the former option, the instant case can, arguably, be regarded as a missed opportunity for the General Court to deliberate on the long standing problematic. Nonetheless, the CJEU compensated for this shortcoming in the following case *Commission v. UK* where it finally 'cut the knot' and gave the much awaited 'in or out' verdict.

V.3.3 Case C-61/03 Commission v. UK

In case *C-61/03 Commission v. UK*[284] the Commission was seeking for a declaration that the UK, by having failed to provide general data relating to a plan for the disposal of radioactive waste regarding the decommissioning of the Jason reactor at Royal Naval College in Greenwich, had breached its obligation stemming from Art.37 Euratom. The Jason reactor was operated by the UK Ministry of Defense and subsequently decommissioned where upon the Commission's request for detailed information concerning the decommissioning the UK responded that the facilities used for military purposes were not caught under the provisions of the Euratom Treaty entailing that the UK was under no obligation to provide the Commission with any general data within the meaning of Art.37 Euratom.

The Court provided a solid argumentation, starting out by looking at the *objectives* of the Euratom Treaty and concluding that the *intention* of the signatories of the Treaty was to emphasize its non-military character, thereby confirming the essentially civil and commercial *objectives* of the Treaty.[285] It provided an

---

282 See, in particular, paras. 71,75 and 76 of the judgment. For a critique of the restrictive stance of the General Court in applying the criteria on legal standing for applicants, see, S. Schikhof, Direct and individual Concern in Environmental Cases: The Barriers to Prospective Litigants, *European Environmental Law Review* October 1998, p. 280.

283 Para. 62.

284 *C-61/03 Commission v. UK*, ECR 2005 p. I-2477.

285 Paras. 26–27.

overview of the events that had preceded the drafting of the Euratom Treaty thereby looking at the respective positions of the representatives of the founding Member States who, in lack of a unanimous solution, decided to leave the issue of military applications unresolved qualifying it as inconclusive.[286] Most importantly, the Court pointed to the significance the Member States attached to their defense interests, making it '[...] inconceivable for them to have impliedly waived the right to establish adequate guarantees in a field as sensitive as that of military applications of nuclear energy'.[287]

As the case concerned the application of the health and safety provisions of the Euratom Treaty (Arts. 30 et seq.), it was acknowledged that Arts. 34, 35 and 37 of the Treaty do not in any way specify that the activities covered by them are exclusively civil, but however esteemed that the application of such provisions to military installations, research programmes and other activities may be liable to *compromise essential national defence interests* of the Member States.[288] In order to further substantiate its reasoning, the Court borrowed the arguments offered by France and the UK which all revolved around the fact that the absence from the Treaty of a derogation laying down detailed rules to be relied upon by the Member States to protect their defense interests indicated that military activities fell outside the scope of the Treaty.[289] Moreover, the UK contended that the derogation contained in ex-Art.296 EC (present Art.346 TFEU) concerning the protection of the essential interests of national security presents a vital asset in safeguarding Member States' security interests, the absence of an analogous provision in the Euratom Treaty constituting '[...] an irremediable "lacuna' militating against the application of this Treaty to the defence sector'.[290]

The Court circumscribed the field of military uses of nuclear energy as falling outside the scope of the Euratom Treaty and thus ruled against the Commission's attempt to rely on Art.37 Euratom in order to require of Member States provision of information on the disposal of radioactive waste from their military installations.[291] It, nonetheless, noted that the former did not in any way undermine the vital importance of the objective of protecting the health of the public and the environment against the dangers related to the use of nuclear energy. Therefore, to the extent that the Euratom Treaty does not

286 Para. 29.

287 Para. 30.

288 Para. 35.

289 Para. 36.

290 Para. 51 of the AG Opinion.

291 Para. 44.

provide the Euratom Community with a specific instrument to pursue the former objective, the Court suggested the use of appropriate measures which would be adopted on the basis of the relevant provisions of the EC Treaty (now, TFEU).[292] The most adequate nexus to attaining the stated objective available within the framework of the TFEU (ex-EC Treaty) would be the corresponding public health (Art.168; ex-Art.152 TEC) and/or the environment protection (Arts.191–193; ex-Art.174–176 TEC) provisions of the TFEU. Consequently, in the future, a TFEU (ex-EC)-based health/environment protection instrument ought to be used in order to counter the potentially harmful effects of waste stemming from military establishments which would further enable the Member States to invoke the Art.346 TFEU (ex-Art.296 EC) derogation whenever they consider their vital security interests threatened.

The judgment in *Commission v. UK* is clearly an example of judicial self-restraint exhibited by the CJEU as it was clearly not the intention of the Court to disrupt the sovereignty ratio between the Member States and Euratom by ruling in favor of an unwarranted encroachment on the Member States' military nuclear industries. The Court was manifestly more inclined to accept the policy-related considerations (the safeguarding of Member States' defense interests) as opposed to the purely legal argumentation offered by both the Commission and the AG Geelhoed which in itself contributed to a colorful legal dispute. The Commission's arguments in the case again confirmed this institution's adamancy toward extending the scope of the Euratom Treaty provisions to the use of nuclear energy for defense purposes.[293] The Commission argued that the Art.37 obligation on provision of general data relating to any plan for the disposal of radioactive waste equally applies to radioactive waste emanating from a military facility.[294] Realizing that it would be highly impossible for the Court to acquiesce to such a broad interpretation of the issue, during the oral procedure the Commission suggested a mid-way approach. It suggested that in applying Art.37, each Member State should decide on the moment in time from which a military source of radioactive waste is to be regarded as waste within the wording of the said article, before communicating the plan for its disposal to the Commission.[295]

A similar approach was suggested by Advocate General Geelhoed who was in favor of the possibility of extending the remit of the Euratom Treaty to the

292 Para. 44.

293 See, para. 36 of judgment in Case C-61/03; para. 51 of the AG opinion in *idem*, and para. 62 in *Danielsson*.

294 Para. 42 et seq.

295 Para. 37.

defense sphere. AG Geelhoed focused on the impending legal void created by the lack of an explicit exclusion of military uses of nuclear energy from the scope of the Treaty. The AG presumed Art.37 Euratom to be equally applicable to military uses; however, in order to avoid any compromising effects that a blanket application of Art.37 to the defence sector would engender, he suggested a case-by-case, dialogue-based approach between the Commission and the Member State concerned.[296] In this way, when supplying the Commission with a plan for disposal of radioactive waste emanating from defence-related activities the State would be entitled to withhold the information it considers indispensable for the protection of essential defence interests.[297] Hence, according to the AG, in the absence of a provision in the Euratom Treaty analogous to ex-Art.296 EC (Art.346 TFEU) and insofar as adequate instruments have not been provided by the Euratom Treaty or the implementing legislation, the former article should be presumed to apply. The AG offered the example of *Opinion 1/94*[298] where the Court examined the European Community's exclusive competence to conclude the Multilateral Agreement on Trade in Goods as regards Euratom products and found that in the absence of specific external trade provisions in the Euratom Treaty, there was nothing preventing international agreements covering the former products to be concluded under ex-Art.133 EC (present Art.207 TFEU; the common commercial policy), thus widening the scope of the EC (TFEU) provisions to also cover Euratom products.[299] Following the same line of reasoning, so long as the Euratom Treaty and implementing legislation have not provided equivalent safeguards for Member State's essential security interests, it is the safeguards offered in Art.346 TFEU that should apply to products covered by the Euratom Treaty.[300] In view of the Court's final conclusion, it seems like AG Geelhoed's Opinion lost the war, but it certainly won some very important battles. Admittedly, the Court yielded to the overwhelming political tenor of the issue by being wary of any undesired effect an 'inclusive' judgment would have on the Member States' defence interests. In this sense, the Advocate General's progressive approach was no match for the compelling political reality of the Member States' military nuclear industries being a notorious 'hot potato' for national governments.[301]

---

296 Para. 117.

297 Para. 114 of AG Opinion.

298 *Opinion 1/94* of 15 November 1994 (ECR 1994 p. I-5267).

299 Para. 105 of Opinion.

300 Para. 107 of Opinion.

301 For further commentary on the Court's approach in this case, see, A. Schrauwen, 'Treaties and Trade-offs', editorial, *Legal Issues of Economic Integration*, 2005 Vol.32 Issue 4,

A case largely similar to the one *supra* and raising the same point of law, was *C-65/04 Commission v. UK*[302] where the Commission demanded that the CJEU declare that the UK, by failing to give the public likely to be affected in the event of a radiological emergency prior information on the local emergency plan existing in Gibraltar, failed to fulfill its obligations stemming from Art.5(3) of *Council Directive 89/618/Euratom on informing the general public about health protection measures to be applied and steps to be taken in the event of a radiological emergency.*[303] The Directive, adopted pursuant to Art.31 Euratom, sets out the common objectives regarding the measures and procedures for informing the general public for the purpose of improving the health protection in the event of a radiological emergency.[304] The Court asserted that the case concerned the possibility of applying the Euratom Treaty to military uses of nuclear energy thereby automatically referring back to its previous judgment in case *C-61/03 Commission v UK* and reiterating the stance that the exclusion of military uses of nuclear energy from the remit of the Euratom Treaty represents a blanket exclusion which does not apply partially but extends to *all* the provisions of the Euratom Treaty.[305]

V.3.4 Joined Cases C-205/10 P, C-217/10 P and C-222/10 P, *Eriksen, Hansen and Lind*

The CJEU had a chance to depart from its restrictive stance in *C-61/03 Commission v. UK*, in a more recent case – *Eriksen, Hansen and Lind v Commission*[306] – that drew on the controversy surrounding the environmental effects of the radiation following the crash of a US military aircraft carrying nuclear weapons in Thule, Greenland in January 1968 in relation to which it was reported by the US Atomic Energy Commission that approximately six kilograms of weapons grade plutonium had been released.[307] In the aftermath of the accident, emergency clean-up operations had begun, the applicants in the cases under examination belonging

---

p. 336,337; I. Cenevska, The exercise of giving way to 'giving in' – some aspects of the Member States' EURATOM obligations revisited, *Journal for European Environmental and Planning Law*, 2009 Vol.6 Issue 4, pp. 487–489.

302 ECR 2006 p. I-2239.

303 OJ 1989 L 357, p. 31.

304 Art.1 of Directive.

305 Para. 26.

306 *Joined Cases C-205/10 P, C-217/10 P and C-222/10 P, Eriksen, Hansen and Lind v Commission* (Order of the Court (Fifth Chamber) of 12 January 2011) ECR 2011 p. I-1.

307 Para. 5 of judgment.

to the group of workers involved in the operations.[308] Initially brought before the General Court, the cases went on appeal before the CJEU as a joinder application.[309] Before the CJEU the applicants claimed compensation for the damage they had suffered as a result of the Commission's alleged failure to ensure implementation of the medical monitoring provisions of *Directive 96/29/Euratom laying down basic safety standards for the protection of the health of workers and the general public against the dangers arising from ionizing radiation* which covered workers who, like Mr Eriksen, Mr Hansen and Mr Nochen, had in the past been potentially exposed to radiation at Thule.[310] They claimed that the harm suffered by them was to be attributed exclusively to the Commission, which had failed to ensure implementation of those provisions in spite of the existence of a Parliament Resolution pressuring the Commission to this end.[311] They insisted that the lethal illness which followed after their exposure to weapons grade plutonium would have been less severe had it been detected and treated earlier to the effect that prompt intervention by the Commission would have alleviated the gravity of the harm they suffered.[312]

Prior to examining the particularities of the case, it is instructive to refer to the European Parliament *Resolution of 10 May 2007 on the public health consequences of the 1968 Thule crash* which was adopted in response to a petition presented to the Petitions Committee of the European Parliament in 2002 by the *Association of Thule workers affected by radiation* that sought implementation of the medical monitoring requirements of Directive 96/29 (Petition 720/2002).[313] The resolution drew on the same issues that subsequently gave rise to the *Eriksen et al.* case, indicating that the petition in question had revealed that workers and members of the public had been irradiated by extremely hazardous weapons

308 Para. 6 of judgment.

309 The protracted element of the case (the Thule accident had occurred in 1968, while the initial applications were lodged before the EU General Court in 2008 and 2009) is due to the fact that the workers concerned were only diagnosed with malignant illnesses as late as in 2002, 2006 and 2007, respectively.

310 Para. 16.

311 Para. 16.

312 Para.17. See, paras. 10 and 11 for the medical condition of the applicants which concerned was malignant diseases, namely, certain forms of lung and kidney cancer.

313 P6_TA(2007)0182 Environmental protection from radiation following the crash of a military aircraft in Greenland: European Parliament Resolution of 10 May 2007 on the public health consequences of the 1968 Thule crash (Petition 720/2002) (2006/2012(INI)).

grade plutonium as a result of the crash at Thule in 1968.[314] As a consequence, in the years that followed a number of the Thule survivors had died of radiation-related illnesses due to the lack of medical monitoring while the other survivors were at the material time still at risk of contracting such illnesses.[315] Furthermore, it was confirmed that some of the radiation-related illnesses could have been detected at an early stage and treated provided that a mechanism of monitoring of the health of the Thule survivors had been put into place.[316] The Parliament invoked the prominence of the health and safety objective of the Euratom Treaty, acknowledging the disagreement arising between the Commission and the Kingdom of Denmark regarding the possibility to apply the Euratom Treaty and the relevant secondary legislation to the health and environment effects of the Thule crash.[317] While taking stock of the CJEU's stance on the inapplicability of the Euratom Treaty to uses of nuclear energy for military purposes, the Parliament considered the CJEU's restrictive approach to the matter as largely determined by the need to protect the national defence interests of the Member States.[318] Nonetheless, the Parliament considered that a restrictive view on the remit of the Treaty should not be taken in relation to the application of the health and safety provisions in "situations where the alleged military purpose concerns a third State (…) and where the only feasibly present connection with a defence interest of a Member State is that the release of nuclear material occurred on its territory".[319]

For these reasons, the Parliament called upon Denmark to apply the relevant provisions of Directive 96/29/Euratom by implementing surveillance and intervention measures[320] and, in the light of the protection of fundamental rights as a general principle of EU law and the positive obligations stemming from Articles 2 (right to life) and 8 (right to home and family life) of the ECHR, urged the Member States engaged in hazardous activities with potential adverse effects to lay down adequate procedures providing the persons involved in such activities

314 Point A of Resolution.

315 Point B.

316 Point C.

317 Point H.

318 Point 4.

319 Point 5.

320 Point 7.

access to all the relevant information.[321] The Parliament noted the failure of the Kingdom of Denmark to fully comply with its obligations under Directive 96/29/ Euratom in countering the after-effects of the Thule crash[322] and requested that Member States implement and apply Directive 96/29/Euratom without any delay thereby insisting that the Commission vigorously pursue any failure to fulfil the former obligations.[323]

The applicants, Mr Eriksen, Mr Hansen and Ms Lind (acting on behalf of her deceased brother), initially brought actions for compensation before the General Court[324] where the latter had taken note of the absence of a concrete reference in the application to the acts or omissions the Commission had allegedly refrained from taking in order to ensure the application of Directive 96/29/Euratom as the applicants focused their claim on the possibility for compensation deriving from the Commission's non-contractual liability.[325] The General Court considered that the only means the Commission had at its disposal in urging the Danish government to implement the medical monitoring provisions of Directive 96/29/Euratom with regard to the Thule workers was to bring infringement proceedings under then, Art.226 EC or Art.141 Euratom against the Kingdom of Denmark.[326] In turn, Mr. Eriksen, one of the applicants, argued that the Commission's alleged inaction had breached the principles of the duty of care and good administration (thereby referring to the Parliament Resolution which had requested of the Commission to pursue any failure by the Members States to respect their obligations under Directive 96/29/Euratom).[327] However, the General Court considered that the only type of omission attributable to the institutions which could potentially trigger the liability of the Union was the instance where the institutions would infringe their legal obligation to act, thereby inferring that there did not exist a legal obligation for the Commission to bring infringement proceedings against Member States and that its decision not to bring proceedings could not be qualified as unlawful and give rise to non-contractual liability for the Union.[328] It was maintained that the former finding could not be affected by the text of

321 Point 8.

322 Point 10.

323 Point 9.

324 See, *Order of 24 March 2010, Eriksen v Commission* (T-516/08, ECR 2010 p. II-40); *Order of 24 March 2010, Hansen v Commission* (T-6/09, ECR 2010 p. II-43); *Order of 24 March 2010, Lind v Commission* (T-5/09, ECR 2010 p. II-42).

325 T-516/08 Heinz Helmuth Eriksen (*ECR 2010 p. II-40*), para. 26.

326 Para. 27 of the judgment.

327 Para. 28.

328 Para. 29.

the Parliament Resolution which was not a legally binding instrument and simply 'urged' the Commission to pursue any existing failures on the part of Member States without prescribing an obligation for the Commission to act in order to initiate infringement proceedings.[329]

> In the judgment on appeal, the CJEU aligned with the reasoning adopted by the General Court, addressing, *inter alia*, the applicant's plea that the latter had failed to consider the fact that the Commission was required to ensure the application of the protective measures foreseen under Directive 96/29/ Euratom to the after-effects of the military accident.[330] In addition, the applicants relied on the European Parliament Resolution as a non-binding instrument in order to support their argumentation regarding the Commission's alleged failure to act where the Parliament urged, in particular, that the Commission tackles any failure [of the Member States] to fulfill their obligations under [Directive 96/29/Euratom]".[331] In response, the Court decreed that it had already been established in cases C-61/03 *Commission* v *United Kingdom* and C-65/04 *Commission* v *United Kingdom* that the Euratom Treaty "has to be interpreted restrictively, that is to say that all military activities should be excluded from its scope".[332] To the contrary, the applicants insisted that the Commission was not entitled to grant exemptions so as to exclude military activities from both the scope of the Euratom Treaty and Directive 96/29/Euratom considering that the former had in any event been under the responsibility to initiate proceedings for failure to fulfill the relevant obligations stemming therefrom.[333] The Court did not further examine the Commission's prerogative to grant the exemptions, centering on the argument that the Euratom Treaty did not apply to military activities as sufficient grounds to reject all of the applicants' pleas as unfounded and dismiss the appeals in their entirety.[334] Hence, it was concluded that the relevant question in the case was not whether the Commission had the power to grant exemptions for that type of activity but rather whether those activities in fact fell within the scope of the Euratom Treaty which the Court's settled case-law clearly indicated did not.[335]

329 Para. 30.

330 Para. 63 of *Eriksen et al.*

331 Para. 12 of *Eriksen et al.*

332 Para. 63.

333 Para. 64.

334 Para. 66.

335 Para. 66.

Dismissing the foregoing actions prevented the General Court and the CJEU from dealing with the issue substantively – the two courts could have arguably offered a more comprehensive argumentation, especially by taking note of (while not necessarily aligning with) the European Parliament's Resolution invoked by the applicants which underscores the significance of tackling the issue of protection of the health of workers that had been exposed to dangerous radiation and furthermore, sheds light on the existence of a gap in the current regime for the protection of the health of the workers and the general public linked to the use of nuclear energy for military purposes, making a plea to the Commission to address the *lacuna*.[336]

Conceivably, properly construing the argument that Denmark is not a nuclear-weapons-state and that the military applications of nuclear energy in the Thule case can be exclusively attributed to the US as a 'third state' could have potentially changed the outcome of the legal dispute. Moreover, the fact that the Parliament Resolution closely predates the original applications before the General Court could plausibly signify that the Parliament was attempting to suggest a possible direction to be taken by the Union courts in this regard. Sadly, the refusal on the part of the Union courts to deal head-on with a substantial issue such as that of the health effects arising from nuclear weapons-related accidents occurring in the territory of the Member States reveals a tendency to downplay the gravity of the problem which can only be explained with the overriding political sensitivity thereof.[337] By contrast, the Parliament's readiness to initiate a broadening of the approach towards this sensitive issue represents yet another of this institution's endeavours to be closely associated with the work and influence the policy of the other Union institutions with greater legal and political leverage under the Euratom construct.

336 Points 11 and 12 of the Parliament Resolution.

337 Academic literature has not covered the *Eriksen et al.* case in any substantial manner; it has, however, been noted that the 'contentious legacy' of the Thule accident persists (see, A.J.K. Bailes, Human Rights and Security: Wider Applications in a Warmer Arctic, *Yearbook of Polar Law*, 2011, Vol.3, p. 533,535).

CHAPTER 5

Euratom and the European Union: Taking Stock of the Present and Mapping Out the Road Ahead

As was established in the preceding chapters, the co-existence between the Euratom and the Union legal frameworks in the past nearly six decades does not come without its own singular setbacks and inherent weaknesses, intrinsic to the very nature of the Union as a *sui generis* creation. The discussion in this concluding chapter sublimates the conclusions of the analyses offered in each of the preceding chapters and provides further insight into what lies ahead for the relationship between the Euratom and the Union frameworks and more specifically, discusses how the existence of the Euratom Community will play out within the EU system in the future. This chapter carries the common thread of the preceding chapters of the book by singling out the actual and potential 'problem areas' that the foregoing analysis has identified in the relationship between Euratom and the Union *stricto sensu*.

The first part of the following discussion outlines the loopholes and inconsistencies the research has detected with regard to the two specific areas of focus – the Euratom health and safety and nuclear safeguards regimes – in the light of their relationship with the policies devised under the Union framework they most immediately interact with – the Union's environmental policy and the Union's non-proliferation policy. This part is organized into four sub-parts corresponding to the respective subject matter covered: the (dis)balance of institutional powers and the democratic deficit under the Euratom system; the relationship between the Euratom health and safety regime and the Union's environmental policy; Euratom's stake in the field of environmental democracy (access to information, participation in decision making and access to courts in matters pertaining to the environment); and lastly, Euratom's and the Union's respective role in the area of non-proliferation of nuclear weapons and the issue of Euratom's relationship with the domain of military applications of nuclear energy;.

The second part of the discussion assumes a broader approach and a more general tone, acknowledging the loopholes and 'weak spots' in the Euratom regime that the analysis has identified and placing them within the overall Union context. In addition, as has been done in the first part, where pertinent, the discussion provides arguments to account for or justify the existence of the weak points that characterise the Euratom system, or, alternatively, suggests possible avenues for overcoming these weak points, pointing, to the extent

 | DOI 10.1163/9789004310414_007

feasible, to possible modifications and adjustments to be made to the current Euratom system.

1 The (Dis)Balance of Institutional Power and the Democratic Deficit under the Euratom System

Prior to going into the two specific areas of focus of the research, the discussion commenced by providing an insight into the nature and purview of the Euratom Community from a constitutional perspective, observing Euratom as a unique creation within the wider context of the Union and the specificity of the Euratom Treaty juxtaposed to the other Union founding treaties. In this sense, the analysis revealed certain deficiencies embedded in the current institutional framework of Euratom and the institutional dynamic created thereunder.

Firstly, a discrepancy was noted between the decision-making patterns set out under the Union framework *stricto sensu* and those under Euratom, the latter having resisted the Lisbon Treaty reforms directed at democratizing the Union's decision-making procedures. Under the Euratom system, the Commission figures as the organ that fully embodies the supranational tendency, being endowed with prerogatives that are manifestly prevalent to those belonging to the Council and the Parliament. Namely, the increase in legislative power for the Parliament introduced by the Lisbon amendments remains confined to the *Union* framework, failing to be matched by a corresponding reform under the Euratom compact. The Parliament is accorded a fairly peripheral role under the Euratom institutional dynamic, disposing of meager decision-making powers which in itself adds weight to the argument on the existence of a democratic deficit within the Euratom institutional system. In spite of the Council acting as the main legislative organ of Euratom, it is effectively the Commission, which enjoys extensive executive and supervisory authority, that carries the 'real' institutional weight.

In order to tackle the foregoing inconsistencies it is necessary that a balanced division of powers is introduced to the Euratom institutional framework matching that of the Union framework, first and foremost, by instituting effective accountability mechanisms with respect to the work of the Commission and the Council along the lines of a 'checks and balances' (or 'weight and counterweight') model. Therefore, it is vital that the institutional dominance of the Commission is curbed and the chances for abuse thereof reduced by vesting one of the Union institutions with the prerogative to regularly overview the work of the Commission. Given that under the Union framework the

Parliament is the institution endowed, for the most part, with prerogatives of supervision over the activities of other Union institutions and bodies, a step in the direction of extending the former mechanism of supervision to the Euratom scope seems pertinent. Such a reform could be accomplished either by Treaty amendment, or, (with a relatively more limited effect) by amending the existing or introducing new Euratom secondary legislation. Thus, some of the modalities in which the Euratom institutions are to discharge of their tasks can be prescribed by non-binding policy documents such as communications, *modus vivendi*, etc.

Secondly, with respect to the applicable legislative procedures, there exists a purely formalistic extension of the relevant articles of the Treaty on the Functioning of the European Union concerning the extension of the ordinary legislative procedure to the remit of the Euratom Treaty (effectuated through Art.106a Euratom). Nevertheless, in spite of the former extension, the Euratom decision-making procedures (under the current, consolidated version of the Euratom Treaty) have not been impacted. The former points to the perfunctory character of the extension, requiring that this important, deliberate or inadvertent, inconsistency be addressed and rectified as soon as possible. The peculiarity of the Euratom decision-making patterns can be plausibly explained by the unique nature of the Euratom Treaty as a sectoral treaty of a prevalently technical character, accounting for the visibly dominant role of the Commission as a key institutional player. The former was considered as instrumental at the initial, promotional stage of Euratom's existence where the nuclear was still a budding industry – however, with nuclear energy in Europe having long since moved on from the promotional era, it is necessary that the pervasive technocratic tendency embedded in the Euratom Treaty is reconsidered in light of the present-day circumstances. Understandably, it is the very nature of the field that the Euratom Treaty covers which makes it less liable to democratic scrutiny, endowing it with a democracy-deficient disposition. Nevertheless, as unique a creation the Euratom Community may be, it should not be considered exempt from the Union's governing principles and standards for democracy, accountability and transparency, making it indispensable that the functioning of Euratom is brought in line with these principles and standards with the Euratom institutions and functioning mechanisms having to undergo a substantial and thorough democratization.

Thirdly, the analysis appraised *the democratic deficit in the Euratom Community* primarily through the spectrum of the above elaborated insufficient involvement of the Parliament in the decision-making processes under the purview of Euratom as well as the options available for direct citizen involvement in the Euratom decision-making. Under the Union framework *stricto sensu*, a significant progressive development was observed in the new role accorded to national parliaments that have been enabled to be active participants in the democratic review of legislative proposals, pursuant to the *Protocol on the role of national parliaments in the European Union* (annexed to the TEU, the TFEU and the Euratom Treaty) and the *Protocol on the application of the principles of subsidiarity and proportionality* (annexed to the TEU and the TFEU). In spite of the legal void created by the fact that the latter protocol has only been annexed to the Union Treaties, this protocol (or at least the relevant provisions thereof) is to be presumed to apply *per extensiam* to Euratom given that Art.3(1) of the *Protocol on the role of the national parliaments* makes direct references to those provisions laying down the procedure involving the national parliaments. Nevertheless, for reasons of legal certainty, it is not sufficient that the applicability of the *Protocol on the application of the principles of subsidiarity and proportionality* to the Euratom purview is merely presumed, therefore necessitating a clarification in this respect and a formal extension of the Protocol to the scope of the Euratom Treaty. Another similar inconsistency is noted with respect to Art.5 TEU which codifies the principles of subsidiarity and proportionality as key principles of Union action, which has not been formally extended to the Euratom remit all the while being manifest that the assessment performed in light of the principle of subsidiarity under the *Protocol on the role of national parliaments in the European Union* is instrumental to the discharge of the newly accorded role of national parliaments in the Union legislative process.

The mechanisms of direct democracy inaugurated by the Lisbon Treaty such as the principle of representative democracy (Art.10(1) TEU) and other direct democracy mechanisms such as consultations with interested parties and citizens' initiatives (Art.11 TEU) have added significant democratic flesh to the Union structure. In this sense what represents a revolutionary step is introducing the option for one million citizens of a significant number of Member States to take the initiative of inviting the European Commission to submit a legislative proposal on matters where citizens consider that a legal act of the Union is required for the purpose of implementing the Treaties (Art.11(4) TEU). Unfortunately, the former direct democracy mechanisms have fallen short of being extended to the Euratom remit which is a missed opportunity for the empowerment of EU citizens to become more actively involved in the Euratom decision-making process. Again, this important drawback of the democracy-deficient Euratom system cannot be compensated by simply employing an extensive interpretation of the relevant provisions of the Union Treaties so that a formal extension to the Euratom purview would be required in this regard.

In terms of Euratom's accessibility for the ordinary citizen, somewhat mitigating the situation, but again confirming the irregularity in approach, is the extension to the Euratom scope of the duty of transparency and good governance of the Union institutions established under Art.15 TFEU, according to which the Union's institutions, bodies, offices and agencies are required to conduct their work as openly as possible and promote good governance and ensure the participation of civil society. In addition, a correlative duty is established for each institution, body, office or agency to ensure that their proceedings are transparent where the details for the execution of the former duty are to be additionally devised in their respective Rules of Procedure (Art.15(3) TFEU).

Arguably, the previously indicated loopholes in the Euratom system reveal a striking democratic deficit which cannot be overcome by relying on a broad construction of the relevant rules of the Union Treaties thereby considering the extrapolation of the relevant Union rules and principles to the Euratom domain as 'implied'. Therefore, in order to overcome the former democratic deficit (to the extent achievable) it is imperative that the Euratom Treaty is amended and/or other relevant legal instruments be adopted to the effect that the detected shortcomings can be overcome. Failing this, it would be impossible to speak of an accomplished balance of institutional powers within the Euratom system with the former continuing to be considered democracy-wise as an anachronistic system.

II The Relationship between the Euratom Health and Safety Regime and the Union's Environmental Policy

The second potential problem area that the research addressed was the interaction between the Euratom health and safety policy and the Union's environmental policy devised under the Union framework *stricto sensu*. For this purpose, the research firstly looked at the possibilities for extending the application of Union rules to the Euratom field and discerned the types of instances where such extension occurs following the *lex specialis derogate legi generali* formula according to which the provisions of the Treaty on European Union and of the Treaty on the Functioning of the European Union *should not derogate* from the provisions of the Euratom Treaty (Art.106(a)(3) Euratom). The former formula for extrapolation of Union rules to the Euratom purview has general applicability and is not confined solely to the interplay occurring between the Union environmental policy rules and mechanisms and the Euratom health and safety domain. It was noted that the spill-over effect of the former kind arises either where an issue of the nuclear domain has not been or cannot be adequately regulated by a Euratom legal rule thus requiring for corresponding Union rules to be applied in order to fill the legal void; or, alternatively, in instances where the competence to regulate a particular issue falls equally under the scope of the TFEU/TEU and that of the Euratom Treaty (concurring competence). In addition, it was observed that the former type of instances occur more frequently, especially in case of absence of relevant Euratom rules to be applied so that Union rules are used to fill in the void (e.g. rules adopted under the Union's common commercial policy, the competition policy, the environmental policy, the health policy, etc.). The latter type of instances which concern the concurring competence between the Union and Euratom are habitually resolved in favor of one of the two potentially applicable legal regimes, depending on the nature and character of the issue and upon an exercise of weighing in on the dominant legal basis has been performed (e.g. as the EU Court of Justice proceeded in *Chernobyl II*).

The relationship between Euratom and the Union's environmental policy was examined in the light of the 'environmental protection' aspect underlying the health protection and nuclear safety provisions of the Euratom Treaty and the Euratom secondary legislation. The analysis established that the dynamic of interaction between the Euratom health and safety policy and the Union environmental policy has primarily been reflected in the number of Union legal instruments adopted in the field of environmental protection which – comprehensively or marginally – cover a particular aspect belonging to the field of nuclear safety or radiation protection (e.g., *Directive 85/337/EEC on assessment of the effects of certain public and private projects on the environment* (codified by Directive 2011/92/EU); *Directive 2001/42/EC on the assessment of the effects of certain plans and programmes on the environment; Directive 2003/4/EC on public access to environmental information*). In turn, the spill-over has cut both ways, given that there are also purely Euratom acts which pertain to the prevention and/or protection from nuclear risks liable to adversely affect the environment and have been underpinned by environmental considerations. With the 'environmental' approach to radiation protection taken to comprise both the human health protection requirements and the requirements specific to the protection of 'air, water, soil, flora and fauna', these Euratom acts can be qualified as endorsing an 'environmental' approach towards radiation protection (e.g., former *Directive 96/29/EURATOM of 13 May 1996 laying down basic safety standards for the protection of the health of workers and the general public against the dangers arising from ionizing radiation* and its successor *Directive 2013/59/EURATOM laying down basic safety standards for protection against the dangers arising from exposure to ionising radiation*; the *Directive establishing a*

Community framework for nuclear safety, the *Directive on the supervision and control of shipments of radioactive waste and spent fuel; Directive 2003/122/ Euratom on the control of high-activity sealed radioactive sources and orphan sources*). Furthermore, the analysis characterised the approach adopted by the majority of EU institutions towards 'radiation protection' as mostly *environmental*, although sometimes short of consistent. Among the majority of institutions, there has been noticeable tendency not to prioritize or in any way favor the health protection over the environmental protection objective, but rather couple the two together into one single objective of protecting 'the population and the environment' against the risks of ionising radiations. The 'environmental' approach towards radiation protection has been further asserted through the activist jurisprudence of the EU Court of Justice with the Court deciding to view the health and safety provisions of the Euratom Treaty as representing a set of rules which are specifically relevant to the protection of populations *and the environment* against ionising radiations (e.g., *Cattenom*; *Commission v. UK*; *Temelin*).

The fully endorsed possibility to extend the scope of the Union environmental provisions to the Euratom domain has further lead to the possibility (if not, duty) to *integrate* the principles of the Union's environmental policy into the Euratom health and safety policy. The discussion focused on two principles – the principles of prevention and the precautionary principle – considering their application to the Euratom scope, in the absence of an express reference in the Euratom Treaty to this effect, as implied given the nature of the health protection objective of the Treaty as one thoroughly underscored by the notion of *prevention*. In this context, the research noted that part of the Euratom secondary legislation is indeed underpinned by a certain aspect of 'prevention' (most salient examples include: *Directive establishing a Community framework for the nuclear safety of nuclear installations*; *Directive* 96/29/EURATOM of 13 May 1996 *laying down basic safety standards for the protection of the health of workers and the general public against the dangers arising from ionizing radiation*; *Directive 2003/122/Euratom on the control of high-activity sealed radioactive sources and orphan sources*). Thus, the principle of prevention is held to be, at the very least, impliedly written into the Euratom Treaty while the same argument could not be extended to the application of the precautionary principle as a relatively novel principle, difficult to reconcile with the longevity of the Euratom Treaty and therefore impossible to have underlain the intentions of the Treaty's drafters. Nevertheless, a dynamic interpretation of the Euratom Treaty provisions should be permitted in this respect, taking into account the new evolved context in which the Treaty provisions are to be interpreted and applied.

Nevertheless, for the purpose of legal certainty, the intention of the Union legislators to extend the principles of prevention and precaution to the Euratom scope cannot simply be presumed and therefore needs to be expressly prorogated either via a Union or a Euratom rule. The prevention and the precautionary principles are legal concepts that have become increasingly prominent in the fields of environment protection and human health protection and are as such inextricably linked to the health and safety aspects of nuclear energy production. The failure to provide a formal extension of these principles (as well as the other environmental principles sanctioned under Art.191(2) TFEU such as the principles that environmental damage should be rectified at source and that the polluter should pay) to the Euratom domain significantly compromises the Euratom standard for health protection and nuclear safety.

Going beyond strictly the scope of application of the principles of the Union's environmental policy, another issue that has arisen in the context of the spill-over of Union rules to the Euratom scope has been the possibility to apply the general principles of Union law as primary sources of law to the Euratom domain. The EU Court of Justice has, to a limited extent, granted the possibility for general principles of law as constitutive components of the legal framework of the Union to be presumed equally applicable to the purview of Euratom. More particularly, with respect to the principle of equality, the Court considered it to be contrary to both the purpose and the consistency of the Treaties for discrimination on grounds of nationality to be prohibited under the Union framework all the while being allowed within the scope of application of the Euratom Treaty (the *Temelin* case). What can be inferred from the Court's reasoning is that it would be equally possible for all the other general principles of Union law to be considered applicable to the Euratom scope (e.g., the principle of protection of fundamental rights, the principle of legal certainty, the principle of proportionality, etc.). However, the activist jurisprudence of the EU Court of Justice in this regard is not sufficient and the matter should be resolved in a more comprehensive manner in the form of a formal extension of the application of the general principles of EU law to the Euratom field, which is to be foreseen either under the Euratom Treaty or the Union Treaties. Failing this, the application of the general principles of Union law to the Euratom field will continue as an irregular and inconsistent practice (i.e. a backdoor-type of application).

III Euratom's Stake in the Field of Environmental Democracy

Bearing in mind that the nuclear field has traditionally being regarded as an area shrouded with confidentiality and notorious for escaping the grip of transparency, primarily attributed to the inherently dual nature of nuclear energy as an energy source potentially catering to both civil and military demands, the research noted the (un)democratic disposition of Euratom specifically in matters related to the environmental field and thus, the environmental democracy mechanisms applicable to Euratom as a problem area that needs to be adressed. Namely, the procedural requirements endorsed under the 1998 *Aarhus Convention on Access to Information, Public Participation in Decision-making and Access to Justice in Environmental Matters* were examined to the extent that the former pertain to Euratom's purview where the analysis established that the respective scope of application of the requirements of the three pillars of the Aarhus Convention – access to environmental information, participation in decision-making and access to justice in environmental matters – coincides in important respects with the purview of Euratom. Consequently, the Union instruments (directives and regulations) transposing the Aarhus Convention requirements to the Union level are equally, to the relevant extent, applicable to Euratom's purview.

As regards the access-to-information pillar of the Aarhus Convention, the Union passed instruments specifically aimed to transpose the former to the EU level (*Directive 2003/4/EC on public access to environmental information*; and *Regulation No 1367/2006 on the application of the provisions of the Aarhus Convention on Access to Information, Public Participation in Decision-making and Access to Justice in Environmental Matters to Community institutions and bodies*). The approach of opening up the national authorities and the Union institutions to requests for environmental information coming from the public is consistent with the requirement that the EU institutions promote transparency and good governance prescribed in Art.15 TFEU (and extended to the Euratom scope), further guaranteeing the right of access to documents to every citizen of the Union. Namely, all citizens of the Union and all natural or legal persons residing or having its registered office in a Member State are granted a right of access to documents from the Union's institutions, bodies, offices and agencies whereby as s a corollary to the former right, a duty is established for each institution, body, office or agency to ensure that their proceedings are transparent.

The Euratom Treaty itself does establish rules regarding access to and exchange of information among the EU institutions and the Member States, however, the aim of these rules is neither one of making the information accessible to the public, nor one of increasing the level of transparency of the information the Euratom Community has at its disposal. For the most part, with the exception of the health and safety provisions of the Euratom Treaty dealing with the human health and environmental effects of radiation and disposal of radioactive waste, the types of information covered by the Treaty are linked to the technical aspects of nuclear energy production which, by their nature, cannot be subsumed under the notion of 'environmental information'. Furthermore, the option for the public or the public concerned to be able to directly address specific requests regarding access to information to the respective national authorities has neither been foreseen under the Euratom secondary legislation, in keeping with the overall tendency of lack of transparency exhibited under the Euratom Treaty. Therefore, what remains as the only applicable regime for requests regarding access to environmental information originating from private persons concerning the nuclear field is the legal regime created pursuant to the Union instruments transposing the Aarhus Convention obligations.

With respect to the participation-in-decision-making pillar of the Aarhus Convention, the analysis looked at the Union instruments transposing the former requirements in EU law, which are also, to the relevant extent, applicable to the Euratom domain: the 1985 *Environmental Impact Assessment Directive*[1] (concerning specific projects which have a significant effect on the environment), the 2001 *Strategic Environmental Assessment Directive*[2] (concerning public plans and programmes that are likely to have a significant effect on the environment) and the *2006 Aarhus Regulation on the application of the provisions of the Aarhus Convention on Access to Information, Public Participation in Decision-making and Access to Justice in Environmental Matters to Community institutions and bodies*). In contrast to the foregoing Union regime on public participation in decision-making which pertains *inter alia* to the Euratom purview, the options for public participation in decision-making available strictly under the Euratom Treaty and the Euratom secondary legislation are practically non-existent and, thus, a far cry from the elaborate transparency mechanisms fostered under the *Union* framework. The striking lack of public involvement mechanisms regarding the access to information and public participation in decision-making concerning health and environmental protection under the Euratom legal framework reveals a dire lack of 'environmental democracy' which can (merely partially and sporadically) be mitigated through the application of Union rules transposing the corresponding Aarhus Convention obligations relative to the Euratom domain.

It follows from the analysis of the available mechanisms under the Euratom system on access to environmental information and participation in decision-making in the nuclear field in matters concerning the environment, that there do exist certain participative mechanisms which the citizens have at their disposal which, nevertheless, originate in the Union instruments that apply to the

1 Directive 85/337/EEC (codified by Directive 2011/92/EU).

2 Directive 2001/42/EC.

Euratom domain and which are in themselves far from being sufficient and offer comprehensive procedural protection. Moreover, there does not exist a Euratom-specific transparency mechanism envisaged by a Euratom rule that provides procedural involvement for the public not only concerning the field of health and environmental protection, but also generally, as far as the entire Euratom purview is concerned. Such a reticent approach towards providing specific democratic mechanisms under the Euratom systems reverts to the democracy-deficient disposition of the Euratom Community – thus, once there is an overall change in approach towards attaching a greater weight to the general democracy mechanisms within the purview of Euratom, the scope of the options for 'environmental democracy' in this regard will follow suit.

The evasiveness exhibited towards giving the 'environmental democracy' mechanisms any real weight under the Euratom construct – and in the nuclear field altogether – has been substantiated by the case law of the international and the Union courts, demonstrating that issues in the nuclear arena pertaining to access to information and public participation in the environmental field are usually tackled in a less straightforward manner than the 'regular' environmental cases. In this sense, what has been manifest is the precaution readily exercised by the courts which, in fear of impinging upon the 'vested' national prerogatives in the nuclear domain, have additionally enhanced the element of confidentiality typically vitiating the nuclear field. In this vein, it is curious that the EU Court of Justice, otherwise considerably prolific in dealing with cases concerning the application of the first and second pillar requirements of the Aarhus Convention,[3] has thus far not dealt with a single case concerning the application of the former requirements to the Euratom domain, which inevitably brings into question the extent to which the Aarhus Convention requirements relevant to the Euratom field can be considered reviewable before the Union courts.

As concerns the access-to-justice requirements of the Aarhus Convention, the discussion addressed the issue of the Union's failure to adopt an access-to-justice directive transposing the Aarhus Convention regime concerning the justiciability of the requirements envisaged under the Convention's first and

3 The seminal cases include: C-266/09 *Stichting Natuur en Milieu v College voor de toelating van gewasbeschermingsmiddelen en biociden; C-204/09 Flachglas Torgau GmbH;* T-264/04 *WWF European Policy Programme v. Council, etc.* – regarding the access-to-information requirements; C-182/10 Marie-Noëlle Solvay and Others; C-*134/09 and C 135/09 Antoine Boxus and Others*; C-115/09 *Bund fur Umwelt und Naturschutz Deutschland, Landesverband Nordrhein-Westfalen eV; C-275/09 Brussels Hoofdstedelijk Gewest et al.; C-416/10 Jozef Križan and others, etc.* – regarding the participation-in-decision-making requirements.

second pillar. The failure to adopt the directive leaves a void in the Union regime pertaining to the implementation of the Aarhus Convention requirements which has been offset to a certain limited degree by the insertion of corresponding access-to justice provisions in the Union acts implementing the first and the second pillar requirements of the Aarhus Convention. It follows that until a directive on access to justice is adopted, there will persist to be an important void in the judicial protection of the participatory rights of the citizens and the non-governmental organizations in matters concerning, *inter alia*, the health and environmental protection in the nuclear domain.

IV Euratom and the Union's Role in the Field of Non-proliferation of Nuclear Weapons and Euratom's Stake in the Field of Military Applications of Nuclear Energy

The last area where the research found there to be potentially problematic issues is the field of non-proliferation of nuclear weapons where Euratom's share of competence concerns the prerogatives exercised by the Euratom Community in the field of nuclear safeguards as a competence exercised *internally* (within the Union borders) whereas the *external* aspect of the competence comes under the scope of the Union's policy on the non-proliferation of Weapons of Mass Destruction and is devised via the mechanisms of the Union's Common Foreign and Security Policy.

The Euratom safeguards regime forms part of a four-tier nuclear safeguards system comprising of the *international level, the primary EU level, the secondary EU level* and, lastly, the *Member State level*. The safeguards regime devised under the auspices of the International Atomic Energy Agency (IAEA) and having its original source in Art. III of the Non-Proliferation Treaty (NPT) stands at the top of the hierarchy with the Euratom safeguards regime acting in strict adherence to the rules and principles established under the former regime and complementing it to the extent necessary. From a legal standpoint, the two safeguards regimes have been secured a smooth coexistence via the *1975 IAEA-Euratom Cooperation Agreement* under which both contracting parties have undertaken to act in close cooperation and in due regard to their respective tasks and objectives, which facilitated the coming into force of the *Safeguards Agreement between the Euratom Member States, the Euratom and the IAEA* in 1977. While it is only the Non-Nuclear Weapon States (NNWS) of the Union that are contracting parties to the Safeguards Agreement with the IAEA, the Nuclear Weapon States (NWS) – France and the United Kingdom – are covered by voluntary offer agreements (VOAs) concluded with the IAEA which, in turn, express the benevolence of the two countries to subject *part* of their civil nuclear programs to safeguards arrangements in spite of there being no legal obligation to this effect.

The Euratom Treaty provides the legal framework for the establishment of a comprehensive safeguards regime which ensures that in the Member States' territories ores, source materials and special fissile materials are not diverted from their *intended use* as declared by the users. The Euratom Treaty's safeguards regime is complemented by the *Commission Regulation (Euratom) No 302/2005 on the application of Euratom safeguards* which comprehensively and in a detailed manner defines the nature and scope of the safeguards requirements laid down in the Treaty. In this respect, coming to the fore is the dominant role the Commission enjoys by acting as the chief authority in overseeing the execution of the safeguards obligations both at the EU and the Member State level. To the difference of the other potential 'weak spots' of the Euratom system in need of amending, the analysis of the Euratom safeguards framework has found the former to be an almost fail-proof system from a legal standpoint.

Lastly, the analysis dealing with the relationship between the Euratom safeguards system and the Union's non-proliferation policy noted two problematic issues. The first one relates to the nuclear weapons sharing arrangements between NATO and a certain number of NNWS of the Union which act as part of NATO's security concept for an 'extended nuclear deterrence' in Europe. The nuclear weapons sharing arrangements are entered into by certain of the Member States, however, in their individual capacity – not in their capacity of Union Member States which, formally speaking, puts the former arrangements away from the scope of Union action. The NATO nuclear sharing arrangements nevertheless have the potential to compromise the Union's non-proliferation efforts since, following the letter and spirit of the Non-Proliferation Treaty, the practice of nuclear weapon sharing should be seen as incompliant with Arts. I and II of the NPT (precluding NWS from transferring nuclear weapons or control thereof to NNWS coupled with the corresponding obligation for NNWS not to accept such transfers of the NPT) and, more generally, as contradictory to the NPT regime's very reason of being. Admittedly, the act of NATO's deployment of nuclear weapons on the territory of the NNWS of the EU can be regarded as a kind of 'transfer' of nuclear weapons or transfer of 'control' thereof – characterizing the practice of nuclear weapons sharing as dubious from a legal standpoint.

Given the delicate political character of the issue, the EU institutions have thus far distanced themselves from confronting it and have avoided making any official statements in this regard – possibly for reasons of exercising caution as not to prejudice the EU-NATO relations. Meanwhile, maintaining these nuclear weapon sharing arrangements runs the risk of the EU being labeled as violator of the letter and spirit of the NPT, potentially compromising the Union's role as global non-proliferation actor and arguably undermining the non-proliferation objective as the central limb upon which the NPT regime rests.

The second problematic issue that the analysis detected in this respect concerns the dividing line between the applicable regimes for civil and military uses of nuclear energy, and more particularly, the issue of the relationship between Euratom and the military uses of nuclear energy and the question as to whether and to what extent the Euratom Treaty can be considered to apply to the domain of military applications of nuclear energy. The fact that the Euratom Treaty is silent on the matter and fails to explicitly exclude or include military applications from its remit has engendered contradicting interpretations of the Treaty text. Moreover, the fact that military uses of nuclear energy have indeed not been *completely* and categorically excluded from the remit of Euratom adds greater ambiguity to the issue and confirms the existence of a loophole peculiar to the Euratom system in this regard.

The EU Court of Justice, almost a half century later, gave its final verdict on this issue which had been considered as contentious ever since the creation of the Euratom Community in its judgment in *C-61/03 Commission v. UK*. The Court declared the military applications of nuclear energy to fall outside of the scope of the Euratom Treaty, grounding its finding on two chief arguments: the lack of intention on the part of the Euratom Community's creators to this effect and the absence from the Euratom Treaty of a specific provision foreseeing the possibility for Member States to derogate from their Treaty obligations in order to safeguard their defense interests (alike the one of ex-Art.296 EC (present Art.346 TFEU)). As regards the latter argument, the Court considered it decisive that the Euratom Treaty did not contain any derogation concerning the protection of the essential interests of national security of Member States, thus inferring that the drafters of the Euratom Treaty would have foreseen such derogation had they considered the military applications as belonging to the purview of the Treaty. By deciding to completely exclude the nuclear defense field from the purview of Euratom and by failing to offer a purposive and non-textual reading of the Euratom Treaty in this context, the Court of Justice showed deference to the national security prerogatives of the Member States which patently indicates that the political climate in the Union is not mature enough for judicial activism in the direction of allowing controlled interference in the Member States' national defense sphere.

The issue of Euratom's stake in the Member States' nuclear defense sphere caused a stark division among certain EU institutions, the Commission having been fervently in favor of placing the contentious field of military applications of nuclear energy (to the extent appropriate) within the purview of Euratom – however, after the judgment in C-65/04 *Commission v. UK* it finally ceded to the Court's stance. The Parliament, in turn, has been persistent in its conviction that – at the very least – the application of the health and safety provisions of the Euratom Treaty needs to be extended to the realm of military applications of nuclear energy. Namely, in the 2007 *Resolution on the public health consequences of the 1968 Thule crash*[4] the Parliament drew attention to the existence of a gap in the current regime for the protection of the health of the general public related to the use of nuclear energy for military purposes, making a plea to the Commission to address the *lacuna*.[5] In this context, it is interesting to note that all the cases in which the CJEU expressed its stance were concerned with the particular issue of applying Euratom's health and safety rules to the realm of military applications of nuclear energy (C-61/03 *Commission v. UK*; C-65/04 *Commission v. UK*; C-205/10 P, C-217/10 P and C-222/10 P *Eriksen et al.*). The major *lacuna* to be observed here is that with the possibility for such an application having been ruled out, there remains to be no Union/Euratom health and safety regime in place that is applicable to military applications of nuclear material, while concomitantly there exists a strong necessity for the Euratom regime pertaining to civil applications of nuclear energy to be matched with a corresponding one in the defense sector.

Bearing in mind that for issues involving activities in the military sphere there can rarely be uniform and catch-all solutions as the former sphere is considered as highly politically sensitive and is often kept in strict confidentiality, it would nevertheless be of utter importance that minimum standards are established at the Union/Euratom level as such (or, at the international level and then subsequently transposed at Union level) for Member States to observe in instances of potentially adverse effects to human health resulting from the operation of military nuclear installations. By preserving the status quo, the population of the EU which is actually/potentially affected from the use of nuclear materials for military purposes will be left to rely solely on the mechanisms provided under domestic law which can vary considerably from one legal system to another.

Therefore, it is indispensable that, especially in light of the plea made by the European Parliament, the Member States and the Union decision-makers look beyond the individual national defense concerns and devise an adequate Union or Euratom-specific legal framework safeguarding the health of the

4 European Parliament Resolution of 10 May 2007 on the public health consequences of the 1968 Thule crash,P6_TA (2007) 0182.

5 Points 11 and 12 of the Resolution.

population actually/potentially adversely affected. The most politically feasible way of accomplishing this is amending the Euratom Treaty by inserting a provision analogous to the national security derogation envisaged under Art.346 TFEU or by extending the application of the former derogation to the Euratom Treaty's remit. The former would be in line with what the Court of Justice observed was missing from the current text of the Euratom Treaty when outlining the main reasons to support its stance against the inclusion of military applications of nuclear energy within Euratom's scope. In the meantime, while waiting for this *lacuna* to be adequately resolved, the caveat suggested by the Court in C-61/03 *Commission v. UK* and C-65/04 *Commission v. UK* can plausibly be utilized – namely, relying on the rules available under the current Union framework in order to tackle the issue of adverse health effects arising from the operation of military nuclear facilities or the handling of nuclear materials destined for military purposes. Unfortunately, the former route would seem exceptionally difficult to follow due to the singular and delicate character of the issue as one that would not as easily yield to a legal solution originating from outside of the Euratom framework *per se*.

V What Lies Ahead for Euratom

The overriding impression gathered from the foregoing elaboration of the problem areas that the research has detected, is that these 'weak spots' or deficiencies of the Euratom system stem from the highly unique character of this system and the legal framework created thereunder. In fact, these deficiencies have been embedded in the Euratom system in such a way that they can be seen as inherent thereto.

The common aspect the majority of the detected problem areas share is that they are a direct or indirect result of the democracy-deficient disposition of the Euratom Community. Namely, going beyond the scope of the Euratom safeguards and health and safety regimes, it is manifest that Euratom is a community in dire lack of transparency and one which persists to be, figuratively speaking, out of reach for the common EU citizen. Resistance to public scrutiny for the matters falling under Euratom's purview was possibly justified in the early days of Euratom when nuclear energy was still being introduced as a novel field in regulatory terms – however, the present-day context of an increasingly more democratic Union bringing its citizens more closely involved in its work does not bode well with a strikingly non-transparent and undemocratic Euratom. There is therefore a pressing need for the Euratom Community to keep pace with the democratic reforms established under the Union framework *stricto sensu* since its current democracy-deficient disposition is liable to compromise the future existence of the Community. This systemic deficiency of the Euratom system, paired with the argument concerning the out-datedness of the Euratom Treaty, figures among the central arguments advocating the need for substantial amendment of the Euratom Treaty and a reform to the Euratom system as such.

Predictions on the future of Euratom have revolved around several scenarios, the most favorable of which concerns a substantial revision of the Euratom Treaty alongside the preservation of the Euratom Community's legal personality. The 'rejuvenation' of the Euratom Treaty text should focus on providing greater involvement for the Parliament in the Euratom decision-making process as well as updating and, if necessary, deleting certain treaty provisions, especially those that have become obsolete with time. The saving grace for Euratom essentially lies in the democratization of the Euratom system which is to be effected primarily by granting the Parliament as the most democratic Union institution greater and more substantial involvement in the Euratom decision-making and by broadening the scope of the available mechanisms for direct citizen involvement in the decision-making process. Unless Euratom's democratic deficit is overcome (or at least, significantly reduced), the legitimacy of Euratom will continue to decrease and possibly lead to the demise of the Community as a self-fulfilling prophesy.

Another plausible scenario for the future suggests that the Euratom Treaty be repealed and the Euratom Community as such abolished, thereby deleting the outdated provisions and the provisions of the Treaty which duplicate the corresponding TFEU provisions, incorporating the remainder of the still 'current' Euratom Treaty provisions into the TFEU, either as a separate chapter or within the existent 'Energy' chapter. With respect to how the former scenario would affect the two areas of focus of the book (Euratom safeguards and health and safety) as prominent areas covered by separate legal frameworks devised to a comprehensive level, it is arguable that such a development will annihilate the autonomy and coherence of the Euratom safeguards and health and safety regimes in a way that would potentially lead to conflict with the existent provisions of the Union Treaties and make the 'imported' Euratom Treaty provisions act as a Trojan horse within the Union framework.

A radical third scenario, mainly supported by the European green political parties, NGOs working in the field of environmental protection and other actors belonging to the European anti-nuclear lobby, suggests that the Euratom Treaty and *all* of the Treaty provisions in their entirety should be repealed. The major claim here is that the Euratom Treaty is an obsolete treaty which does not reflect the EU's nuclear reality and necessitates for the EU's nuclear policy to be brought back to the national level i.e. become re-nationalized. On the face of it, the former scenario proposes that the Union dispenses with an undemocratic and out-dated treaty and the governing rules and principles for the civil nuclear industry are reinstated to Member States competence. It is important to remind that the Euratom safeguards and health and safety regimes have become so vital to the civil nuclear energy industries of the Member States that it would seem counterintuitive – let alone unreasonable – to bring them back under solely Member State competence. The former development is liable to open the Pandora's box in the nuclear field for the Union: all the problems associated with giving full control over the implementation of the nuclear safeguards arrangements to the national authorities will surface increasing the national security of Member States since the chances for uncontrolled and illicit diversion of nuclear material will effectively multiply. Moreover, abolishing the Euratom policy on health and safety and re-nationalizing the standards for health and safety in the nuclear domain will lead to unwarranted and dangerous discrepancies reflected in the multitude of applicable national legal regimes, acting primarily to the detriment of the Member States' general population.

In a Declaration attached to the Final Act of the Intergovernmental Conference on the Lisbon Treaty, the governments of five Member States (*Germany, Ireland, Hungary, Austria and Sweden*) expressed their support for the convening of a conference of representatives of the governments of the Member States as soon as possible and for the purpose of bringing the Euratom Treaty provisions up to date. The hour for deciding on the definitive future of Euratom and the convening of a conference of the former kind will possibly strike soon based on the increasingly divergent attitudes towards the use of nuclear power in the EU, which include Member States with active phase-out policies in place (Austria, Germany) at the one end of the spectrum, and Member States which continue to rely on the nuclear as a vital energy source catering not only to the demands of their civil industry, but also their military industry (France, the UK). The highly diverse nuclear landscape of a Union of twenty-eight significantly departs from the initial nuclear consensus among the six founding members out of which the Euratom Community was born and it is this very consensus that will be put to the test in the years to come.

Back in 1958, an American scholar speaking about Euratom posed the following question: '*Can supranational regulation of atomic energy contribute, by way of example, to the realization of the vision of a united region of the old continent, an entire and perfect union in itself?*'[6] With the benefit of hindsight, the

6 H.J. Hahn, 'EURATOM – The Conception of An International Personality', *Harvard Law Review*, 1958, Issue 71–76, p. 1056.

lingering question is whether Euratom as we know it today indeed comes close to an entirely successful model for supranational regulation in the nuclear field and whether the Union's decision-makers are willing to invest the necessary effort in order for the former question to be answered in the affirmative nearly sixty years on.

Bibliography

Books and Chapters in Books

Balme, R. and Chabanet, D., *European Governance and Democracy: Power and Protest in the EU*, Rowman & Littlefield, 2008.

Birnie, P., Boyle, A. and Redgewell, C. (eds.), *International Law and the Environment*, Oxford University Press, 2009.

Bodansky, D., *The Art and Craft of International Environmental Law*, Harvard University Press, 2010.

Burroughs, J., *Two Legal Issues Confronting NATO And The Non-Proliferation Regime: US Presidential Decision Directive 60 Versus Pledges of Non-Use of Nuclear Weapons Made to Non-Nuclear Weapon States and NATO Nuclear Sharing versus the Nuclear Non-Proliferation Treaty*, Lawyers' Committee on Nuclear Policy, 1999.

Cameron, P.D., Energy: Efficiency, Security and the Environment, in, Dougan M. and Currie S. (eds.), *50 Years of The European Treaties: Looking Back and Thinking Forward*, Hart Publishing, 2009.

Camps, M., *Britain and the European Community 1955–1963*, Princeton University Press, 1964.

Cardwell, P.J., (ed.), *EU External relations law and policy in the post-Lisbon era*, Springer, 2012.

Crowley, J. and Giorgi, L., The Political Sociology of the European Public Sphere in, Giorgi Von Homeyer and Parsons (eds.), *Democracy in The European Union: Towards the Emergence of a Public Sphere*, Routledge, 2006.

De Sadeleer, N., The Principles of Prevention and Precaution: Two Heads of the Same Coin? in, Ong Merkouris and Fitzmaurice (eds.), *Research Handbook on International Environmental Law*, Edward Elgar Publishing, 2011.

Dhondt, N., *Integration of Environmental Protection into Other EC Policies*, Europa Law Publishing, 2003.

Ebbesson, J., Chapter 2: European Community, in, J. Ebbesson (ed.), *Access to justice in environmental matters in the EU*, Kluwer Law International, 2002.

Ebbesson, J. and Okowa, P., Environmental Justice in Situations of Armed Conflict, in, Okowa P. (ed.), *Environmental law and justice in context*, Cambridge University Press, 2009.

Edward, D. and Robinson, W., The Court of Justice and Environmental Protection, in, MacDougall D.S. and Wälde T.W. (eds.), *European Community Energy Law: Selected topics*, Graham&Trotman/Martinus Nijhoff, 1994.

Epiney, A., Environmental Principles, in, Macrory, R (ed.), *Reflections on 30 Years of EU Environmental Law: High Level of Protection?* Europa Law Publishing, 2006.

Falk, R., The Second Cycle of Ecological Urgency: An Environmental Justice Perspective, in, Ebbesson, J and Okowa P. (eds.), *Environmental Law and Justice in Context*, Cambridge University Press, 2009.

Fischer, G., *The Non-Proliferation of Nuclear Weapons*, Europa Publications, 1971.

Fitzmaurice, M.A., *International Protection of the Environment (Collected Courses of the Hague Academy of International Law)*, Martinus Nijhoff Publishers, 2001.

Fitzmaurice, M., The European Convention of Human Rights and the Human Right to a Clean Environment, in, This is a chapter of the book authored by M. Fitzmaurice (Contemporary Issues...), fully cited in following.

Fitzmaurice, M., *Contemporary Issues of International Environmental Law*, Edward Elgar Publishing, 2009.

Goens, J.R., The Opportunities and Limits of European Co-operation in the Area of Non-proliferation, in, H. Muller (ed.), *A European Non-Proliferation Policy: Prospects and Problems*, Clarendon Press, 1987.

Goldschmidt, B., Proliferation and Non-proliferation in Western Europe: A Historical Survey, in H. Muller (ed.), *A European Non-Proliferation Policy: Prospects and Problems*, Clarendon Press, 1987.

Govaere, I., Beware of the Trojan Horse: Dispute Settlement in (Mixed) Agreements and the Autonomy of the EU Legal Order, in, Hillion C. and Koutrakos P. (eds.), Mixed agreements revisited: The EU and its Member States in the World, Hart Publishing, 2010.

Grunwald, J., Euratom Treaty History and The Way Forward in, *Nuclear Inter Jura 2007 Proceedings*, Bruylant, 2008.

Harris, D.J., O'Boyle, M., Bates, E.P. and Buckley, C.M., *Law of the European Convention on Human Rights*, Oxford University Press, 2009.

Duffield, J.S. and Birchfield, V.L. (eds.), *Toward a Common European Union Energy Policy: Problems, Progress, and Prospects*, Palgrave Macmillan, 2011.

Howlett, D.A., *Euratom and Nuclear Safeguards*, Macmillan Press, 1990.

Jans, J.H. and Vedder, H.B., *European Environmental Law*, Europa Law Publishing, 2008.

Jendroska, J., Public Information and Participation in EC Environmental Law: Origins, Milestones and Trends, in Macrory, R. (ed.), *Reflections on 30 Years of European Environmental Law: A High Level of Protection*, The Avosetta Series: Proceedings of the Avosetta Group of European Environmental Lawyers, Europa Law Publishing, 2006.

Jendroska, J., Public Participation in Environmental Decision-making, Interactions Between the Convention and EU Law and Other Key Legal Issues in its Implementation in the Light of the Opinions of the Aarhus Convention Compliance Committee, in, Pallemaerts M. (ed.), *The Aarhus Convention at Ten: Interactions and Tensions between Conventional International Law and EU Environmental Law*, Europa Law Publishing, 2011.

Klein, N., Settlement of International Environmental Law Disputes, in, Ong D.M., Merkouris P. and Fitzmaurice M. (eds.), *Handbook on International Environmental Law*, Edward Edgar Publishing, 2010.

Kohler-Koch, B. and Rittberger, B., Charting Crowded Territory: Debating The Democratic Legitimacy of The European Union, in, Giorgi Von Homeyer and Parsons (eds.), *Democracy in The European Union: Towards the Emergence of a Public Sphere*, Routledge, 2006.

Kramer, L., *EC Environmental Law*, Sweet and Maxwell, 2003.

Kramer, L., *EC Environmental Law*, Sweet and Maxwell, 2000.

Kramer, L., The Genesis of EC Environmental Principles, in, Macrory, R. (ed.), *Principles of European Environmental Law* (Proceedings of the Avosetta Group of European Environmental Lawyers), Europa Law Publishing, 2004.

Kramer, L., Environmental Justice in the European Court of Justice, in Ebbeson J. and Okowa P. (eds.), *Environmental law and justice in context*, Cambridge University Press, 2009.

Lamm, V., The Utilization of Nuclear Energy and International Law, Akademia Kiado, Budapest, 1984.

Lavrysen, L., The Aarhus Convention: Between Environmental Protection and Human Rights, in, *Liège, Strasbourg, Bruxelles: parcours des droits de l'homme. Liber amicorium Michel Melchior*, Anthemis, 2010.

Lunn, S., A Crucial Decision: NATO's Nuclear Weapons in the Twenty-First Century, in, Chalmers M. and Lunn S. (eds.), NATO's Tactical Nuclear Dilemma, Royal United Services Institute, 2010.

M. Maresceau, A Typology of Mixed Bilateral Agreements, in, Hillion C. and Koutrakos P. (eds.), Mixed agreements revisited: The EU and its Member States in the World, Hart Publishing, 2010.

Merrills, J.G. and Robertson, A.H., *Human Rights in Europe: A study of the European Convention on Human Rights*, Manchester University Press, 2001.

Müller, H., Non-Proliferation Policy in Western Europe: Structural Aspects, in, Müller H. (ed.), *A European Non-Proliferation Policy: Prospects and Problems*, Clarendon Press, 1987.

Nikpay, A. and Faull, J., *The EC Law of competition*, Oxford University Press, 1999.

Polach, J.G., *EURATOM: Its Background, Issues and Economic Implications*, Oceana Publications, 1964.

Ribeiro, B., Le role de l'arme nucleaire dans la mise en oeuvre d'une PESCD, in, P. Buffotot et N. Vilboux (dirs.), *Vers une politique europeenne de securite et de defense: Defis et opportunites*, Economica, 2003.

Sands, P., Principles of International Environmental Law (2nd ed.), Cambridge University Press, 2003.

Schram, F., From a General Right of Access to Environmental Information in the Aarhus Convention to a General Right of Access to All Information in Official Documents: The Council of Europe's Tromsø Convention, in, The contribution by Schram is part of an edited volume by M. Pallemaerts (The Aarhus Convention at Ten...), fully cited in following.

Pallemaerts, M. (ed.), *The Aarhus Convention at Ten: Interactions and Tensions between Conventional International Law and EU Environmental Law*, Europa Law Publishing, 2011.

Scott, J., The Precautionary Principle before the European Courts, in, Macrory R. (ed.), *Principles of European Environmental Law (Proceedings of the Avosetta Group of European Environmental Lawyers)*, Europa Law Publishing, 2004.

Shelton, D., Describing the Elephant: International Justice and Environmental Law, in J. Ebbeson and P. Okowa (eds.), *Environmental law and justice in context*, Cambridge University Press, 2009.

Shelton, D., Human Rights and the Environment: Substantive Rights, in, Ong D.M., Merkouris P. and Fitzmaurice M. (eds.), *Research Handbook on International Environmental Law*, Edward Elgar Publishing, 2010.

Shelton, D., Resolving Conflicts between Human Rights and Environmental Protection: Is there a Hierarchy? in, de Wet E. and Vidmar J. (eds.), *Hierarchy in International law*, Oxford University Press, 2012.

Von Bogdandy, A., A Disputed Idea Becomes Law: Remarks on European Democracy as a Legal Principle, in, Kohler-Koch B. and Bittberger B. (eds.), *Debating the Democratic Legitimacy of the European Union*, Rowman & Littlefield, 2007.

Zweifel, T.D., *Democratic Deficit? The European Union, Switzerland, and the United States in Comparative Perspective*, Lixington Books, 2002.

Journal Articles

Allen, D., The Euratom Treaty, Chapter VI: New Hope or False Dawn, *Common Market Law Review*, 1983, Vol.20, Issue 3.

Ayllon Diaz-Gonzalez, J.M. Derecho Nuclear, Granada, Comares, 1999 (cited in N. Prieto Serrano, Wakening the Serpent: Reflections on the Possible Modification of the Euratom Treaty, *International Journal of Nuclear Law*, 2006, Vol.1, No.1).

Bailes, A.J.K., Human Rights and Security: Wider Applications in a Warmer Arctic, *Yearbook of Polar Law*, 2011, Vol.3.

Bar, M., Towards Implementation of the Aarhus Convention Third Pillar: Draft EU Access directive Compared with the Situation in Poland, *Environmental Liability*, 2004, Vol.12 Issue 2.

Barnes, P.M., The nuclear industry: A particular challenge to democracy in Europe, *Managerial Law*, 2006, Issue 48.

Bouquet A., How Current are Euratom provisions on Nuclear Supply and Ownership in view of the European Union's enlargement? *Nuclear Law Bulletin*, December 2001, No.6.

Cameron, P.D., The Revival of Nuclear Power: An Analysis of the Legal Implications, *Journal of Environmental Law*, 2007, Vol.19 No.1.

Capek, S.M., The 'Environmental Justice' Frame: a Conceptual Discussion and an Application, *Social Problems*, 1993 Issue 40.

Casteleiro, A.D., EU Declarations of Competence to Multilateral Agreements: A Useful Reference Base?' *European Foreign Affairs Review*, 2012, Vol 17, No. 4.

Cenevska, I., The exercise of giving way to 'giving in' – some aspects of the Member States' EURATOM obligations revisited, *Journal for European Environmental and Planning Law*, 2009 Vol.6 Issue 4.

Churchill, R. and Scott, J., The MOX Plant Litigation: The FirstHalf-Life, *International and Comparative Law Quarterly* 2004 Vol.53.

Cusack, T., A Tale of Two Treaties, *Common Market Law Review*, 2003, Vol.40 Issue 117.

De Abreu Ferreira, S., Passive Access to Environmental Information in the EU: An Analysis of Recent Legal Developments, *European Energy and Environmental Law Review*, August 2008.

De Abreu Ferreira, S., The Fundamental Right of Access to Environmental Information: a Critical Analysis of WWF-EPO v. Council, *Journal of Environmental Law*, 2007, Vol.19, Issue 3.

Deubner, C., The expansion of West German Capital and the Founding of Euratom, *International Organization*, 1979.

Dupont-Lassalle, J., Accès aux documents et confidentialité des enquêtes de la Commission, *Europe*, January 2014, Comm. n 1.

Ebbesson, J., Public Participation and Privatisation in Environmental Matters: An Assessment of the Aarhus Convention, *Erasmus Law Review*, 2011, Vol.4 Issue 2.

Efron, R., and Nanes, A.S., The Common Market and Euratom Treaties: Supranationality and the Integration of Europe, *International and Comparative Law Quarterly*, 1957, Vol.6.

Efron, R., and Nanes, A.S., The Emerging Concept of Supranationality in Recent International Agreements, *Kentucky Law Journal*, 1955, Issue 44.

Emmerechts, S., Environmental Law and Nuclear Law: A Growing Symbiosis, *Nuclear Law Bulletin*, 2008-I.

Govaere, I., Case commentary, cases C-70/94 and C-83/94 (Leifer and Werner) of the European Court of Justice concerning dual use goods, *Common Market Law Review*, 1997, Vol.34.

Hahn, H.J., Control under the Euratom Compact, *The American Journal of Comparative Law*, 1958, Vol.7.

Hahn, H.J., Euratom: The Conception of an International Personality, *Harvard Law Review*, April 1958, Issue 71–6.

Hedemann-Robinson, M., EU Implementation of the Aarhus Convention's Third Pillar: Back to the Future over Access to Environmental Justice? (Part 1), *European Energy and Environmental Law Review*, June 2014.

Helm, D., The European framework for energy and climate policies, *Energy Policy*, 2014, Issue 64.

Houben, P.M., The Merger of the Executives of the European Communities, *Common Market Law Review*, 1965–1966, Vol.3 Issue 37.

Hymans, J.E.C., When Does a State Become a 'Nuclear Weapon State'? An Exercise in Measurement Validation, *Non Proliferation Review* , March 2010, Vol.17 Issue 1.

Inglis, K., Anticipating New Union Competences in Energy, *Maastricht Journal of European and Comparative Law*, 2008, Vol.15 Issue 1.

Jendroska, J., Aarhus Convention Compliance Committee: Origins, Status and Activities,*Journal of European Environmental and Planning Law,* 2011, Vol.8 Issue 4.

Jendroska, J., Citizen's Rights in European Environmental Law: Stock-Taking of Key Challenges and Current Developments in Relation to Public Access to Information, Participation and Access to Justice,*Journal of European Environmental and Planning Law*, 2012, Vol.9 Issue 1.

Jendroska, J., Citizen's Rights in European Environmental Law: Stock-Taking of Key Challenges and Current Developments in Relation to Public Access to Information, Participation and Access to Justice,*Journal of European Environmental and Planning Law*, 2012, Vol.9 Issue 1.

Joerges, C. and Neyer, J., 'Deliberative Supranationalism' Revisited, *EUI Working Paper*, LAW No.2006/20.

Joerges, C., 'Deliberative Supranationalism' – Two Defences, *European Law Journal*, 2002, Issue 8.

Kanellakis, M., Martinopoulos, G., and Zachariadis, T., European Energy Policy – A Review, *Energy Policy*, 2013, Issue 62.

Kobia, R., The EU and Non-Proliferation: Need for a Quantum Leap? *Nuclear Law Bulletin,* June 2008, No. 81.

Koester, V., Review of Compliance under the Aarhus Convention: A Rather Unique Compliance Mechanism, *Journal of European Environmental and Planning Law*, 2005, Issue 1.

Koutrakos, P., Case note on Case C-29/99 Commission v Council (re: Nuclear Safety Convention), *Common Market Law Review*, 2004, Vol.41.

Lavranos, N., The Epilogue in the MOX Plant Dispute: An End Without Findings, *European Energy and Environmental Law Review*, June 2009.

Lee, M. and Abbot, C., The Usual Suspects? Public Participation under the Aarhus Convention, *Modern Law Review*, 2003, Vol.66 Issue 1.

Leino, P., Just a Little Sunshine in the Rain: The 2010 Case Law of the European Court of Justice on Access to Documents, *Common Market Law Review*, 2011, Issue 48.

Lierman, S. and Veuchelen, L., The Optimisation Approach of ALARA in Nuclear Practice: An Early Application of the Precautionary Principle? Scientific Uncertainty versus Legal Uncertainty and its Role in Tort Law, *European Environmental Law Review*, 2006, Vol.15 Issue 4.

Mallard, G., Can the Euratom Treaty Inspire the Middle East: The Political Promises of Regional Nuclear Communities, *Non Proliferation Review*, November 2008, Vol.15 Issue 3.

Maltby, T., European Union Energy Policy Integration: A Case of European Commission Policy Entrepreneurship and Increasing Supranationalism, *Energy Policy*, 2013, Issue 55.

Mariolina, E., Collective Redress in Environmental Matters in the EU: A Role Model or a 'Problem Child'? *Legal Issues of Economic Integration*, 2014, Vol.41 No.3.

Marsden, S., MOX Plant and the Espoo Convention: Can Member State Disputes Concerning Mixed Environmental Agreements be Resolved outside EC Law? *Review of European Community and International Environmental Law*, 2009, Vol.18 Issue 3.

Mason, M., Information Disclosure and Environmental Rights: the Aarhus Convention, *Global Environmental Politics*, August 2010, Vol.10 Issue 3.

Mathijsen, P., Some Legal Aspects of Euratom, *Common Market Law Review*, 1965–1966, Issue 3.

Mollet, G., *Vital Speeches of the Day (15 March 1957)*, Vol.23 Issue 11.

Molodstova, E., Nuclear Energy and Environmental Protection: Responses of International Law, *Pace Environmental Law Review*, 1994, Vol.12 Issue 1.

Molodstova, E., Nuclear Energy Law and International Environmental Law: an Integrated Approach, *Journal of Energy and Natural Resources Law*, 1995, Vol.13 Issue 4.

Nanda, V.P., International Environmental Norms Applicable to Nuclear Activities, with Particular Focus on Decisions of International Tribunals and International Settlements, *Denver Journal of International Law*, 2006, Vol.35 issue 1.

Nanes, A., The Evolution of Euratom, *International Journal*, 1957–1958, Vol.13 Issue 1.

Norman, P., The Accidental Constitution: The Story of The European Convention, *Euro-Comment*, 2003.

Pedersen, O.W., European Environmental Human Rights and Environmental Rights: A Long Time Coming? *Georgetown International Environmental Law Review*, 2008, Vol.21 No. 1.

Pedersen, O.W., The Ties that Bind: The Environment, the European Convention on Human Rights and the Rule of Law, *European Public Law*, 2010, Vol.16 Issue 4.

Pointvogl, A., Perceptions, Realities, Concessions – What is Driving the Integration of European Energy Policies? *Energy Policy*, 2009, Issue 37.

Portela, C. and Jasper, U., EU Defense Integration and Nuclear Weapons: A Common Deterrent for Europe? *Security Dialogue,* 2010.

Portela, C., *The Role of the EU in the Non-Proliferation of Nuclear Weapons: The Way to Thessaloniki and Beyond* (Research Report no.65), Peace Research Institute – Frankfurt, 2003.

Reyners, P., Le droit nucléaire confronté au droit de l'environnement: autonomie ou complementarité? *Revue québécoise de droit international,* 2007, Hors-série.

Ruhle, M., NATO and Extended Deterrence in a Multinuclear World, *Comparative Strategy*, 2009, Vol.28 No. 1.

Sand, P., The Precautionary Principle: Coping with Risk, *Indian Journal of International Law*, January–March 2000, No.1.

Schärf, W., 'The Temelín-Judgement of the European Court of Justice', *Nuclear Law Bulletin*, Vol.2010/1.

Scheinmann, L., Euratom: Nuclear Integration in Europe, *International Conciliation*, Carnegie Endowment for International Peace, May 1967, No. 563.

Scheinmann, L., Transcending Sovereignty in the management and control of nuclear material, *IAEA Bulletin*, 2001, Vol.43 Issue 4.

Schikhof, S., Direct and individual Concern in Environmental Cases: The Barriers to Prospective Litigants, *European Environmental Law Review*, October 1998.

Schrauwen, A., 'Treaties and Trade-offs', editorial, *Legal Issues of Economic Integration,* 2005, Vol.32 Issue 4.

Serrano, N.P., Wakening the serpent: reflections on the possible modification of the Euratom Treaty, *International Journal of Nuclear Law*, 2006, Vol.1 No. 1.

Shelton, D., International Decision: *Tatar c. Roumanie*, App. No. 67021/01 European Court of Human Rights, Jan. 27, 2009, *American Journal of International Law*, 2010, Issue 104.

Smith, D.D., The European Atomic Energy Community (Euratom): The Limits of Supranationalism, *California Western International Law Journal*, 1970, Vol.1 Issue 33.

Steiger, H., An Evaluation of Legal Development on a Regional Basis: The Search for European Unity, *Ohio State Law Journal*, 1961, Vol.22.

True, C., Legislative Competences of Euratom and the European Community in the energy sector: The Nuclear Package of the Commission, *European Law Review*, 2003 Vol.28 Issue 5.

Usher, J.A., International Competence of Euratom (Comment on Ruling 1/78 of November 14, 1978), *European Law Review*, 1979, Vol.4.

Van Ham, P., The European Union's WMD Strategy and the K: A Critical Analysis, *Non-Proliferation Papers*, September 2011.

Veuchelen, L., The Legal Value of General Principles, Technical Norms and Standards in European Nuclear Safety Law: The Imbalance Between Soft and Hard Law and the Need for Global Regulatory Governance, *European Energy and Environmental Law Review*, 2009, Vol.18 Issue 4.

Wates, J., The Aarhus Convention: A Driving Force for Environmental Democracy, *Journal of European Environmental and Planning Law*, 2005, Issue 1.

Wetter, A., Enforcing European Union Law on Exports of Dual-use Goods, Stockholm International Peace Research Institute – Research Report No.24, Oxford University Press, 2009.

Wolf, S., Euratom, the European Court of Justice, and the Limits of Nuclear Integration in Europe, *German Law Journal*, 2011, Vol.12 No.8.

Woodliffe, J., Making Sense of Article 37 of the Euratom Treaty, *European Law Review*, 1989, Vol.14 Issue 2.

Yondrof, W., Monnet and the Action Committee: The Formative Period of the European Communties, *International Organization*, 1965.

Articles, Reports and other Documents on the Internet

Butcher, M., Nassauer, O., Padberg, T. and Plesch D., *Questions of Command and Control: NATO, Nuclear Sharing and the NPT*, British American Security Information Council Research Report, PENN Research Report Vol.1 2000 (http://www.basicint.org/pubs/Research/2000nuclearsharing3.htm).

Chalmers, M., NATO Dual-Capable Aircraft: A Stocktake, in, Chalmers M. and Lunn S. (eds.), *NATO's Tactical Nuclear Dilemma*, Royal United Services Institute, 2010, accessible at http://www.rusi.org/downloads/assets/NATOs_Nuclear_Dilemma.pdf.

Chalmers, M., NATO's Nuclear Weapons: An Introduction to the Debate, in, Chalmers M. and Lunn S. (eds.), NATO's Tactical Nuclear Dilemma, Royal United Services Institute, March 2010, (accessible at http://www.rusi.org/downloads/assets/NATOs_Nuclear_Dilemma.pdf).

Foti, J. et al., *Voice and Choice: Opening the Door to Environmental Democracy*, World Resources Institute, 2008 (available at http://pdf.wri.org/voice_and_choice.pdf).

Fouquet, D., 'The Legal Perspective: The Euratom treaty and the new Constitution', prepared for the conference entitled 'The Euratom Treaty and Future Energy Options: Conditions for a Level Playing Field in the Energy Sector', organized by Friends of the Earth-Denmark, The Danish Ecological Council and The Danish Organisation for Sustainable Energy, September 23rd 2005 (http://www.energyintelligenceforeurope.dk/conf_p6.html).

Gadbois, S. et al., Final Report: Situation concerning public information about and involvement in the decision-making processes in the nuclear sector, May 2007, commissioned by the Commission's DG TREN, Contract Number: TREN_04_NUCL

_S07-39556, available at http://ec.europa.eu/energy/nuclear/doc/governance/2007_05_summary_en.pdf.

Grip, L., The EU Non-proliferation Clause: A Preliminary Assessment, Stockholm International Peace Research Institute Background Paper, November 2009 (http://books.sipri.org/files/misc/SIPRIBP0911.pdf).

Keohane, D., *The EU and Armaments Co-operation*, Centre for European Reform Working Paper, December 2002 (www.cer.org.uk).

Kilb, W., The European Atomic Energy Community and Its Primary and Secondary Law, in, *International Nuclear Law: History, Evolution and Outlook*, OECD NEA publication, 2010 (downloadable at http://www.oecd-nea.org/law/isnl/10th/isnl-10th-anniversary.pdf).

Kristensen, H.M., *U.S. Nuclear Weapons in Europe: A Review of Post-Cold War Policy, Force Levels, and War Planning*, Natural Resources Defense Council, February 2005 (accessible at http://www.nrdc.org/nuclear/euro/euro.pdf).

Kristensen, H.M., Non-Strategic Nuclear Weapons, Federation of American Scientists, Special Report No. 3 May 2012 (http://www.fas.org/_docs/Non_Strategic_Nuclear_Weapons.pdf).

Kulesa, L., Global Zero: Implications for Europe, in, Jean Pascal Zanders (ed.), European Union Institute for Security Studies Chaillot Papers, April 2010 (http://www.iss.europa.eu/uploads/media/cp120.pdf).

Meier, O., 'NATO Sticks with Nuclear Policy', *Arms Control Today*, June 2012, (https://www.armscontrol.org/act/2012_06/NATO_Sticks_With_Nuclear_Policy).

Mölling, C., The Grand Bargain in the NPT: Challenges for the EU beyond 2010, in Zanders J.P. (ed.), European Union Institute for Security Studies Chaillot Papers, April 2010 (http://www.iss.europa.eu/uploads/media/cp120.pdf).

Nassauer, O., *Die Nuklearwaffen der USA in Europa – Doch kein Ende in Sicht? Wissenschaft und Frieden,* August 2012, No.3/12 (downloadable from the website of the Berlin Information center for Transatlantic Security http://www.bits.de/frames/publib.htm).

Nassauer, O., Nuclear Sharing in NATO: Is it Legal? *Newsletter of the Institute for Energy and Environmental Research: Science for Democratic Action* Vol.9 No.3, May 2001 (accessible at http://www.ieer.org/sdafiles/vol_9/9-3/nato.html).

Pélopidas, N., Non-proliferation through International Norms: A European Preference? *Cahiers Europeens N°02/2006* (accessible at, http://www.portedeurope.org/IMG/pdf/Cahier_norme_1_Pelopidas.pdf).

Ptasekaite, R., *The Euratom Treaty v. Treaties of the European Union: limits of competence and interaction*, Swedish Radiation Safety Authority, July 2011 Report number: 2011:32 ISSN: 2000-0456 (available at www.stralsakerhetsmyndigheten.se).

Spagnuolo, L., *NATO nuclear burden sharing and NPT obligations,* BASIC Getting to Zero Papers Number 13, April 2009 (accessible at http://www.basicint.org/sites/default/files/gtz13.pdf).

Sauer, T., 'How "common" is European nuclear non-proliferation policy', Joint Session of Workshops of the European Consortium for Political Research, Edinburgh, 2003 (http://ecpr.eu/events/paperdetails.aspx?paperid=14273&eventid=48).

Wolf, S., Euratom Before the Court: A Political Theory of Legal Non-Integration, *European Integration Online Papers*, 2011 Vol.15, Article No.10 (http://eiop.or.at/eiop/texte/2011-010a.htm).

United Nations Economic Commission for Europe (UN ECE), *The Aarhus Convention: An Implementation Guide*, ECE/CEP/72 (prepared by S. Stec and S. Casey – Lefkowitz in collaboration with J. Jendroska (Editorial Adviser)), December 2000 (available at http://www.unece.org/fileadmin/DAM/env/pp/acig.pdf).

United Nations Environment Program (UNEP), *Compendium on Human Rights and the Environment: Selected International Legal Materials and Cases*, UNEP, 2013, (http://www.unep.org/environmentalgovernance/Portals/8/publications/UNEP_Compendium_HRE.pdf).

Conference report: The Euratom Treaty and Future Energy Options: Conditions for a Level Playing Field in the Energy Sector, September 23rd 2005, at the Danish Parliament Building Christiansborg, Conference by NOAH – Friends of the Earth Denmark, The Danish Ecological Council and The Danish Organisation for Sustainable Energy (http://www.energyintelligenceforeurope.dk/conf_p6.html).

Friends of the Earth Europe, 'Will the New EU Constitution Promote Nuclear Energy? Paper Analyzing the Role of the EURATOM Treaty in the New EU Constitution', May 2005 (available at *http://www.foeeurope.org/publications/2005/euratom_and_constitution_may2005.pdf*).

Proceedings of the European workshop on practical implementation of the Aarhus Convention in the nuclear field (24–25 June 2009, Luxembourg) organized by the Belgian Nuclear Research Center, (http://www.sckcen.be/en/Events/AARHUS).

Summary of a Working paper circulated by the Association Nationale des Comités et Commissions Locales d'Information (ANCCLI). The Working paper was prepared in the framework of the conference on public participation in decision making in the nuclear domain (Luxembourg 12–13 March 2013), accessible at (http://www.anccli.fr/Europe-International/ACN-Aarhus-Convention-Nuclear/European-round-tables-Tables-rondes-europeennes/Quatrieme-Table-Ronde-Europeenne-surete-nucleaire).

Special Eurobarometer Report 271: Europeans and Nuclear Safety (Fieldwork October–November 2006), February 2007 http://ec.europa.eu/public_opinion/archives/ebs/ebs_271_en.pdf .

Special Eurobarometer Report 297: Attitudes to radioactive waste, published July 2008 http://ec.europa.eu/public_opinion/archives/ebs/ebs_297_en.pdf.

Special Eurobarometer Report 324: Europeans and Nuclear Safety, March 2010, http://ec.europa.eu/public_opinion/archives/ebs/ebs_324_en.pdf.

Special Eurobarometer Report 271: Europeans and Nuclear Safety (Fieldwork October–November 2006), February 2007 http://ec.europa.eu/public_opinion/archives/ebs/ebs_271_en.pdf.

Special Eurobarometer Report 324: Europeans and Nuclear Safety, March 2010, http://ec.europa.eu/public_opinion/archives/ebs/ebs_324_en.pdf.

Other Websites Consulted

http://ec.europa.eu/energy/nuclear/doc/nuclear_power_plants.pdf).

http://ec.europa.eu/energy/nuclear/index_en.htm.

www.world-nuclear.org/info/Country-Profiles/Countries-G-N/Germany.

http://www.un.org/disarmament/WMD/Nuclear/Repository/submissions_2014.shtml).

http://www.europarl.europa.eu/parliament/archive/elections2009/en/turnout_en.html [Accessed March 31, 2010]).

(*http://ec.europa.eu/environment/aarhus/*).

(*http://ec.europa.eu/energy/nuclear/governance_en.htm*).

http://european-convention.eu.int/EN/bienvenue/bienvenue2352.html?lang = EN.

http://archive.greens-efa.eu/cms/topics/dok/172/172579.euratom_50_years_too_much@en.htm.

http://archive.greens-efa.eu/cms/default/dok/173/173688.nuclear_error_since_1957@en.htm

http://million-against-nuclear.net/.

http://www.ctbto.org/fileadmin/content/treaty/treaty_text.pdf.

The text of the most recently updated 2010 edition of the Covenant can be found at http://www.portals.iucn.org/library/efiles/documents/EPLP-031-rev3.pdf.

www.ctbto.org/map/#status.

http://www.anccli.fr/Europe-International/Nuclear-Transparency-Watch).

http://www.epa.gov/environmentaljustice/.

http://www.unece.org/env/pp/ratification.html.

http://treaties.un.org/Pages/ViewDetails.aspx?src =TREATY&mtdsg_no = XXVII-13&chapter = 27&lang = en) http://www.environ.ie/en/Environment/News/MainBody,30480,en.htm.

(http://conventions.coe.int/Treaty/EN/Summaries/Html/205.htm.).

(http://conventions.coe.int/Treaty/Commun/ChercheSig.asp?NT = 205&CM = &DF = &CL = ENG.).

http://www.sckcen.be/en/Events/AARHUS.
http://www.anccli.fr/Europe-International/2013-ACN-Aarhus-Convention-Nuclear.
http://www.unece.org/env/pp/cc.html).
http://ec.europa.eu/environment/eia/home.htm.
http://www.iaea.org/safeguards/.
http://www.un.org/News/Press/docs/2009/sc9679.doc.htm. http://www.iaea.org/NewsCenter/Focus/IaeaDprk/chrono_pre2002.shtml; (http://www.iaea.org/About/Policy/GC/GC53/GC53Resolutions/English/gc53res-17_en.pdf).
(http://www.fissilematerials.org/ipfm/pages_us_en/fissile/production/production.php).
(http://www.un.org/disarmament/WMD/Nuclear/NPT.shtml).
http://unhq-appspub-01.un.org/UNODA/TreatyStatus.nsf/NPT%20%28in%20alphabetical%20order%29?OpenView).
http://treaties.un.org/doc/Publication/MTDSG/Volume%20II/Chapter%20XXVI/XXVI-4.en.pdf.
http://www.unog.ch/80256EE600585943/%28httpPages%29/6286395D9F8DABA380256EF70073A846?OpenDocument.
http://www.unog.ch/80256EE600585943/%28httpPages%29/2D415EE45C5FAE07C12571800055232B?OpenDocument.
http://www.nti.org/treaties-and-regimes/proposed-fissile-material-cut-off-reaty/.
http://www.iaea.org/About/statute.html).
http://www.iaea.org/About/statute_text.html.
http://www.iaea.org/OurWork/SV/Safeguards/safeg_system.pdf, p. 1.
http://www.iaea.org/OurWork/SV/Safeguards/safeg_system.pdf, p.2.
http://www.iaea.org/OurWork/SV/Safeguards/safeg_system.pdf, p.4.
http://www.iaea.org/OurWork/SV/Safeguards/safeg_system.pdf, p.4.
http://www.iaea.org/safeguards/documents/AP_status_list.pdf; http://www.iaea.org/OurWork/SV/Safeguards/protocol.html.
http://www.iaea.org/OurWork/SV/Safeguards/sir_table.pdf
http://www.consilium.europa.eu/uedocs/cmsUpload/09-06-22_speech_Sopot_AG.pdf).
http://www.consilium.europa.eu/eeas/foreign-policy/non-proliferation,-disarmament-and-export-control-/wmd?lang = en.
http://www.consilium.europa.eu/eeas/foreign-policy/non-proliferation,-disarmament-and-export-control-/ms-clara-ganslandt?lang = en.
http://www.eeas.europa.eu/non-proliferation-and-disarmament/index_en.htm.
http://eeas.europa.eu/delegations/un_geneva/documents/eu_statments/conference_disarmament/2014_05_02_npt_prepcom_cluster_1_eu_statement_final.pdf).
http://www.nato.int/issues/nuclear/sec-environment.html.
http://archives.lesoir.be/arme-nucleaire-en-europe-pas-de-retrait-sans-accord_t-20100422-00VYHQ.html?query = armes + atomiques&queryand = armes + atomiques,+OTAN&queryor = armes + atomiques&firstHit = 0&by = 10&when = -1&sort = datedesc&pos = 1&all = 65&nav = 1).

http://www.nato.int/nato_static/assets/pdf/pdf_topics/20091022_NATO_Position_on_nuclear_nonproliferation-eng.pdf.

http://www.nato.int/issues/nuclear/sec-environment.html.

http://www.nato.int/issues/nuclear/sec-environment.html

http://www.nato.int/nato_static/assets/pdf/pdf_topics/20091022_NATO_Position_on_nuclear_nonproliferation-eng.pdf.

http://www.nato.int/lisbon2010/strategic-concept-2010-eng.pdf).

http://www.spiegel.de/international/germany/0,1518,druck-618550,00.html.), http://www.nti.org/gsn/article/belgian-senate-to-consider-nuclear-weapon-ban/).

http://archives.lesoir.be/arme-nucleaire-en-europe-pas-de-retrait-sans-accord_t-20100422-00VYHQ.html?query = armes + atomiques&queryand = armes + atomiques,+OTAN&queryor = armes + atomiques&firstHit = 0&by = 10&when = -1&sort = datedesc&pos = 1&all = 65&nav = 1.

http://nypost.com/2014/09/10/russia-developing-new-nuclear-weapons-to-counter-us-nato/).

http://www.washingtonpost.com/opinions/nato-based-nuclear-weapons-are-an-advantage-in-a-dangerous-world/2014/08/17/059d0ddc-23ba-11e4-8593-da634b334390_story.html.

Legislative Acts and other Documents of the EU Institutions

Regulation (EEC) No. 3954/87 of 22 December 1987 laying down maximum permitted levels of radioactive contamination of foodstuffs and of feedingstuffs following a nuclear accident or any other case of radiological emergency [1987] OJ L 371/11.

Regulation (EEC) No. 3955/87 on the conditions governing imports of agricultural products originating in third countries following the accident at the Chernobyl nuclear power-station of 22 December 1987 [1987] OJ L 371/ 14.

Regulation No. 1049/2001 regarding public access to European Parliament, Council and Commission documents, [2001] OJ L 145/43.

Regulation (Euratom) No 302/2005 of 8 February 2005 on the application of Euratom safeguards, [2005] *OJ L 54, pp. 1–71.*

Regulation No 1367/2006 on the application of the provisions of the Aarhus Convention on Access to Information, Public Participation in Decision-making and Access to Justice in Environmental Matters to Community institutions and bodies (the Aarhus Regulation) [2006] OJ L 264/13.

Regulation No 428/2009 setting up a Community regime for the control of exports, transfer, brokering and transit of dual-use items [2009] OJ L134/1.

Directive 80/836/Euratom of 15 July 1980 amending the Directives laying down the basic safety standards for the health protection of the general public and workers against the dangers of ionizing radiation [1980] OJ L 246, p.1.

Directive 85/337/EEC of 27 June 1985 on the assessment of the effects of certain public and private projects on the environment [1985] OJ L 175, pp. 40–48.

Directive 89/618/Euratom of 27 November 1989 on informing the general public about health protection measures to be applied and steps to be taken in the event of a radiological emergency OJ [1989] L 357/31.

Directive 90/313/EEC of 7 June 1990 on the freedom of access to information on the environment [1990] OJ L 158/56.

Directive 92/43/EEC of 21 May 1992 on the conservation of natural habitats and of wild fauna and flora, [1992] OJ L 206/7.

Directive 96/29/Euratom laying down basic safety standards for the protection of the health of workers and the general public against the dangers arising from ionizing radiation [1996] OJ L 159/1.

Directive 2001/42/EC of the European Parliament and of the Council of 27 June 2001 on the assessment of the effects of certain plans and programmes on the environment [2001] OJ L 197, pp. 30–37.

Directive 2003/35/EC providing for public participation in respect of the drawing up of certain plans and programmes relating to the environment, [2003] *OJ L 156, pp. 17–25.*

Directive 2003/4/EC on public access to environmental information, [2003] *OJ L 41,* pp. *26–32.*

Directive 2006/117/Euratom on the supervision and control of shipments of radioactive waste and spent fuel, [2006] OJ L 337/21.

Directive 2006/117/Euratom on the supervision and control of shipments of radioactive waste and spent fuel, [2006] OJ L 337/21.

Directive 2008/99/EC on the protection of the environment through criminal law [2008] OJ L 328/28.

Directive 2009/71/Euratom establishing a Community framework for the nuclear safety of nuclear installations, [2009] OJ L172/18.

Directive 2011/70/Euratom of 19 July 2011 establishing a Community framework for the responsible and safe management of spent fuel and radioactive waste, [2011] OJ L 199, pp. 0048–0056.

Directive 2011/92/EU of the European Parliament and of the Council of 13 December 2011 on the assessment of the effects of certain public and private projects on the environment (codification) [2011] OJ L 26, p.1–21.

Directive 2013/59/EURATOM laying down basic safety standards for protection against the dangers arising from exposure to ionising radiation [2013] OJ L 13/1.

Directive 2014/87/Euratom amending Directive 2009/71/Euratom establishing a Community framework for nuclear safety of nuclear installations, [2014] OJ L 219/42.

Proposal for a Council Directive (Euratom) laying down basic obligations and general principles on the safety of nuclear installations, COM (2004) 526 final.

Proposal for a Directive of the European Parliament and the Council on access to justice in environmental matters, Brussels, 24.10.2003, COM (2003) 624 final, 2003/0246 (COD).

Proposal for a Council Directive laying down basic safety standards for protection against the dangers arising from exposure to ionising radiation, European Commission, Brussels, 30.5.2012 COM(2012) 242 final 2011/0254 (NLE)).

Commission Decision 90/413/Euratom of 1 August 1990 relating to a procedure in application of Article 83 of the Euratom, OJ L 209/8.

Commission Decision of 21 February 1994, 94/285/Euratom, OJ 1994 L 122/30.

Commission Decision 2005/844/EURATOM of 25 November 2005 concerning the accession of the European Atomic Energy Community to the Convention on Early Notification of a Nuclear Accident, OJ L-314 of 30/11/2005 p.21–22.

Commission Decision 2005/845/EURATOM of 25 November 2005 concerning the accession of the European Atomic Energy Community to the Convention on Assistance in the case Nuclear Accident or Radiological Emergency, OJ L314 of 30/11/2005 pp. 27–34.

Commission Decision 2006/626/Euratom of 15 February 2006 pursuant to Article 83 of the Treaty establishing the European Atomic Energy Community, OJ 2006 L 255/5.

Commission Decision 2008/50/EC of 13 December 2007 laying down detailed rules for the application of Regulation (EC) No 1367/2006 of the European Parliament and of the Council on the Aarhus Convention as regards requests for the internal review of administrative acts, OJ 2008 L 13/24.

Commission Decision 2008/401/EC, Euratom of 30 April 2008 amending its Rules of Procedure as regards detailed rules for the application of Regulation (EC) No 1367/2006 of the European Parliament and of the Council on the application of the provisions of the Aarhus Convention on Access to Information, Public Participation in Decision-making and Access to Justice in Environmental Matters to Community institution and bodies, OJ 2008 L 140/22.

Commission Recommendation 1999/829/Euratom of 6 December 1999 on the application of Article 37 of the Euratom Treaty, OJ L 324, 16/12/1999 pp. 0023–0043.

Commission Recommendation 2000/473/Euratom of 8 June 2000 on the application of Article 36 of the Euratom Treaty concerning the monitoring of the levels of radioactivity in the environment for the purpose of assessing the exposure of the population as a whole (notified under document number C(2000) 1299).

Commission Recommendation of 15 December 2005 on guidelines for the application of Regulation (Euratom) No 302/2005 on the application of Euratom safeguards (notified under document number C(2005) 5127), OJ L 028, 01/02/2006 P. 0001–0085.

Commission Recommendation 2010/635/Euratom of 11 October 2010 on the application of Article 37 of the Euratom Treaty OJ L 279, 23.10.2010, pp. 36–67.

European Commission, Communication to the Council, The Development of Community measures for the application of Chapter III of the Euratom Treaty 'Health and Safety' COM/86/434FINAL.

European Commission, Communication of 2 February 2000 on the Precautionary principle, COM/2000/0001 final.

European Commission, Communication to the Council and the European Parliament: Nuclear Illustrative Programme (Presented under Article 40 of the Euratom Treaty for the opinion of the European Economic and Social Committee), COM (2006) 844 final, Brussels, 10.1.2007.

European Commission, Communication on the Application of Article 35 of the Euratom Treaty: Verification of the operation and efficiency of facilities for continuous monitoring of the level of radioactivity in the air, water and soil, Report 1990–2007, Brussels, 20.12.2007 COM (2007) 847 final.

European Commission, Communication to the European Parliament, the Council and the Economic and Social Committee: Update of the Nuclear Illustrative Programme in the context of the Second Strategic Energy Review, COM (2008) 776 final, Brussels 13.11.2008, p.6.

European Commission, Communication from the Commission to the Council and the European Parliament, Communication on nuclear non-proliferation, Brussels, 26.3.2009, COM (2009) 143 final.

European Commission, Report from the Commission to the Council on Civil Protection, Tourism and Energy, SEC 1996 496 final.

European Commission, Aarhus Convention Implementation Report, Brussels 14 April 2011, COM (2011) 208 final.

European Commission, Report from the Commission to the Council and the European Parliament on the experience gained in the application of Directive 2003/4/EC on Public Access to Environmental Information; COM (2012) 774 final; Brussels, 17.12.2012.

European Commission (Directorate-General for Energy), Report on the Implementation of Euratom Safeguards in 2013, Ref. Ares (2014) 1534607 – 14/05/2014, April 2014.

European Commission White Paper: 'An Energy Policy for the European Union', COM (1995) 682 final.

Report on the annual accounts of the Euratom Supply Agency for the financial year 2009, OJ C 338, 14/12/2010 pp. 0006–0009.

Report on the annual accounts of the Euratom Supply Agency for the financial year 2008, together with the Agency's replies, OJ C 304 , 15/12/2009 P. 0006–0009.

European Commission Green Paper, The dual-use export control system of the European Union: ensuring security and competitiveness in a changing world, COM (2011) 393 final.

Report 'A Target for Euratom', submitted by Louis Armand, Franz Etzel and Francesco Giordani at the request of the governments of Belgium, France, German Federal Republic, Italy, Luxembourg and the Netherlands in May 1957, can be consulted at http://www.cvce.eu/obj/report_by_the_three_wise_men_on_euratom_4_may_1957-en-e72917a4-3c9d-48b1-b8cb-41307736731e.html (the website of the Centre Virtuel de la Connaissance sur l'Europe).

Council Decision 80/565/Euratom of 9 June 1980 approving the conclusion by the Commission of the International Convention on the physical protection of nuclear material, OJ L149 1980 p.41.

Council Decision 87/600/Euratom of 14 December 1987 on Community arrangements for the early exchange of information in the event of a radiological emergency OJ L 371, 30.12.1987, p.76.

Council Decision of 25 July 1994 regarding the preparation for the 1995 Conference of the States parties to the NPT, OJ L 205/0001–0002.

Council Decision 2005/370/EC of 17 February 2005 on the conclusion, on behalf of the European Community, of the Convention on access to information, public participation in decision-making and access to justice in environmental matters, OJ L 124, 17.5.2005, pp. 1–3.

Council Decision 2007/513/Euratom of 10 July 2007 approving the accession of the European Atomic Energy Community to the amended Convention on the Physical Protection of Nuclear Material and Nuclear Facilities (*OJ L 190, 21.7.2007, pp. 12–14*).

Council Decision 2010/212/CFSP of 29 March 2010 relating to the position of the European Union for the 2010 Review Conference of the Parties to the Treaty on the Non-Proliferation of Nuclear Weapons, OJ L 90/8.

Council Decision 2010/430/CFSP of 26 July establishing a European network of independent non-proliferation think tanks in support of the implementation of the EU Strategy against Proliferation of Weapons of Mass Destruction OJ L 202/5.

Council of the EU, Resolution of 18 June 1992 on the technological problems of nuclear safety (92/C 172/02), Council Resolution of 18 June 1992 on the technological problems of nuclear safety, OJ C 172, 8.7.1992, pp. 2–3.

Council of the EU, Action Plan for the Implementation of the Basic Principles for an EU Strategy against Proliferation of Weapons of Mass Destruction, 10354/1/03 Rev 1, 13 June 2003.

European Council, A Secure Europe in a Better World: European Security Strategy, Brussels, 12 December 2003.

Council of the EU, EU Strategy against proliferation of weapons of mass destruction, 15708/03, 10 December 2003.

Council of the EU, EU Strategy against the proliferation of WMD : Effective multiaterlaism, prevention and international cooperation, November 2008 (www.consilium.europa.eu/uedocs/cms_data/librairie/PDF/EN).

Council of the EU, EU Strategy against the proliferation of WMD: Monitoring and enhancing consistent implementation, 16694/06.

Council Common Position of 29 July 1999 (OJ L 204/1–2) relating to EU's contribution to the promotion of the early entry into force of the Comprehensive Test Ban Treaty.

Council Common Position 2000/297/CFSP of 13 April 2000 relating to the 2000 Review Conference of the Parties to the NPT (L 97/1–3); Council Common Position of 25 April 2005 relating to the 2005 Review Conference for the NPT (OJ L 106/32–35).

Council Common Position 2000/297/CFSP of 13 April 2000 relating to the 2000 Review Conference of the Parties to the NPT (L 97/1–3).

Council Common Position of 13 April 2000 relating to the 2000 Review Conference of the Parties to the NPT (L 97/1–3); Common Position of 25 April 2005 relating to the 2005 Review Conference for the NPT (OJ L 106/32–35)).

Council of the EU, Action Plan for the Implementation of the Basic Principles for an EU Strategy against Proliferation of Weapons of Mass Destruction, 10354/1/03 Rev 1, 13 June 2003.

Council of the EU, Note on the implementation of the WMD clause 5503/09 (2003–2008 period) of 19 January 2009.

Council of the EU, Six-monthly progress report on the implementation of the EU Strategy against the Proliferation of Weapons of Mass Destruction (2009/I) 11490/09, 26 June 2009.

Council of the EU, Six-Monthly Progress Report on the Implementation of the EU Strategy Against the Proliferation of Weapons of Mass Destruction (2013/I), *OJ 2013/C 228/05*; Council Six-Monthly Progress Report on the Implementation of the EU Strategy Against the Proliferation of Weapons of Mass Destruction (2013/II) *OJ 2014/C 54/01*.

Council of the EU, Conclusions on the Ninth Review Conference of the Parties to the Treaty on the Non-Proliferation of Nuclear Weapons, 20 April 2015, CONOP 29 CODUN 9 CFSP/PESC 61.

European Parliament, Resolution on measures to safeguard the Non-Proliferation Treaty, OJ C262, 14 October 1985, p. 84.

European Parliament, Resolution on the importance of the Non-Proliferation Treaty Review Conference, OJ C262, 14 October 1985, p. 85.

European Parliament – Directorate-General for Research, Working paper: The European Parliament and the Euratom Treaty: past, present and future (*Energy and Research* Series) ENER 114 EN 2-2002, pp. xvi–xvii.

European Parliament, Report on Non-Proliferation of Weapons of Mass Destruction: A Role for the European Parliament, Committee on Foreign Affairs, 2005/2139, FINAL A6-0297/2005, 12 Oct. 2005.

European Parliament, Resolution on the problem of nuclear safety fifteen years after the Chernobyl accident, B5-0321/2001; European Parliament *Legislative Resolution on the draft Council regulation establishing an Instrument for Nuclear Safety and Security Assistance* (9037/2006 – C6-0153/2006 – 2006/0802(CNS)A6-0397/2006).

European Parliament, Summary of the meeting of the Committee on Foreign Affairs (AFET) and the Subcommittee on Security and Defence (SEDE), Public hearing: '*The Future of the Nuclear Non-Proliferation Treaty (NPT)*', Brussels, 12 July 2006 Brussels, 13157/06 PE 294.

European Parliament, Opinion of the Committee on Constitutional Affairs of the European Parliament (included in the *Report on Assessing Euratom – 50 Years of European Nuclear Energy Policy* (*Maldeikis Report*) A6-0129/2007 final) (2006/2230(INI)).

European Parliament, Committee on Industry, Research and Energy, Rapporteur: E. Maldeikis, Report on Assessing Euratom: 50 years of European nuclear energy policy (*Maldeikis Report*) A6-0129/2007.

European Parliament, Resolution of 10 May 2007 on the public health consequences of the 1968 Thule crash (Petition 720/2002) (2006/2012(INI)).

European Parliament, Report on the proposal for a Council Directive (Euratom) setting up a Community framework for nuclear safety of nuclear installations (*Hökmark Report*) A6-0236/2009.

European Parliament Committee on the Environment, Public Health and Food Safety (Draft Report) on the proposal for a Council directive laying down basic safety standards for protection against the dangers arising from exposure to ionising radiation (COM (2012)0242–C7-0151/2012–2011/0254(NLE)).

European Parliament, Resolution of 14 March 2013 on risk and safety assessments ('stress tests') of nuclear power plants in the European Union and related activities (2012/2830(RSP)).

European Parliament, Resolution of 14 March 2013 on risk and safety assessments ('stress tests') of nuclear power plants in the European Union and related activities, 2012/2830(RSP) (COM (2012)0571).

Archives historiques du Conseil de l'Union européenne, Bruxelles, Négociations des traités instituant la CEE et la CEEA (1955–1957), CM3. Réunion des ministres des affaires étrangères, Messine, 01-03.06.1955, CM3/NEGO/006, (http://www.ena.lu/resolution_dopted_foreign_ministers_ecsc_member_states_messina_june_1955-2-24617).

Comité intergouvernemental créé par la conférence de Messine, Rapport des chefs de délégation aux ministres des Affaires étrangères. Bruxelles: Secrétariat,

21 avril 1956, pp. 9–135. (http://www.ena.lu/report_heads_delegation_foreign_ministers_brussels_21_april_1956-2-25213).

Cooperation Agreement between the EURATOM and the IAEA, OJ L 329, 23/12/1975, p.0028-0029.

Agreement between the Kingdom of Belgium, the Kingdom of Denmark, the Federal Republic of Germany, Ireland, the Italian Republic, the Grand Duchy of Luxembourg, the Kingdom of the Netherlands, the European Atomic Energy Community and the International Atomic Energy Agency in implementation of Article III (1) and (4) of the Treaty on the non-proliferation of nuclear weapons (78/164/Euratom OJ L 051 , 22/02/1978 P. 0001–0026).

Contribution to the Convention on the future of Europe, Mr Klaus Hänsch, member of the Convention: 'Future of the Euratom Treaty', Brussels, 14 October 2002, CONV 344/02.

Contribution to the Convention on the future of Europe, Mr Hannes Farnleitner, Mr Caspar Einem and Mr Reinhard E. Bösch, members of the Convention: 'A single legal personality – On the future of EURATOM' Brussels, 22 October 2002, CONV 358/02.

Contribution to the Convention on the future of Europe, Ms Marie Nagy, Ms Renée Wagner and Mr Neil MacCormick, alternate members of the Convention: 'The Future of the Euratom Treaty in the Framework of the European Constitution' Brussels, 18 February 2003, CONV 563/03.

Note of the Presidium of the Convention on the future of Europe, dated from 14 March 2003, CONV. 621/03.

Final report of the Convention's Working Group on Legal Personality, 1 October 2002, CONV 305/02.

Stabilisation and Association Agreement between the European Communities and their Member States, of the one part, and the Republic of Montenegro, of the other part, OJ L 108/3, 19.2.2008, p. 1.

EU Statement By Mr Jacek Bylica Principal Adviser and Special Envoy for Non-Proliferation and Disarmament European External Action Service Third Session of the Preparatory Committee for the 2015 Review Conference of the States Parties to the Treaty on the Non-Proliferation of Nuclear Weapons (Cluster 2), United Nations, New York, 1 May 2014 (http://eeas.europa.eu/delegations/un_geneva/documents/eu_statments/conference_disarmament/2014_05_01_eu_statement_cluster_2_final.pdf).

EU Statement By Mr Jacek Bylica Principal Adviser and Special Envoy for Non-Proliferation and Disarmament European External Action Service, Third Session of the Preparatory Committee for the 2015 Review Conference of the States Parties to the Treaty on the Non-Proliferation of Nuclear Weapons (General Debate), United Nations, New York, 29 April 2014 (http://eeas.europa.eu/delegations/un_geneva/documents/eu_statments/conference_disarmament/2014-04-29-npt-2014-prepcom-eu-general-statement_final.pdf).

International Atomic Energy Agency (IAEA) Documents

IAEA, INFCIRC/290, December 1981, Agreement of 27 July 1978 between France, the European Atomic Energy Community and the International Atomic Energy Agency for the application of safeguards in France, accessible at: (http://www.iaea.org/Publications/Documents/Infcircs/Others/infcirc290.pdf).

IAEA, INFCIRC/263, October 1978, Agreement of 6 September 1976 between the United Kingdom of Great Britain and Northern Ireland, the European Atomic Energy Community and the Agency in connection with the Treaty on the Non-Proliferation of Nuclear Weapons, point 1 et seq. of Preamble; (http://www.iaea.org/Publications/Documents/Infcircs/Others/infcirc263.pdf).

IAEA Safety Series No. 115, IAEA 1996, International Basic Safety Standards for Protection against Ionizing Radiation and for the Safety of Radiation Sources (http://www-pub.iaea.org/MTCD/publications/PDF/Pub996_EN.pdf).

IAEA Additional Protocol with France, INFCIRC/290/Add.1, Date: 24 February 2005; and Additional Protocol with the UK, (INFCIRC/263/Add.1, Date: 24 February 2005).

IAEA Safety Glossary: Terminology used in Nuclear Safety and Radiation Protection, 2007 edition, IAEA, 2007.

IAEA Safety Standards for protecting people and the environment: Radiation Protection and Safety of Radiation Sources: International Basic Safety Standards, IAEA, 2014 (http://www-pub.iaea.org/MTCD/Publications/PDF/Pub1578_web-57265295.pdf).

Model for the IAEA safeguards agreements, INFCIRC/153(Corrected).

IAEA, Model Protocol Additional to Agreement(s) between State(s) and the IAEA for the Application of Safeguards (INFCIRC/540 (Corrected).

List of Cases

Court of Justice of the European Union

C-22/70 *Commission v Council* (*ERTA* (*European Agreement on Road Transport*)) ECR 1971 p.0263.

Ruling 1/78 ECR 1978 p.02151.

C-188-190/80 *France v Commission, Italy v Commission, UK v Commission* ECR 1982 p.2545

C-328/85 *Deutsche Babcock* ECR *1987 Page 05119.*

C-187/87 *Land de Sarre and others v Ministre de l'Industrie* ECR *1988 p.I-05013.*

C-62/88 *Greece v Council* ECR 1990 p. I-1527.

C-70/88 *Parliament v Council* ECR 1991 p. I-4529.

Opinion 2/91 ECR 1993 p. I-01061.

Opinion 1/94 ECR 1994 p. I-5267.

C-36/98 *Spain v Council*, 2001 ECR I-779.

C-157/96 *The Queen / Ministry of Agriculture, Fisheries and Food and Commissioners of Customs & Excise, ex parte National Farmers' Union and others,* ECR 1998 p. I-2211.
C-180/96 *United Kingdom v Commission,* ECR 1998 p. I-2265.
C-29/99 *Commission v Council (Nuclear Safety Convention)* ECR 2002 p. I-11221.
C-281/01 Commission v Council (*Energy Star Agreement*), ECR 2002 p. I-12049.
C-459/03 *Commission v Ireland,* ECR 2006 p. I-4635.
Opinion 1/03 ECR 2006 p.I-1145.
C-459/03 *Commission v Ireland (MoX)*, ECR 2006 *p. I-4635.*
C-176/03 Commission v Council, ECR 2005 p. I-7879
C-115/08 *Land Oberösterreich v ČEZ,* ECR 2009 p. I-10265.
C-39/03 Commission v Artegodan and others, ECR 2003 p. I-7885.
C-61/03 *Commission v UK,* ECR 2005 p. I-2477.
C-65/04 *Commission v UK,* ECR 2006 p. I-2239.
C-266/09 *Stichting Natuur en Milieu v College voor de toelating van gewasbeschermingsmiddelen en biociden,* ECR 2010 p. I-13119.
C-204/09 *Flachglas Torgau GmbH,* ECR 2012 I-0000.
C-240/09 *Lesoochranárske zoskupenie VLK v Ministerstvo životného prostredia Slovenskej republiky,* ECR 2011 p.I-1255.
C-134/09 and C-135/09 *Antoine Boxus and Others,* ECR 2011 p. I-9711.
C-115/09 *Bund fur Umwelt und Naturschutz Deutschland, Landesverband Nordrhein-Westfalen eV,* ECR 2011 p. I-3673.
C-275/09 *Brussels Hoofdstedelijk Gewest et al., ECR 2011 p. I-1753.*
C-182/10 *Marie-Noëlle Solvay and Others,* ECLI:EU:C:2012:82.
C-416/10 *Jozef Križan and Others,* ECLI:EU:C:2013:8.
Joined Cases C-205/10 P, C-217/10 P and C-222/10 P *Eriksen, Hansen and Lind v Commission* (Order of the Court (Fifth Chamber) of 12 January 2011) ECR 2011 p. I-1
Joined cases C-514/11 P and C-605/11 P *Liga para a Protecção da Natureza (LPN) and Republic of Finland v European Commission,* ECLI:EU:C:2013:738.
C-48/14 *Parliament v Council,* ECLI:EU:C:2015:91.

General Court of the European Union

T-458/93 and T-523/93 *ENU v Commission,* ECR 1995 p. II-2459.
T-219/95 *R, Danielsson and Others v Commission,* ECR 1995 p. II-03051.
T-74/00, T-76/00, T-83/00, T-84/00, T-85/00, T-132/00, T-137/00 and T-141/00 *Artegodan and Others v Commission,* ECR 2002 p. II-4945.
T-264/04 *WWF European Policy Programme v. Council,* ECR 2007 II-00911.
T-429/05 Artegodan v Commission, ECR 2010 p. II-491.
T-516/08 *Eriksen v Commission (Order of 24 March 2010),* ECR 2010 p. II-40.
T-6/09 *Hansen v Commission (Order of 24 March 2010),* ECR 2010 p. II-43.
T-5/09 *Lind v Commission (Order of 24 March 2010),* ECR 2010 p. II-42.

European Court of Human Rights

Lopez Ostra v. Spain (1994) 20 EHRR 277.

Guerra v. Italy (1998) 26 EHRR 357.

Balmer-Schafroth v. Switzerland (1998) 25 EHRR 598.

McGinley and Egan v. UK (1998) 27 EHRR 1.

L.C.B. v. United Kingdom (1998) 27 EHRR 212

Athanassoglou v. Switzerland (2001) 31 EHRR 13.

Hatton and Others v. United Kingdom, no. 36022/97, ECHR 2003

Roche v. United Kingdom, no. 32555/96, ECHR 2005.

Tatar c. Roumanie, no. 67021/01, ECHR 2009.

Di Sarno et autres c. Italie , no. 30765/08, ECHR 2012.

International Court of Justice

Nuclear Tests (New Zealand v. France), Judgment, I.C.J. Reports 1974, p. 457.

Nuclear Tests (Australia v. France), Judgment, I.C.J. Reports 1974, p. 253.

Request for an Examination of the Situation in Accordance with Paragraph 63 of the Court's Judgment of 20 December 1974 in the Nuclear Tests (New Zealand v. France) Case, I. C. J. Reports 1995, p. 288.

Legality of the Threat or Use of Nuclear Weapons, Advisory Opinion, I. C.J. Reports 1996, p. 226.

Legality of the Use by a State of Nuclear Weapons in Armed Conflict, Advisory Opinion, I.C. J. Reports 1996, p. 66.

UNCLOS Arbitral Trbunal

MOX Plant Case (Ireland v. United Kingdom), case no. 10, Order of 3 December 2001, on Susprension of Proceedings on Jurisdiction and Merits (http://www.pca-cpa.org/showpage.asp?pag_id = 1148).

OSPAR Convention Arbitral Tribunal

Final Award 2 July 2003, Ireland v UK, Dispute concerning access to information under Article 9 of the OSPAR Convention (http://pca-cpa.org/upload/files/OSPAR%20 Award.pdf).

Aarhus Convention Compliance Committee

Findings and Recommendations Communication ACCC/C/2009/41 concerning compliance by Slovakia, adopted on 17 December 2010 ECE/MP.PP/2011/11/Add.3.

Findings and recommendations with regard to communication ACCC/C/2008/32 (Part I) concerning compliance by the European Union, Adopted on 14 April 2011 ECE/MP.PP/C.1/2011/4/Add.1.

Index

Aarhus Convention
  Aarhus Convention Compliance Committee 158–159, 212, 218–220, 230–231
  environmental democracy 142–146, 150–151, 179–189
  pillars of 12, 155, 160, 167, 171
Aarhus Convention and the EU
  direct effect 223–225
  EU implementing legislation 171–179, 189–200, 225–232
  Findings and recommendations - Communication ACCC/C/2009/41 concerning compliance by Slovakia (Mochovce Nuclear Power Plant) 218–220
  Findings and recommendations - Communication ACCC/C/2008/32 concerning compliance by the European Union 230–231
Access to environmental information in the EU
  Directive 2003/4/EC on public access to environmental information 12, 46, 126, 138, 148, 171, 173, 228
Access to justice in environmental matters in the EU
  Commission Proposal for a Directive on access to justice in environmental matters 226–227
Amsterdam Treaty 1(n1), 66(n250), 168, 189(n280)
Article 203 Euratom ('flexibility' clause) 38, 40, 43, 67(n255), 68–70
Article 106a Euratom ('bridging' clause) 28, 37, 40, 45(n141), 70, 80, 141, 168, 190

Benelux Memorandum 19

Civil uses of nuclear energy 4, 151, 235, 245, 265, 285, 289, 291
Convention on Assistance in the case of a Nuclear Accident or Radiological Emergency 136, 179(n145)
Convention on Early Notification of a Nuclear Accident 179(n145)
Convention on Environmental Impact Assessment in a Trans-boundary Context (Espoo Convention) 91, 180
Convention on the Future of Europe 71–72, 75
Convention on Nuclear Safety 54, 55(n184), 56, 90, 136, 245(47)
Convention on the Physical Protection of Nuclear Material and Nuclear Facilities 52, 90, 137, 245(n47), 297
Convention for the Protection of the Marine Environment of the North-East Atlantic (OSPAR Convention) 91, 102, 132, 212
Convention on Spent Fuel and Radioactive Waste Management 90, 177, 199
Council of the EU
  competences under Euratom 31–38, 39–41, 43, 45–48, 50, 123
  involvement in EU non-proliferation policy 261, 264, 268, 271–272

Draft International Covenant on Environment and Development 93

Environmental Impact Assessment (EIA) 91, 97, 126, 184–186, 190–193, 195, 207, 220
European Coal and Steel Community (ECSC) 8, 17, 19, 20, 23–27, 79, 81, 289
European Commission
  competences under Euratom 8, 16, 18, 24, 28, 40, 43, 45, 48–51, 54, 56–57, 59–60, 63–65, 71–73
European Convention of Human Rights
  Art.2 ECHR (right to life) 105, 110, 211, 305
  Art.6 ECHR (right to a fair trial) 105, 208
  Art.8 ECHR (right to respect for private and family life) 104–106, 109, 205
European Council 71–72, 261, 263–264
European Court of Human Rights
  Balmer-Schafroth v. Switzerland 10, 107–108, 211
  McGinley and Egan v. UK 13, 109, 136, 208, 210

European Court of Human Rights (cont.)
L.C.B. v. United Kingdom 110, 136, 211
Athanassoglou v. Switzerland 10, 108, 211
European Defense Community (EDC) 15, 19, 284–286, 289
European Economic Community (EEC) 1, 8, 17, 19–20, 23, 25–27, 35, 81
European Parliament
competences under Euratom 38–40, 45–50
democratic deficit 38–39, 42, 46–47, 49, 69, 231
Hőkmark Report 42, 46(n142), 113(n161), 120(n183), 121(n184–189)
Maldeikis Report 42, 46(n142), 67(n251,n255), 69
Chernobyl I case 84, 114(n162), 123
Chernobyl II case 9, 40, 56–57, 84
Parliament v Council (C-48/14) 41(n118), 42(n118)
External relations of Euratom 35–36, 53–54, 56, 59, 302

Integration, principle of
applicability to Euratom domain 84, 95, 134–135, 139–141
International Atomic Energy Agency (IAEA)
IAEA Safety Standards 118–119
IAEA Safeguards Agreements with Non-Nuclear Weapons States 14, 234, 242, 247–248
IAEA Safeguards Agreement with Euratom and the Member States 249–251
IAEA Statute 118, 242(n37), 245–246, 252, 254
IAEA Cooperation Agreement with Euratom 250
Voluntary Offer Agreements 251–253
International Court of Justice
Nuclear Tests I (New Zealand v. France) 10, 96
Nuclear Tests II (Australia v. France) 10, 96, 134(n266), 136
Advisory Opinion on the Legality of the Threat or Use of Nuclear Weapons 10, 95, 98, 241
Advisory Opinion on the Legality of the Use by a State of Nuclear Weapons in Armed Conflict 95, 100–101

Legislative procedures under Euratom 37–39, 41–42, 45–49, 122
Lisbon Treaty
amendments to Euratom Treaty 1, 3, 6, 8–9, 27, 37, 39–40, 45, 47, 49–50, 67, 71–72, 77, 79, 234, 261, 264, 266

Messina Resolution 19, 289
Military uses of nuclear energy, Euratom and
Commission v UK (C-61/03) 16, 82, 124, 235(n7), 255, 299–303
Commission v UK (C-65/04) 16, 124, 303, 307
Danielsson case 298–299
Erkisen and Others case 16, 303–308
Ruling 1/78 9, 31(n71) 36, 52–54, 297–298
European Parliament Resolution on Thule crash 44, 67(n251), 303–306, 308
MOX *Plant* litigation
Court of Justice of the EU (C-459/03 *Commission v Ireland*) 9, 59–62, 103, 212(n296), 218
UNCLOS Arbitral Trbunal (*Ireland v. United Kingdom*) 10, 59–61, 102–104, 136, 212(n296)
OSPAR Convention Arbitral Tribunal 13, 102, 212–217
Monnet, Jean 20–21, 292(n258)

NATO nuclear sharing 15, 276–281
Non-discrimination, principle of 63, 86–87, 259
Non-diversion of nuclear material 13, 233, 242, 245–246, 250(n80), 254, 259
Non Proliferation Treaty (NPT)
disarmament (see *Nuclear disarmament*)
non-proliferation (see *Non-diversion of nuclear material* and *Nuclear safeguards*)
promotion of civil uses of nuclear energy (see *Civil uses of nuclear energy*)
Nuclear disarmament
concept of disarmament 14, 236, 237–241, 265, 267, 269–270, 272, 274, 282, 290
Conference on Disarmament (CD) 240, 270(n161)
Fissile Material Cut-Off Treaty 240
Nuclear safeguards

Euratom safeguards system 254–260, 287–288, 293–296, 298
IAEA Safeguards (see *International Atomic Energy Agency*)
IAEA-Euratom Cooperation Agreement (see *International Atomic Energy Agency*)
IAEA-Euratom-Member States Safeguards Agreement (see *International Atomic Energy Agency*)

Nuclear safety
Convention on Nuclear Safety (see *Convention on Nuclear Safety*)
Directive 2009/71/Euratom establishing a Community framework for the nuclear safety of nuclear installations (Nuclear Safety Directive) 42(n143), 44, 56(n190), 89(n14), 120–122, 127, 138, 176–177
Directive 2014/87/Euratom amending Directive 2009/71/Euratom establishing a Community framework for nuclear safety of nuclear installations 89(n44), 121(n190), 138(n276), 176(n131,n132), 199–200
Nuclear Safety Convention case 9, 36(n98), 54–56, 116, 123(n193)
Temelin case 9, 59, 62–66, 86–87, 124

Nuclear security 137(n275), 296

Nuclear testing
Comprehensive Nuclear Test Ban Treaty (CTBT) 98, 240, 244(n46), 268, 270, 275(n185)
Partial Nuclear Test Ban Treaty (PTBT) 89, 97, 98(n82), 244(n46)
Nuclear Tests I and *II* (see *International Court of Justice*)
McGinley and Egan v UK (see *European Court of Human Rights*)
L.C.B. v UK (see *European Court of Human Rights*)

Nuclear waste 57, 60, 82, 91–93, 112, 123, 125–127, 137, 154, 170, 172, 175–177, 182, 192, 199, 202, 233, 245, 299–302

Nuclear waste from military uses
Cattenom case 9, 56–57, 123–124
Commission v UK (C-61/03) (see *Military uses of nuclear energy*)
Commission v UK (C-65/04) (see *Military uses of nuclear energy*)

Nuclear weapons
Nuclear-Weapon States (NWS) 2, 14, 237–238, 242, 248, 251–253, 265, 266(n137), 278, 282
Non-Nuclear-Weapon States (NNWS) 14, 238, 241–244, 252, 266, 278–279, 282
Security Assurances 243–244
South Pacific Nuclear Free Zone Treaty (Rarotonga Treaty) 97
Voluntary Offer Agreements (see *International Atomic Energy Agency*)

Participation in decision-making on environmental matters in the EU
Directive 85/337/EEC on assessment of the effects of certain public and private projects on the environment (Environmental Impact Assessment Directive) 125, 148, 149(n31), 190–194
Directive 2001/42/EC on the assessment of the effects of certain plans and programmes on the environment (Strategic Environmental Assessment Directive) 126, 190, 194–199
Directive 2003/35/EC providing for public participation in respect of the drawing up of certain plans and programmes relating to the environment 12, 46, 149, 191
Directive 2011/92/EU of the European Parliament and of the Council of 13 December 2011 on the assessment of the effects of certain public and private projects on the environment (codification) 149(n31), 190

Peaceful uses of nuclear energy (see *Civil uses of nuclear energy*)

Penelope document (Feasibility study on the Constitution of Europe) 73

Precautionary principle
as principle of EU environmental policy 128, 130–135
applicability to Euratom domain 135–141
Commission Communication on the Precautionary Principle 132–133

Prevention principle (Principle of preventive action)
as principle of EU environmental policy 128, 130–135

Prevention principle (cont.)
  applicability to Euratom domain 135–139, 141
Protocol amending the Treaty establishing the European Atomic Energy Community 45
Protocol on the application of the principles of subsidiarity and proportionality 47–48, 141(n289)
Protocol on the role of national parliaments in the EU 47–48, 141(n289)

Radiation protection
  Basic Safety Standards (Euratom) 55, 60, 64, 119–121, 128, 138, 178
  Directive 96/29/Euratom laying down basic safety standards for the protection of the health of workers and the general public against the dangers arising from ionizing radiation 44, 119, 121, 128, 304–307
  Directive 2013/59/EURATOM laying down basic safety standards for protection against the dangers arising from exposure to ionising radiation 119, 138, 178
  environmental approach 5, 45, 114–115, 119–120, 123, 125, 133
  IAEA Safety Standards (see *International Atomic Energy Agency*)

Radioactive waste (see *Nuclear waste*)
Rio Declaration (1972) 99, 131, 132(n246), 146, 180

Single European Act (SEA) 111, 131, 139–140
Spaak, Paul Henri 19, 21, 290–291
Spaak Report 15, 19, 235, 284, 289–291
Stockholm Declaration (1992) 99, 146
Strategic Enviromental Assessment (SEA) 186, 190, 194–195

United Nations Convention on the Law of the Sea (UNCLOS) 59, 61, 102, 103, 212(n296), 218

Venice Conference 15, 19, 235, 284, 290–291
Vienna Convention on the Law of Treaties (VCLT) 68, 216

Weapons of Mass Destruction (WMD), EU policy on
  EU Strategy against Proliferation of WMD 261(n107), 263–264, 271(n165), 274(n180)
  European Security Strategy 263
  European nuclear deterrent 265
  NATO nuclear sharing 15, 276–281
  WMD clause in EU agreements 271–276
Western European Union (WEU) 15, 284, 286–288

Printed in the United States
By Bookmasters